THE ORIGIN OF THE SOUL
IN ST. AUGUSTINE'S
LATER WORKS

THE ORIGIN OF
THE SOUL IN
ST. AUGUSTINE'S
LATER WORKS

ROBERT J. O'CONNELL, S.J.

NEW YORK
FORDHAM UNIVERSITY PRESS
1987

PUBLICATION OF THIS BOOK
WAS AIDED BY A GRANT FROM
THE HENRY AND IDA WISSMANN FUND

Printed in the United States of America

In tribute to
Mlle ANNE-MARIE LA BONNARDIÈRE

Facta est quasi navis institoris
de longe portans panem suum.
(Prov. 31:14)

CONTENTS

ACKNOWLEDGMENTS

For generous help received in the preparation of this study, my thanks must go, first of all, to the authorities of Fordham University who awarded me the two Faculty Fellowship years that went into its inception and completion, respectively. I am also especially grateful to Dr. Eugene TeSelle and J. Patout Burns who read and offered valuable suggestions on an earlier version of this work; to Rev. W. Norris Clarke, s.j., and Rev. Thomas V. Bermingham, s.j., whose combined knowledge of Plotinus and of the Greek and Latin languages helped sharpen a number of statements touching on their fields of expertise.

I must thank, also, the authorities of Fairfield University, and particularly Rev. Christopher Mooney, s.j., Academic Vice President; and of Vanderbilt University, and particularly Dr. Jack Forstman, Dean of the Divinity School. They both accorded me warm hospitality, along with the privileges of Visiting Scholar, at their institutions during the year spent researching and writing the preliminary drafts that eventually, somehow, became this printed volume. For the alchemy that went into that transformation, I hold as chiefly responsible Mrs. Karen Harris and Dr. Mary Beatrice Schulte, the former for her typing, the latter for her editing, but both for highly professional skills unfailingly applied with enspiriting cheerfulness.

ABBREVIATIONS

AM	*Augustinus Magister*. Acta of the International Augustinian Congress. 3 vols. Paris: Etudes Augustiniennes, 1954.
AS	*Augustinian Studies*.
BA	Bibliothèque Augustinienne series of the works of St. Augustine; BA 48, for example, indicates Volume 48.
CCL	Corpus Christianorum, series latina, plus Volume number, e.g., CCL 50.
CSEL	Corpus Scriptorum Ecclesiasticorum Latinorum, plus Volume number, e.g., CSEL 58.
NRT	*Nouvelle Revue Théologique*.
RA	*Recherches Augustiniennes*.
REA	*Revue des Etudes Augustiniennes*.

Note: The texts in the Bibliothèque Augustinienne editions regularly reproduce the latest critically established text available, so I have made generous use of them. The critical edition of the *De Trinitate* in the CCL series, however, postdates the one used by the editors of the BA version, so I have checked, against the CCL edition, all the texts employed to support my contentions about that work. For those of Augustine's writings not yet published in the BA, CCL, or CSEL series, I have regularly worked from the texts recommended by Eligius Dekkers and Aemilius Gaar, editors of the *Clavis patrum latinorum*, 2nd ed. (= *Sacris Erudiri* III), published in Steenbrugge in 1961. All translations are my own.

In citing from Augustine's works, I have regularly omitted the chapter numbers, except in places in those works where they are indispensable (as occurs in certain passages of the *De civitate Dei* and the *Retractations*); only the book and paragraph numbers are given. Thus, for example, *Confessions* 5.10.19 is shortened to *Confessions* 5.19.

When giving a running commentary within a book of a single work, I cite the paragraph numbers only, in parentheses in the text, where the discussion of the material contained in that paragraph comes to a close.

All references to Alois Goldbacher's chronological essay on Augustine's *Letters* are from Appendix III of CSEL 58. I abbreviate to CSEL 58 plus arabic page number.

ABBREVIATIONS FOR AUGUSTINE'S WORKS
USED ONLY IN NOTES

Acad	*Contra Academicos*
Adim	*Contra Adimantum Manichaei discipulum*
AnOrig	*De anima et ejus origine*
Civ	*De civitate Dei*
Conf	*Confessiones*
CorGrat	*De correptione et gratia*
Cresc	*Ad Cresconium grammaticum*
De Div QQ	*De diversis quaestionibus 83*
Enchir	*Enchiridion ad Laurentium sive de fide, spe, et caritate*
En(n)	*Enarratio(nes) in Psalmos*
Ep(p)	*Epistula(e)*
ExpRom	*Expositio quarundam propositionum ex Epistula ad Romanos*
GenImp	*De Genesi ad litteram opus imperfectum*
GenLitt	*De Genesi ad litteram*
GenMan	*De Genesi contra Manichaeos*
Gest	*De gestis Pelagii*
Immort	*De immortalitate animae*
InJo	*Tractatus in Joannis evangelium*
Jul	*Contra Julianum Pelagianum*
JulImp	*Contra secundam Juliani responsionem opus imperfectum*
Lib	*De libero arbitrio*
LitPel	*Contra duas epistulas Pelagianorum*
Mer	*De peccatorum meritis et remissione*
Mor	*De moribus ecclesiae*
NatGrat	*De natura et gratia*
Nupt	*De nuptiis et concupiscentia*
Ord	*De ordine*
Oros	*Ad Orosium presbyterum*
Pecc	*De gratia Christi et de peccato originali*
Persev	*De dono perseverantiae*
Praed	*De praedestinatione sanctorum*
Quant	*De quantitate animae*
Retr	*Retractationes*
Ser(r)	*Sermo(nes)*

Simp	*Ad Simplicianum de diversis quaestionibus*
Sol	*Soliloquia*
Spir	*De spiritu et littera*
Trin	*De Trinitate*
Ver	*De vera religione*
Vita	*De beata vita*

THE ORIGIN OF THE SOUL
IN ST. AUGUSTINE'S
LATER WORKS

INTRODUCTION

Our advance in understanding St. Augustine depends on the concerted efforts of a multitude of scholars from a wide array of disciplines. Philosophers and theologians would naturally prefer to enter the scene only after a number of more "scientific" issues have been settled. They would relish the luxury of firm assurance that a critical text has been properly established, that translators and philologists have done the work their special skills fit them for, and that relevant questions of history, notably those affecting the chronological interrelationships of Augustine's works, have ripened into a consensus that gives, at least on major points, reasonable promise of irreversibility.

But when it comes to the chronological relationships of Augustine's later works, nothing is clearer than that confusion reigns. This is particularly, and painfully, true in the case of the *De Trinitate* and the *De peccatorum meritis et remissione*; but similar confusion besets the interpreter of the *De Genesi ad litteram* and, though slightly less so, the *De civitate Dei*. There was a time when such chronological questions awakened little or no trepidation in the breasts of Augustine's interpreters; there seemed no cogent reason to doubt that strong binding threads of consistency knit his thought together into a relatively seamless whole. Development there may have been, as scholars more or less consciously acknowledged; but the confidence prevailed that Augustine's thought serenely advanced, deepened perhaps and broadened, but never encountered major contradiction with itself.

One could peacefully suppose, for instance, that the theories of *memoria* in the *Confessions* and the *De Trinitate* could be made to illumine each other, viewing whatever differences that cropped up as complementary, perhaps slightly corrective, but surely in no

way contradictory one of the other.[1] Augustine's earlier works
might manifest an exploratory tendency, but surely his views on
the human situation had solidified by the time he wrote the Confessions. The contours of that view of man, accordingly, might be
assumed to remain substantially firm from that point on through
the intervening works and up until the final pages of the De civitate Dei.[2]

Perhaps the chronological problem assumes the importance it
does for me precisely because of the hypothesis I have been brought,
over the years, to adopt about Augustine's theory of man. Some
will be inclined to think it my problem, and uniquely mine. But
whatever its special importance for my hypothesis, the chronology
of Augustine's later works is unquestionably a problem in and for
itself. Nor is it a problem that my professional training, or indeed
my philosophic inclinations, equip me to tackle with the confidence
that my conclusions will finally settle the issue. I enter this dusty
arena only because I must.

The reasons for that "must" may be familiar to some readers
already. My interpretation of Augustine's theory of the human
condition compelled me to conclude that his early works enshrined
a view of man as "fallen soul";[3] that this view of our journey
through "this" life persisted in his Confessions;[4] but that, sometime

1. See, for example, Michael Schmaus's pages on this topic in his Die psychologische Trinitätslehre des hl. Augustinus (Münster: Aschendorff, 1927). Etienne
Gilson, on pp. 310–11 of his Introduction à l'étude de saint Augustin, 3rd ed. (Paris:
Vrin, 1949), which remains substantially unchanged from the first edition printed
in 1928, and which was published in English as The Christian Philosophy of Saint
Augustine, trans. L. E. M. Lynch (New York: Random House, 1960), claims to have
uncovered not "the slightest properly philosophical variation in any of [Augustine's]
essential theses." But that judgment was written some years before a new wave of
studies compelled a closer and more informed look at the Neoplatonic language
and thought-world Augustine was employing in his "understanding of the faith." It
would be difficult to conceive of anyone's taking Gilson's approach to Augustine's
thought in 1960, when the translation (p. 364) left this judgment unaltered, much
less in the 1980s. I refer to these two works henceforth as, respectively, Introduction
and Christian Philosophy.
    2. Erich Dinkler, in his Die Anthropologie Augustins (Stuttgart: Kohlhammer,
1934), pp. 4–5, explicitly makes this assumption of continuity into something like
a methodological principle.
    3. See St. Augustine's Early Theory of Man, A.D. 386–391 (Cambridge: The Bel-
knap Press of Harvard University Press, 1968). Henceforth, Early Theory.
    4. That hypothesis, presented at first in a more hypothetical vein in St. Augus-
tine's CONFESSIONS: The Odyssey of Soul (Cambridge: The Belknap Press of Harvard
University Press, 1969) (henceforth: Odyssey), I would consider this present study as
verifying. I had long been baffled by both the grounds for, and surprising rancor of,

around the year 415, the issues surrounding the Pelagian controversy awoke him to the realization that it might be difficult to square his earlier theory with St. Paul's teaching in the Epistle to the Romans.[5] One would be led to expect, then, that the works he published after 415—and the final publication of the *De Trinitate* now appears surely to have occurred well after that date[6]—should have been rinsed clear of that "fallen soul" theory. It was puzzling to find that I could devise no way of interpreting the view of man embodied in the *De Trinitate* except as substantially consistent with that earlier, and presumably discarded, theory![7] To add to my embarrassment, the *De Genesi ad litteram*, on which accepted chronologies tell us Augustine worked over many of the same years he devoted to the *De Trinitate*, seemed, at least on the face of it, to be applying the text of Romans to refute this very theory. At the same time, all the accepted accounts of the *De civitate Dei* stressed the view that Augustine's repudiation of Origen in that work implied unambiguous rejection of the "fallen soul" view that history associates with his name. As for the *Retractations*, the accepted view concluded, nothing could be clearer than Augustine's repudiation of Origenism in that work.

One way out of this anomaly would have been to deny that the *De Trinitate* does, after all, embody the offending theory; but diligent re-examination of that work persuaded me that honesty forbade that escape route. How to reduce the anomaly? Here, a point of chronology assumed fascinating suggestiveness. Sometime around that pivotal date, 415,[8] two things seem to have happened:

Goulven Madec's persistent criticisms of my views; for evidence that he has seriously misunderstood me, and attacked what he terms my "methodology" from a seriously questionable standpoint of his own, see my *St. Augustine's Platonism* (Villanova: Villanova University Press, 1984). (Henceforth: *Platonism.*) There I endeavor to clear up his confusions on what I really hold, as well as indicate where his counterview bears more searching examination. (This same work contains references and replies to several other critics of the above two books, as well as of subsequent articles.)

5. See "Augustine's Rejection of the Fall of the Soul," AS, 4 (1973), 1–32. Henceforth: "Rejection."

6. See Anne-Marie La Bonnardière's *Recherches de chronologie augustinienne* (Paris: Etudes Augustiniennes, 1965), esp. pp. 165–77. (Henceforth: *Chronologie.*) This work is a nearly impeccable model of how this sort of thing must be done.

7. See "The Human Being as 'Fallen Soul' in St. Augustine's *De Trinitate,*" *Mediaevalia*, 4 (1978), 33–58. Henceforth: "Fallen Soul."

8. This date must be left somewhat vague for the moment. We shall see that the chronology of this entire period, including that of Augustine's *Epp*, calls for careful re-examination. Note that Eugene TeSelle, in *Augustine the Theologian*

Augustine's discovery of Romans' bearing on the "fallen soul"
theory, and the theft of the major portion of the *De Trinitate*.
Coincidence? Perhaps. But in any event, the possibility dawned
that Augustine may have felt obliged, willy-nilly, to finish the
twelfth of that fifteen-book work, and to write the three concluding
books, in grudging consistency with a theory of man he had already
seen he must abandon.[9]

This was the hypothetical possibility—temporarily entertained—
which brought me to test the conclusions of others, more appropriately trained than I, perhaps, but working with those serene assumptions that might account for the fact that, in Augustine's phrase,
securius loquebantur. What had become a gnawing problem for me
had never been a live issue for them; they could well afford to hand
down conclusions that, though at times conjectural, seemed both
reasonable and uncontroversial at the time. My primary focus had
to be on the publication history of the *De Trinitate*, but it soon
became clear that the relationship of that work to the *De Genesi
ad litteram* had constantly to be kept in view. My working hypothesis may have forced me to pour more skeptical acid than is
considered decent on the inferences drawn by my predecessors, but
I was brought to suspect numerous places where argumentation
grew alarmingly circular, and where threads of conjecture and
tatters of evidence were suddenly presented to us, *presto*, as the
imperial garment of historical truth. Even my doubts, however, I
must sometimes put forth as hypothetical; the art of attaining
historical knowledge is exactly that, and I can scarcely claim to be
a master of it. The fool may have more questions than the wise
historian can answer; and yet, the fable assures us, even when less
than tutored, but prompted by a sharper set of questions than
others have felt compelled to ask, the fresh look at accepted truths

(New York: Herder & Herder, 1970) (henceforth: *Theologian*), p. 257, dates
Augustine's rejection of this "possibility" as occurring in *GenLitt* 6.15-17, which
"probably comes from the same period," i.e., 406. That probability he buttresses
with some suggestive doctrinal parallels between *GenLitt*, *Trin*, and *InJo*, none of
them, however, touching on this precise issue. I find it much more plausible that
this rejection in *GenLitt* represents a later "emendation." But the evidence for that
contention must await examination further on.

9. Subsequent study of the question has persuaded me that this hypothesis was
ill-conceived. When Augustine finally came to incorporate his "fallen soul" theory
in Books 13 and 14 of the *Trin*, he did so with far less reluctance than I had originally supposed.

may rightly ask whether the emperor's clothes are real, after all.

To ward off a possible misunderstanding: I mean neither to question that historians *must* often work from shreds of evidence, nor to deny that intelligent conjecture must frequently intervene in the effort to weave the pattern that makes most reasonable sense of that evidence. Nor do I mean to call "Foul!" because, in phases of the process, the unifying power of the pattern inevitably influences one's reading of the evidence. It would be naïve, even perverse, to deny the magical (and often *legitimately* persuasive) power the master historian brings to this patterning task. But any shred of evidence may be more ambiguous on re-examination than it first appeared; not every historical conjecture is as compelling as it might be. And when an entire historical pattern begins to unravel, worn through by the abrasion of new evidence and/or equally cogent counter-conjecture, it may sometimes be the best policy to dismiss the old pattern in its entirety for the moment, submit each atom of evidence to critical re-examination, and experiment with various alternative patterns that suggest themselves to the imagination. The initial stages of such a re-examination may appear excessively, almost unreasonably, corrosive; but to clear the mind of the older pattern, one may be obliged to examine each of its constituents "out of all connection," so to speak, in the hope of isolating first what we can be *sure* that constituent points to— whether to one, or to one of several, possible new arrangements.

Permit me to illustrate my meaning by an examination of Ephrem Hendrikx' "Note Complémentaire" to the Introduction of the Bibliothèque Augustinienne edition of the *De Trinitate*,[10] treating the chronology of that work. Hendrikx first accepts a correction to the date given in the *Retractations* for Augustine's disputation with Felix the Manichee: instead of 404, this event must have occurred in the year 398. This permits him, along with others,[11] to date the inception of the *De Trinitate* shortly after the *Contra Felicem*, as indicated by the order given in the *Retractations*: in

10. See BA 15 (Paris, 1955), pp. 557–66. This "Note" is substantially the reproduction of Hendrikx' article on the same question: "La date de composition du *De Trinitate* de saint Augustin," *L'Année Théologique Augustinienne*, 12 (1952), 305–16.

11. Those others include distinguished scholars like Gustave Bardy, Seraphim Zarb, and Paul Monceaux: see William Mountain's list of references in CCL 50, pp. lxxxii-xcvi.

the year 399, very close to the brief Trinitarian meditation on man which occurs in Book 13 of the *Confessions*. "It seems very acceptable," Hendrikx then infers, "that on that occasion [of composing *Confessions* 13.12] the idea came to Augustine to write a special work on the subject." *De fait* (the inference once provisionally made has somehow jelled into fact), after completing the *Contra Felicem* and the six brief opuscula listed after it—they *could not* have taken him much time—Augustine went to work, toward the summer of 399, on his *De Trinitate*.

Even should I pass over several other shaky inferences Hendrikx permits himself,[12] the highly speculative tone of his argument should be clear already. But alas, his whole case depends on a change of dating for the *Contra Felicem* which has more recently been found to defy the data of the Julian calendar;[13] the only year that satisfies those data is 404, after all, and if the *Retractations* are to be believed, Augustine is telling us he began his *De Trinitate* sometime *after* that date.

There is a similarly speculative cast to Hendrikx' arguments for 419 as the date of the final publication of the *De Trinitate*.[14] Though it may be "difficult" to believe that Augustine worked on completing this treatise during the busy and literarily productive years 420–425, Mlle La Bonnardière's far soberer researches have shown this to be the fact;[15] and while Augustine's *De Trinitate* citations of passages in the *De civitate* and *In Joannem* "can suggest" that the cited passages were dictated or written only a short time before the passages citing them, they can do little more than that. Such arguments are transparently risky.[16] What, though, accounted for

---

12. These inferences concern, among other things, the dating of *Conf* 13 and the composition of the entire work. Hendrikx imagines that the first nine books had been distributed and read before Books 10–13 were composed. This is a highly questionable supposition, given what we are daily discovering about the unity of the entire work.

13. See the note by Régis Jolivet and Maurice Jourjon, in their edition–translation of *Six Traités anti-manichéens*, BA 17 (Paris, 1961), pp. 787–88.

14. BA 15, pp. 558–59; Hendrikx confidently concludes that "the only possible remaining date for the completion and the publication of the *De Trinitate* is the year 419."

15. See note 6, above.

16. BA 15, p. 559. Hendrikx' conjecture that Augustine was subjected to a "general assault" from his fellow-bishops, insisting that he publish *Trin* without further delay, and that this assault took place "sans doute" during his sojourn in Carthage in 418, turns out to be another flight of historical fancy; see La Bonnardière, *Chronologie*, p. 70n5. (Compare Hendrikx' "il va de soi" on the same question,

Augustine's long hesitations about final publication? "It is clear," we are assured, that the great difficulty of the subject treated in Books 5–7, the theory of "relations" as applied to the Trinity, along with the "novelty" of Augustine's treatment, "slowed up the rhythm" of his advance.[17] Possible, even probable, but factual? It would be wrongheaded to complain that Hendrikx' reading of the evidence was influenced by the pattern he thought capable of making sense of that evidence; we all do that, and must. But that pattern does seem to have exerted, at various points, so excessive a magnetic power as to soften his judgment on how much the evidence warranted.[18]

But Hendrikx' attempt to reconstruct the publication history of the *De Trinitate* is partially dependent on a pattern he inherited from Irénée Chevalier's study of Trinitarian "relations" theory.[19] Though this theory is developed in Books 5 through 7 of the *De Trinitate*, Chevalier's contention was that this section was a later insertion. Augustine, he thought to demonstrate, could be shown to have worked out this theory sometime between the years 413 and 416.[20] As Hendrikx noted, Augustine's correspondence during those years shows him again and again postponing his publication

p. 566.) *Ep 143*, as we shall see, tells us much about the pressure "the brothers" like Marcellinus (speaking for his fellow-*believers*) were applying to persuade Augustine to hurry his publication. But that letter tells us other things as well; closer study of it could have obviated the need for many of Hendrikx' ungrounded speculations.

17. BA 15, p. 561. But there is a question of consistency here. Hendrikx later writes as though this long delay occurred around the year 412 or afterward, whereas his theory seems here to suppose a unity of conception and composition implying that Books 5–7 were written by the end of 401.

18. I pass over a number of Hendrikx' questionable affirmations in BA 15, pp. 562–66, but two of them are worth noticing. He supports his claim that Augustine must have written *Cresc* after having written the first draft of the entire *Trin* "dans un premier jet" (p. 562) by the circular argument that the latter was finally published in 419 (p. 563), as well as by forced interpretations of *Epp 120, 143*, and *162* (pp. 563–64); that same publication date also underlies his proposal that the famous theft of Books 1–12 of *Trin* must have occurred in 416 (p. 565). On this dubious notion of the unitary conception of *Trin*, compare TeSelle, *Theologian*, pp. 223–37, esp. 224. La Bonnardière, *Chronologie*, p. 169, places this theft after 417 or even 418, but future scholars may have to ask if her evidence and argument point to the date of the actual *theft*, or to the date of Augustine's subsequent *resumption* of the work. Then the question becomes: How long were his labors on *Trin* interrupted?

19. *Augustin et la pensée grecque: Les Relations Trinitaires* (Fribourg: Librairie de l'Université, 1940). Henceforth, *Relations*.

20. *Relations*, pp. 16–36. TeSelle, *Theologian*, pp. 294–95, places more faith in Chevalier's case than I am able to do.

of, indeed even his progress on, the *De Trinitate*. What more likely reason for these delaying tactics than the difficulty involved in thinking out this new, and brain-testing, theory?

Chevalier's method of demonstration takes the following turn: if we look into Augustine's other works for where and when he speaks and writes of the Trinitarian relations, we may find when this problem was uppermost in his mind—*prima facie* evidence, at least, for when he was thinking out the implications of relation-theory. Chevalier's results are at first blush impressive. He uncovers five different works[21] in which Augustine discusses Trinitarian relations, and they all seem to occur within the three-year span running from 413 to 416. A strong convergence, indeed! Conclusion: Augustine was working on Books 5 to 7 of the *De Trinitate* between those years.

Later research, alas, has taken most of the starch out of Chevalier's case. His dating of the first Sermon of *Enarratio in Psalmum 68* remains valid; it would seem to have been preached during the summer of 414. But *Letters 238* to *241*, Augustine's exchange with the crypto-Arian Pascentius, which Chevalier claims for the year 414 or thereabouts, could have been written a number of years before,[22] or a number of years afterward;[23] we have no solid evidence to go on.[24] But Mlle La Bonnardière has shown, convincingly I think, that *Letter 170*, to Maximus, must be dated as of 418 at the earliest,[25] whereas the *Tractatus in Joannem 39* could date anywhere from 419 at the earliest to 421 at the latest.[26] The last text Chevalier adduces is from the *De civitate Dei* 11. He notes, rightly, that Orosius' dedication to his *Adversus paganos*, a work he finished

21. *Relations*, pp. 16–37; these five works I deal with immediately below.

22. See, for example, Frits G. L. van der Meer, *Augustine the Bishop*, trans. Brian Battershaw and G. R. Lamb (New York: Sheed and Ward, 1961; henceforth: *Bishop*), pp. 120–21, who places the exchange with Pascentius in 408, though without producing his support for this dating.

23. La Bonnardière, in *Chronologie*, pp. 91–101, points out the evidence for an intensification of activity on the part of Arian heretics around the year 418; this exchange *could* have occurred in that same period.

24. Chevalier refers to the fact that Alois Goldbacher, in the chronological introduction to his edition of Augustine's *Epp*, CSEL 58, 44–45, "thinks" Augustine may have been somewhere near his sixtieth year—an educated guess, but little more than that.

25. *Chronologie*, p. 98; but see the supporting discussion, which may someday have to undergo review.

26. *Chronologie*, p. 117. The supporting discussion for this conclusion starts on p. 87.

in 417, speaks of Augustine's having completed Books 1 to 10, and presumably moved on to Book 11, at the time Orosius took up his own pen. Chevalier candidly admits that this gives us a *terminus a quo*, but no firm indication of when Augustine might have completed Book 11; but since Book 12 of the *De civitate* is actually cited in Book 13 of the *De Trinitate*, we may have, there, evidence for the *terminus ad quem*. Chevalier's argument now supposes that the *De Trinitate* was completed in the year 419, and that Book 13 must therefore date from 418 or thereabouts. That argument, too, Mlle La Bonnardière has rendered somewhat porous by showing that the *De Trinitate* was not completed before the year 420, and that its completion could conceivably date from a year or even several years after that.[27]

But even were one to grant Chevalier's date for *De civitate* 11, the imposing convergence he hoped to present has unraveled; *Enarratio 68* may well date from 414, and *De civitate* 11 from 417 or 418, but all the connecting tissue between these two texts has vanished. Others, true, have sought to buttress his failing case with other indications.[28] *Letter 151*, for instance, dating from 413/414,[29] has Augustine expressing his determination to employ whatever leisure he can find in the study of "ecclesiastical sciences"; he could conceivably have intended to read the Eastern Church writers on the Trinity, but can we know this? *Letter 148*,[30] written shortly before, may be thought to corroborate that conjecture, since Augustine refers to both Athanasius and Gregory as bearing on the question under discussion; but the question being discussed is precisely whether God can be seen with corporeal eyes![31] Did Chevalier's

27. *Chronologie*, pp. 69, 77, 165–66; though La Bonnardière, p. 167n4, thinks *Civ* 13 dates from 417/418.
28. Notably TeSelle, in *Theologian*, pp. 294–95.
29. TeSelle refers especially to *Ep 151* 13.
30. Specifically, *Ep 148* 10.
31. Note that TeSelle, *Theologian*, p. 294, refers to *Ep 173* as supporting the view that Augustine first sent off Books 1–12 to Aurelius in Carthage. He is repeating an error originally made by Chevalier, *Relations*, p. 26, for the letter to Aurelius in question is *Ep 174*. That mistake, however, was necessary for Chevalier's argument, for Goldbacher had discovered a letter, which he numbers *173A*, in which Augustine writes to his "literary agent," Deogratias, as though he were at long last ready to "edit" the (presumably *final* version of?) *Trin*. Goldbacher then argues from the date he *assumed* for the final publication of the work, 416, that *Ep 173A must* have been written sometime in 416, and *Ep 174* to Aurelius, accordingly, only a short time afterward, i.e., in 416 as well. But Chevalier overlooks the fact that Goldbacher's whole argument depends on his assumption that *Trin* was published in 416, and

convergence still hold strong, these conjectures might still have some plausibility; but without that convergence to rest on, they hang inconclusively in midair, and add nothing to our knowledge.

But besides removing prop after prop from under his apparent convergence, more recent research has called into question Chevalier's whole angle of attack. Instead of speaking and writing about the Trinitarian relations because the subject—and the composition of Books 5 to 7 of the *De Trinitate*—happened to be his temporary preoccupation, as Chevalier's hypothesis ran, it is now clear that Augustine wrote and spoke on this subject over a long span of years, precisely when the needs of his flock demanded it. When, for instance, the barbarian invasions promoted the influx of a number of Arians into Africa, the occasion to speak on Trinitarian doctrine presented itself with greater frequency and urgency. Hence, the comprehensive list of Trinitarian heresies Mlle La Bonnardière has been able to draw up,[32] representing the foci of Augustine's concern in *Tractatus in Joannem 26* to *53*, all of them—including Chevalier's *Tractatus 39*—preached between the years 419 and 421, when this Arian challenge reached its acutest stage. The scholar's psychology may direct his conversations toward the topics he is writing on; but a busy preacher, his eye on the needs of his congregation, can less often afford that luxury.

It is difficult to criticize the achievements of scholars, especially more eminent scholars, without appearing graceless. But this negative moment in my argument was unavoidable: it was meant to free the reader's mind of prevailing patterns, to entertain with at least initial sympathy the pattern I hope to propose in their place. A brief summary of that alternate pattern may serve as a road map through the often heterogeneous chapters of this study.[33]

---

that he himself was assuming a publication date of 419; Chevalier then goes on to infer that *Ep 174* to Aurelius, which his mind still "dates" as 416, *could not* have referred to the *entire* work. The lesson is one we shall relearn at several other junctures in this study: change one date in an accepted chronology, and you must be alert to the need for changing *a number of other* interdependent dates as well. But we shall have occasion to see that a more careful reading of *Ep 174* itself, as well as Augustine's remarks on this whole episode in *Retr*, should have obviated Chevalier's error: it could not be clearer that *Ep 174* accompanied *Trin* in its *completed* state.

32. *Chronologie*, pp. 91–92.

33. The evidence for all of these claims will be developed below, of course; for the moment, I am only furnishing a road map of what might otherwise seem an aimlessly meandering journey.

My central contention is this: one important key to understanding Augustine's later development as a thinker is found in his protracted wrestling with the question of the "origin" of the human soul. In his *De libero arbitrio*, Augustine had sketched the "hypotheses" regnant in his time as four: creationism, traducianism, and two variants on the soul as pre-existent: either it was divinely "sent" or it sinfully "fell" into the body. Crucial to his thought on that troubling question was his eventual realization that St. Paul, in Romans 9:11, seemed peremptorily to have excluded the fourth of these: that the soul pre-existed its incarnate state, sinned, and "fell" into this world of bodies. That theory, Augustine was to learn in time, was Origen's; one service it rendered was that of lending God's election of this soul rather than that—of Jacob rather than Esau, for example—an appearance of "justice." But, Origen's adversaries argued, Romans 9:11 precisely rejects the notion that God's election of Jacob rather than Esau was contingent on any previous merits they might have had: before they were born, they had done neither good nor evil.

In Africa, far from the scene of these controversies, and occupied with the Manichaean heresy and the Donatist schism by turns, Augustine knows very little of the controversy stirred up by Origen's views. He catches muted echoes of it, writes to Jerome in Bethlehem to have them clarified, with no result. Simplician writes to him, posing a series of questions, one of them directly on Romans 9:11 and its implications. Augustine answers him, and finds himself compelled to reverse his own earlier interpretation of the text and to exclude now all divine consideration of merits: God's election is perfectly free, else grace would not be truly grace. But he makes no application to the question of the soul's origin. Indeed, events show that he sails serenely on, assuming that, as far as Scriptural evidence is concerned, the four hypotheses he had outlined in his *De libero arbitrio* remain in equal contention; his mind is, understandably, elsewhere.

But in the year 410, just as he and his fellow-bishops were busy tying up the Donatist controversy, the fall of Rome brings a wave of refugees to the shores of Africa. Among them are Pelagius and his lieutenant, Caelestius. It is Caelestius who mounts an attack against the African Church's understanding of infant baptism; it could not be for the "remission" of any sin, since infants are

sinless. Caelestius bases his argument on the creationist hypothesis
of the soul's origin: it is an insult to their Creator to contend that,
fresh from the creative hand of God, unborn souls can be sinful.
The African theology of the matter was understandable, of course,
since they were all following Tertullian in his erroneous espousal
of the traducianist hypothesis; but, Caelestius implies, the creationist wisdom of the more intellectual Eastern Churches will soon
dispel that error.

Baptismal theology had been at the very center of the Donatist
controversy; Caelestius could scarcely have chosen a more neuralgic
point for his attack. Here was the doctrine of grace, linked explicitly with the question of the soul's origin, and infant baptism
made the very nub of the issue. The loyal Catholics of Carthage
are thrown into a mixture of rage and confusion. But they have an
able and zealous spokesman in the Count Marcellinus: he has
already had cordial dealings with Augustine, not only with respect
to the Donatist schism, but also regarding the growing pagan re-
sentment of Christianity brought on by the fall of Rome. He writes
repeatedly to Augustine, off in Hippo, bringing him abreast of
events in Carthage, and prodding him to bring some clarity into
the confusion stirred up by Caelestius' Pelagian propaganda.

Marcellinus is aware that Augustine is already hard at work on
two lengthy treatises, his *De Trinitate* and his *De Genesi ad litteram*,
and aware, as well, that both treatises must touch on issues inflamed
by this new controversy. In addition to eliciting from him a number
of other writings—the first two books of the *De civitate Dei*, the *De
spiritu et littera*, and the *De peccatorum meritis et remissione*, all of
which Augustine dedicates to his revered friend—Marcellinus keeps
urging him to publish, as rapidly as he can, the two great treatises
the Catholic "brethren" impatiently await from him. Also aware
of Augustine's Trinitarian preoccupations is Consentius: he makes
a visit to Hippo to consult him, but Augustine is away, recovering
from an illness, so he leaves a letter asking for help on some questions that bother him.

To both Consentius and Marcellinus Augustine makes it clear
that he is having difficulty finishing his *De Trinitate*, and the *De
Genesi ad litteram* as well. But where does the difficulty lie? Not
with Trinitarian relations theory—he never once mentions that.
The difficulty to which he directly points has to do with the human

soul and, more precisely still, with the problem of the soul's origin. The Pelagian controversy has made him see that this is a far more "dangerous" question than he had realized.

About this time a young priest, Paul Orosius, presents himself at Augustine's door; he has come from Spain, where his fellow-believers are being propagandized with a potpourri of Priscillian-ism and Origenism, including Origen's adventurous speculations on the origin and destiny of human souls. Foiled in his repeated attempts to extract such information by correspondence from Jerome in Bethlehem, Augustine welcomes this new knowledge, and responds with a little work (the *Ad Orosium*) refuting the contentions, some heretical, others highly questionable, about which he had just learned. His treatment of Origen's theory of the soul's repeated cycles of fall and return is labored and roundabout; he obviously has no apodictic Scriptural grounds for rejecting it out of hand. The bearing of Romans 9:11 on the issue has not yet occurred, or been communicated, to him. A letter from Marcellinus on the same topic prompts a reply that shows he still considers all four hypotheses as possible options for believing Catholics. Marcel-linus appeals to Jerome; some time afterward, Jerome answers briefly, but in essence puts the ball back into Augustine's court.

Meantime, in September 413, Marcellinus is put to death. Some time after his death, Augustine replies, "consulting" Jerome on the question. Pelagianism has made it a burning issue and, what is more, based the rejection of infant baptism for remission of sin precisely on the hypothesis Jerome is known to favor, creationism. Both he and Jerome agree that—excluding Manichaeism—the same four hypotheses are up for adjudication. Augustine shows his dis-taste for the cyclic implications of the Origenist hypothesis Orosius had explained to him, as well as for the materialistic coloration of traducianism; but as far as the evidence of Scripture goes, he must leave all four hypotheses "open," while awaiting Jerome's reply to the glaring difficulties he sees as affecting the creationist proposal.

The year is 415; Marcellinus has been dead since September 413; and yet, at two distinct junctures in a work dedicated to him, the *De peccatorum meritis et remissione,* Augustine treats the soul's origin, and twice rejects the fourth, pre-existent–fall, hypothesis. That rejection, to all appearances, is crisp, firm, and unambiguous. He settles the matter quite simply by adducing the single text from

Romans 9:11. How can he so confidently reject, presumably in the year 412/413, an hypothesis that he still considers an open possibility a year and then two years later? The answer I propose is that the *De meritis* we read today is an emended version, still prefaced by the dedication written to Marcellinus when he was alive, but finally published some years after his death. But in what year? Surely subsequent to Augustine's discovery of the bearing Romans 9:11 had on the "fall" of the pre-existent soul; and the earliest independent evidence we have for that dates from the year 417/418.

But 417 was an interesting year indeed. Our best evidence suggests it as the year when some of Augustine's over-zealous friends, long out of patience with his repeated excuses and delays, purloined what he had completed of his *De Trinitate* and had it copied and distributed. Augustine is furious; he resolves never to finish the *De Trinitate*; but then, he is finally prevailed upon to do so. When? The best information we now have points to the year 420 or 421, at the earliest. He sends the completed work to Aurelius, Primate of Africa, with a covering letter. That letter, exposing the unhappy theft and what he subsequently felt compelled to do about it, he prescribes should stand as introduction to all future editions of the *De Trinitate*; it will alert his readers to the fact that he could do no other than complete the work in basic consistency with the books that had been filched from him. Those books, I am suggesting (Books 1 to 11, with a substantial portion of Book 12), were composed *before* Augustine came to realize that Romans 9:11 precluded exactly the theory of the soul he had embedded in his *De Trinitate*: the theory of the soul as pre-existent and "fallen" into the world of bodies. But the same cannot be said, I am now convinced, of Books 13 and 14. By the time he wrote these closing books, Augustine had come, or been brought, to see that Romans 9:11 appeared, at least, to preclude the "fallen soul" hypothesis. Was it possible that he could have written that theory into these books for the sake of consistency with the earlier books that had been purloined and in spite of his conviction that Paul's authority stood against that view of our human condition? Given the seriousness Augustine had come to attach to this question, and its close connection, as he saw it, with the *fundatissima fides* Pelagius had attacked, that notion struck me as highly implausible. It forced me to re-examine Books 11 through 14 of the *De Trinitate*. But there was no other way of interpreting the anthropology of those books; the offending view of souls as fallen remained stubbornly encased in them. Perhaps some light could be gleaned from his other works from the same period and, notably, from the *De Genesi ad litteram*.

For Augustine still had the *De Genesi ad litteram* safely in his possession when the force of Romans 9:11 dawned on him; this enabled him to "emend" sections of that work, composed earlier, in such a way as to warn believers of the dangers that text pointed to in the "fall" hypothesis. After two inconclusive brushes with the problem of the soul's origin, however, Augustine finds himself obliged to return to it. He breaks the forward progress of his work and invents a pretext for according the question a full-scale treatment in the tenth book of the *De Genesi*. But this time his starting point is frankly derived from St. Paul. Which of these four hypotheses, he asks, can be squared with the Pauline affirmations that we all, even infants, stand in need of Christ's redemptive grace conferred in baptism? Only two hypotheses survive the examination Augustine brings to the issue: precisely those two which can account for the soul's being sinful from birth if not before—the "fallen soul" and the traducianist theories. This leaves Augustine in a painful quandary; for Romans 9:11 would appear, at least, to exclude the "fallen soul" alternative, whereas the traducianist view comes laden with a materialistic notion of the soul which Augustine finds entirely repulsive.

In his dilemma, Augustine begins to toy with a distinction: Romans 9:11 *may* only have meant to exclude our having committed any sin before we were born into our "proper" lives in this body and into our individual personal histories in time. Does this leave room for some kind of sin we might have committed even before those proper lives began? The distinction implied by that notion of "proper" lives blinks on and off through the works of his later period, until he gains a certain guarded confidence that it may, indeed, provide a way out of his dilemma. We may be fallen souls, after all, but the implications of that fall must be importantly different from the ones which Origen drew; one may, then, hold firm to a theory of souls as fallen, and still reject the theory which Origen proposed.

Once he sees that avenue open out before him, I submit, Augustine felt himself freed to finish off both his *De Trinitate* and *De civitate*, encasing in both those works a view of human beings as contemplative souls, plunged into the misery to which the painful "mortality" of our present bodies clearly attests. For we must once have lived a "common" life, not only "in" Adam, but a life which made us identical with Adam. We sinned in his sinning; his sin was truly ours; and so, the punishment that "this" human life represents is just, and only Christ's redemptive grace can wipe it away.

Even this highly condensed summary will give the reader some idea of the readjustments required in our view of the later Augustine if all I claim here is true. But our picture of the early Augustine is also affected. The development sketched here tends to confirm the view that up until, and well after, the composition of his *Confessions*, Augustine's preferred theory was that human beings were fallen souls. But no such summary can indicate the number of points at which I have felt both obliged and entitled to overturn the currently accepted consensus on very particular questions. Some of those questions are chronological. If I am even remotely right, we need a serious overhaul of the chronologies once so heroically established by scholars like Zarb, Bardy, and Goldbacher. Which brings us back to the array of scholars, varied in training and competence, to which a work like this is inevitably addressed—and modestly addressed. No single student of Augustine should have the temerity to publish a book like this; it represents the results of much long digging, but, even more than that, it raises a shout to fellow-workers on how much digging remains to be done, and where. This, then, is an unfinished book; but if my fellow-diggers find it worth their attention, someone else, some thirty years from now, may find he has meanwhile been furnished the tools required to finish it. Keenly aware of how specialized and therefore limited each of our individual efforts is, I have nonetheless succumbed to one last sin of presumption: I have chosen to dedicate this work to one whose years of generous, tireless, and self-effacing labors have turned up so much pure gold that enriches us all.

1

THE
De Libero Arbitrio III

ANY APPROACH TO Augustine's later theory of man must begin with
a close review of the third book of his *De libero arbitrio*.[1] Though
completed sometime around 395, well before the presentation of
the theory encased in the *Confessions*, this work is pivotal for several
reasons. First, it shows Augustine entertaining the famous four
"hypotheses" on the origin of the soul, a central feature of any
theory of man during his century; and, secondly (partly because
of his handling of those four hypotheses), it becomes a target for
later objectors to his views. That makes it a benchmark for deciding
how his later theory of man relates to his earlier view.

But a decisive reason for making such a close review of this book
is its inherent difficulty. The controversy that raged some years
back[2] among such scholars as de Montcheuil, Boyer, de Lubac,
Trapè, and LeBourlier is testimony to that. When men of such
talent, and fundamental good will, cannot agree on what Augustine
said and meant at crucial turnings of this relatively compact work,

1. My citations and translations are based on the BA 6 edition of *Lib* (Paris,
1976), edited, translated and commented on by Goulven Madec. Where my translations differ from Madec's French version, I shall footnote that fact, and explain
my grounds for differing.
   Since virtually all references are to *Lib* 3, I indicate, in my text, only the paragraph
number being discussed.
2. For ample bibliography, and some history of this controversy, see Madec's
note in BA 6, pp. 578-80. The contributions of central concern to us here are: Yves
de Montcheuil, s.j., "L'hypothèse de l'état originel d'ignorance et de difficulté
d'après le *De Libero Arbitrio* de saint Augustin," *Mélanges théologiques* (Paris:
Aubier, 1946), pp. 93-111; Charles Boyer, s.j., "Dieu pouvait-il créer l'homme dans
l'état d'ignorance et de difficulté?" *Essais sur la doctrine de saint Augustin* (Paris:
Beauchesne, 1932), pp. 237-71; and Henri de Lubac, s.j., "Note sur saint Augustin,
De Libero Arbitrio," AM III, pp. 279-86. Madec avows his own inability to resolve
this controversy; the reason, I shall try to show, is that he accepts too many of the
questionable assumptions shared by de Montcheuil, Boyer, and de Lubac.

one begins to wonder whether the work itself is a model of clarity. True, that controversy was complicated and occasionally beclouded by the intrusion of issues extraneous in varying degrees to the interpretation of Augustine's text. Some of those issues concerned the theology contemporary with the controversy, notably those raised by de Lubac's *Surnaturel*; one had to wonder whether such contemporary concerns truly illuminated Augustine's own.[3] Other issues were more historical, focusing on the Augustinian interpretations of Jansenius, Baius, and Noris; it was not always clear how what these men said, or, indeed, "would have said," clarified what Augustine himself meant to say. But even when it came to what Augustine did say, advocates of one side or the other appealed to an array of much later texts, drawn from more mature stages in his developing thought on grace and nature, when different adversaries chose to use his earlier affirmations against him; but in those later texts, it is not always immediately evident how much Augustine's self-defense takes the form of exact interpretation, "retractation," or even *re*interpretation of his thinking in this less mature work. Those complications did not always make the task of interpreting *this* work, as it stands, an easier one; but the fact remains that the work itself is scarcely easy of interpretation, so that the difficulties it has inspired may be to a large degree of Augustine's own making.

AUGUSTINE'S COMMANDING INTENTION

The first challenge to the interpreter is to uncover, if he can, Augustine's own point of view, his precise preoccupations in the work, uncomplicated by the differing preoccupations and points of view commanding later discussions. And here all partisans in the controversy agree, first, that his principal target in this whole discussion is the Manichaean heresy, and second, that his governing preoccupation is to defend the "Catholic" view of human freedom (as he understands that view) against Manichaean objections.[4]

First, then, Augustine's target is the Manichaean heresy. But the

3. Madec (p. 580) quotes de Lubac ("Note," 279) as characterizing de Montcheuil's treatment as a "model of analysis"; one could question whether this was an entirely disinterested judgment, as we shall see.
4. While all parties in the debate agree in principle that this is Augustine's preoccupation, not all of them remain consistently faithful to the ground rules that perspective should have imposed.

common ground he shares with his adversaries is this: the experience of human beings attests to the fact that we encounter "evils" in our world. Now, the Manichaean claim was that, to "understand" this problem of evil, one had to admit a substantial Principle of Evil, an anti-God, so to speak, as source of them; for piety forbids us to blame God for evil. As applied to the present question, the Manichaean position went, the Catholic teaching on human freedom and responsibility for sin, if pushed to its ultimate roots, logically wound up blaming their one God for the evils for which Catholics hold that human freedom is responsible.

In a word, then, the third book of the *De libero arbitrio* represents a Catholic "theodicy" of free will, against Manichaean objections.[5] Other aspects of Manichaean teaching Augustine feels he has adequately treated elsewhere; he will not concern himself directly with them here. Nor will he take the more aggressive tack of carrying the battle into the Manichaean camp—of arguing, for example, that the suppositions *behind* their objections are questionable, absurd, or in their own way more impious than the "impiety" with which they charge the *Catholica*. No, his consistent intention throughout this book will remain that of *neutralizing* a variety of Manichaean objections, of showing that the conclusions they thought evident were not valid conclusions after all. And, grossly put for now, all their objections come down to claiming that if God gave us free will, He must ultimately be blamed for the sins we freely commit, and therefore is not the loving, just God Catholics proclaim as the object of their praise and adoration.

God, for instance (the first objection runs), infallibly foresees our future sins; hence, He must bear ultimate responsibility for them (4–11).[6] This objection countered, another takes its place: God could have abstained from creating creatures who could sin (and who He foresaw would sin). Augustine replies at considerable length (12–50) to this objection and to the various forms it assumes.

5. Madec, indeed, p. 184, extends this theodicean intention to the entire three books of *Lib*, and I tend to agree with that view. That unity of intention, however, should not beguile us into forgetting that Augustine seems to have strung out the composition of the work over three, four, and, more probably, eight years; see Madec, p. 157. That factor may well have introduced a certain jaggedness in the way he executed his original intention; see Madec's discussion of Olivier DuRoy's proposals, pp. 158–62.

6. Madec, pp. 167–70, gives a valuable content summary of the work; my exposition here quite deliberately follows his summary.

He does so by appealing to the magnificent order of a creation in which God makes "all things" (*omnia*), from highest angelic to lowest material beings, not only exist, but exist each in its proper "place" in that hierarchic order. This architectonic vision permits him to refute the would-be suicide's claim that he would prefer not to exist at all (18–23), and to justify the existence of unhappy souls, whose very misery chimes in with the universal harmony. Divine justice has accorded them, too, the "place" they freely merited by sinning (24–31). The whole moral order of the universe, indeed, elicits our praise for the God Who so ordered it (32–50).[7]

THE ORDERED *Omnia*

This argument from the beautifully ordered "all," the *omnia*, will have a long history in Augustine's writings; it represents one of the major insights he came to in his early period. Its anti-Manichaean thrust provides a good entryway for understanding the point Augustine is making with it. For the Manichee was convinced that the order detectable in the visible world is ultimately traceable to the primal catastrophe whereby souls were captured and borne down from the supernal region of "Light" and plunged into the evil darkness of "Matter." The Manichees accounted for our unfortunate presence in this lower world without assigning any culpability on the part of our souls; the evil anti-God, Matter, was responsible. Their fundamental conviction was that this lower, visible world should never have existed, and they professed pious shock at the Catholic contention from Genesis that the one true God made things both visible and invisible, made this "all" and found it "very good."

Augustine's reply to that contention rests on the claim that it is more eloquent proof of God's creative goodness and fecundity that He made "all" things, visible and invisible, instead of restricting Himself to making only higher, spiritual realities. The appeal enclosed in that reply is ultimately aesthetic: the beautiful hierarchic "order" we behold—higher spiritual realities in their lofty places, lower and lower realities each in the lower places of the

7. This section includes the sentence, in paragraph 34, stating that the soul, *post peccatum*, has less control over the body than it formerly did. This later becomes a bone of contention in *Ep 143*. We shall be obliged to return to that controversy below.

universe which are perfectly appropriate to them—would have been impossible had God not created "all" things, *omnia,* and like the master artist He is continued providentially to "order" them.

But Augustine was aided in elaborating this argument by the fact that Plotinus, too, had been compelled to face a group of Gnostic adversaries whose estimate of the visible world strongly resembled that of the Manichees. The argument he uses against them so directly parallels Augustine's here, and appears in treatises we can be quite certain Augustine read and pondered in connection with his conversion at Milan, that scholars have found no difficulty in inferring an "influence" of the one thinker upon the other.[8] Indeed, at that central point in his *Confessions* where Augustine is relating the positive fruit he drew from reflecting on those "books of the Platonists," he admits that he once "complained" as a Manichee would about the very existence of this lower, bodily world, and found in this argument the cure for such "madness." He was brought to see that it was "better" that "all things" exist, and not just higher, spiritual realities.[9] We shall meet this argument again, at a crucial turning in Augustine's career; it will serve us well to remember its genealogy.

"IGNORANCE" AND "DIFFICULTY"

But there is still another objection. It would seem that man does not "have it in his power to be good," either because of "ignorance," i.e., "not seeing what sort [of man] he ought to be," or through a sort of moral impotence, "not being able to be the sort [of man] he sees he ought to be" (51). How can the God responsible for our being in such moral ignorance and powerlessness hold us responsible for sinning?

These two features of human experience will occupy Augustine

8. Madec, pp. 557–61, presents a suggestive summary of the various Neoplatonic "influences" that have been proposed as active in *Lib,* as well as in Augustine's early works more generally.

9. See *Conf* 7.13–16, esp. 7.19, where *absit, iam ut dicerem non essent ista* refers to his former temptation as a Manichee, and *non iam desiderabam meliora quia omnia cogitabam* [and hence] *iudicio saniore pendebam* to his subsequent "healthier" and "saner" judgment on the rightful existence of the beautifully ordered "all." Note that Plotinus used this very same anti-Gnostic argument in a treatise, *Ennead* 5.8, which, I have argued, wielded a decisive influence on the early Augustine; see *Early Theory,* pp. 207–24. On DuRoy's rejection of this treatise, see *Platonism,* pp. 11–14 and notes.

for most of the remainder of *De libero arbitrio* 3. Augustine himself abbreviates reference to them by using the terms "ignorance" and "difficulty"; but for clarity and consistency, I shall refer to them as moral "ignorance" and moral "impotence," respectively, since those are the meanings Augustine gives them in his first introduction of the ideas, meanings he assumes he shares with his Manichaean adversaries. Still, the interpreter must remain sensitive to the possibility that the meaning attributed to the terms in paragraph 51 may receive additional clarification as Augustine's analysis proceeds, clarification that may hold certain surprises for the contemporary reader.[10]

One cannot but be struck by the weight Augustine and, presumably, the Manichaeans attach to these two obstacles to moral activity. Consider what he says of ignorance. There are, he concedes, certain acts done "through ignorance" (*per ignorantiam*) which Scripture esteems both "blameworthy and in need of correction" (*improbanda et corrigenda*). He argues similarly about our moral impotence: certain acts are "blameworthy" (*improbanda*) even if they are "done out of necessity" (*necessitate facta*)—like the *non enim quod volo facio* Paul speaks of in Romans or in Galatians. *Improbanda, corrigenda* they may be, but "sinful"?[11] It would depend, a modern would answer, on how insuperable, or culpable, the ignorance and impotence in question are. Augustine seems to be thinking exactly along those lines. But how dense is the moral ignorance he is thinking of? How crippling does he imply this moral impotence is? His answer may be surprising, but it comes to this: our moral ignorance can assume such density that we become incapable of knowing what sort of being we ought to strive to become; but even when that ignorance assumes more attenuated form, so that we can see what we ought to do, our moral

10. One factor that introduced additional confusion into the Boyer–de Montcheuil controversy was, I submit, their shared inability to credit the density Augustine attributes to our ignorance and moral impotence, a density that is more intelligible in the "fallen soul" hypothesis than in any of its rivals, except traducianism.

11. De Montcheuil, "L'hypothèse," pp. 94–95, interprets these terms with the expression "nous sont reprochés," thereby muddling the very distinction that Augustine is here striving to make: namely, that such acts may be reprehensible, and need correction, but still not be "sinful" in the strict sense of the term. It all depends, as Augustine is acute enough to see, on the amount of free responsibility we bring to their commission. From this point on, de Montcheuil's treatment becomes something less than a "model of analysis."

impotence is such that we are simply incapable of doing it. In either combination, however, the acts Scripture refers to as *improbanda* and *corrigenda* are, all other considerations apart, acts that we are incapable of *not* committing and, therefore, non-sinful.

A modern reader might object that other considerations *should* have intervened to qualify Augustine's thinking here. How could the human being depicted in such somber tones make any moral progress whatever? By divine assistance, one might suggest. But it should be noticed that Augustine himself, precisely at this stage in his argument, makes no allusion whatever to either the need or the possibility of divine assistance. Nor does he advert in any way to the issue of moral progress. Every step in his reasoning is directed to driving home a single, even a single-minded, point; nothing extraneous is permitted to deflect the drive of an argument that is fashioned to prove that the condition into which humans are born is, and must be, a "penal" one. For only on this condition, as he sees matters now, can God be exonerated from responsibility for these objectively "sinful" acts.

But sinful they truly are, Augustine is convinced, and not merely objectively so, but imputable to us as sinful agents. What makes such acts sinful in that plenary sense, however, is that this combination of ignorance and impotence, insuperable though it is, is *culpable*; it is a condition we have brought on ourselves by a sin knowingly and freely committed. This is the force of the words quoted from St. Paul and the Psalmist about the ignorance and impotence they experienced. They are words uttered by men "coming from that deadly damnation,"[12] men consigned justly and rightly to a "penal" condition.

If, on the other hand, the condition they were speaking of were, not a punishment laid on mankind, but a "natural" state in which God had created them, none of these acts would be "sins." Augustine's use of the indicative mood states the case as brutally as one might wish: *nam si non est ista poena hominis, sed natura, nulla*

12. Madec translates (p. 479) *ex illa mortis damnatione* as "de la *première* condamnation à mort"; the text gives no warrant for that term "première," and it makes a difference to the way one understands Augustine's thought. Madec seems to have read the Latin through the lens of the creationist theory of the soul's origin he assumes Augustine espoused, whereas Augustine's wording can *best* be reconciled to either of those two "penal" hypotheses among the four we are about to see him introduce for consideration. Those two are traducianism and the "fallen soul" hypothesis.

ista peccata sunt (51). Man as we experience his existence literally "cannot become better" (*ita ut melius esse non possit*). But if this helplessness were due to the way God created us, then when man "does these things," objectively reprehensible though they are, he nonetheless "does what he ought" (*ea quae debet facit*). Hence, God would have to be assigned responsibility for those acts—the precise conclusion Augustine is determined to avoid.

We shall have to remain alert to how consistent Augustine remains in this understanding of our moral ignorance and moral impotence as his analysis progresses. But it should be clear that in these initial paragraphs both he and his Manichaean adversaries must agree in attaching surprising density to the operative terms: man as we know him neither "is good" nor "has it in his power to become good" (51).[13] It is this density that enables us to understand why Augustine must take the Manichaean objection so seriously. Were God responsible for our present helpless condition, then God must bear responsibility for the sins that we cannot but commit, for acts that cannot, accordingly, be considered truly "sinful" on man's part. The only way one can relieve God of this responsibility, therefore, is to show that the insuperable ignorance and impotence themselves are something for which *we* must bear the responsibility; that they are, in modern terms, "culpable," or, in Augustine's terms here, not "natural" but "penal"—resulting from some previous sin. The drunk may plead innocence for the accident he caused while drunk, but he must bear the guilt for becoming so drunk as to cause the accident! But what if God Himself made us all incurably drunk? In that case, clearly, He would have to bear responsibility for our drunken actions; and the Manichee triumphs.[14] Hence, God *could* not have so created us as to make this our "natural" condition.

13. Again Madec mistranslates, and apparently for the same reason as above; for *Si autem bonus homo esset, aliter esset*, both expressions for the *present* contrary-to-fact conditional, he gives us a *past*: "si l'homme *avait été* bon, il *aurait été* autre." This momentarily distorts the argument Augustine is making, though in the next sentence Madec is back on the tracks with the present tense.

14. I use Aristotle's classic example for clarity's sake, and mean no irreverence. Note, however, the plain and obvious implications of Augustine's consistent use of the indicative mood: we humans *are* not "good," *are* afflicted with moral ignorance and impotence such that we *do not* "have it in our power to be good"; the logical consequence is that the acts we perform out of this condition cannot be accounted "sinful" —*unless* the condition itself is a "punishment" for prior sins. But *whose* sins? The reader who has followed his argument to this point, and with no preternatural antici-

So, at least, Augustine seems to imply by the opening paragraph of his answer to this objection. Were the reader to vault over the intervening thirteen paragraphs to 64, however, he would be in for a rude shock. For there Augustine seriously entertains the very possibility that he would seem peremptorily to have excluded here: that the moral ignorance and impotence we experience may be "natural" to us, after all! Is there some inconsistency, or at least discrepancy, in his thinking?

That question may be answered in Augustine's favor if a much later explanation he gives of this entire intervening section is judged satisfactory. In the *De dono perseverantiae*, written more than thirty years afterward, in answer to objections from Pelagians rather than Manichees, he explains a polemic strategy he chose to employ, and puts it in parallel with the strategy he claims to have employed here. There were two views on the subject of the "ignorance and difficulty without which no man is born"; the first, that they are "punishments" (*supplicia*) ; the second, that they are *primordia naturae*, "natural" to man as originally constituted by God. His strategy against the Manichees, he tells us, was to entertain both views (*sensus*) and to refute the Manichees in terms of either supposition—and that, despite the fact that he "holds" one of those views to be the true one, and evidently to the exclusion of the other. Further, Augustine claims, he expressed himself even then *satis evidenter*, in unmistakable terms, in the *De libero arbitrio* itself, as clearly holding the view he now prefers: that our moral ignorance and impotence are not features of the "nature of man [as he was] established," but rather "the punishment [of man inasmuch as he was] condemned."[15]

Now, one rather obvious point Augustine is making in the *De dono perseverantiae* is this: simply because he momentarily accepted, purely for the sake of argument, a particular Pelagian supposition—or, in this case, Manichaean—with the intention of proving that, even on that supposition, their case would not hold,

---

pation of what is to follow in later paragraphs, could not but draw the obvious conclusion: *our* sins.

15. *Persev* 29. Note that Madec quotes this text, p. 580, but seems either to assume or to draw the curious conclusion that the creationist hypothesis is coherent with the claim that our ignorance–impotence condition is "penal." We shall have to be alert during Augustine's discussion of the four hypotheses further on to see whether his analysis of them admits of any such coherence.

his adversaries have no right to interpret such polemic strategy as implying he did, in fact, accept the adversary supposition as true. *Dato, sed non concesso,* as the Medievals will express the same tactic: I do not concede the truth of your supposition, but *even if I did,* your conclusion would not follow.

So far, so good. Perhaps! But is the argumentative strategy as clear as all that from the text of the *De libero arbitrio* itself? Manifestly not. In paragraph 51, at the very first mention of the two alternative possibilities, Augustine's "preferred view" has already pushed him to take sides so strongly—and in such categorical terms —that one would scarcely dream he was proposing an "hypothesis" and fully intended to treat "the other side" in terms of the strategy he outlines in the *De dono perseverantiae.* Ah, one might object, but he has told us in the *De dono perseverantiae* that he did *two* things, and, apparently, *pari passu,* if not simultaneously. He did, purely for the sake of argument, assume the Manichaean hypothesis as true—with the intention of then showing that its conclusion did not follow—but he claims *also* to have shown plainly his unmistakable preference for the contradictory hypothesis. It must be allowed that such a tack would cohere with the *dato, non concesso* mode of argument; it is far less certain that the Augustine of the *De libero arbitrio* was successful in bringing it off. For there is not a single phrase in paragraph 51 which warns the reader that he was arguing hypothetically, or reminds him that Augustine was embarked on such an elegant tightrope walk: that of holding one view, showing clearly that he held it, yet at the same time treating it *as though* the opposing view were later to be dealt with as a counter-possibility on the same dialectical footing as his own. So confusing is this whole performance to the reader that one is tempted to ask whether the counter-hypothesis of paragraph 64 might even have been introduced later, as a kind of afterthought, such that this balancing of hypotheses may not have been Augustine's original intention, after all!

Meantime, however, without yet committing ourselves on that question, let us refer to these as two "hypotheses"; the first, Augustine's "penal" hypothesis, and the second, the competing "natural" hypothesis. We have already seen the density he attaches to our condition of "moral ignorance" and "moral impotence"; this conjoint obstacle to right moral activity he views, initially, as so insuperable as to liberate man from the responsibility that would máke his acts genuinely "sinful"—*unless*, that is, it were the consequence of some antecedent (and fully responsible) sin, and therefore *culpable* in origin. "Who can doubt," Augustine asks rhetorically, that man's "is a penal condition" (*Poenam istam esse quis dubitet?*) (51)?[16] But, Augustine concludes, if it is penal, then it is a punishment leveled by none other than God and therefore a "just recompense for sin" (51).[17] Augustine's language could hardly be more "categorical."

Thus, it should be no cause for "wonder" that man "does not [now] have the freedom of will to choose what he ought . . . or cannot see what he ought to do or fulfill it when he will." It is the "most just penalty for sin that man should lose what he was unwilling to make good use of when he could have done so without difficulty if he wished." The implication is clear: man, before deservedly incurring this penal condition, both was able to know what was right and had the power to do what he knew was right. His proneness to error and his present moral impotence "do not belong to the nature of man as he was created; they are the penalty of man as condemned."[18] The "freedom of the will" Augustine has been discussing throughout the *De libero arbitrio*, therefore, is the "freedom wherein man was created," not the sorely impaired condition that sinful, and condemned, mankind now experiences (52).

Up to this point, then, several things are clear about Augustine's argument. First, the combination of moral ignorance and moral impotence mankind currently experiences is considered to be insuperable—so insuperable, in fact, that Augustine can speak here of our "erring against our will" and "not being able" to resist the attractions of the flesh.[19]

---

16. Augustine momentarily envisages the possibility that this punishment might be an unjust one, inflicted (it would appear) by the devil; that possibility refuted, the conclusion returns that the punishment must be God-ordained and therefore "just."

17. One *might* have entertained a doubt about whether Augustine (in 52) meant to include *both* ignorance and impotence as features of our penal state, but these final statements remove any such doubts.

18. *Non est natura hominis sed poena damnati* (52). Observe the indicative *est*.

19. Note the expressions *ut erret invitus* and *non posse . . . temperare* (52). Augustine could scarcely be clearer.

Secondly, this very insuperability makes it necessary for him to conclude that it cannot be the state in which God created mankind; otherwise the Manichees would be right in blaming Him for those reprehensible actions for which our helplessness makes us non-responsible.

Who, then, is responsible for this moral helplessness? Clearly, "we" must be. Mankind once enjoyed both the wisdom and the freedom required for being sufficiently responsible for reprehensible actions as to make them genuinely "sinful" and deserving of the just punishment that our present moral helplessness constitutes.

Augustine is unequivocally clear about this: so unobstructed was the freedom in which God created "man" that man must take full responsibility for the penal reduction of that freedom he now experiences. Our present condition is, therefore, "penal" in the strict sense of the term. Not only do all Augustine's expressions lend themselves to this interpretation; they call for it both as their most natural meaning and as the one required for the cogency of his argument against the Manichees. *We* are the ones both ignorant and impotent, the ones being punished. Unless God is unjust, *we* must have been the ones who sinned.[20]

Thirdly, Augustine seems consistently to be implying this reasoning: the more insuperable our moral helplessness, the more urgent it becomes to prove that God did not create us in that condition and that we were sinfully responsible for having incurred it as the appropriate "punishment" for that sinfulness. Hence, the implied equation: the greater the insuperability, the greater our own culpability for it, and vice versa. Any reduction in insuperability must logically entail a reduction in our original culpability, just as any reduction of our original culpability *should* have resulted in a less disastrous condition as its penal consequence.

---

20. Augustine's language from start to finish supports this view; see, for example, *peccatrix anima* (16); *quia peccatrices esse voluerunt* (25); *peccans creatura, tali peccato detectus, peccatrix anima* (27); *peccati poena tenebatur, ad hoc diminutionis* [of its original, plenary freedom] *redacta* (30); *peccaturas, non ut peccarent* (32); *quae peccatura praecognita est* (33); and *etiam si ista peccare noluisset, etiam si peccaret, qui etiam corporalem peccantibus* (35). It is always the soul itself, or souls themselves, who sin, sinned, or would sin. The two final sections (33 and 35) will be of particular interest to us further on; they come from the same argumentative unit as the sentence drawn from 34, which becomes the focus for consideration in *Ep 143*.

A NEW POSSIBILITY: THAT THE SIN WAS NOT "OURS"

Whether as thesis or preferred hypothesis, however, Augustine's "penal" account must now confront a new objection, one that will shatter the neatness of his reasoning to this point and force it to proliferate into tortuous complexity. The objection is especially interesting in that Pelagius' lieutenant, Caelestius, will later make it his own and aim it squarely at Augustine's developed view of grace and free will. The "sin" that lies at the root of our penal condition and makes it a "just" punishment, he will argue, is the sin of Adam and Eve. But then, as Augustine puts it here (53), "what have *we* unhappy creatures done, to deserve being born in the darkness of ignorance and in the torments of difficulty"? And for the very *first time* in this entire book, Augustine must deal with the possibility that the sin for which we are being punished *may not be ours* in the strict sense!

His opening move is to remind us of what is uppermost in his mind: "To them I reply: keep quiet and stop murmuring against God." For God is "present everywhere," coming to man's aid and helping him to overcome the ignorance and moral impotence into which each of us is born. "Had no one ever been victorious" over ignorance and impotence, Augustine admits, the objector might have grounds "rightly to complain" of God's justice; but this (newly introduced) possibility of moral progress removes the sting from his objection. But notice what has happened: faithful to the implicit equation governing his argument so far, Augustine has been compelled to reduce the insuperability of our moral helplessness,[21] and precisely in view of a reduced culpability on "our" part. Despite our ignorance and impotence, it is now possible for us to be "victorious" over them and to make moral progress. True, Augustine accounts for this possibility of moral progress primarily in terms of God's omnipresent "helps" to Adam's children; but he also insists that no one has been stripped of the power[22] to "know

21. Nowhere do I find either Boyer or de Montcheuil taking note of this crucial argumentative shift on Augustine's part. This is another factor that introduces inextricable confusion into the controversy between them.

22. One might question whether the *ablatum* of 53 has the force my translation gives it (as does Madec's "à nul homme n'a été ôtée") but the paragraphs following confirm the correctness of that interpretation.

[enough] to seek" what he needs to know and to "confess" the weakness from which God is always willing to deliver him. Man's incapacity for the moral life is no longer the insuperable matter it was just a paragraph earlier; the entry of Adam and Eve into the discussion has compelled Augustine to change the terms of his argument, even though remaining faithful, so far at least, to the equations between culpability and insuperability which previously governed it. Is it possible that Augustine wrote those previous portions about our moral helplessness *without* anticipating the eventual need of answering this Adam–Eve objection? That question must be kept in mind as we proceed further with this confusing book.

Meanwhile, Augustine continues, along this road of moral progress, men may do some things wrongly, having not yet overcome either ignorance or moral impotence. These wrong deeds are rightly called "sins," but *only* in a derived and extrinsic sense of that term; they are the "deserved consequences of" and "have their origin in the first sin of the will when it was free." In this hypothesis, only that first sin is "*properly* called sin" since it alone was committed "knowingly and with free will." The wrongs *we* commit, however, while still in the bondage of ignorance and impotence are sins in a derived and quite obviously attenuated sense of the term.[23] The balder *nulla ista peccata sunt* of paragraph 51 has yielded here to more qualified language: what we do out of our moral ignorance and impotence is "sin" in *some* sense, after all. But even so, we see Augustine manfully striving to preserve his original equation between our original culpability and our present accountability: reduce the one, and he must admit a reduction in the other. They are *not* sins in the strict sense!

So too, he now further illustrates his point, we speak of human "nature" in two distinct senses. "Properly speaking" the term refers to the "blameless nature with which man was originally created." But we also apply the term, in a less proper sense, to the "nature with which we are born mortal" and prey to the ignorance and moral impotence that are all "really the penalty of sin."[24] Indeed, Augustine goes on to say, the power[25] that remains to us, God aid-

23. Need one stress that, if squarely asked whether sins in this "improper" sense are or are not truly sins, Augustine's answer would be simply "No."

24. Here, too (54), this nature in the "improper" sense is, simply speaking, *not truly* our nature.

25. I take this as implied by *volentem non prohiberi . . . oportebat* (55).

ing, to transcend the penal ignorance and impotence into which we are born is itself testimony to "how easily man might have retained the nature with which he was created if he had so willed."[26]

Once again, one could scarcely claim that Augustine keeps his reader alert to the notion that he is entertaining this "penal" account of our ignorance and moral impotence as merely one of two competing hypotheses: the whole cast of this section would lull one into supposing, as his categorical view, that Adam and Eve were created with a knowledge and power of choice that they misused, and justly lost, both for themselves and for all their "mortal" progeny. The term "human nature," then, applies "properly" to their pre-fallen condition and only in a derived sense to the "human nature" of our condemned existence. What all this eventually means, *after* the counter-hypothesis has been introduced and dealt with, remains to be seen.

AUGUSTINE BECOMES "HYPOTHETICAL"

But even in terms of the "penal" hypothesis, Augustine has not said his last word. And now he will shift unmistakably into the hypothetical key.[27] The last objection has raised the crucial point of our

26. Note the twin suppositions here (55): that "man" enjoyed an original plenary type of freedom, and that the restriction imposed on the freedom we now enjoy is not the insuperable obstacle it was in Augustine's argumentation *before* he was forced to deal with this nettlesome Adam–Eve objection.

27. Having introduced the Adam–Eve objection in 53, Augustine seems first to have tried to deal with it in general terms (53–55). But now, in 56 and following, he will address it more specifically in the light of the four possible modes of explaining the "origin of souls." But the very terms in which the objection was posed in 53 would seem to have implied a distinction between "us" who are being punished (justly? and, therefore, punished in the *proper* sense?) and the Adam and Eve who properly sinned and were both justly and properly punished. That implied distinction between us and those first parents, therefore, has *already* put us into one or other of the four hypotheses Augustine now outlines: whichever of them, that is, imply this distinction.

But this is the hypothesis Augustine's supposed *objector* seems to assume as true; unsurprisingly, Augustine answers him on his own terms. Madec, p. 582, claims to find creationist overtones in the terms *de illo primo coniugio* (55); he aids his case somewhat by translating (p. 485) the phrase *ex illius damnati poena* of 54 as "par suite de la peine que subit le *premier* homme condamné" when the text gives no warrant for that "premier." Augustine could have in his *own* mind the meaning that *primum coniugium* had for him in his first exegesis of Genesis (see *Early Theory*, pp. 156–58); but even if that is not true here, it does not seem legitimate to saddle him with an hypothesis that is really his objector's and not necessarily his own. In fact, the introduction of these four hypotheses on the soul's origin has the implied force of reminding any such objector that there are two of them in which "we" are *not*, in the deepest sense of the term, "other" than Adam and Eve!

relationship to the Adam for whose sin, it would appear, *we* are being punished and, Augustine means to show, justly punished. In any case, that relationship with Adam is the pivotal point he means to consider now. It can be conceived of in a number of ways. Augustine sketches four, and makes each of them turn on the question of the soul's "origin"; that question he presents as intimately connected with the question of how the soul became "embodied."[28]

To grasp that connection, anticipate Augustine's argument for a moment. Consider what one might well imagine as the most "intimate" relationship possible between Adam and the human souls coming after him: that subsequent humans drew their souls from Adam's soul in much the same way as they drew their bodies from his—in such a way, in fact, that their souls were contained "in" his. In this case, it would seem implied that when Adam sinned, "they" sinned "in" Adam's sinning—and would justly be punished with, indeed punished *in*, Adam's own punishment. Both sin and punishment here assume their "proper" senses.

But now consider a more "distant" relationship. Imagine God producing post-Adamic souls as disembodied creatures, somehow, somewhere; they would exist entirely independent of any derivation from Adam. It would make no sense, then, to claim (as in the relationship above) that they could have sinned "in" Adam.

Suppose, though, that these disembodied souls became "embodied," and in a flesh derived from Adam's, a flesh that bore a taint from Adam's sinfulness. One might now imagine the sinful Adamic flesh communicating its taint to the soul that entered it. Now one might speak of the soul as "sinful" (extrinsically) with "Adam's" sinfulness—but "sinfulness" would mean something importantly different from the (intrinsic) "sinfulness" affirmed of a soul that itself actively "sinned *in* Adam's sinning." If one went on to speak of merited "punishment" for sin, moreover, an Adam-derived soul that "sinned in" Adam's sinning obviously merits "Adamic" punishment in a far more proper sense of the term "punishment" than a soul that, itself sinless, becomes tainted by the sinfulness of flesh derived from Adam. The connection of questions, therefore, is clear enough: say something of the soul's origin, and you say some-

28. Madec, p. 579, is even stronger: asking about the origin of our souls amounts "more exactly" to asking how our souls became "embodied." See Augustine's *Ep 166* 19.

thing about the soul's embodiment—*and* about the soul's relationship to sinful Adam and the punishment Adam merited by his sin.

Augustine is now about to entertain four such hypotheses about the soul's origin.[29] But why *just* four, and *precisely* the four he proposes? One might be tempted to dream of him, a Germanic Rembrandt "philosopher" below the turning stair, conjuring up these four hypotheses as the only thinkable possibilities.[30] Indeed, the disjunctive quality of those possibilities at moments seems to argue that he generated these hypotheses out of his own head, as it were.[31] But a number of indications point to a somewhat humbler derivation. When asked about the origin of the soul, Jerome produces the very same four hypotheses[32] and intimates that any well-read person knew they were the ones taken seriously in learned discussions of the time. Evodius, too, speaks in much the same tones.[33] It seems, then, much more plausible that Augustine was brought to inform himself about contemporary learned opinions—he actually refers to them as *sententiae*—and chose to deal with the four that were deemed to represent the serious choices open to a thinker of his time.

The first hypothesis Augustine deals with is the traducianist theory: that "only one soul was originally created, and the souls of all men born since derive their origin from it." In this hypothesis, is our penal condition just? Yes, Augustine replies, for if our souls were contained in Adam's, "who can say that he did not sin when the first man sinned?" In Adam's sin, we sinned; we are now being punished for that sin. Here, the connection between sin and merited punishment is unambiguously clear, but qua souls, we are not "other" than Adam!

But in the second, creationist, hypothesis, that connection is far more ambiguous. In this supposition, "souls are created separately

29. Again, we are at 56.

30. De Lubac, "Note," p. 279, has Augustine thinking these up as though out of his own head.

31. The logic of the "division" would then run this way: the soul either existed before embodiment or it did not; then, in either of those two hypotheses, the soul itself was sinful or it was not. Result: four hypotheses.

32. See *Ep 165* in the Augustine corpus. Jerome adds a fifth, i.e., the Manichaean hypothesis that the soul was divine and part of God. The remaining four, however, pair up easily with the four Augustine is about to propose here, as he himself makes clear in *Ep 166*, replying to Jerome.

33. See *Ep 163*. Evodius writes as though they were so familiar he did not even have to enumerate them explicitly. *Ep 143*, moreover, shows both Augustine and his critics implicitly accepting these terms of discussion.

in individual men as they are born";[34] they are not, therefore, "contained" in—hence, do not "sin" in—that first man's sin. Indeed, Augustine makes clear, the soul in this hypothesis receives a relatively damaged state *"before any sin [of its own] and even before it was born."* Nevertheless, he argues, "it is nothing perverse, but appears, rather, most appropriate and in accordance with right order, that the evil [condition] an earlier soul [Adam's] has merited should become the nature [i.e., natural condition] of later souls, and that later souls should [by their good deeds] merit to regain the state which was natural to the earlier one."[35] Even in this diminished state, moreover, the soul should "give thanks to its Creator." For it has been endowed with a nature "superior to any bodily being, however perfect." It has, moreover, been given the "power" and "natural judgment"[36] enabling it, with the Creator's aid, to cultivate itself, to progress in virtue, and in time to free itself of the blinding ignorance and tormenting moral impotence of its incarnate condition; it can, thereby, ultimately attain to the happiness the Creator means to grant souls that grow in love for Him.

The reduction in the soul's own culpability compels Augustine to stress this reduced insuperability. In such an hypothesis, moreover, Augustine makes another crucial admission: the term "punishment" (*poena*) can rightly (*recte*) be applied to the first soul that actually sinned (*peccatrix*), since its transition into ignorance and moral impotence was from a state "better" than this punitive state (*ideo poena recte dicitur, quia melior ante hanc poenam fuit*). The implication is clear: the term *poena* cannot rightly be applied, in its proper sense, to the situation of later souls, which never enjoyed the superior condition their sinful progenitor experienced. Augustine now makes it explicit: their ignorance and moral impotence are not a "punishment of sin" (*supplicium peccati*), but an "admonition toward progressing, and the first stage on the way to perfec-

---

34. Observe that Augustine's expression of the creationist hypothesis is quite exact here; it is free of any suggestion that the soul was created *before* its embodiment. The fact that he was once given to such careful statement of creationism will become of interest to us further on in this study.

35. Notice the much stronger form this Latinism assumes in the paraphrase de Montcheuil ("L'hypothèse," p. 96) presents: "Mais il n'aurait pas été normal qu'Adam et Eve engendrassent des enfants qui fussent meilleurs qu'eux. . . ."

36. Augustine uses the terms *facultas* and *iudicium naturale*; again, the original insuperability of our ignorance and impotence has been, and in this hypothesis must be, seriously diminished, for the culpability involved is not truly "ours."

tion" (56). If their condition is to be regarded as "penal," therefore, it is so only in some looser and derived sense of the term.

But does the term *poena* require *only* this passage from a superior to a lower condition of existence? Or would it require also, for its most proper application, that the soul be *peccatrix*, and so, through *its own sin*, deserve its relatively diminished condition? Augustine's language leaves us wondering about this point; his notion of divine justice surely suggests that a *poena* in the proper sense of the term *should* imply sinful responsibility on the part of the soul receiving a divine punishment.[37] Indeed, the language and reasoning he used earlier, when introducing this "penal" explanation of our ignorance and moral impotence (51), was boldly explicit on the point. Now, however, the very hypothesis he is entertaining precludes his satisfying our minds on that expected connection between punishment decreed and sinful desert. His language in justifying God has a nervously defensive ring: *immo convenientissimum et ordinatissimum apparet . . . Quid enim indignum si . . . ?* But clearly the term "penal" as accounting for our hapless, and unhappy, condition has drastically changed its sense.[38] Does it, even in Augustine's own mind, still satisfactorily answer the original Manichaean objection? All the indications are that, even now, Augustine was less than comfortable with this, the creationist hypothesis. It is not the last time that discomfort will show.

Augustine now considers a third hypothesis: that "souls preexist in some secret place and are sent out to quicken and rule the bodies of individuals when they are born." In this case, too, they themselves have not sinned; but God has assigned them a "mission": to "govern the body well," to "discipline" and "subject" it to "an orderly and legitimate servitude, so that in due order and due time men may attain the place of heavenly perfection." Again, as in the creationist hypothesis, this possibility of progress is an important consideration in the argument. But these souls must "undergo for-

37. De Montcheuil ("L'hypothèse," p. 98) assumes this *condicio* is both necessary (which is obvious) and *sufficient* for a punishment in the true and proper sense; Boyer ("Dieu," p. 74) finds this entirely un-Augustinian, a point which de Lubac ("Note," pp. 282–84) seems implicitly to grant for the *mature* Augustine, but not for the author of *Lib*, whose thought is still "en devenir." But this paragraph makes it abundantly clear that whatever may be true of Adam and Eve, the creationist hypothesis makes it impossible to speak of "our" condition as *truly* penal. See notes 15, 22, 23, above.
38. Again, neither Boyer nor de Montcheuil takes account of these changes of sense.

getfulness of their former existence" apart from the body, at the
same time as they submit to the "labors of their present existence"
—including the ignorance and moral impotence that are always at
the center of Augustine's attention.

Again, though, as in the creationist hypothesis, that ignorance
and impotence are not strictly "punishment" for these souls (as
they were for Adam's); they represent, rather, a "doorway" toward
the spiritual progress that, even in the mortal flesh, remains both
possible to and required of them. Once again, therefore, our moral
ignorance and impotence must be, in this hypothesis, "penal," but
not in the proper, only in a wider, sense of the term; in consequence,
the reduction of the soul's culpability obliges Augustine to stress
the superability of that ignorance and impotence. Those same properties, he goes on to say, cannot properly be denominated "sin" for
which either the soul or the Creator Himself is directly culpable;
the "sin" in the proper sense of the term was Adam's and Adam's
only. Nor can the soul itself be considered "sinful"; it is the "flesh
coming from [Adam's] sinful stock," the "body born under the
penalty of the first man's sin," the penalty of "mortality," which
is the subject of punishment in the strict sense. The body, or flesh,
infects the innocent soul sent into it, accounting for the moral
ignorance and impotence that afflict it.

Now Augustine enters a further qualification that drastically
attenuates the "ignorance" with which this entire discussion began.
It is, he assures us, not so total as he previously gave us to believe,
for God has given the soul the "way of faith" to temper the "blindness of its forgetfulness." He has given it more. As he did in the
creationist hypothesis, Augustine stresses God's gifts of the "power"
(*facultas*) of doing good despite "toilsome" difficulty, and the "judgment" (*iudicium*) "that it must seek to know what it does not
know" and persevere, God aiding, in the effort to overcome its
moral impotence. For God will always "aid" those who "try" to
overcome, and who implore that aid from Him. The insuperable
moral ignorance and impotence described in paragraph 51, at the
start of this lengthy reply to the Manichaean objection, has undergone a transformation, indeed.

The fourth and final hypothesis, like the third, features the supposition of "souls existing in some place," obviously apart from the
body. These, however, are not "sent by the Lord God, but come

of their own accord [*sua sponte* . . . *veniunt*] to inhabit bodies."
Now, argues Augustine, "it is easy to see that whatever the ignorance or difficulty that follows on [*secutum fuerit*] their own choice,
the Creator cannot in any way be considered culpable." This is
Augustine's central point, and he stresses it: "He [God] would be
entirely without blame." Even in the third hypothesis, Augustine
now points out in a curious move of thought, God provides divine
aids toward spiritual progress; so too, here.[39] The Manichaean objection does not take sufficient account of this, Augustine is saying;
however miserable our soul's initial embodied condition may be,
it can be the starting point, with God's omnipresent aid, of progress
toward eventual beatitude.

But if this hypothesis represents our *de facto* situation, we certainly have nothing to complain about. We wake up into this life
to a penal condition, but as a consequence of our own free, sinful
choice. We have elected to "come"—Augustine will later say "fall"
—into a world of bodies infected by Adam's punishment, and in
Letters 143 and *166* Augustine makes it plain that the pre-embodied
choice involved in this hypothesis of the *De libero arbitrio* is correctly understood as a sinful one.[40] Accordingly, not only did we
deserve, we perversely chose, the condition that God's all-ordering
power awarded us as punishment.

AUGUSTINE's *Dimissio* INSIGHT

It is necessary to pause here in order to point out the kinship, if
not the identity, of this mode of thinking with a central feature of
Augustine's thought, early and late. Indeed, one of the triumphs
of his early theory of the human condition was his painstaking

39. The move of thought seems curious, since the point has been covered at great
length already. Could it be a sign of Augustine's discomfort with the third hypothesis?
Or does he have at the back of his mind the peculiar fashion in which his *dimissio*
notion welds the third and fourth hypotheses into one? For that notion, see below.

40. In 59, the *sua sponte veniunt* of 58 is rephrased as *sua sponte labantur*; study
of *Epp 143* and *166* will show that Augustine can employ various verbal expressions
for this hypothesis, but every one of those expressions points unmistakably to the
same hypothesis *in substance*. Madec, in his review of my "Rejection" article, in REA,
21 (1975), 394, claimed to find this equivalence unconvincing; in BA 6, pp. 581–82,
he seems just on the point of raising that same objection, but instead veers off to
object that *Ep 143* would discourage one from holding that this fourth was (ever?)
Augustine's preferred hypothesis. Does this mean he now admits at least that the
fourth hypothesis remains identical beneath the various expressions Augustine gives
of it? Madec does not say; hence, I shall be obliged further on in this study to attend
to both these objections: see below, chap. 3.

elaboration of the notion of *dimissio*.[41] The prologue of the *De beata vita* saw him asking a complex question about the soul, but it is important to notice *what kind* of question is being asked. How and why did the soul wind up foundering in this "stormy sea" of human life? Was the cause "God," Augustine asks, "or nature, or necessity, or our own will—or a combination of some or all of these"? The possibilities may be condensed into two: Is our presence in this unhappy condition due to some sin we willed and for which God has punished us; or is it the result of some natural necessity, the working of cosmic law? The second member of that question is freighted with significance, for Augustine is tacitly convinced that it *must* be a "combination" of both these alternatives— but both of them operating in such an intimate conjunction that the one is the convex, so to speak, to the other as concave; the causality of "fault" must be one and the same as the working of cosmic— read "divine"—law.

This is the idea he somehow fumbled with in his *De ordine* and subsequently grappled with more effectively in the first two books of the *De libero arbitrio*. But his formulation of it can be placed with reasonable confidence at that point in the *De Genesi contra Manichaeos* when he is interpreting the phrase that God "dis-missed" Adam and Eve from their (obviously "spiritual") paradise.

The key insight, I submit, he found in Plotinus' *Ennead* 4.3.12– 13. For Plotinus, in that ingenious section of his works, is wrestling with the very same problem: how to reconcile the view that our souls "fall" through their own fault with the apparent counter-view that they are "sent" to govern and beautify the lower world of bodies? We must think, Plotinus proposes, of the soul's desire to govern bodies as a kind of natural, spontaneous desire—somewhat like a "weight" the soul takes on. Weighed down, the soul moves naturally—the force of its desire acting in perfect concert with the cosmic laws of spiritual gravity—to the "place" appropriate to that weight.

---

41. See *Early Theory*, pp. 169–73. Some years ago I published a study of the *"De libero arbitrio* I: Stoicism Revisited," in AS, 1 (1970), 49–68, before it became clear to me that something like this *dimissio* notion was what Augustine, even that early, was endeavoring to fashion. I would write that article differently now, with that point kept firmly in view. For an exposé of an analogous view (but only that), see John Rist's "Augustine on Free Will and Predestination" (henceforth: "Free Will"), *Journal of Theological Studies*, 20 (1969), 420–47.

Amor meus pondus meum—"My love is my weight." Augustine will subsequently sound that theme in a thousand variants. But for him the term "weight," *pondus,* always carries a *moral* connotation. Desires, when evil, draw us downward toward immersion in the miserable world of mortal bodies; when good, they lighten us to ascend to the higher, spiritual world. So man's soul in its spiritual paradise became "weighted" with the desire—the "proud" desire—to govern a body of its very "own" (*proprium*). God did not have to "send" or "expel" the soul from paradise, accordingly: so Genesis tells us He "dis-missed" the soul as one does a visitor who desires to depart. Human and divine activity form a perfect interlock.

Again and again in the works we are about to study that *dimissio* theme will make its appearance under one or other of its several garbs;[42] it is one to which Augustine was dearly attached. It assures us that the "place" God accords us in His ordered universe is the one perfectly appropriate to our inmost desires, whether good or evil. We have no grounds for complaint, as though He treats us arbitrarily. The world is moral, through and through. For God's "justice" is one with His omnipresent Providence, ordering everything, high and low, from one end of the universe to the other, exactly as it "ought" to be.

Augustine now envisages two classes of souls whose condition of ignorance and moral impotence result from this sinful choice to enter bodies. The first class would be "zealous and well-disposed"; on these, he assures us, God "would bestow the power [*valere praestaret*] to overcome such ignorance and difficulty and gain the crown of glory." Again, progress from this unhappy condition to eventual beatitude is possible, and God will confer on well-disposed souls the "power" and aid to make that progress. The Manichees should have no complaints on that. Consider the opposing class, however. "They are neglectful and wish to defend their sins on the grounds of their weakness" (58). Will God respond by objecting that their very weakness—their ignorance and moral impotence—is itself a sin? No, says Augustine, *non ipsam ignorantiam difficultatemque pro crimine objiceret.* But He will "punish them justly"

42. Its original exegetical connection will explain why I refer to this notion of a perfect "interlock" between freedom and divine law as Augustine's *"dimissio* theme." For illustration of how persistent this theme becomes, see my "The God of Saint Augustine's Imagination," *Thought,* 57 (1982), 30–40.

precisely on this account: that "they have chosen to remain" in that state of ignorance and moral impotence "rather than zealously seeking and learning, and humbly confessing and praying, and [thereby] arriving at truth and ease [in moral activity]." Even in these sinners, then, the condition of ignorance and moral impotence they allege as excuse is not, itself, a sin (crimen). It is, though, clearly the penal consequence of their pre-embodied sin, and penal in the proper sense of the term.

DID AUGUSTINE HAVE A PREFERRED HYPOTHESIS?

Which of these four hypotheses on the soul's embodiment does Augustine consider the most likely? He will imply later on, in Letter 143, to Marcellinus, that he couched this entire discussion of them in such careful terms as not to argue from any one of them as a preferred position; for that mode of argument would only have weakened his endeavor to show that God, pace the Manichees, must in no hypothesis be held accountable for our sins, or unjust in having consigned us to the miserable condition in which we find ourselves.

And yet, as we saw, he admits in the De dono perseverantiae that he preferred the theory that our miserable condition is a penal one, and that he let that preference show satis evidenter in the way he wrote this book.

There is at least a trace of incompatibility between these two later interpretations: in explaining the two hypotheses in which the soul itself is innocent of sin—whether "created" for insertion, or "divinely sent" into the body—the Augustine of the De libero arbitrio is at pains to point out that our condition may be termed "penal," but only in an improper sense of that term. Are we to infer that he preferred one of the hypotheses—traducianism or "fall"—in which the term "penal" may be used in its "proper" sense?

The argumentative line that presides over the book, up to and including paragraph 52, would seem to support this understanding of the interpretation given in the De dono perseverantiae.[43] Before the intrusion of the Adam–Eve difficulty in paragraph 53, as we saw, Augustine appears to be telling the Manichees that we sinned, and

43. So too, as we shall see, his Carthaginian critics will later argue; see Ep 143 and my treatment of it further on in this study.

therefore *we* plainly deserve the condition that he portrays, in categorical terms without a hint of the hypotheses to come later, as "penal" in the proper sense of the term. The Adam–Eve objection has compelled the simplicity of that earlier argumentative line to branch out into a series of complexities, not all of them, clearly, equally potent to answer the Manichaean objections. Did Augustine already anticipate those complexities and attenuations when writing the trenchant, confident prose of paragraphs 51–52? His answer in *Letter 143*, to the criticism reported to him by Marcellinus, would appear to claim that he did so anticipate them; our verdict on this question must await, accordingly, a close examination of that letter. Suffice it to say, for now, that if we had nothing but the *De libero arbitrio* to judge by, the compositional difficulties, even confusions, of this third book would leave us in a state of bafflement indeed.

SUMMARY OF AUGUSTINE'S ARGUMENT

It may help to summarize the progress of Augustine's argument to this point. He is presenting a theodicy, endeavoring to neutralize Manichaean objections to the Catholic view that God made all things, endowed humans with freedom of choice, and remains a just God, worthy of praise and adoration. In time, he comes to the objection that a God responsible for the moral ignorance and impotence that characterize our human condition must bear the responsibility for the evil acts we commit out of that ignorance and impotence. For he implicitly agrees with his adversaries in viewing this sorry condition as simply insuperable: humans are not good, do not have it in their power to be good—with the result that all they do is unavoidably "reprehensible."

Reprehensible, Augustine agrees, but not, for that reason, truly "sinful"; for their insuperable moral ignorance and impotence would, all other considerations apart, reduce to zero their culpability for the acts they perform. But does this make God, accordingly, responsible for those acts? No, Augustine's argument runs, for the very condition of moral ignorance and impotence is one for which human souls themselves are culpably responsible; their original "natural" state, the state in which God created them, was one of moral wisdom and unfettered freedom of choice. They have *merited* their present sorry state as a punishment, in the proper sense of that term, for a sin or sins—again, in the proper sense—*they* themselves committed. The fullness of their original freedom, and hence the culpability of the sin committed out of such sovereign freedom, are in perfect proportion to the insuperability of the moral ignorance and impotence that is now their punishment.

So Augustine's argument has run, both simply and with seamless consistency, up to and including the unambiguously categorical summary he presents in paragraph 52. But suddenly, without the slightest warning, paragraph 53 introduces a difficulty that all his previous argumentation seems never once to have anticipated. Everything up to this point would be unobjectionable, that difficulty implies, on one condition: *if* it be granted that the sin for which we are being so severely punished was truly "ours" in the first place. Supposing, though, that our condition is a punishment for a sin that "we" never committed: the sin of an Adam and Eve who are, the objector implies, "other" than ourselves? Could God truly punish us for a sin *we* never committed and still be just in doing so?

At first, Augustine tries to answer the objection in general terms. In order to do so he accepts, if only for the sake of argument (*dato, non concesso?*), the objector's supposition that we, as moral agents, are not identical with Adam and Eve. On such a supposition, he realizes, his earlier straightforward proportion between the insuperability of our penal ignorance and impotence, and our presumed original culpability, has had the bottom knocked out of it. Reduce our culpability to the extent this objection supposes, and you must admit that one can no longer speak of "our" having sinned at all or of "our" being "punished" in any proper sense of either term. Indeed, our otherness from Adam radically eliminates all grounds for speaking of *us* as having sinned, of *ourselves* as being "justly punished."

The willingness to fight on the terrain dictated by his adversary's objection has gotten Augustine into a seemingly inextricable difficulty. How was he to fight his way out of it? There were, I suggest, two avenues open to him. The first of them was to remain consistent with the argumentative concession his objector has asked him to make: that we are truly "other" than Adam and Eve. In that case, he would have been compelled to jettison the principle that has guided his defense of God up to this point: the principle of just proportionality between culpability and punishment. That principle, however, seems to have been much too dear to his ethical heart; he will remain faithful to it. But then, admit reduced culpability, and you must reduce proportionately the weight of the punishment; and this is precisely what Augustine has done. He abandons his estimate, unquestioned until now, that our moral ignorance and impotence are simply insuperable, and argues that they must be superable after all, that we can make moral progress and even attain our ultimate beatitude, that God will aid us along that road. And lo! all justified complaints against God's justice have been laid to rest—or, nearly so.

But now he catches sight of a second exit road. Need one so easily grant the "otherness" of Adam and Eve which his objector is supposing? No, for there is at least one theory on the origin of our souls —traducianism—which actually asserts our identity with Adam, so that we did indeed sin "in" his sinning and are therefore being rightly punished for that sin. Here, both sin and punishment retain the "proper" sense Augustine's original line of argument required.

There was yet another theory. It held that our souls pre-existed their entry into this post-Adamic existence, and from that pre-existence freely chose to "come" or "fall"—sinfully—into bodies; here, too, one could speak of both sin and punishment, both in the proper senses of those terms. What, though, of our relationship with Adam and Eve? Augustine may well have thought that the spiritual interpretation he had already given in his *De Genesi contra Manichaeos* remained a satisfying answer to that question, for there our souls were all mysteriously contained in, and identical with, the paradisiac "human nature" Genesis could be thought to mean by that "first couple," *primum conjugium*, Adam and Eve. And, coincidence that may not have been purely coincidental, this same identity of post-Adamic "men" with an Adam viewed as Archetypal "Man" was a common feature of most "fallen soul" theories of the time.

There were, it must be admitted, two other theories regnant on the "origin" of our souls. Our souls could have been created individually, or divinely "sent" into post-Adamic bodies. In these cases his objector's supposition is correct. Our "otherness from Adam" obliges Augustine to repeat the performance in paragraphs 53–55:

eliminate culpability and punishment in the proper sense; hence, renege on the insuperability of our formerly penal condition, turn that condition into an "admonition," and allow for—indeed, stress —the possibility of moral progress.

Now, however, Augustine contents himself with warning us that none of these four hypotheses should be affirmed "rashly"; the question of adjudicating between them is fraught with "obscurity and perplexity," so that either Catholic Scripture commentators have failed to resolve it or, if they have, their writings have not come into Augustine's hands. But choosing between these positions, he tells us, may be left a secondary matter, as long as our belief holds no "false or unworthy opinion concerning the substance of our Creator," to Whom we are bidden to wend our way along the path of piety. To hold a wrong opinion about the soul, a creature, is "no danger" to us so long as we "do not hold it as if it were assured knowledge." But a false opinion on God—one that would claim Him mutable, for instance, or either more or less than a Trinity— is far more lethal (60). And when it comes to questions concerning "temporal" realities, including, evidently, the past history and future destiny of our souls, "expectation of things to come is more important than research into things past," and our main concern is rightly bestowed "on what is hoped for in the future" (61). "What disadvantage is it to me," Augustine asks, "not to know when I began to be, when I know that I exist now and do not cease to hope that I shall continue to exist?" The voyager to Rome may have forgotten the shore he set out from; no problem in that so long as he keeps in mind the port to which he is directing his course. So, too, with us. The principal thing is not "holding unworthy opinions of God Who is the sole end of the soul's labors" and the "end" in which our souls are to "find rest" (61).

Augustine would not go so far as to "forbid those who have the ability" and the "leisure" to inquire about which of these four hypotheses may represent the true past history of the soul. "Such inquiries and discussions are justifiable if reason demands them in order to answer some necessary question, or if leisure from more necessary matters is available." But such inquiries should not produce contentiousness and "rash" seizures of anger at those who might disagree with our opinion; nor should one with a "clear and certain understanding" of the matter, based on Scripture, "suppose that another has lost all hope for the future because he does not remember the soul's origin in the past" (62).

Now Augustine reminds his readers of the central point of all this long discussion: whether one pass over or defer the question of the soul's origin for later consideration, "there is no obstacle preventing us from answering the question with which we are dealing at present," and from answering it in such a way "as to make clear that souls pay the penalty for their own sins [*peccatorum suorum*], by the upright, just, unshaken and changeless majesty and substance of the Creator." Again, it is a *theodicy* of freedom he is concerned with; he has been forced to scout a number of secondary and side issues in order to exculpate God, but secondary issues they remain for him, and, he hopes, for us as well. The condition that prompts Manichaean complaints about God is a just "punishment" for souls' "own sins," and "these sins, as we have explained at great length, are to be ascribed to nothing but to their own wills" (*non nisi propriae voluntati earum*). God, therefore, is not to be held responsible for them (63).

There are several puzzles involved in this terse summary, however. The first of them is already familiar: Augustine's expression of it gives the reader no hint that this "penal" account of our moral ignorance and impotence was only one of two hypotheses he had intended to entertain. He is about to introduce that second, competing, hypothesis for consideration: that such ignorance and impotence may be our "natural" condition. But instead of preparing his readers' minds for it, this concluding summary makes its introduction an even greater mental shock.

Yet apart from that, his summary of the preceding discussion is surprisingly simplified. Our ignorance and impotence are surely, in the traducianist hypothesis, "punishment" for a sin that (Augustine feels) is truly "our own"; the same must be said of the "fall" hypothesis, the pre-embodied "choice" implied being both "ours" and sinful. But this bald way of characterizing our human condition hardly fits the two other hypotheses, wherein a perfectly innocent soul was either "created" or "sent by God." Again, Augustine has been forced to concede that in neither of these cases can the

sin accounting for our condition truly be called "our own" or
the condition resulting from it be termed a "punishment" in the
"proper" sense of that term. Was he so preoccupied by his main,
theodicean point that he would almost prefer to forget the qualifications that so seriously complicate, and by complicating attenuate,
the force of his argument in God's defense?

Or is this conclusion an unemended residue from an earlier
version of the work—a conclusion quite in line with the simpler
argumentative thrust of paragraphs 51–52 and a conclusion coherent, accordingly, with only the "fall of the soul" and traducianist
hypotheses? However one chooses to answer that question, one
must admit that the question itself is real![44]

In any event, Augustine has left no doubts in his readers' minds
that this defense of God was, in fact, his main preoccupation
throughout this book. Much has been made of the silence he pre-
serves here on his own preferred theory of the soul's origin, and of
the reasons he submits for it. More than one writer has concluded
that he simply had no preferred theory during this period and,
indeed, positively refused to choose among the theories competing
at the time he wrote the De libero arbitrio. Hence, any attempt to
read such a theory of the soul's origin out of this, or out of the
works bracketing it in time, is doomed from the outset.

Even were we left with nothing but the third book of the De
libero arbitrio, however, that conclusion can be shown to go dangerously beyond the evidence. Despite all his strategic disclaimers,
we saw Augustine admit that inquiries into the origin of the soul
are "justifiable if reason demands them in order to answer some
necessary question, or if leisure from more necessary matters is
available." He is entering a period of his life when the relative

---

44. One is reminded of Henri-Irénée Marrou's famous "Augustin compose mal."
After I had finished reading this study, the idea occurred to me that Marrou may
have been perfectly correct in regard to those works which Augustine saw fit to
"emend" after completing them; a thorough study of his emendatio technique would
add considerably to our knowledge. At all events, there is real danger in absolutizing
the context of any single sentence pulled out of the context of his writings.

J. Patout Burns has suggested to me that in 63 Augustine may have meant to
affirm no more than that God punishes only those sins for which a person is responsible. But this would imply that Augustine had momentarily lost sight of the point
presiding over this entire section: that of explaining the condition of ignorance and
impotence into which humans are de facto born. This I find an awkward supposition,
especially given Augustine's immediate return to that central preoccupation at the
beginning of 64.

"leisure" he enjoyed at Cassiciacum and Thagaste must yield to the press of priestly and, later, episcopal, duties; but those very duties will bring him closer to the time when a very "necessary question" will arise to show that "reason" does indeed "demand" a renewal of inquiry into this troubled question.

Did he, though, in that earlier period of "leisure" which ended with publication of the *De vera religione* attempt to argue for one or other of these *sententiae* on the soul's origin and incarnate condition? It is at least suggestive that later, when the question heats up again, he will explain his silence in the *De libero arbitrio* in terms that reduce several of the "reasons" given here to distinctly secondary rank. Any argument in favor of one preferred hypothesis over the others, he will say, would only have weakened the force of his argument for the main point of this book: namely, that God (*pace* the Manichees) is not to be blamed for our sins. This is sound argumentative strategy, surely. But, just as surely, there are joints where the argumentative strategy of *De libero arbitrio* 3 seems to creak. Yet compare the looseness of Augustine's handling of them with the tight control and frequent, almost tiresome, reminders of this, his central strategic intention, and the evidence supports his later interpretation of the work, of its main intention, and of the reasons he later gives for not, *in this precise work*, laming his argument by injecting any preference he might have had for one or other hypothesis on the soul's origin. He *could*, therefore, have had a preference, after all.

Indeed, the *De dono perseverantiae* avows that, between the "penal" and the "natural" hypotheses, not only did he have a preferred position but he allowed that preference to show clearly in the course of composition. Granted: he does not permit such a preference to show so plainly as we might like; but it remains true that the only way to discover whether he had an equally "preferred" hypothesis on the soul's origin is to read his earlier works with that question in mind, and with both mind and question sufficiently open for the answer he gives.[45]

45. This, I have to think, seems scarcely the open attitude to be found in Gerald J. P. O'Daly's several contributions to this question. For references and evaluation of his position, see my "Pre-Existence in the Early Augustine" (henceforth: "Pre-Existence"), REA, 26 (1980), 176–88. His recent "Augustine on the Origin of Souls" (henceforth: "Origin"), *Platonismus und Christentum*, Jahrbuch für Antike und Christentum Supplement 10 (1983), 184–91, does little to change that judgment.

Now, however, without any warning, Augustine turns our attention to the counter-hypothesis: that ignorance and moral difficulty are, not "penal," but "natural to man" (64). *Si naturalis est*: the *si*, so strangely absent from his introduction of the "penal" hypothesis much earlier, at least alerts us that we are dealing with an hypothesis *now*. Will God's justice—still Augustine's main concern —be impugned in this hypothesis? No, he argues, all this supposition entails is that we accept this starting point as the one from which the soul begins its advance toward overcoming both ignorance and moral impotence, to arrive at eventual perfection and happiness.

The argument, with its stress on the superability of our moral ignorance and impotence, essentially parallels those marshaled in the hypotheses that the soul is either created or sent. Again, reduce or eliminate the soul's culpability for its helpless condition, and you must perform a comparable reduction respecting the insuperability of that state, along with stressing the possibility of moral progress. So, too, Augustine must admit, the ignorance and difficulty man begins with are not, in this hypothesis, to be considered penal, though God would rightly hold man guilty and punish him were he willfully to neglect to progress toward knowledge and moral capacity; in such a case, the punishment would be to fall into a "still graver state" of both ignorance and moral impotence.[46]

Moreover, since God does not deny man the "capacity" (*facultas*) to make such progress, all imputation of injustice on His part is excluded. On the contrary, the "Creator is to be praised on all counts" since He gave man the "power" (*capacitas*) to rise from such beginnings to attaining the chief good," "renders aid as [man] advances," and "completes and perfects his advance." Again, Augustine stresses, the soul created even in this relatively humble state still excels all bodily creation, and has its very existence from the Creator's goodness; its progress takes time and effort, but each successive effort is rewarded by new gifts from God, both of moral

46. Here, in 64, Augustine gives the interesting parallel: one would not "blame" an infant for its inability to speak, since that inability is "natural" to the infant as such. This hints at the very remote sense that terms like "sinful" and "penal" would have in this "natural" hypothesis, if sense it can be called. Notice, however, that the status of this "natural" hypothesis is substantially equivalent to those of the creationist and "divinely sent" hypotheses, so that Augustine must deal with each and all by essentially the same argumentative strategy.

knowledge and of facility in moral action. "Why" then, Augustine asks, "should not the author of the soul be praised with due piety ..." (65)?

So he ends his reply to the Manichaean objection concerning our moral ignorance and impotence—a condition that at the outset seemed so dense and relatively insuperable that it must have been penal, and we culpable of falling into it, but a condition which now, in three distinct hypotheses,[47] turns out to be not insuperable, not penal, and not culpable. One wonders whether Augustine—or the Manichaean objector—was quite content with this highly quali-fied response. Surely Augustine's taste for the vigorous, unatten-uated penal theory of paragraphs 51–52, before the Adam–Eve objection was introduced, is easy to understand.

Now Augustine passes on to another objection against God's way of acting: His creation of infants who die before attaining any capacity for personal moral development, some of whom, innocent though they be, suffer all manner of bodily torments (66–68).[48] We shall return to this set of objections later on, to compare his position with the one he is compelled to assume in the face of Pelagianism.

THE ORIGINAL HUMAN CONDITION

Of more immediate concern now is his closing set of speculations on human nature's original condition. Was man created "wise"— in which case, how did the devil ever succeed in seducing him? Was he created "foolish"—in which case, since "folly" is the greatest of all vices, "how is God to escape being held the author of vice"?

The force of the objector's question here is difficult for us mod-erns to grasp immediately. Why could a "wise" man not be seduced into evil-doing? And what can it mean to call "folly" the greatest of all vices? Could not God have created man in a condition of un-wisdom, but an un-wisdom that by growth and human develop-ment could naturally yield to the acquisition of wisdom? Augus-tine's answer to this objection is equally difficult to follow. I have

47. Three, that is, if one count creationist, "sent," and "natural" as distinct hypotheses. Analysis will show, however, that creationism and divine sending really turn out to be two species of the more general hypothesis claiming that our ignorance and moral impotence are "natural" and not penal. See note 46, above.

48. Augustine's consideration of the sufferings of animals (69–70) does not directly concern us here.

found no commentator on the *De libero arbitrio* who has anything truly helpful to say about the obscure considerations he puts forward in the paragraphs[49] that follow. And yet, Augustine obviously thought the objection important enough to answer at some length; his answer may turn out to be more revealing than it initially seems. But so obscure is the argument here, and so unfamiliar to us the terms in which Augustine conducts it, I can find no other way of throwing some clarity on it than to present a kind of running paraphrase *cum* interpretation of it.

To understand both the force of the difficulty and Augustine's reply to it, one must grasp from the outset how he is using the terms "folly" (*stultitia*) and "wisdom" (*sapientia*).[50] First, it is obvious that he is speaking of *moral* folly and *moral* wisdom. But secondly, as he himself makes clear further on,[51] he is using these terms as "contraries," denoting opposite *extremes* on the spectrum of moral orientations. Indeed, as his argument will show, he tends to understand these terms much the way an ancient Stoic would. Moral "folly" is not simply moral "ignorance," the simple nescience of how one ought to conduct one's life.[52] Much more positive than that, it amounts to an entrenched set of moral inclinations that guide the moral agent in precisely the *wrong* direction. *Stultitia,* as Augustine uses the term here, tends to resemble a culpable ignorance, a moral state that follows on the guilty rejection, refusal— Augustine will say "neglect"—of its opposite alternative, moral

---

49. This discussion runs from 71 to 74. Note that while Madec (BA 6, pp. 582–83) assures his readers that Augustine's meditations are conducted "on the historical plane" implying the sin of a "first couple" which accounts, in his mind, for the "misery of [our present human] condition," he fails to support that contention by any explicatory analysis illuminating the extraordinarily difficult paragraphs in question.

50. I shall give references from the text itself to support this contention; but the test of its truth must also be its value as an hypothesis that helps us read the whole of Augustine's analysis with some measure of understanding.

51. See below, 73; Augustine writes that the *medium* sought between *sapientia* and *stultitia* supposes that "humans in this life" must think of these as "contraries" (*ab hominibus in hac vita non nisi ex contrario datur intelligi*). The context shows that Augustine himself unreservedly accepts the legitimacy of thinking of them in that way.

52. See his analysis of "infant" un-wisdom, below (71). No one, he argues, would rightly call this *stultitia* in the proper sense. Compare the related assertion here that those are truly *stulti* who *per neglegentiam sapientia carent*, so that their lack of wisdom is due to *vitium* and not to *natura*. Hence, *stultitia* (in the way he wishes us to understand the term) is *non quaelibet, sed vitiosa ignorantia*, a "vicious ignorance."

"wisdom." As such, it might be thought of as analogous to a moral "blindness"[53] that has been voluntarily chosen by the person, who is then, consequently, responsible for that moral blindness.[54]

Moreover, *stultitia* tends to characterize the *total* moral orientation of the person, not only his moral perception, but his moral affections as well; he both sees and loves as his good the evil he has chosen to set both mind and heart on, "making" it his good,[55] as it were. At this point, it is tempting to think of the *stultus* as so "acting out of" the total personal orientation that is his chosen *stultitia* that it becomes difficult to imagine his acting in any way other than "foolishly" (*stulte*).[56] We are, in fact, back with a close analogue of the insuperable moral ignorance and impotence of paragraphs 51–52! Hence, the force of the objector's question: if God created man *stultus*, He must be held the author of the "vices" flowing from that *stultitia*.

Moral wisdom, *sapientia*, on the other hand, is an equally positive, one might say "accomplished," state. It is not merely a "knowing"—as contrasted with a nescience of—how one should conduct one's life;[57] it is much more positive; it must be thought of as analogous to the state resulting from one's having chosen, and firmly chosen, to follow the right path that leads to what is genuinely the "good."[58] Having set one's heart upon what one has seen to be the

53. Compare 72: *Stultitia quippe caecitas quaedam est*, but a blindness tantamount to an *obscuratio*; that (self-)darkening issues *ex aversione a lumine Sapientiae*, out of a "turning away from the Light of Wisdom." (The capitals in *Sapientiae*, Light, and Wisdom anticipate somewhat my eventual interpretation of this entire section; the reader has a right to remain skeptical about them for the moment.)

54. See 71. Genuine *stultitia* further implies, and requires, that *vitiosae stultitiae sit voluntas rea*, that the will be "guilty" of it. This supposition is entirely parallel to Augustine's account (see 51) of our "ignorance and difficulty" as culpable; indeed, the insuperable ignorance–impotence couple is simply another way of expressing the moral *stultitia* now under discussion.

55. See 72: *sibi ipse vult esse bonum suum*. The *stultus* "wills" to be his own "good," thus "turns away" (from God) and becomes "darkened."

56. Compare Augustine's reply to the difficulty entertained in 73, with the argumentation concerning ignorance and moral impotence in 51. There are overtones here of the rigid antithesis (some) ancient Stoics posed between moral *stulti* and accomplished *sapientes*, but the deeper implicit, I shall try to show, is a Neoplatonic one.

57. See 72: *Aliud enim esse rationalem, aliud esse sapientem*; rationality and "wisdom" are not one and the same.

58. So, in 72, Augustine writes: *praecepti observatio meritum est accipiendae sapientiae*. Obey God's command, and you will "merit" the (consequent) "reception" of Wisdom—which, once "tasted," as it were, ensures the soul's continued union with It.

good, one sees it as the good in all the more compelling terms; seeing issues into choosing, but choosing in its turn issues into an even more imperative seeing. At this point, it is tempting to think of the *sapiens* as so acting "out of" his chosen *sapientia* that it becomes difficult to imagine his acting in any way other than *sapienter*, with moral "wisdom." Hence, the force of the objector's question: If God created man "wise," how could the devil succeed in seducing him?

So much for the force of the objection. The same senses of "folly" and "wisdom" allow us to understand how Augustine chooses to answer it. If both "folly" and "wisdom" are contrary states that *follow* on a choice to assume, to congeal oneself in, the total personal posture of being either "foolish" or "wise," then (he argues) there must have been an *antecedent* posture, before that choice and its inevitable consequences, a posture in which one was not yet settled in either orientation, had not yet chosen the life-direction of being either foolish or wise. "Only then," Augustine affirms, "does a man *begin* to be either *stultus* or *sapiens*, in such wise as necessarily to be called either the one or the other, when he is *able* to possess wisdom, unless he neglect [to do so], in such wise that his will is guilty of the vicious *stultitia* [his negligence entrains]."[59] The choice between folly and wisdom, then, supposes a certain development on the part of the chooser; and if the resultant *stultitia* is both vicious and morally culpable, it follows that a chosen *sapientia* would be the opposite of those qualities.

SEARCHING FOR AN INTERMEDIATE STATE

But if there be some prior, intermediate state, neither wise nor foolish, how is it to be conceived? First of all, Augustine reasons, one may exclude certain ways of conceiving of it. The animal,[60] for example, is not even radically able to make the choice for either moral wisdom or moral foolishness. Ignorant, morally nescient though it may be, one could not sensibly accuse the animal of being morally "foolish," in the sense described above. Compare its state of nescience with the state we designate as "blindness." A newborn

59. The italics here are my own.
60. I have inverted, for clarity, the order of Augustine's considerations of animals and infants; see 71.

puppy cannot, for a certain period of days, see; but does that entitle us to call it "blind"? No, Augustine confidently asserts. Its inability to see is perfectly consonant with its state of development; at that state of development, it is not *meant* to see. We may rightly say that it is "unable to see," but to call it "blind" is to imply that it was unable to see when it was meant to be able to see. In Aristotelian terms, Augustine might have said, "blindness" is not a mere negation, a mere inability to see; the term, in its proper sense, implies a *privation*, the absence of an active ability that *should* be there.[61]

Having discarded the animal parallel, Augustine examines the situation of the human infant. Infant though it is, it is nonetheless a *human* infant. Unlike the animal, it has, therefore, the *radical* capacity for (eventually) making the kind of moral choice that could congeal it into the posture of either moral folly or moral wisdom. But the capacity is only a radical one; the infant's humanity must undergo development before it arrives at the insightfulness required for a moral choice. One might say that it is "able" to confront the moral choice for either moral folly or moral wisdom, but that ability, rooted in its human nature as "rational," is not yet actualizable; the infant is not yet sufficiently developed as a being of reason and insight to confront that choice. Translate that choice into Edenic terms: the infant is not yet able to "receive" the "precept" God presented to Edenic man—not yet developed enough to "take in," and respond willingly to, God's command for obedience both to Him and to the way He has set down for the "wise" conduct of human life. One cannot yet, therefore, call the infant either "wise" or "foolish" as those terms are being applied here. Indeed, as we shall see, the infant is not even ready to make the initial choice that would enable us to designate it either wise or foolish.[62]

It may just be that Augustine's argument becomes a trifle foggy from this point on. To begin with, he seems confident we will allow him this much: in the developmental view he is proposing, one can understand that man could so be "made" that "although he may not have yet been wise, he could nonetheless [be equipped to] receive the precept which he ought to obey"; man was ready for that

---

61. But note that even this parallel is not exact. *Stultitia* adds to the notion of *privatio* the qualifications that it be both culpable and self-inflicted.

62. See 72, and the analysis to follow, which, the text being obscure and elliptical, is necessarily conjectural in spots.

much, at least. But, he reminds us, this readiness did not amount to accomplished wisdom; hence, still short of wisdom, "it is no wonder that [man] could be seduced." So far, so good. But, Augustine continues, "it is not unjust, either, that, disobeying that precept, he should have to pay the penalty" (for that disobedience). "Nor" can we say "his Creator is the author of [his] vicious actions [*vitiorum*] since the non-possession of wisdom was not yet a vice for man if he had not yet received the power of possessing [wisdom]."

Not yet wise or even granted the power of possessing wisdom, man is nonetheless at a stage where he is sufficiently able to "receive" God's commandment of obedience to Him—to understand it sufficiently and to understand his obligations in the face of it— that he can justly be punished for not obeying it.[63] For, Augustine goes on to explain, man was equipped with "reason," and it is reason which makes him "capable of [receiving] the commandment," of seeing that he "ought to be faithful to it so as to do what is commanded." And just as reason naturally equips him for "taking in" God's command, so his "observation of the commandment" issues into his reception of "wisdom."

That "observation" of the commandment is also within reach of the "nature" God has given him in that the "will," in addition to his reason, is part of that nature, and his observation of the commandment "merits," entitles him to "receive wisdom." But again, this fully developed wisdom is not required for man's responsibility for his actions; "man begins to be able to sin from the moment he begins [in virtue of his natural reason-power] to be able to receive the commandment."

We have seen that such sin can take the form of "receiving" but not observing God's commandment; but in his developmental state, there is a second way in which man can sin: by not "accommodating himself" to receiving the commandment. Augustine is implying

63. See 72. Observe that Augustine seems here to have abandoned the conviction that presided over his earlier argument (52); cf. 33–35, where genuine culpability for this original choice required a plenary kind of freedom quite different from the more limited freedom we now experience. The more developmental kind of thinking he has been compelled to embark on now seems far more consonant with the emphasis on man's capacity to "progress" in virtue, an emphasis which, we have seen, he was (for the first time in this work) compelled to entertain when dealing with the "non-penal" hypotheses on the origin of the soul (56–58). Here, too, accordingly, we may well be faced with the insertion of a later stratum of both thought and composition.

here that there is a measure of moral responsibility involved in the way we manage our development. If we arrive at the moment when God presents us with His commandment ill-prepared in the sense (apparently) of being "unreceptive" toward it, that unreceptivity is the result of our own doing, and accordingly can be—in fact is— sinful. The question occurs to the reader: Would that unreceptivity be due to a lack of insightfulness, or to a lack of willingness to submit obediently to the precept? Augustine does not answer that question; he leaves this whole process of "self-accommodation" to God's commandment a matter for our own inference and specu- lation.[64]

But he has given us enough indications about how he envisages the subsequent stages of that process. The phase of self-preparation having reached its culmination, Augustine supposes a moment when the divine commandment is presented to man. Now man, capable of doing so, must choose, either consenting to or rejecting the divine command. If he refuses, the consequence of that refusal is that he becomes, now in the fullest sense, "foolish." If he con- sents, then his consent merits, entitles him to, the "gift" of "wis- dom" God then confers upon him.[65]

That gift comes to man as an "illumination" from the Divine Wisdom itself, flooding his soul. Is that illumination merely a cognitive affair? The context of the entire discussion would appear to argue otherwise. The "wisdom" man has now attained to is moral wisdom in the very intense meaning of that term Augustine has been employing from the beginning;[66] the implication is that the moral insight involved is a thoroughly "loving" knowledge of the beauteous Wisdom, the contemplative union with which is man's ultimate beatitude.

That interpretation is borne out in Augustine's enumeration of the stages in human development. For even when merely "cap- able" (in the radical sense) of eventually receiving God's precept,

64. Though the text itself is ambiguous, it remains a question of the "moral wisdom" which, for Augustine here, implies both insight and resolve, mind and will; compare the formula just above (72): *Quod est autem natura ad capiendum praeceptum* [scil., *ratio*], *hoc est voluntas ad observandum.*
65. The connection between "merit" and divine "gift" is worth noting; how "free" this "merited" gift remains, or how "owed" in justice to the one meriting, remains unclear. It would be risky to interpret the early Augustine by the later, on this as on so many other points.
66. This seems to confirm my remarks in note 64, above.

man is for that reason "rational" and "good," and "better" than the brute creation. But he is even "better" when he has received the precept, and better still when he has "obeyed" it. Yet he is in a better state than all these when he is "happy on account of the eternal light of Wisdom," a happiness Augustine rephrases as the "contemplation of Wisdom." Man's wisdom, then, is not merely a developed moral insight into what he ought to do; that insight coincides with a loving, contemplative union that is beatifying. What man ought to do and what man wants to do have become one and the same; perfect rectitude and perfect beatitude coincide.

Augustine's brief description of this ultimate stage in human moral development now makes it even easier to understand the density of the term "wisdom" as he has been using it throughout this discussion. One can understand the objector's reluctance to admit that a soul established in this contemplative happiness, "wise" through the light of Divine "Wisdom" flooding into its entire being, could turn away into the darkness of *stultitia*; one can also understand Augustine's implied sympathy with the objector's position: the initial choice in the direction either of "wisdom" or of "folly" would indeed seem to require a state of soul "intermediate" between both folly and wisdom.

ANOTHER TURNABOUT: NO INTERMEDIATE STATE IS NEEDED

Now, the entire discussion just summarized was aimed at showing that such an intermediate state was conceivable: if both conceivable and indispensable, it must have been man's original state. It implied a developmental view of man, and Augustine had to sketch the plausible phases of that development. And yet, just at the point of outlining man's responsibility for "accommodating himself" for eventual reception of God's command, Augustine surprises his reader by suddenly[67] undercutting the basic premiss that had forced him into this discussion in the first place. "The wise man," he asserts in passing, *can* "sin" after all, "if he turns himself away from Wisdom"—the supernal object of his contemplative beatitude. It is not a slip of the pen, for he repeats it: while "sin" can occur

67. This reversal of field occurs, without the slightest warning, in the very middle of 72.

in terms of a "negligent" reception, or a negligent observance, of the precept, it can also occur in terms of a negligent "guardianship"[68] of the contemplation of Wisdom"! This latter possibility, Augustine now informs us, helps us to understand that, "even if the first man was made wise, he was nevertheless capable of being seduced" away from the contemplation of Divine Wisdom that makes him truly "wise."

"Wise" though he may have been, man was nonetheless capable of sinning. The need to search for an "intermediate" state has been denied. We are left to speculate on why Augustine has so unexpectedly shifted his ground.[69] Does this mean that he has changed his meaning of the key terms "wise" and "foolish," so that they are no longer the contraries they were originally? He has given no indication of such a change; the sequel, moreover, clearly implies he is still employing these terms in the same way.[70]

How, then, he must ask, could man, so established in "wisdom," make the choice to become "foolish"? "It is pride," Augustine begins his reply, "that turns man away from Wisdom" into folly; that folly, moreover, is both "the consequence of turning away from Wisdom" and the "just penalty" which "divine law" decrees should "follow"—i.e., as a natural "consequence" of that turning away. We must think of the "Light of Wisdom" as the object of the wise man's blissful contemplation, Augustine's language suggests, and of "folly" as a "kind of blindness" that "darkens the hearts" (Rom. 1:22) of the foolish. "Whence came this darkness, if not from turning away from the Light of Wisdom?" Augustine asks; for one cannot turn away from the Light without turning toward the opposing darkness. Blindness is both punishment for and nat-

68. Compare the interpretation of Gen. 2:15 that Adam was given the task of "guarding" (*custodire*) the contemplative beatitude God had conferred on "human nature" in *GenMan* 2:15; Augustine seems plainly to have this same interpretation in mind here.

69. One might speculate that he has returned to a confidence in his *GenMan* interpretation of "human nature's" paradisiac state of establishment in "Wisdom" and therefore to contemplative happiness; this would cohere with the *custodire* allusion above, note 68. That, however, would signify a return to the hypothesis of the soul as "fallen" which, I am arguing, was the foundational stratum left from the first version of this work. This may be part of that unemended stratum.

70. Note that the interpretation of wisdom and foolishness as "contraries" occurs in 73; compare above, note 51. Augustine has unaccountably abandoned the "developmental" sort of thinking he has been experimenting with.

ural consequence of that turning, as the sublime perfection of "divine law" requires.[71]

But the root of this "turning away," we have been told, is "pride." How are we to understand its operation? "Man," Augustine replies, "whose good is God, willed to be his own good, as God is God's own good." Psalm 42:6 (in Augustine's personal exegesis of it) intimates this teaching when it depicts the soul, turned to itself (*ad meipsum*), as inevitably "disturbed" or "troubled" (*conturbata*); that "turn to oneself" also corresponds to the devil's deceptive promise to Adam and Eve that their disobedience would make them "like gods." Pride, then, is a turning away from the Divine Light which is our beatifying Good, by the very fact that it is a turning "to oneself"; but, one infers, since we ourselves are not the Light and remain enlightened only when turned toward the Light, turning to ourselves is *eo ipso* a turn toward darkness, blindness, *stultitia*.[72]

SEARCHING FOR AN INTERMEDIATE Transitus

Augustine seems satisfied that this explanation, in terms of "pride," allows us to understand that man, even though established in wisdom, could nonetheless freely choose to become "foolish." The necessity for the "intermediate state" between folly and wisdom would appear to be eliminated. It is thinkable that man should have "departed" from the Light of Divine Wisdom after all.

But now he sees another difficulty.[73] Does "folly" only ensue from this turning, or does it precede it? Man may be thought either to have turned away and departed from God *out of* "folly" or to have become "foolish" in consequence of, and "after," that turning away. If one chooses the first alternative, it follows that man was "foolish *before* departing from Wisdom, so that foolishness would be the cause of his departing." But this hypothesis flies in the face of the supposition that man was "wise," in the intense meaning Augustine pours into that term—i.e., "wise" on account of his bliss-

71. This interlock of elements recalls Augustine's cherished *dimissio* theme; see above, notes 41 and 42.
72. Augustine interprets the phrase about John the Baptist's being "not the light" as referring to the soul; see *Conf* 7.13. Hence, he can image this turning of the soul to itself as a turning away from the Divine (beatifying) Light toward the "darkness."
73. See 73.

ful contemplation of Wisdom's Divine Light. No room for any *stultitia* here![74] It would appear we are left with the second alternative: that man became *stultus* only *after* turning away. But no; for that would mean that man turned away from God *out of* "wisdom," hence "wisely," and if wisely, "rightly," so that he committed no sin (*nihilque peccavit*).[75]

But that consequence is equally unacceptable. So, once again, Augustine is compelled to entertain *quiddam medium*, to seek some middle ground between the objector's two alternatives. It is not, though, the middle ground he contemplated earlier, an "intermediate *state*" in which man, poised for the choice between folly and wisdom, would be neither foolish nor wise before making that choice. Augustine is quite bravely continuing with the supposition that man was established in wisdom; the *quiddam medium* he seeks now must provide a *transitus* "whereby" (*quo*) that first man passed from that summit of wisdom (*ex arce sapientiae*) to folly, a *transitus* that must be effected in such a way that the *transitus* itself is neither wise nor foolish.

Now mortal humans, Augustine observes, are compelled to think of "wise" and "foolish" as, not contradictories, but "contraries."[76] So, if we take the case of a man who progresses (as all men must) from *stultitia* to *sapientia* and consider the *transitus* he makes from the one state to the other, we are inclined to argue this way: if he makes it *stulte*, foolishly, then he cannot make it *bene*, well; but, if we are talking of a *transitus* from folly to wisdom, it is madness to claim it was not "well" made. It cannot, then, have been made *stulte*, foolishly. Does it follow that it was made "wisely," *sapienter*? If so, we must suppose there was already "wisdom" in the man *before* he made the *transitus* "to" wisdom—a supposition which

74. This supposition would also threaten to make God responsible for this "foolish," i.e., sinful, turning.

75. Again, *sapientia* and *stultitia* must be understood in that very "strong" sense that makes them "contraries."

76. Augustine begins this sentence as though he were about to express a reservation on this "human" way of looking at things, but the context shows that no such reservation is intended. The question then arises: Given these strong senses of both *sapientia* and *stultitia,* is the developmental cast of thought he has been experimenting with any longer admissible? The sequel answers that question in the negative. Madec's translation of *adparet* (BA 6, p. 521) as "on voit" is strong, but his "termes opposés" for *ex contrario* is weak. Contraries, like contradictions, are "opposed," but the former are at opposite *ends* of their shared spectrum. This is crucial for appreciating Augustine's reasoning here.

Augustine, by dint of the fact that he himself treats wisdom and folly as "contraries" to each other, pronounces "no less absurd" than the insane conclusion just rejected above.

What, then, are we to conclude? That there must be a "middle" sort of *transitus* that is neither wise nor foolish; "such that when the first man made the *transitus* from the citadel of wisdom [*ex arce sapientiae*] to folly, that *transitus* itself was neither foolish nor wise."[77] A humble illustration may help. Both "going to sleep" and "waking up" are types of *transitus* from sleep to wakefulness, but neither is the accomplished state of either "being asleep" or "being awake." Only an illustration, Augustine admits, but let it serve.[78] The illustration is patently inadequate, but it is the best Augustine can do with a problem his use of terms has made intractable. He simply drops it, and passes on.

Here, then, we have another curious passage of arms, replete with self-contradictions resulting, in all likelihood, from a series of self-corrections injected into the text without Augustine's having lifted out the original phases of his thought he later found objectionable. Starting with an understanding of *stultitia* and *sapientia* as contraries, Augustine finds it impossible to envisage how a passage from one to the other could be effected. How, in particular, could there be any possibility of the moral progress and development so crucial to his thinking on the creationist, divinely sent, and "natural" hypotheses if *stultitia* and *sapientia* are defined this way? He then tries to envisage an intermediate *state* between them, one which is neither insuperable *stultitia* nor accomplished *sapientia*; this permits him to begin thinking of stages in man's moral development. Yet, in mid-explanation of those stages, he abruptly reverts to his earlier definitions, affirms that man was originally established in *sapientia*, and must now set himself the

77. Note that this supposition would entail the very un-Augustinian corollary that the *transitus* from "happiness" to the "misery" that he considers genuinely penal would involve no "sin" on the part of the soul. Hence, the embarrassing conclusion that the soul would be punished without having merited punishment.

78. Augustine goes on to remind us of a difference (*verum interest*) that is vital: the passage from sleeping to waking often (*plerumque*) does not involve an act of the will (*sine voluntate . . . fiunt*) to which one could assign either moral culpability or moral merit. The opposite is true of the *transitus* he is searching to understand: *illa autem numquam nisi per voluntatem*, so that in such a case *iustissimae retributiones consequuntur*. Punishment, to be just, requires this voluntary choice. It is curious, given this embarrassed admission, that this "sleeper" illustration seems to live on in the famous *modo, et modo, sed modum non habebat modum* in *Conf* 8.12.

new problem of envisaging an intermediate *transitus* from *sapientia* to *stultitia*.

This problem is merely the obverse of the one above: both *stultita* and *sapientia*, conceived as contraries with no intermediary stages between them, are such "established" conditions that neither sinful fall from *sapientia* nor moral progress from *stultitia* seems thinkable! The illustration from waking or falling asleep simply points to the reality of *transitus* in general, somewhat like Dr. Johnson's kicking a stone to refute Zeno. Augustine himself admits that such *transitus* examples do not quite fit the bill, since "willing" need not be involved in them. But, one must add, he has made the voluntary passage from established *sapientia* to its contrary, insuperable *stultitia*, a problem of such a special sort that the gradual transition of waking from sleep is scarcely a parallel at all. How, one wonders, did Augustine ever get himself into this quandary? Before hazarding an answer to that question, we shall be better advised to examine the next topic he feels obliged to take up.

THE DEVIL'S FALL—AND "MAN'S"

He ends his book with a brief meditation on the difference between man's first sin and the sin of the fallen angels. The question he has in mind is this: What put it into the angel's mind, so to speak, to commit the act which resulted in his fall from on high? In man's case, Augustine feels, the explanation lies more directly to hand, for there were two opposing appeals being made to his choice: from on high, the appeal of God's precept; from below, the appeal of the devil's tempting suggestion.

To understand Augustine's mode of argument here, it is necessary to recall how he conceives of "free choice" (*liberum arbitrium*). The term itself suggests that he thinks of it primarily as free "judgment." He envisages the choosing subject as confronted with at least two opposing "goods," but goods in the precise sense of *attractive* or *desirable* goods, goods that promise, each in their distinct ways, to make the subject "happy." The subject is then called upon to "judge between" attraction and counter-attraction; in consequence of that "judgment," the "will" is prompted to pursue whichever "good" is deemed more attractive, more conducive to happiness.

So, Augustine asserts here, no "choice" is explicable except in function of something "perceived" (*visum*) and, evidently, perceived as an attractive good. Nor is it in the power of the free creature to determine what objects will make their appeal to the will; what is in his power is the choice of accepting or rejecting the appeal of those objects. The misery or blessedness that follows upon that choice is, accordingly, merited.

Apply this to man in paradise, presented with the appeal of two opposing realities, God's command and the devil's suggestion. Both these realities confronted him entirely independent of his power to will that they confront him or not; but, Augustine insists, what lay in the power of man's will was the choice "not to yield to the vision of inferior seductions" (*non cedere visis inferioris illecebrae*), a vision suggested to him by the devil.

How can we know that this choice lay in man's power? Augustine now makes it explicit that he envisages paradisiac man as "established in the healthy state of wisdom" and "free of all the chains of difficulty" (free, therefore, of the ignorance and moral impotence discussed earlier[79]) and argues this way: the proof that paradisiac man had it in his power to resist the devil's tempting suggestion lies in the fact that "even *stulti*, about to pass over to *sapientia*, conquer [these seductions], even with [or: despite] the burdensomeness involved in doing without the poisonous sweetness of their [former] ruinous habits." The echoes ring pure from his own conversion experience; the facts are clear, so there must be some way of understanding them. But it is no less clear from what we have seen that precisely this "passage" from *stultitia* to *sapientia* so far defies Augustine's categories of moral understanding.

So much for the case of man's sin. But understanding how and why the devil himself first sinned is not quite so simple. For in his case what is missing is precisely the counter-appeal his tempting suggestion offered to paradisiac man. What was it that stood in opposition to God's commandment and "suggested to the devil himself the resolution to follow after impiety, whereby he fell from his supernal abode"? For "whoever wills, surely wills *something*"; if the devil

79. And originally established, therefore, in that plenary kind of freedom he was thinking of in paragraphs 1 to 52, but momentarily abandoned in the more "developmental" cast of thinking the non-penal hypotheses of the soul's origin compelled him to entertain.

were affected by nothing seen, he would not have chosen to do what he did; for unless something had entered his mind, there is no way that he could have turned his intention toward wrong. Whence, then, did it enter his mind, whatever it was that entered his mind, so that he undertook those things whereby, from good angel, he became devil [75]?

There are three sorts of things the devil could have "seen." The first is the sort of persuasive suggestion the devil himself made to man; but from the nature of the case, there being as yet no devil, we may exclude this possibility. Two other possibilities remain. The devil's "vision" may have arisen from "realities lying beneath": that is, either beneath the mind's own attention (*intentio*) or beneath the bodily senses. What, though, lies beneath the "mind's" (*animus*) attention?[80] "First of all, the mind itself, whereby we also [*nos etiam*] are conscious that we are living" beings; "next, the body which [the mind] governs." What lies beneath the bodily senses are, obviously, bodily realities of all sorts. Note that unfallen angels, like unfallen souls, nonetheless enjoy (to Augustine's way of thinking) a superior kind of "corporeity."

But Augustine means to explain the devil's fall without invoking the appeal of lower corporeal delights. So, he assures us, even when it is engaged in the contemplation of the Unchanging Highest Wisdom, the devil's

mind, which is changeable, beholds itself as well, and so, somehow or other, comes into mind. This is owing to the difference that makes the mind other than what God is; and yet, the mind [*animus*] is something that, after God, can be a pleasing reality [76]

and, obviously, become the pleasing object of its own gaze. But that pleasingness of the mind to itself can be an entrapment for the mind. For the mind, Augustine tells us, is in a "better state" when it forgets itself "out of charity [i.e., desire] toward the unchangeable

80. The soul, or mind, is spoken of throughout this passage as *animus*, and the term is applied indifferently to human souls, angelic and diabolical minds. Madec, in BA 6, p. 522n120, asserts that *visum* in this entire context is the "translation of *phantasia*, proposed by Cicero" in his *Prior Academics*; hence, he translates *visum* each time it occurs by the term "representation," except in 76 (p. 527), where he reverts to the more natural "la *vue* [d'un] objet." He gives no reasons for our accepting this Ciceronian interpretation, and the text he cites from GenLitt 9.25 in no way supports that interpretation: its *visis* lends itself much more naturally to the translation "by objects *seen*" i.e., as "good" or attractive.

God," even to the point of wholly despising itself in comparison
with Him.

> If, however, it takes pleasure in itself, as though encountering itself
> [as something between itself and God], to the point of imitating
> God perversely, wishing to delight in its own power, then the
> greater it desires to be, the less it [actually] becomes. And this is
> what is [meant by the expressions]: "The beginning of all sin is
> pride," and "The beginning of pride is man's turning away from
> God."[81]

So, Augustine is persuaded, he has answered the difficulty proposed to him. There was no need of an "inferior" kind of counter-
suggestion, rivaling God's commandment, to explain the angel's
sinning with the sin that made him devil. Such a counter-suggestion
makes it *easier* to understand how paradisiac man could have sinned,
but in the devil's case, his own mind, object of an intuition exercised alongside the beatifying contemplation of God, provided the
"*some*thing" he saw, the something whose pleasingness drew him
away from the "piety" of that contemplation into "impiety," an
impiety whose very heart was pride: the creature's delight in its
own power, so inebriating as to bring it to imitate, perversely,
God's own creative power.

This difference between the devil's and man's first sin also serves
to explain the difference between the punishments God leveled
on the two of them. The devil "persuaded" man to commit a sin
of pride much like the one he knew had damned him, but his appeal
to man *also* involved the "seductions" of "inferior" bodily delights.
Behind that diabolical persuasion, and intensifying its malice, there
worked a "most malevolent envy" of man, who still enjoyed his
unfallen condition. Hence it is that man, though having committed the sin of pride "in imitation of the devil" (but a sin rendered less serious through the appeal of bodily delights?), receives
a punishment meant to "correct," rather than "kill," him, and that
Christ the Lord came to elicit a counter-imitation of His own

---

81. Compare, once again, the application (and interpretation) of these same texts
in the GenMan description of the fall of "human nature"; see my *Early Theory*, pp.
169–83. Madec's translation of the *ad me ipsum* from Ps. 41 as "A l'égard de moi-
même" (BA 6, p. 521) raises a doubt about whether he understood the force Augustine
is *giving* that phrase: the soul's "turn" to itself is a turn away from God which
inevitably entails "disturbance." Compare *En 41* 12, which Madec footnotes, but
does not seem to have studied closely.

humility, our way to eternal "life." His blood shed for us, we can hope to "adhere" to Him after inexpressible toils and miseries, in such a way that, "snatched away [in]to Him by His so great brightness, nothing we see from out of the lower realms [of being] may twist away our upward-tending gaze." [82] And were it to happen that our "appetite for lower realities" should temptingly "suggest" such a turning, the devil's eternal damnation and sufferings will serve to call us back to our enraptured contemplation of God. [83]

"For so great is the beauty of Justice, so joyful the vision of Eternal Light, that is to say, Unchangeable Truth and Wisdom," Augustine concludes, that "even if it were permitted us to abide in it for the space of only a day, we should, in exchange for that day alone, rightly and deservedly despise [the alternative of] countless years of this life, full though they were with delights, and teeming with temporal goods." And with this paean to our contemplative bliss, Augustine ends the De libero arbitrio. [84]

MORE PUZZLES—AND AN HYPOTHESIS

This closing meditation contains some features that must seem puzzling to the contemporary reader. Why, for example, did Augustine find it so necessary to ferret out a possible motivation for the devil's "fall" from the citadel of contemplative wisdom and happiness he once enjoyed? And what are we to make of the language of animus, used of both devil and human soul as though it fitted them in perfectly parallel ways, such that the devil, too, seems to have had a body and corporeal senses, and the fall of man's "soul" or "mind" (mind-soul?) can be spoken of on the model of the devil's own?

Those puzzling expressions are, however, revelatory; they may

---

82. The language of contemplative beatitude is once again in evidence. The soul derives that beatitude from contemplative union with the Christ Who, as God, is its Wisdom, Light, and Life. This, I am suggesting, is both the soul's original and eventual terminal condition. Madec, BA 6, p. 527, blurs the thought by translating eius (i.e., Christ the Word's) claritate as "une clarté."

83. See 76, and note 82, above.

84. Compare these final indications with their parallels in Lib 2 and Ver, and it becomes plain that our "end" is the same as our "beginning": a contemplative beatitude we shared with angels as well. See my Early Theory, pp. 52–64 and 146–83, as well as Olivier DuRoy's L'Intelligence de la foi en la Trinité selon saint Augustin (Paris: Etudes Augustiniennes, 1966) (henceforth: Trinité), pp. 132–33, 204–205, 233–36, 240n6, and 288–97.

provide us the final missing keys to unlock the entire cluster of problems with which this confusing work has confronted us. But, first, it must be squarely acknowledged that the anomalies uncovered by a careful reading of De libero arbitrio 3 are real and that the very reality of those anomalies represents a problem to be solved. How did Augustine ever come to write a book so bristling with shifts of argumentative register, inconsistencies, inner contradictions, and repeated self-corrections? His thought, de Lubac observes, is "en devenir," but does that bland phrase really take the measure of the problem this confusing work constitutes?

We know that Augustine spent several years in completing the De libero arbitrio, and that he may have devoted as many as three years to finishing off this third book. In the meantime, we may think, he was learning, pondering, finding elements of his earlier views that might not have stood up to the challenge of later discoveries; this is not surprising, for this was the way of it for Augustine to the very end of his life. Let these two observations, then, entitle us to frame a working hypothesis: that the third book of the De libero arbitrio dramatizes the clash between different strata of Augustine's developing thought, later strata coming into conflict with earlier, and calling for the complications, self-corrections, and shifts of argumentative register he, oddly enough (to our way of thinking), allowed to stand in the final redaction side by side with residues of his original earlier thought.

Now, add a second hypothesis growing out of this first, that the original stratum of Augustine's thinking was the one he informs us about in the De dono perseverantiae: that he considered mankind's condition of moral ignorance and impotence a "penal" condition rather than a "natural" one. The very antithesis he uses entitles us to take that term "penal" in the proper, rather than the improper, sense he admits it must assume in the "natural" hypothesis; otherwise he is making a distinction without a difference! Which, therefore, of the four "hypotheses" on the soul's origin would the original stratum of his thinking have supposed? We are left with only two choices: traducianism or the voluntary and sinful "fall of the soul." But Augustine, as we shall repeatedly see further on, manifested a lifelong antipathy to the traducianist hypothesis, and the evidence of his earlier works makes this much unmistakable: if these are our only two choices, the palm must go to the "fall of the soul."

Suppose, then, we assume that in the original stratum of his thinking, Augustine considered mankind as so many souls, each of which freely and sinfully chose to come down into the world of human bodies. Does this assumption illuminate the *De libero arbitrio* 3, even to the point of permitting us to understand how it came to be such a tangled work? I submit that it may, and that it may allow us to understand as well both why the famous Boyer–de Montcheuil controversy still seems unresolvable[85] and how one might resolve it.

Strictly speaking, a hypothetical view of the sort I mean to propose should be expressed in conditional and subjunctive moods; but in the interests of straightforward prose, I shall use indicatives. And first, the "fallen soul" hypothesis permits us to understand what Augustine repeatedly tells us here about mankind's original condition. Before incurring the ignorance and impotence that mark our fallen, "penal" condition, we were established in "wisdom" and plenary freedom. We were souls, embodied, with a celestial kind of body quite unlike the "mortal" flesh of our present experience. This means that we enjoyed the fullness of both wisdom and happiness that consists in gazing contemplatively on the Light, Truth, Wisdom, and Beauty of God. So Augustine can express our original condition in the same terms used for the devil's while he remained an unfallen angel:[86] both devils and human souls are *animi*, "mind-souls," made for and fallen from the same contemplative bliss, so that the central mechanism of man's "fall" is a proud apostasy in imitation of the devil's.[87] The fullness of their beatitude, moreover, coincides perfectly with accomplished "rectitude," obedience to God's "precept" that they remain in the status for which He created them.

The difficulty with this view, the classic difficulty in the Neo-

85. Again, see Madec in BA 6, pp. 579–80, for this judgment. Indeed, given his position, he cannot come to any other conclusion.
86. Note again that, in Augustine's thought, angels, like human souls, are "spiritually" embodied; indeed, the devil even now boasts a kind of "aerean" body.
87. See 72 (*Superbia enim avertit . . . sibi ipse vult esse bonum*) where this parallelism is clear; see also 76 and note 80, above. The devil's "seductive" appeal to bodily delights only *reinforced* the lure of pride, and, hence, made man's fall *easier* to understand.

68   THE ORIGIN OF THE SOUL

platonic view of the soul, is that of understanding why and how a
mind soul so "established" in blissful wisdom could ever "turn
away" from the beatifying object of its contemplative rapture.
Sapientia in its perfectly achieved state would seem, in its way, as
"insuperable" as the moral ignorance and impotence—read now,
the stultitia—which are its absolute contrary.[88] Hence, the need
Augustine feels to produce a plausible mechanism for the devil's
"fall"—a mechanism wherein superbia, "pride," operates very much
the way Plotinus' τόλμα does. The fall of the human soul may be
easier to understand by reason of the devil's counter-appeal, but its
pride mechanism is essentially the same.

But if one grant this as human souls' original (and "natural")
condition, one may understand that the fallen soul may make no
appeal to the ignorance and diminished freedom we now experience
as extenuating the culpability of that original sinful act; it was
committed out of the unimpaired fullness of both wisdom and
liberty, and so we fully merited what we both chose and received
as punishment. The dreadful seriousness of the act accounts for the
dreadful insuperability of the moral ignorance and impotence Augustine—originally—conceived of as its punishment.[89]

In this hypothesis, Adam and Eve are symbolic names for the
original coniugium,[90] that blissful marriage of contemplation and
undistracted action that paradisiac "human nature" was. So Augustine explains that term in his De Genesi contra Manichaeos, where
every element of the foregoing interpretation receives its most explicit formulation.[91] In this hypothesis, "we" were and are Adam
and Eve, "their" sin was and is truly ours, so that the direct linkage
between our culpability and the penal condition it merited is clear
and uncomplicated. Hence, the relative simplicity and vigor of the

88. The position of some Stoics on this contrareity has now, for Augustine,
received Neoplatonic underpinning: turn away from the Light, and you must turn
toward the opposing darkness. See above, note 56.
89. One may think that Augustine would have been brought in time to sever
the strands of this rigid position; but it might have made some difference in
the result had his adversaries here not been the Manichees, with their "complaints"
against God's justice.
90. See note 27, above, for the meaning this term can take in the "fallen soul"
hypothesis. Madec, however, in BA 6, p. 582, is quite correct in giving the term the
more "historical" sense called for in the context of the hypothesis Augustine is considering in 55. But change the hypothesis, and the meaning of coniugium can change
accordingly.
91. See Early Theory, pp. 146–83.

"penal" explanation Augustine was supposing from the outset: up until paragraph 53, when the Adam–Eve difficulty was thrust upon him.

For there are, Augustine has since learned, other ways of understanding Genesis, other hypotheses on the soul's origin and consequently on the relationship of our individual selves to "Adam" and "Eve." There are *sententiae*, opinions regnant among Catholic thinkers, which would hold, for instance, that our souls are "created" for insertion into bodies inherited from two historical individuals who lived in their own bodies long ago. In that hypothesis, Adam and Eve are "other" than ourselves. Would it be just of God to mete out to "us" the dreadful punishment of insuperable moral ignorance and impotence when we ourselves, our souls, were innocent of their sin? Indeed, to complicate matters even further, there are even those in the Church who seem to claim that this ignorance and impotence are not a punishment at all, but the "natural" condition in which God placed mankind at its creation.

Suppose, now—for despite all these indicatives, we are still dealing with a hypothesis—that Augustine learned of these counter-theories, and of the respectable status they held among Catholic thinkers, only *after* composing his entire third book of the *De libero arbitrio* in the simpler key his own preferred view permitted him. He could, of course, have scrapped what he had written, from start to finish, and begun afresh; the resulting work would then show none, or far fewer, of the anomalous turns and shifts this surviving version betrays. He does, we saw, at one point entertain the notion that mankind may originally have been established, not in "wisdom," but in some "intermediate" state, but his experiment with this idea was short-lived. He reverts to his original conviction that the nearly insuperable "wisdom" of his earlier view still obtained, thus forcing him to conjure up the notion of an intermediate form of "transition" from wisdom to *stultitia*. But that, he must admit, does not entirely satisfy either. Neither of these intermediary notions, therefore, offered much promise for a thorough reworking of his position. And besides, Augustine may have been profoundly attached to that original position.[92] What, then, ought he to do? His own preferred position on this controverted question would provide only a con-

<hr />

92. See notes 27, 42, 68, 69, 81, above; it should also be kept in mind that Augustine had been plunged into the busy round of priestly and, later, episcopal duties.

troversial premiss for proving something that should be placed beyond all possible controversy: that God is just in all His dealings.

And so, my hypothesis runs, he sets about patching up his book as best he can, with the result that it turns out to be the patchwork we read today. On a foundation running from paragraph 1 to paragraph 52, a foundation that supposes "we" are truly Adam and Eve, he adds a shaky second storey to deal with the possibility that Adam and Eve may, after all, be "other" than ourselves, and a third to deal with the possibility that our ignorance and impotence may be "natural," not penal after all: two "hypotheses" which he had not even envisaged when composing the foundational stratum of his work, and which, when all is said, he did not take sufficient care to weave into that work in such a way as to prepare his readers' minds to accept his own original *thesis* precisely as one of several competing hypotheses.[93] And so they interlace in the finished product: original thesis, hypothetical consideration of competing theses, and then, at the end, sections on the fall of devil and man which suppose the original thesis as though nothing in the interim had called it into question or reduced it to only one hypothesis competing with others.

Three of those competing hypotheses supposed that the embodied soul was innocent of sin; in doing so, they snapped the thread of Augustine's direct argumentative line that ran from the soul's dreadful culpability to the dreadful penal condition he felt warranted in portraying originally in such dense and insuperable terms. Not only must he admit that our condition would not be penal, in any proper sense of the term; he must both soften the insuperability of that ignorance and impotence because it no longer makes sense for a good and just God to punish innocent souls as cruelly as He might "fallen" souls, and "justify" even this punishment by stressing the possibilities of moral progress and eventual beatitude it still leaves open to unfortunate humankind. Hence, the experiments with intermediary states and transitions; hence, too, the tentative outline of those progressive stages, from radical to mature rationality, through the self-accommodation for receiving, to the eventual "reception" of, God's "precept"—an outline which, as we

---

93. Indeed, a thorough revision of Book 3 would have implied comparable revision of Books 1 and 2, as well.

have seen, Augustine abandons in mid-career, only to revert to those original notions of *sapientia* and *stultitia* with which his meditation began, and which consorted so much more naturally with the hypothesis with which he was much more at home, the hypothesis with which he terminates his work. Our end is contemplative bliss, fullness of freedom, rectitude, and happiness; this is what is truly "natural" to us and the way we were created at the beginning. God *could* conceivably have created man in such a way that concupiscence—that is, moral ignorance and impotence—would be "natural" to him; the requirements of his theodicean intentions forced Augustine to take those regnant *sententiae* as respectable hypotheses; and so Boyer was right to build his argument on phrases taken from Augustine's treatment of the creationist and "natural" hypotheses. But while God *could* conceivably have created man that way, Augustine is convinced that He *did* not; select a series of texts from sections of the work where this preferred "thesis" is at work, and de Montcheuil's conclusion results. What neither of them took sufficiently into account was the unevenness—indeed, the tangle of confusions—the finished work represents; and what both of them supposed was that Augustine's preferred opinion *must* have been either creationism or traducianism.[94] Approached that way, I am convinced, the *De libero arbitrio* will never yield its secrets.

A careful reading of the works leading up to the *De libero arbitrio* supports the view, I am still persuaded,[95] that Augustine did indeed prefer the hypothesis that we are all "fallen souls." But can the same be said for the later works we must now examine? Quite specifically: some twenty years later, Count Marcellinus will write to Augustine, informing him that certain critics of his in Carthage have proposed an interpretation of the *De libero arbitrio* seriously resembling the one hypothesized here. In *Letter 143*, it would appear that Augustine effectively refutes that interpretation.

94. De Montcheuil argues for traducianism ("Dieu," p. 97) largely on the basis of its being a "penal" hypothesis. The premiss is correct, but he never seriously entertains the possibility of that other penal hypothesis, the fall of the soul. Boyer, "Dieu," passim, on the other hand, laboring under the assumption that Augustine was a creationist, sees clearly that this cannot be conceived of as a penal hypothesis.

95. See my *Early Theory*, pp. 146–200. There, I did not give a close analysis of this baffling book, *Lib* 3; for that omission, this chapter may stand as *amende honorable*.

But that refutation needs to be seen in context, and the letter as a whole read against the background of a vastly altered thought-situation. In any event, this hypothesis must remain exactly that until we have mapped that altered background and taken the measure of Augustine's "refutation."

2

ALL QUIET ON THE
AFRICAN FRONT

BETWEEN THE YEARS 395, when he completed the *De libero arbitrio*, and 411/412, which scholars have until now accepted as the date of his *De peccatorum meritis et remissione*, it would appear that the question of the soul's origin slumbered in unbroken peace at the back of Augustine's mind. Initially, this may seem hard to credit, for precisely during these years the topic became a burning one for Catholic thinkers in other quarters of the Mediterranean basin. In an epoch of instant communications, we can too facilely suppose that a theological explosion in Rome or Jerusalem must have wakened immediate echoes in Africa. But even without falling into such anachronisms, it is not easy to believe that noises of the tempest this question began to stir in the year 393 reached Augustine's ears in Hippo Regius only some eighteen years later. This long delay is even more difficult to imagine if one accept the suggestion made in the preceding chapter: that Augustine's "four hypotheses" on the soul's origin were very probably *sententiae* that he had learned, somehow or other, were the regnant opinions among respectable Catholic thinkers. How could he have learned this much about the state of theological discussion, and so little more?

That is the first question about this interlude of relative quiet which begs for an answer. But answering it will show that the very text that later becomes central to Augustine's thinking on the soul's origin, Romans 9:11, had elsewhere already become pivotal to the same discussion as early as 393. To understand Augustine's developing thought on this issue, we shall be well-advised to ask how aware he was of this text and how he went about his earlier interpretations of it.

There is still a third question. We have seen what a conundrum the *De Trinitate* represents for tracing the development of Augustine's theory of the soul; their interpretations of his *Letter 120*, to Consentius, figured prominently in the story of that development as told by Hendrikx and Chevalier. It will constitute a first test of the counter-view presented in this study to show whether it can weather a close examination of that crucial document better than its competitors.

The final question raised by this period is one that could quite conceivably call into question the very legitimacy of the present study; for there are those who have claimed that *the* question about the soul which galvanized Augustine's interest was, much less its origin, much more its mode of union with the body. The secondary claim in that position would also contest what later pages will show is a claim, distinctly secondary, but nonetheless a claim of this essay: that Plotinus' writings continue to provide sharper illumination of Augustine's views on the soul than those of his editor and disciple, Porphyry. Scrutiny of those issues will require that we pay close attention to Augustine's *Letter 137*, to Volusian.

RUFINUS, JEROME, AND ORIGENISM

First, then, what was the status of theological discussion on the soul's origin during these years, and how adequately was Augustine informed about it?

Having finished the third Book of the *De libero arbitrio* in 395, Augustine seems to have begun composing his *Confessions* some two years later, in 397.[1] Meanwhile, in the East, a storm was brewing, one that would eventually sweep over Africa as well, and test a number of the views Augustine tranquilly held up until that time.

The storm center was Origen. Dead he may have been, since 251, but the spirit of this restless genius lived on, bringing restlessness wherever it invaded. His commentaries on Scripture were read, plundered, cited, or copied, by platoons of followers, Jerome among them. His more adventurous works of theological synthesis were not always known to those who fed on his Scriptural commentaries.

---

1. Since my *Odyssey* has already furnished an interpretation of the *Confessions* in line with the thesis being defended here, I shall omit any express treatment of that work.

Jerome, for instance, will claim that he never knew the tenor of Origen's *De principiis* until long after making enthusiastic use of his Scriptural works.[2]

But even in those Scriptural commentaries, Origen's theories on the origin of human souls were kept no secret. Our souls, he proposed, were created before our bodies, indeed, before the existence of any visible, bodily creation. One in nature with angels and archangels, they sinned; to purify them of their sins, God thereupon created the visible world as a sort of purgatorial "prison," into which He plunged them, more deeply if their sin was grave, less deeply if it was light. The condition and position, as it were, of any human soul at its birth, including its intelligence, environment, and attendant possibilities of living wisely and virtuously, and thus returning to the spiritual world from which it had fallen —all these were in direct proportion to the gravity of that sin in its pre-embodied existence. Did some infants seem to die prematurely? No. Their early death was explained by the lightness of their pre-incarnate sin, which entitled them to an early release from the bondage of the body.

This theory of souls, however, was set inside a more general theory; call it a cyclic theory of creation, or, better, of multiple creations. The universe we know now was preceded by another, indeed, perhaps by countless others; and others, maybe countless others, would succeed ours. Each universe presumably goes through the same cycle of fall and return—not only of souls, but of angels and archangels become demons and archdemons. And each "return" would be a *complete* return; even the most obdurate archdemon, even Satan himself, would enter into the eventual reconciliation, the full reintegration, ἀποκατάστασις, which crowned the cycle of that particular universe.[3] The devils' punishment, accordingly, though spoken of in Scripture as *aeternum*, "everlasting," would only, given God's "mercy," be *diuturnum*, "long-lasting," after all.

Origen's ambitious synthesis of Platonizing Christianity won a

2. See Jerome's *Apologia contra Rufinum* 1.11 and 14. Compare also J. N. D. Kelly's *Jerome: His Life, Writings, and Controversies* (New York: Harper & Row, 1975), pp. 143, 250, and 252, on Jerome's translation of Origen's *Homilies on St. Luke's Gospel.* His rejection of Origen's adventurous theological speculations, Kelly admits, came only later.

3. More accurately, one might speak of one "period" in the multiple cycles of creation, fall, and return.

number of adherents, particularly in his native Alexandria and its environs. Among his followers were Didymus the Blind, Synesius of Cyrene, Nemesius of Emesa, Pierius of Alexandria, and, eventually Rufinus, longtime friend and colleague of Jerome's.[4]

It is not always easy, even possible, to know the ways in which the growing anti-Origenist mood of the East became known to Augustine, but two things are clear: first, that he remained long in ignorance of events occurring far from Thagaste and Hippo, and, second, that Jerome could have been a key informant on these events, but turned out to be far less informative than he could, perhaps should, have been.

Jerome's Stormy Silence

Jerome may have had his reasons for being less than forthcoming. His earlier reverence for Origen was blazoned on the pages of his *De viris illustribus*, where he referred to him as second only after the Apostles as teacher to the Church. His regard and affection for Didymus the Blind, propagator and then defender of Origen's doctrines, led him to refer repeatedly to that saintly man as "master," even after he had swung over to opposing Origen himself. And, much to his later embarrassment, his earlier commentaries on Scripture frequently cited Origen's views, including those on the origin of souls, without the faintest note of criticism.[5]

The anti-Origenist reaction, in its most dramatic form, may be dated from 393, two years before Augustine became bishop. Gregory of Nyssa had published his opposition to Origen's views, as had Peter of Alexandria and Methodius of Olympus; controversy had begun to simmer.[6] But in 393, at the urging of Epiphanius, who had drawn up a catalogue of Origen's "errors," Atarbius leads a raid on Jerome's peaceful monastery in Palestine: Jerome must join in condemning Origen. Jerome capitulates. Not so his longtime friend, Rufinus, in his neighboring monastery; in the face of a similar raid, he bars the door and remains incommunicado. Five years later, in 398, Jerome's opposition to the cyclic theory of the

4. See Johannes Quasten's *Patrologia*, 3 vols. (Westminster, Md.: Newman, 1960), III 89–99, 107, and 353, for further details.
5. For documentation and closer detail, see Kelly, *Jerome*, esp. pp. 54 (on the *De viris illustribus*), 125, 143, 150, and 178.
6. See Kelly, *Jerome*, pp. 197ff., and Quasten, *Patrologia*, II 115 and 129, III 289.

soul shows clearly in his *Commentary on Matthew*,[7] but Rufinus' old Origenist loyalties remain intact.

In that year, Rufinus is prevailed upon to issue a translation of Origen's *De principiis*; he has not, like Jerome, yielded to the bullying of the anti-Origenists. The once-famous friendship between Rufinus and Jerome is becoming seriously strained. But Rufinus strains it even further. He omits, in his "translation," a number of Origen's proposals which would offend contemporary orthodoxy; others he doctors, sometimes by astute paraphrase, sometimes by interpolating parts from others of Origen's writings. The result is an Origen in his Sunday best. To cap off his strategy, Rufinus writes a Preface cleverly calculated to associate his effort with Jerome's own name.[8]

Jerome, predictably, explodes. His *Letter 84*, an "open" letter to Rome and to the Romans, is a thorough repudiation of Rufinus' publication, and, typical of Jerome, reads in parts like a repudiation of Rufinus' person as well. He singles out for special attack the doctrine on the origin of souls, claiming (not entirely truthfully) that his commentaries on both Ecclesiastes and Ephesians show he had long since rejected it; he marvels that Rufinus has implicitly or explicitly rejected other features in Origen's teaching, but left this theory intact, as though it remained "matter still open for discussion" among the churches. And yet, despite Jerome's proclaimed opinion to the contrary, Rufinus' estimate of the matter appears to have been more in line with the facts of the time.[9]

In the following year, 399, an eastern synod at Nitria issues a round condemnation of Origen's questionable teachings. In 400, the new pope, Anastasius, is persuaded, by communications from the East, to convene a Roman synod to issue similar condemnations. He then writes to Simplician, at Milan, and other North Italian bishops to join Rome in their condemnation of "Origenism."[10]

In Hippo, however, Augustine's hands are full with the waxing Donatist controversy. In 394, he had written to Jerome,[11] in Beth-

7. See Kelly, *Jerome*, p. 223.
8. Ibid., pp. 230–31.
9. Ibid., pp. 238ff.
10. Ibid., pp. 203ff.
11. On the personal dynamics between Augustine and Jerome, which have their importance in interpreting the force of Augustine's contentions, see my "When Saintly Fathers Feuded: The Correspondence between Augustine and Jerome," *Thought*, 54 (1979), 344–64. But research toward this present study compelled some

lehem, raising a question about his interpretation of Paul's Letter to the Galatians. His partial familiarity with Jerome's works (and unfamiliarity with his leonine temper) shows in Augustine's unsolicited advice that Jerome suspend his translation of the Bible from the Hebrew, and instead furnish people like Augustine with translations of the Biblical commentaries of Greek Fathers, and particularly those of Origen, "whose name" Jerome seems "to have singular pleasure in sounding forth" in his writings.

That letter fails to reach its destination; yet it manages to turn up in Rome and elsewhere, revealing to the world that the brilliant young presbyter from Africa has made bold to differ with Jerome's interpretation of Galatians and to question the value of translating the Bible from Hebrew! Three years later, in 397, Jerome writes a brief and cordial note to Augustine, the tenor of which betrays that he had never received the letter of 394. So, in 397, the year in which he was setting to work on his *Confessions*, Augustine writes again (*Letter 40*). He repeats his objection to Jerome's exegesis of Galatians, expands upon it, and summons Jerome to recant! He presses his less than diplomatic recommendation that Jerome abandon his work of translating from the Hebrew, and proceeds to question Jerome on several other matters, all unwitting that a storm is brewing over in Bethlehem. A report of, then a copy of, the original *Letter 28* have finally reached Jerome; his prickly sensitivity about his competence and reputation sputters into flame, and there is no want of willing hands to fan the flame into a blaze. Wagging tongues interpret Augustine's act as a deliberately engineered attempt to shine at Jerome's expense, to show the world, so much of it eager to see it happen, that here at last is one both daring and brilliant enough to close the fearful old lion's jaws.

In 402, eight years after the original offending letter, Jerome emits a warning growl (*Letter 68*); even the now-famous bishop of Hippo had better think twice before baiting *him*. But a year or two later, the minatory growl has become a roar. More of the dossier of Augustine's letters, querying, suggesting, cajoling, objecting, arguing, is before his unbelieving eyes; the impertinence, ambition, and (most unforgivable, perhaps) shameful ignorance of his adver-

revisions to the views expressed both there, and (especially) in its more doctrinal companion-article, "Rejection." The numbering of Jerome's letters to Augustine is given according to the Augustine corpus of *Epp.*

sary are all laid bare. *Letter 72* is fired off in a towering, incoherent rage. A messenger arrives with the final pieces of evidence. Now Jerome shifts (*Letter 75*, written in 404) into the register of biting, clawing sarcasm; page upon page of argumentation, scalding refutation, sneering allusions to Augustine's relative youth, insult thinly veiled or not at all, are all overlaid with a majestic pose of superior learning. This, surely, will batter the enemy into whimpering submission.

Augustine's replies to this onslaught of furious irrationality (*Letters 73* and *82*, written in 404 and 405 respectively) show the measure of the man. Requests for pardon, occasional concessions, frank admissions of his ignorance, pleas for some re-entry of sweet reason into this tumbling fray—with all this he is ready and generous. And yet, let none of it be mistaken for weakness. There are important features of Christian truth at stake, and bullying tactics leave him unintimidated. Soberly, lucidly he exposes the contradictions in Jerome's irate demands, the unconvincingness of his arguments; strongly, he stands his ground.

It is comforting, it has its amusing side, that Jerome seems later to have come to Augustine's view of the central issue that divided them during this fierce exchange.[12] But for the understanding of his subsequent *Letter 166*, to Jerome, it is important to observe that Augustine approaches that discussion with a keen appreciation of the risks involved in disagreeing with Jerome, with a wary knowledge of how the old fighter must be handled.

Origen's Busy Ghost

But throughout this correspondence threads the magic name of— Origen. In 394 Augustine asks Jerome to set himself to translating the great Greek commentators on Scripture, and notably Origen, on whom he has lavished such signal praise.[13] Three years later (Augustine is by now at work on his *Confessions*) he inquires about the title of a work Jerome had written (and Augustine read) on various ecclesiastical writers; later, we are told, the book was in fact the *De viris illustribus*, in which the name of Origen glitters

12. See Hugh Pope, *St. Augustine of Hippo* (London: Sand, 1937), pp. 222–26, for suasive evidence of this change of mind (on whether St. Paul was "dissimulating" at the Council of Jerusalem).
13. *Ep 28* 2.

with a luster second only to that of the Apostles.[14] But the winds of Jerome's favor may have shifted slightly. He is right, Augustine allows, to warn us to take from Origen, "that remarkable man," what is true and to discard what is false. But what, specifically, he asks, did Origen *say* that was false and mischievous?[15] Clearly, he does not know, and seeks illumination from Jerome. A moment later we glimpse what may be a partial reason for his ignorance: Jerome must write another book on ecclesiastical writers, giving not only the names of heretics, but details on what their heresies are; a work like this is "most necessary" for those (and Augustine seems to class himself among them) without either the leisure (he is, by now, a very busy bishop) or the knowledge of the Greek language needed for reading and understanding so many things.[16]

It is five years later, 402. Augustine's *Confessions* have been written and published. So far as we know, he has never gleaned from Jerome the knowledge he desired on the dangers of Origen's teaching, particularly of his teaching on the "fall" of the soul. Only now does Jerome dispatch a partial copy of his *Apologia against Rufinus*.

That copy, we may safely infer, comprised only the first two books of his *Apologia*. For in *Letter 68* 3 Jerome clearly indicates that he had recently received a copy of Rufinus' own *Apologia*: he refers to him, sarcastically, as Calphurnius. To that work, he tells Augustine, he had already replied *breviter*, but only in part (*ex parte*). With *Letter 68*, he is sending along copies of that partial reply (*libelli ejus*), since he has learned that copies of Rufinus' own work have already reached Africa. He then promises to send along, at his earliest opportunity, a *latius opus*, a "more extensive work"— quite obviously, I submit, the eventual whole of his *Apologia*, comprising Books 1 through 3.

If this reconstruction of events is sound,[17] one could scarcely

14. *Epp 40* 2 and *72* 3.
15. Mlle La Bonnardière, in her article on "Jérome Informateur d'Augustin au sujet d'Origène," in REA, 20 (1974), 42–54, shows how unresponsive Jerome remained to these appeals for information.
16. *Ep 40* 9.
17. Mlle La Bonnardière, in "Jérome Informateur," 44n16, confidently affirms that Jerome is referring here to his *Apologia against Rufinus* (of which there can be little doubt), but that this already included the *third* book of the *Apologia*. The evidence for that second affirmation, however, is far less peremptory than Mlle La Bonnardière

expect Augustine to have gleaned much about Origen's position from Jerome's treatment of it in *Apologia* 2.8–10, except that Rufinus was being laid out as an ignorant fool. (The treatment in 3.28–29, by comparison, is somewhat more revealing; against Rufinus' more waffling typification of it, Jerome identifies Origen's view squarely as a "fall of the soul" theory.) He then answers Rufinus' objection—why would God create innocent souls to be born of adulterous unions?—with a reply with which Augustine later (in *Letter 166*, written in 415) indicates he is familiar. But this direct acquaintance with *Apologia* 3 is evidenced only at that much later date. In any event, the interpretation of Origen was the central issue dividing Jerome and Rufinus, and in 404, Augustine, significantly, admits that he has not yet taken the measure of Rufinus' side of the argument.[18] He must, he says, guess at the ferocity of his attack on Jerome from the obvious "restraint" of Jerome's reply!

The final mention of Origen occurs in connection with Jerome's defense of his reading of Galatians: he claims to have done little else than distill the opinions of the *majores* on this nettling issue.[19] The first of them, whether surprisingly or not, is Origen, who heads an impressive list of Greek Scriptural commentators.[20] Origen again

---

seems to imagine. For we know (see Kelly, *Jerome*, pp. 251–55) that Rufinus composed his *Apologia* against Jerome in Rome, during the year 401. A copy of that work reached Bethlehem only *after* Jerome had finished composing Books 1 and 2 of his *Apologia* replying to the tack he had indirectly learned Rufinus was taking. These first two books of Jerome's *Apologia* reached Rufinus in spring or early summer of 401, prompting Rufinus to send Jerome a copy of his own *Apologia*. *Ep 68* 3 seems clearly to mention Jerome's recent reception of Rufinus' work, Jerome's partial reply to it, and his promise to send the *latius opus*, i.e., the eventual whole of his *Apologia*.

Notice that Kelly, *Jerome*, p. 265nn25 and 27, argues circularly: in note 27 he opines that *Ep 68* 3 "seems" to refer to Jerome's "second Apology," i.e., Book 3, but in note 25 he has already reasoned that Jerome's letter must date from mid-402 since only by then had he finished that second *Apology*. Goldbacher, in CSEL 58, p. 21, dates *Ep 68* in similar dependence on the dating of the Jerome–Rufinus exchange, but otherwise agrees with the analysis I give above. Mlle La Bonnardière lists several other references (*Epp 73* 6, and *82* 1 and 23) to support her contention, but close examination of them will show they could refer to either Jerome's "first" or his "second" *Apology*; she is, though, on more solid ground in claiming that *Ep 166*, written in 415, shows that Augustine had, *by that time*, learned the content of Jerome's *Apologia* 3. But when and how that book reached Augustine remains cloudy; the evidence from *Ep 68*, however, clearly suggests he did *not* receive it along with that letter from Jerome.

18. *Ep 73* 6.
19. *Ep 75* (from 404).
20. Ibid. 4.

heads the list of commentators on the Psalms which he throws up against Augustine's "novel" *Enarrationes*.[21] Has Augustine read them? No, Augustine answers, none of them. But Jerome himself has impugned the authority of four of them; "as to Origen and Didymus, I read in some of your more recent works censure passed on their opinions, and that in no measured terms, or in regard to insignificant questions, though formerly you gave Origen marvelous praise."[22] The year is 405. In addition to part of his *Apologia* against Rufinus, what did these "recent works" of Jerome include? And how much did they illumine Augustine on the "fallen soul" theory? Subsequent events will show that on that crucial question Jerome managed to radiate more heat than light; Augustine, in any case, seems to have learned almost nothing from him.

Jerome's explosive reaction may be partially understood from the background of these years. He felt himself already a fiercely beleaguered man. Rufinus had replied, in 399, to the Roman synod's condemnation of Origen, with an *Apologia* written to Pope Anastasius; there, he repudiated a number of Origen's condemned teachings, but persisted in considering the question of the soul's origin a matter for debate among theologians. He then sets to work on his reply to Jerome's *Letter 84*, and by 401 is ready with his *Apologia* against Jerome. But before the work is published, informants have transmitted much of its tenor to Jerome, in Bethlehem. Without awaiting the published text itself, and working on the basis of these reports and of other relevant documents, Jerome reels off the first two books of his own *Apologia* against Rufinus.[23]

Neither *Apologia* makes for very edifying reading now, our taste for ecclesiastical billingsgate being much blander than that of earlier centuries. But certain aspects of both works vividly illustrate the way issues stood in the year 401.

For and Against Origen

In the course of summarizing Jerome's accusations, Rufinus quotes his characterization of Origen's claim that "souls have been made

21. Ibid. 20.
22. *Ep 82* 23.
23. See Kelly, *Jerome*, pp. 248ff.

before their bodies, and have been brought down from heaven and inserted into their bodies."[24] He defends himself for having written both preface to and translation of the *De principiis* the way he did, comparing his approach with Jerome's way of doing such things (1.10–21). And as for Jerome's proclaimed "rejection" of Origen's views, Rufinus quotes liberally from his commentary on Ephesians to show the contrary. Was Paul, for example, or Jeremiah, "predestined" from his mother's womb, without any previous merit on his part? Jerome cites this interpretation, Rufinus suggests, full knowing it would imply that God did not act justly, "which, of course, is contrary to the faith" (1.26). This explains why Jerome then proceeds to cite a contrary interpretation, attributing it to an "other" who is left anonymous. But that "other . . . tries to show that God is just," so that Jerome "evidently wishe[d] to exhibit [this second interpretation] as being what is everywhere held for Catholic and indubitable, to give a testimony by which he [Jerome] will, as he asserts, seek to show that God is just." That anonymous "other" is, of course, Origen, who, in Jerome's paraphrase of him, "seeks to vindicate the justice of God [and accordingly] argues that it is not according to His own pre-judgment and knowledge, but according to the merit of the elect that God's choice of men is determined."

Jerome is then quoted as paraphrasing Origen's claim that "before the creation of the visible world, of sky and earth and seas and all that they contain, there existed other invisible creatures, among which were also souls"; that these souls, for reasons known to God alone, were "cast down" into this "vale of tears, this place of our mournful pilgrimage" (1.26). Rufinus then combats Jerome's attempts to dissociate himself from this Origenist view: "those souls, *you* say, who in a former age had been inhabitants of heaven, now dwell here, on this earth, and that not without reference to certain acts which they had committed while they lived there" (1.27); no argumentative twists and turns can deflect that indictment of Jerome. This same (obviously laudable) concern for God's just ways of dealing with souls according to their merits had persuaded Jerome to reproduce the Origenists' argument that "it would be

---

24. *Apologia in Hieronymum* 1.10. Subsequent references to this work will appear in parentheses in the text.

impossible . . . to explain" the various inequities of the human condition, among them

> the fact that some are born poor and barbarous, in slavery and weakness, while others are born as Roman citizens, wealthy and free and strong of health; that some are born in a low, some in a high, station; that they are born in different countries, different regions of the world.

Such inequities, the argument runs, cannot be understood unless

> there are some antecedent causes for which each individual has its lot assigned according to its merits. . . . [T]he difference of conditions under which men are born would impugn the justice of God unless they were the results of the soul's previous deserts.

And now Rufinus continues from Jerome's own text, applying the same reasoning to a particular Scriptural instance:

> God could not have loved Jacob before he came forth from the womb, and hated Esau before he had done anything worthy of hatred, unless there were some antecedent causes which would, if we knew them, prove that God is just [1.28].

The Pivotal Text: Romans 9:11

Rufinus goes on to associate Jerome with Origen's related view of the body as "chain" and "prison" of the soul (1.40–41), then regales his readers with Jerome's many past expressions of enthusiastic admiration for Origen (2.13–20).

But that mention of Jacob and Esau merits close attention. For Paul, in his Epistle to the Romans, 9:11–13, brings up this precise example to illustrate his teaching on election and predestination. Rebecca, he notes, was told by God that "the elder" of her unborn twins "would serve the younger"; Esau would serve Jacob. Now, this was told her before the twins were even born, "and before either had done good or evil," in order to "stress that God's choice is free, since it depends on the One who calls, not on human merit." And yet, in the very next verse, Paul asks: "Does it follow that God is unjust?" and answers his own question, "Of course not."

One can understand the quandary of those early commentators. Stress the freedom of election without any regard for previous merits, and it makes God appear to act arbitrarily, even unjustly; but vindicate His justice, and what becomes of this free, unmerited election? Crudely put: Origen's interpretation tends to "vindicate God's justice" by pointing back to merits or demerits gained in a previous existence, a "pre-human" existence before strictly "human merit" could come into question.

Reread in the light of this "either/or," Augustine's own *De libero arbitrio*, and quite especially its third book, seem clearly more sensitive to defending God's justice than to defending the freedom of election. But, *securius loquebatur*, the question was not so sharpened for him as an awareness of this exegetical controversy might have made it. More aware of the dangers emanating from the Manichaean objections, he may have sailed a bit too close to the opposing danger: that of reducing God's freedom in electing whom He will. Augustine's awareness of that danger will grow with time; it would be fascinating to know whether Rufinus' *Apologia* ever reached him to illuminate him on it. But Rufinus' work suggests the terms in which the controversy was cast, not only for himself and Jerome, but for the broader world of theological discussion.

When Augustine is finally apprised of those terms, he will make that text from Romans 9:11–13 the very crux of the discussion; and the question as he frames it then will be: How to defend God's freedom of election, and still not impugn His justice? Pelagius and his colleague Caelestius will prod him into putting the issue that way; they will make him see how the question of the soul's origin intersects with such questions as election, grace, and Original Sin.

Jerome on the Origin of Souls

Jerome's reply, his *Apologia* against Rufinus, is in three books. But the first two of them were written before Rufinus' work had reached him; the third (which may *later* reach Augustine) was added sometime after, on the basis of his reading Rufinus' own *Apologia*. Our chief point of interest in these first two books is Jerome's remarks on the origin of souls. He has read Rufinus' *Apologia* to Pope Anastasius, and found him saying that:

> I have read a great many writers on this question, and I find that they express diverse opinions. Some of those whom I have read hold that the soul is infused together with the material body

through the channel of the human seed; and of this they give such proofs as they can. I think this was the opinion of Tertullian or Lactantius among the Latins, perhaps also of a few others.

Others assert that God is making new souls every day, and infusing them into the bodies which have been framed in the womb; while still others believe that the souls were all made long ago, when God made all things out of nothing, and that all He does now is to plant out each soul in its body as it seems good to Him. This is the opinion of Origen and of some others of the Greeks.

As to his own opinion on the matter, Rufinus proclaims that "up to the present moment I am unable to hold any of them as certain or absolute"; he "remains in ignorance on the subject" except for the Church's article of faith that God is Creator of souls as well as bodies.[25]

Jerome's mockery of this profession of "ignorance" is nothing less than cruel, but something less than honest. He is correct in questioning whether Lactantius sided with Tertullian;[26] Lactantius seems to have advocated the creationist, not the traducianist, opinion. But he accuses Rufinus of refusing to condemn the traducianist opinion purely in order to avoid the duty of condemning Origen's opinion as well. Jerome's distaste for traducianism, and clear preference for creationism, are evident. But then he expostulates:

> The Lord says in the Gospel: "Father, I have revealed Your name to men." Did He Who revealed the Father keep silence on the origin of souls? And are you[, Rufinus,] astonished if your brethren are scandalized when you swear that you know nothing of a thing which the churches of Christ profess to know?

Jerome's most recent biographer can do no better than quote Henry Fremantle's mildly devastating comment on this rhetorical flight: " 'perusal of [Jerome's] subsequent correspondence with Augustine shows that he was in the same perplexity as Rufinus, but less ingenuous in confessing it.' "[27] To claim, as Jerome claims here, that the "churches" had a clear and certain teaching on the origin of human souls, and that this doctrine was none other than

25. Compare Rufinus' *Apologia ad Anastasium* 6 and Jerome's *Apologia contra Rufinum* 2.8.
26. *Apologia contra Rufinum* 2.10, 3.28.
27. See Kelly, *Jerome*, p. 252n54.

Jerome's opinion of the moment, creationism, is not only the "bluster" Kelly rightly calls it; it is little short of plain dishonesty. The question of the soul's origin remained, at this moment in history, far more "open" than that—as open, in fact, as Rufinus held it to be.

But later, in one of those mood swings so typical of him, Jerome will insinuate that the question was even more open than Rufinus' estimate of the possibilities would have it be. Compare Rufinus' three with the four possibilities Augustine deals with in the *De libero arbitrio*. Both creationism and traducianism eschew the theory of the soul's pre-existence; but of the two versions Augustine presents as involving the pre-existence of the soul, Rufinus seems to have considered only one; or, perhaps more exactly, he seems to have telescoped these two distinct alternatives into one formulation—that "souls were all made long ago, when God made all things out of nothing, and that all He does now is to plant out each soul in its body as it seems good to Him." Souls then exist prior to their entrance into bodies. But despite the mention of Origen's name, Rufinus makes no reference to the feature of Origen's theory which held that souls in this pre-existent state sinned, so that God "plants" each into an embodied existence perfectly proportioned to the gravity of its sin in that pre-embodied existence. Rufinus' formulation only too closely resembles the other alternative: that the soul pre-existed, but was simply "sent" by God into this or that body. That "sending" would, on the face of it at least, require no appeal to any previous "sin" to account for God's sending the soul into a body; nor would it, ostensibly, invoke the gravity or lightness of some such sin to explain the higher or lower condition in which the soul, once embodied, finds itself.

Rufinus' vagueness here may have been a calculated one, but Jerome will not let it pass without remark. For he agrees with Augustine in seeing the pre-existent possibility as branching out into two alternative theories: either the soul "fell," or it was divinely "sent," into the world of bodies. So, on receipt of Rufinus' *Apologia*, Jerome sets to work on a further reply: the third book of his *Apologia against Rufinus*.[28]

28. We may infer (see note 17, above) either that Jerome eventually sent a copy of this third book to Augustine, or that the latter was able at some time before 415 to get his hands on a copy.

Taking up the question of the soul's origin, Jerome twits Rufinus at length on his pious profession of ignorance on the matter. One need not claim to be privy to all the secrets of nature before professing knowledge about this one vital question. "The church's doctrine," Jerome implies again, "is that God forms souls every day, and sends them into the bodies of those who are born";[29] but this opinion Rufinus presumably thinks is held only by "us simple and foolish men, who do not see that, if our opinion is true, God is thereby shown to be unjust" (3.30). He will doubtless reply with all Origen's further objections about the justice of granting souls to those born of adultery or incest, or with his own "mysterious question": "Why do infants die?" Rufinus had once addressed this very question to Didymus the Blind, who replied to it in perfectly Origenist fashion: those who die in infancy could not have sinned very gravely in their pre-embodied existence, so that "it was enough punishment for them just to have touched their bodily prisons" (3.28). Clearly, then, Jerome is interpreting Rufinus' vague account of the "pre-existence" possibility in Origenist terms; and the question of God's "justice" is at the heart of the matter.

But, he now asks Rufinus, "outside of these three opinions, tell me whether any truth can be found so that all three may be false? . . . If there is some other possibility, why do you confine the liberty of discussion to such a closely drawn line?" (3.30). Perhaps Rufinus' profession of ignorance is only a mask, donned in order to avoid condemning Origen's opinion "that our souls existed before our bodies and committed some sin, because of which they have been tied to these gross bodies."

Or could Rufinus possibly be entertaining another version of the pre-existence theory: namely, that between their creation and their divine implantation in bodies, souls may be thought to have "slept like dormice in a state of torpor and slumber"? Such a slumbrous condition would obviously exempt the soul from the possibility of sinning. Did Jerome think this theory up on his own, or were there actual historical proponents of it? Our historical information grows cloudy at this point, but it would seem that Jerome himself thinks of some such "torpor" as part and parcel of the hy-

29. *Apologia contra Rufinum* 3.28. Further references to this work will be given in the text.

pothesis that souls, all created in the beginning, are successively "sent" by God into bodies, without any pre-incarnate sin on their part.

AUGUSTINE LEFT IN THE DARK

This stormy controversy, then, may explain some of the passion, not to say paranoia, Jerome unleashes upon Augustine in his letters of 402 and 404. Had there not been a series of other disagreements dividing them personally, Jerome might have conveyed more useful knowledge to Hippo on the issues dividing the larger Christian community. How much Augustine could hope to glean from the portion of Jerome's *Apologia* he was sent is difficult to guess; even the later treatment of the origin of souls (3.28–31) shows Jerome more willing to mock and taunt than to air the issues in a truly enlightening way. Augustine's only references to this work show him far more impressed, perhaps even thoroughly distracted, by the rivers of personal venom he finds running through Jerome's reply; and he is left to guess at the ferocity of Rufinus' antecedent provocation. He dwells with sadness on the disintegration of this once-famous friendship between Rufinus and Jerome, and all the more movingly, perhaps, in that he fears a similar fate may overtake his relationship with Jerome.

But still, in the year 404, he makes no allusion to the issue of the soul's origin.[30] *Letter 82*, written the following year, betrays that Augustine has taken note of Jerome's more recent critical attitude toward Origen, but no specifics of doctrine are brought into focus. Augustine is too preoccupied with saving his threatened relationship with Jerome to enter into that kind of discussion. Five years pass, with no evidence of any further correspondence between the two men. In 410, in *Letter 123*, Jerome breaks the silence with a brief, but apparently cordial, greeting; still, no matters of substance are discussed. Not until some years later, when Count Marcellinus writes to Jerome inquiring about the origin of human souls, does

30. This curious obloquy on Augustine's part may lie behind Mlle La Bonnardière's carefully phrased observation ("Jérome Informateur," 45) that, while Jerome's *Apologia* 3.28–31 did contain some information on this subject, it is only in 415, when Augustine writes his *Ep 166* to Jerome, that we can be confident that he had, "by that time," closely *attended* to that information.

Jerome reply in such a way as to bring Augustine into the discussion—an Augustine who, events will show, is far less convinced of Jerome's infallibility than the latter might have wished. But that is another chapter in our story; we must get to it in its place.

The battle royal waged by Jerome and Rufinus makes it clear that by the year 393 the text from Romans 9:11 had become crucial to the debate over God's freedom in "election." But that debate had also spilled over into a question on the origin of souls. For, the inference went, if neither Esau nor Jacob had done either "good or evil" before they were "born," the Origenist proposal that our souls pre-existed our birth in this bodily world, and sinned in that pre-existence, was peremptorily excluded.

But that is the conclusion of an inference: the text bears primarily on the question of election, only inferentially on the question of the soul's origin. It was possible to draw the obvious conclusions about God's freedom of election, and still not take the inferential step concerning the origin of the soul.

Defending God's "Justice"

This, in fact, seems to have been the story of Augustine's earlier dealings with this text. In his *Expositiones* on "certain propositions from the Letter to the Romans," written while he was still a presbyter, sometime around 394, Augustine is brought in the course of his work to confront this text. If there were any doubt about his sensitivity, at this stage of his career, to the issue of God's justice in the process of election, his interpretation in this work removes it.

Election,[31] he argues, is not exercised among perfect "equals"; there must be some ground in the individuals elected which justifies God's election of them and not of others. Can this ground be the good "works" (*opera*) of those elected? No, says Augustine. This is what Paul clearly excludes in his reference to Esau and Jacob, and, indeed, throughout the Letter to the Romans. Is God's election, then, entirely arbitrary—which is to say, no genuine "election"

31. *ExpRom* 60–61. This emphasis is even stronger in the (earlier?) *De Div QQ 83*, q. 68.4–5. But there is no mention of Rom. 9:11.

at all? No, argues Augustine. God "foresees" which of us will "believe" and on the ground of this future *belief* elects and saves us. The supposition is that belief is not a human "work" in the meaning of that term which Paul's epistle would exclude as the basis for God's election of one person rather than another. An awkward supposition, at best, and one which Augustine soon abandons; but it, and his appeal to God's foreknowledge, show to what lengths he was willing to go in order to make the "justice" of God's election at least moderately understandable to his readers—and, perhaps, to his persistent Manichaean objectors.

It is significant for the interpretation of that work that these *Expositiones* were written just around the time when Augustine was busy with the third book of the *De libero arbitrio*; there, too, his primary concern is to defend the "justice" of God.

To Simplician: God's "Freedom" in Election

By the time he writes his answers *To Simplician*, in 396, the winds have shifted. His old counselor, soon to become bishop of Milan, faces him squarely with the issue embodied in Romans 9:11. Augustine tells us elsewhere[32] that in the face of that challenge he struggled to uphold the human being's power to will and, by freely willing, to merit salvation, but "God's grace won out" in spite of all. Even faith, he sees, is a "work" in the sense Paul excludes as preceding God's gracious election; the appeal to God's foreknowledge is a tactic which the unmerited graciousness of grace will no longer permit him to entertain. God elects us, he now proclaims, with no consideration whatever of any merits of ours, whether past or foreseen as future. What kind of "justice," then, is this? The inscrutable justice proper to God's dealings with human creatures, Augustine replies, a justice beyond both our understanding and our right of complaint.[33]

There are, Augustine admits, a series of texts that would seem to raise objection to this radical position on the mystery. One by one he deals with them, and removes their sting. In the course of doing so, he reveals his persisting conviction that concupiscence—

32. *Retr* 2.1.1.
33. *Simp* 2.2–16. Further paragraph references to this work are given in parentheses in the text.

compare the "ignorance and difficulty" of the *De libero arbitrio*—
is the "penal" result of our having sinned (20); lays the ground-
work for his later explanation of the working of grace, by arguing
that progress toward salvation must imply God's graciously granting us a "delight" in the "good" we are meant to pursue (21); and
alludes to the appeal which Origen, and others after him, had
made to the various talents with which we are equipped in starting
life.[34] They cannot, he pronounces firmly, be thought to serve as
grounds for God's electing this one rather than another (22).

No Light on the Soul

God's election, then, is perfectly free and, yet, not demonstrably
unjust. This is the point to which Simplician's questioning had
directed Augustine's attention, and to this single point he sticks.
Despite the closeness of the two questions, he never makes reference
to that of the soul's origin; nor does he draw any conclusions with
respect to it.

That same single-minded attention prevails in the year 411/412,
when he was preaching his *Enarratio* on Psalm 134. Romans 9:11,
he proclaims, shows us that Jacob was "elected" in the purest sense
of that term; God does not base that election on any merits whatsoever.[35] No occasion arises to treat of the soul's origin, and no allusion is made to that question. The Pelagian controversy is already
beginning to occupy Augustine's attention; as time goes on, the
issues of that controversy will compel him to make the connection
between freedom of election and the origin of the human soul. That
connection once established, it will appear so obvious that one may
wonder why Augustine did not make it earlier. But progress in sys-

---

34. Augustine here interprets Origen as having made double employment of the
"fallen soul" theory: not only would it explain the conditions into which each of us
is born *retrospectively*, as proportioned to the seriousness of our sin in pre-existence,
but it would also explain *prospectively* our future eligibility for God's (all-just)
election of us. This may be a hint that Augustine sees these two questions as distinct,
even separable, so that, in his later thinking, "fall" theory may still legitimately be
invoked for the retrospective explanation of our (universally) "miserable" condition,
even after it has been rightly discarded as a prospective explanation of our (individual)
election from out of that sinful misery. However the case may stand for Augustine's
thinking, the logical separability of the two questions may be important for an
understanding of how he could have remained sympathetic to "fall" theory despite
his progress on the election question.

35. *En 134* 5.

tematic thought is always an uneven thing, and gaps often occur where we would least expect them to do so. Enough, perhaps, that Augustine has digested this major revolution in his thinking, that God's election was, despite all his concern for divine justice, radically free from all considerations of previous merit on the human being's part.

This much, accordingly, is clear: until the year 411/412, and even amid the first volleys of the Pelagian onslaught, there is no evidence whatever that Augustine has seen how Romans 9:11 bears upon the question of the soul's origin and, specifically, excludes the hypothesis of a "fall" accounted for by some pre-incarnate sin. No evidence whatever, a purely negative conclusion. We are about to deal with evidence that argues more positively than that. The Pelagians will very shortly face Augustine directly with the issue of the soul's origin; his uncertain reaction, when this occurs, is simply unintelligible if one suppose that the bearing of Romans 9:11 on that question was already clear in his own mind.

PROGRESS ON THE *De Trinitate*:
Letter 120, TO CONSENTIUS

Meanwhile, Augustine has been working on the *De Trinitate*. He began that work, as we saw, not in the year 399, as Hendrikx supposed, but in 404. We have also seen that the theory of man he proposes in that work, and quite particularly his views on the origin of the human soul, create something of a puzzle. Resolving that puzzle requires that one pay close attention to any hints he may drop concerning the problems he encountered in the process of writing the *De Trinitate*.

The first clear reference we have to the *De Trinitate* occurs in *Letter 120*, to Consentius.[36] Hendrikx dates this letter as of 410, in substantial agreement with the Maurists who propose the year 411. Goldbacher makes the observation that there is nothing in the letter itself to confirm that date, except the way Augustine speaks of the *De Trinitate*; it is not yet, it appears, in its finished state.[37] But the

36. Gustave Bardy, in BA 12, p. 579, wrongly describes this letter as written to Evodius.

37. See Goldbacher's remarks in CSEL 58, p. 35; notice that he assumes *Trin* was finished by 416, and hence dates *Ep 174* to Aurelius in that year (p. 45). But if, as more recent research suggests, *Trin* was completed much later (in 421, for example),

Maurist date, as Hendrikx has noticed, has more solidity than that, for Consentius' *Letter 119*, to Augustine, speaks of the latter's having left Hippo for reasons of health, a fact mentioned in *Letters 121–124* as well. That rest cure can reliably be dated as having occurred shortly after Augustine's illness in 410.[38]

Consentius' letter to Augustine shows he is asking for advice as to how we can come to some knowledge of the Trinity from created realities. He writes of having published some blunders on the more general subject of our knowledge of God from our knowledge of creatures; his thinking about God, he has come to see, was insufficiently purified of corporeal imagery. He appears even to have succumbed to a seizure of discouragement; he candidly avows his temptation to give up all such attempts to seek an "understanding" of the faith, and to settle back into a position that later theologians would characterize as fideist.

The temptation may have been a momentary one, for he is, after all, writing in the hope that Augustine may succeed in illumining the "eyes of [his] heart." But even now strong traces of corporeal imagery remain in Consentius' thinking about God, and particularly about God's omnipresence; that style of thinking also affects his conceptions about God as Trinity. He seems conscious of this himself, for he reminds Augustine of his own warnings that "God must not be thought of in the terms appropriate to a material body," goes on to admit that he can "scarcely grasp the fine point of [Augustine's] argument," and details the reasons for his continuing difficulty.[39] Can Augustine give him help on this matter?

It is revelatory of Augustine's mind-set at this epoch that, before entering into the substance of Consentius' difficulties, he moves decisively and at considerable length to combat his fideist temptation. *Intellectum valde ama.* That celebrated phrase occurs at the height of an impassioned defense of the legitimacy of pursuing an "understanding" of the faith, an understanding which Augustine

---

then *Ep 174* needs re-dating as well. We shall see further on that factors like these introduce nettling confusions into the way various scholars employ Goldbacher's datings as premisses for their own inferences.

38. See van der Meer, *Bishop*, pp. 235–37 and relevant notes.

39. "Justice," Consentius admits, cannot be conceived of in corporeal terms. But, he objects, justice does not seem to be self-subsistent, as God must be. Therein lies his difficulty in following Augustine's argumentation proving God's incorporeality. This could well provide a clue to which of Augustine's works Consentius was familiar with.

still conceives of as an intermediate stage toward the fullness of direct "vision."[40] Only then does Augustine finally address himself to the central issue.

Or perhaps one should speak of several issues; for there is, first of all, the more general question of how we can come to some knowledge of God from created realities, and then the question of how we may come to some such knowledge of God as Trinity. Augustine reminds Consentius that he has already written a great deal (*multa*) on this first, more general question, and urges him to read, or reread, those works of his. This, I suggest, is the most natural way of understanding his injunctions in paragraph 13 of this letter:

> [I]nterim volo ut legas ea quae ad istam quaestionem pertinentia jam multa conscripsimus; illa etiam quae in manibus habemus, et propter magnitudinem tam difficilis quaestionis, nondum possumus explicare.

> Meanwhile, I would have you read the many writings we have written together pertaining to that question; and those [other] writings also, which we have to hand, and cannot as yet disentangle, on account of the greatness of so difficult a question.

Now, Hendrikx would have us take the vague phrase *ea quae . . . jam multa conscripsimus* as pertaining precisely to the question of God as Trinity, and argues that it must refer to the portion of the *De Trinitate* which Augustine has already completed. The *illa etiam quae in manibus habemus* would then refer, he goes on to argue, to the remainder of the work which Augustine must have had completed in rough copy. All of this would fit very nicely with his curious conviction that the entirety of the *De Trinitate* was written in a single burst of activity, though in rough form, by the year 405.[41] But his argument rests on the acceptance of two dates which later scholarship has shown to be incorrect. We can now be confident that Augustine began work on the *De Trinitate* in 404, not 399, and that he completed the work, not in 419, but sometime after the year 420.[42]

40. *Ep 120* 2–5.
41. BA 15, pp. 563–64. If Augustine had begun writing the *De Trinitate* as early as 399, as Hendrikx supposed, this would be a thinkable possibility.
42. See Introduction, note 18, above.

To what works, then, does the term *multa* refer? The most natural interpretation, and the one that is strongly suggested by the text of *Letters 119* and *120*, would take this phrase as including any number of Augustine's earlier works. In the opening paragraph of his reply to Consentius, he expresses the wish to have him near while he examines *quaedam nostra opuscula,* "certain of our little works," especially since Consentius has been laboring through copies that he has found manifestly deficient. That term *opuscula* would fit the early works very well; and the *ista quaestio* referred to would then refer to the more general question, so often the theme of those early works, of attaining some knowledge of God by transcending all corporeal imagery. Is this interpretation strengthened by that curious verb-form *conscripsimus,* "which *we* have written *together*"? Does it refer to the fact that these *opuscula* were regularly cast in dialogue form? It would be risky to attach too much weight to that frail indication, but it is suggestive.

In any event, his interpretation of *Letter 120* shows Hendrikx once again allowing the lure of his synthesis to bring him running well ahead of the textual evidence. But there is another point where this same letter raises a small question to that synthesis. For alongside the general question of our spiritual knowledge of God and, be it noted, of God as "omnipresent," Augustine speaks of the more precise question of knowing God as Trinity. Neither effort at knowledge may base itself on what we know of corporeal realities; but can we hope, Augustine asks, to rise from what we know of the human *soul* to some understanding of the Trinitarian Godhead? This is the precise project on which Augustine is now embarked, and he admits to finding it fraught with peculiar difficulties; it is a "great" and "difficult question" which he does not yet find himself able to disentangle (*explicare*).

But far be it from him to surrender to the fideist temptation so attractive to Consentius. For Paul's words in Romans 1:20 assure him that such a quest is not beyond the reach of our understanding (*non . . . a nostro intellectu omnino abhorrere*). It is not, accordingly, entirely absurd, perhaps (*non erit fortassis absurdum*), to hope that we may glean some understanding of the Trinity from created realities. But the created reality from which that understanding must start is, Augustine specifies, that "rational and intellectual soul." For this is precisely what was "made in the image" of the Trinity. Indeed, Augustine is even more specific than that: he is determined to focus on the principal feature of that rational soul (*quod habet praecipuum*), the "mind and intelligence itself."[43]

Augustine's exalted view of the human understanding, along with his hopes for gaining an understanding of the faith, even an understanding of the Trinitarian mystery itself, remain remarkably sanguine. And yet, he must express them as hopes, for the move of the mind he is striving to make, from the human intelligence to the Trinitarian Godhead, has disclosed itself to him as beset with difficulties he may not have anticipated earlier. He has no hesitation in recommending his earlier works to Consentius, but there it was question of rising from creatures to God as Creator, and of purifying thought of bodily imagery in the process. But on the issue that now engages his attention, his *nondum possumus explicare* is blunt and unvarnished. He is, for the moment, stumped.

The issue that has stumped him, however, is not the explanation of the Divine Persons in terms of relation theory—as an older view of the *De Trinitate*'s composition would have us believe. That explanation takes up Books 5 to 7 of the completed work. The question Augustine explicitly mentions as so "great" and "difficult" is the one he treats of in Books 8 to 14: the ascent from the soul as intellectual to the Trinity in whose "image" it has been created.

This same difficulty, or nest of difficulties, will haunt Augustine for some years to come. For the evidence strongly suggests that his long delays in completing his *De Trinitate* stemmed from the same root difficulty to which he points in his letter to Consentius. He will be brought even more sharply than now to the piercing recognition that the soul itself is more mysterious than he had once thought. That mystery enwraps its marvelous powers, surely, as well as its mode of union with the body; but both those questions, he will come to realize, plunge roots into another locus of mystery: the mystery of the human soul's origin. And that question, Pelagius will challenge him to see, is not only fraught with difficulties, but bristling with dangers as well. Augustine's loyal efforts to resolve those difficulties while at the same time side-stepping those dangers

43. *Ep 120* 12.

will even call into question the sturdy reliance on the powers of human understanding to which he bravely summons Consentius in the year 410 or 411.

ENTER FLAVIUS MARCELLINUS

At this juncture, a remarkable man appears on the North African scene: Count Flavius Marcellinus. Augustine's correspondence with him stretches over no more than two years, and yet comprises no fewer than seven letters still extant, several of Marcellinus' letters to Augustine having been lost to us.[44]

Marcellinus was sent to Carthage in 411, to assume duties as Imperial Commissioner for Africa. He was a man of extraordinary qualities; it would be a serious blunder to consider him just another political figure. He was, in Peter Brown's phrase, typical of a "new generation of Catholic politicians";[45] religion, for him, was the very soul of his political activity. In his Roman days, he may well have frequented those circles of Catholic intellectuals in which such notables as Jerome and Rufinus could also be found.[46] No sooner is he in Africa than his serious theological interests declare themselves in, among other ways, this spate of letters with the bishop of Hippo. Zealous and informed, he will follow developments in Carthage, relating not only to the Donatists, but to the pagan charges against Christianity on the occasion of the fall of Rome, and to the early stages of the Pelagian controversy as well. He often apprises Augustine of Carthaginian developments, and elicits his views on them. As time goes on, the two become linked both by cordial friendship and by mutual admiration, and Marcellinus does not hesitate to take advantage of that friendship by playing the insistent gadfly to the bishop, prodding him, as often as not, into theological activity he might not otherwise have taken. Augustine will repay his zeal by dedicating to him the first two books of the *De civitate Dei*, as well as the *De peccatorum meritis et remissione* and the *De spiritu et littera*.

44. Madeleine Moreau brings out (though a trifle inflatedly) the importance of this exchange of letters with Marcellinus, in "Le Dossier Marcellinus," RA, 9 (1973), 1–181.

45. *Augustine of Hippo* (Berkeley: University of California Press, 1967), p. 292.

46. See Louis Duchesne, *Early History of the Christian Church* III, trans. Claude Jenkins (New York: Longmans Green, 1924), pp. 131, 146.

VOLUSIAN'S QUESTION ON THE INCARNATION

Augustine's first two letters to Marcellinus are of an official nature.[47] But Marcellinus is soon asking Augustine to compose a long letter to his pagan friend Volusian, explaining points of Catholic doctrine. The ensuing correspondence[48] he follows with active interest, circulates the bishop's writings in coteries of Carthaginian intellectuals, both pagan and Christian, and does all of this in addition to his official duties, central among them the task of reconciling Catholics and Donatists.

Marcellinus' friend Volusian, then, has questions. He writes Augustine listing a number of them. One of them engages Augustine's particular attention: it focuses on how the Divine Son of God could be enclosed in an infant body, that body itself enclosed in Mary's womb.[49] Augustine moves against this question in familiar fashion.[50] The objection, if objection it is, "belongs to men who are not able to imagine any substance except what is corporeal" and, hence, incapable of "being wholly everywhere." The old lessons on how to understand omnipresence, learned so well from Plotinus' masterful treatise on the topic,[51] are adduced, one by one, and applied both to God's presence to the world and to the soul's presence to the body.[52] An *exercitatio animi*, very like the one in *De libero arbitrio* 2, is brought forward to help sharpen Volusian's mental vision.[53] Finally, Augustine is ready to make the application

47. *Epp 128* and *129*.
48. *Epp 132, 135, 136, 138,* and *139* all have to do with this pious conspiracy; Augustine is justified in commenting on Marcellinus' apostolic zeal in this and other connections.
49. *Ep 135* 2.
50. *Ep 137* 4–8.
51. *Ennead* 6.4–5. For the importance of this treatise to Augustine's thinking from 386 up to and including his *Conf*, see *Early Theory*, pp. 36–64. But the omnipresence insight maintains its importance throughout his life; see, for example, in addition to *Ep 137*, to Volusian, *Epp 140* 7, *147, 148, 162* 8–9, *187* passim, but esp. 10–11, 12–14, 16–19. In Augustine's thought, the spirituality of the soul is regularly linked with its capacity to transcend "carnal" and bodily modes of thought in coming to know God as integrally omnipresent.
52. That parallel relationship, of the "divine" to lower realities, and of soul to body, is solidly Plotinian. Compare *Enneads* 6.4–5, passim, and 4.2; see *Early Theory*, pp. 36–38, on the kinship between these two treatises.
53. The set of analogies between the argumentation of this letter and *Lib* 2 would be worth exploring. Note that *Lib* 2 provides the most telling evidence for the influence of *Ennead* 6.4–5 on Augustine's early thinking, as Olivier DuRoy confirms in *Trinité*, p. 252. But DuRoy's loyalty to the method of "verbal identities" prevents

to the Divine Word's relationship with His human body, one
which makes the Omnipresent no less Omnipresent after than
before His Incarnation.[54]

A Link to the Soul–Body Problem

But how, Volusian may object, can God be "joined to man as to
become the single person of Christ"? As though the difficulty of
conceiving that union were all so unique, Augustine retorts, and
proceeds to disarm his objector by citing the everyday mystery of
"how the soul is joined to the body so as to form the single person
of a man." If Volusian is ready to accept this everyday mystery without being able fully to understand it, he should a fortiori be willing
to accept the union of Incarnation in Christ; for the "mingling
[mixtura] of two incorporeal things"—God and human soul—baffles
the mind somewhat less than the mingling of incorporeal soul with
corporeal body.[55] And Augustine rounds out his meditation on the
Word Incarnate by running through that familiar litany of paradoxical predicates drawn from his personal vocabulary of omnipresence: "present and hidden, nowhere confined, nowhere divided,
nowhere extended, but, without corporeal mass, everywhere totally
present."[56]

   This letter has been invoked as a texte de base[57] to argue that
Augustine's view of "the problem of the soul" derives from a stream
of fourth-century thought which, among other things, took this
question of the "mingling" of soul and body as a central concern.
And likely it is that Augustine here shows contacts with that problematic and with some of its representatives.[58] But instead of a

---

his detecting the same Plotinian "patterns" already at work in Augustine's Cassiciacum writings. For a discussion of this methodological difference between us, see
my notes 36–38 and 88, 89, in Platonism.
   54. Ep 137 8; compare 12, also.
   55. Ibid. 9–11.
   56. Ibid. 12 (praesens et latens, nusquam conclusa, nusquam discissa, nusquam
tumida, sed sine mole ubique tota . . .).
   57. By Ernest L. Fortin, A.A., Christianisme et culture philosophique au cinquième
siècle: La quérelle de l'âme humaine en Occident (Paris: Etudes Augustiniennes,
1959), p. 113.
   58. See Fortin's evidence for this, ibid., pp. 114–15. Compare in the same sense
Jean Pépin, Ex Platonicorum persona: Etudes sur les lectures philosophiques de saint

texte de base, the letter to Volusian is a relatively exceptional text, even a *texte minoritaire*; it shows Augustine making a foray onto terrain which is, if anything, almost alien territory for him.[59] He has been drawn into this discussion, moreover, not through any direct interest in the "mingling" question for itself, but precisely in order to fend off an objection on the Incarnation. Finally, far more striking than his speculations on this "mingling" of soul and body, are his repeated applications of the omnipresence relation he learned, and never forgot, from Plotinus.[60] Again, I suggest, it is less accurate to claim that the "hypostatic" relation of soul to body is modeled on the hypostatic relation of Word and humanity than to claim that both those relations are modeled on the omnipresential relation of the "higher" spiritual world—Soul, Noûs, and perhaps even One—to the "lower" world of spatially extended bodies.[61]

This was the relationship of soul to body on which Augustine settled in his earliest works, notably in the *De quantitate animae* and in the second book of the *De libero arbitrio*.[62] Once satisfied with this solution of the matter, Augustine no longer views this as "the problem" of the soul. Far from it. *The* problem, for him, from *De libero arbitrio* 3 until now, and from this point onward with increasing urgency, turns on the "origin" of the soul. And the question of the soul's "origin," for him, boils down to discovering how the soul ever became embodied in the first place.

Augustin (Amsterdam: Hakkert, 1977), pp. 211–67. Both authors find that Augustine's conclusion on this "mixture" issue stems from Porphyry; neither of them even seriously considers whether that conclusion, if indeed it be Porphyrian, has not been "reset" (as Augustine so regularly does) into a frame (in this case omnipresential) which makes the total resultant at least as "Plotinian" as Porphyrian. Given the frequent close kinship between these two thinkers, it is dangerous to regard their influence as mutually exclusive one of the other.

59. Although, as Pépin, *Ex Platonicorum persona*, pp. 252–67, points out, Augustine returns to this "mixture" problematic in *Trin* 9.7–8, the components are no longer soul and body, but mind, knowledge, and love.

60. DuRoy, *Trinité*, rightly observes that Augustine regularly speaks of the Incarnation of the Word as the "appearance" to mankind of Him Who was already integrally omnipresent; see p. 202 and the texts adduced in his notes. The same omnipresence–appearance device often recurs in his Christmas sermons: *Ser 184–196*.

61. See *Early Theory*, pp. 274–75.

62. Note that as early as *Immort* Augustine excludes such soul–body relationships as entelechy and harmony on the score of their "materialism"; see *Early Theory*, pp. 135–45.

AUGUSTINE'S THOUGHT SITUATION IN 411

This survey of the interlude between 395 und 411 shows several important features of Augustine's thinking as he approaches a threshold that will prove crucial in his further development. On the problem of the soul's origin, we have seen that he seems to have remained remarkably innocent of the issues raised by the anti-Origenist reaction in the churches beyond the sea from Africa: the Jerome who could have informed him about those issues proves obstinately unhelpful until, some time after the year 402, he sends a copy of the third book of his *Apologia* against Rufinus to the bishop of Hippo. What genuine illumination Augustine might have gathered from Jerome's rantings is difficult to conjecture.

But Augustine's earlier interpretations of Romans 9:11, the pivotal text in the anti-Origenist debate, have, with his replies to Simplician in 396, undergone a minor revolution: he shifts from defending the "justice" of God's "election," which was Origen's principal concern, to proclaiming a divine liberty in terms that herald, in important respects, the understanding of "grace" he incorporates in his *Confessions* and later in his anti-Pelagian polemic. But there is no sign that he leapt over the inferential gap between that premiss on election to the conclusion that would reject Origen's "fall" of the soul; Romans 9:11 does not yet speak to him in those terms.

And yet, the problem of the soul concerns him in another connection. His reply to Consentius gives us strongly to suspect that his slowed progress in writing his *De Trinitate* stems, not from some imagined grapple with relations theory, but from the difficulty he sees in moving upward from the soul to God precisely as Trinity, a move he finally makes and encases in Books 8–14 of the work. And since evidence to the contrary has largely evaporated, we may now return to the very natural assumption that by the year 411 his writing of the earlier books on relations theory was already well behind him.

But what precise shape did the problem of the soul assume for Augustine at this time? Volusian's queries on how we might conceive of God as joined to human flesh prompt Augustine to use the more familiar union of soul and body as his starting point to help his correspondent to admit the possibility, at least, of union between divinity and humanity. But does this mean that "the problem" of the soul has come to center, for Augustine, on the modality of that union, and his interest shifted to Porphyry's manner of understanding it? Surely not. His answer to Volusian encases whatever details he may have gleaned from Porphyry in those familiar terms he long ago learned, once for all, from Plotinus' great treatise on omnipresence. And the chapters that follow will show beyond doubt that for Augustine *the* central problem of the soul invariably focused on how and why the soul became embodied.

Augustine's letter to Consentius, however, taken together with his replies to Simplician, serves to point up a feature of his thinking which is about to undergo a severe test. His reading of Romans still persuades him that the human mind can indeed rise from things created to "catch sight" (*conspicere*) of God's *invisibilia*, "understood." Even the knotty problem of making this ascent from the soul to the Trinity, though it sobers him and seems to have him momentarily baffled, has not quenched his enthusiasm for the task and possibilities of understanding. And yet, in pondering the questions Simplician sent him, he has been compelled to take a step the long-term consequences of which must be watched. His former defense of God's "justice" was to a great extent a product of human understanding. It had to knuckle under to the text of Romans affirming peremptorily that God's election must be radically free, with a freedom that transcended all such human conceptions of justice and injustice.

The year is 411, a fateful year for Augustine. For it brought him from across the seas that staunch and inspiring Catholic, Flavius Marcellinus. But the same year brought him Pelagius and his lieutenant, Caelestius, fleeing from the barbarians overrunning Italy. They will bring with them a vision of God's dealings with His people more "enlightened," so they claim, than the one prevailing in Africa's theological backwater. Their theory will proceed from what they consider an unassailable premiss: that each and every human soul came clean and unsullied from the creative hand of a perfectly just God. On that premiss they will erect an elegantly reasoned view of Christian truth, and pit it against Augustine's growing trust in God's word in Scripture. Augustine will perceive with growing clarity that he must choose between the sometimes baffling and inscrutable message of The Book, and his residual claims for human modes of understanding.

The acid test of this growing reliance on Scripture will be, once again, Romans 9:11. This time, however, Augustine will be compelled to attend to that phrase "before they were born, they did neither good nor evil." But when did Augustine see that text as bearing on the question of the soul's origin? The conventional wisdom would have it that this insight occurred during the winter of 411/412, when he published his *De peccatorum meritis et remissione*. But the evidence for that received position is hardly so solid as scholars have come to think. Showing that, and showing the difference it makes in our estimate of Augustine's evolution on this tormenting issue, will be my next task.

De peccatorum meritis et remissione

Romans 9:11, we have seen, became a crucial text in the discussion of the soul's origin; that discussion was carried on outside of Africa, without Augustine's being able to follow its progress. But in the *De peccatorum meritis et remissione* we suddenly find him applying that text, with considerable confidence, to exclude the very theory of man as "fallen soul" which may well have been his preferred theory when writing the *Le libero arbitrio* and, indeed, when composing the *Confessions*. There is an anomaly here: the usual date proposed for the *De meritis* is 411/412, whereas in a series of works written well after that date, Augustine remains totally unaware of the bearing of this text on the issue of the soul's fall. That anomaly can be cleared up, I submit, by re-examining the evidence that has led scholars to date the *De meritis*—in the form in which we read it today—much earlier than that evidence warrants.

The pivotal piece of evidence for the dating of the *De meritis* is Augustine's *Letter 139*, to Marcellinus. He does speak of the work elsewhere, as we shall see, but interpretation of those other statements inevitably turns on one's reading of *Letter 139*.[63]

---

63. Bardy, in BA 12, pp. 584–85, fails to keep clear the distinction between Books 1–2 and the later Book 3 in averring that *Mer* was "written" in 412. Charles Urba and Joseph Zycha, in CCL 60, p. i, repeat that dating. Jacob H. Koopmans, in "Augus-

Letter 139 seems clearly to have been written during the winter months of 411/412.[64] We do not have the letter from Marcellinus to which Augustine is replying, but it is obvious (he is prodding again!) that he has inquired about a "book" that Augustine had previously written and sent to him, a book on the baptism of infants. "I have forgotten," Augustine admits,

> why I received back the copy of the book on the baptism of infants which I had sent your Excellency—unless, perhaps, it was because I found it faulty when I looked it over, and wanted to correct it; but I have been so unbelievably busy that I have not done so.
> There was also a letter to be written and added to the manuscript, and I began to dictate it while I was there [presumably at Carthage], but you must know that I have added little to it and it is still unfinished. If I could give you an account of my days and of the labor I expend at night on other pressing duties, you would be surprised and very saddened at the great burdens which weigh me down, which cannot be put off, and which prevent me from doing those things which you ask and urge me to do, willing though I am and more grieved than I can say at not being able to do them. When I get a little time . . . there are plenty of details having priority over the scraps of time devoted to dictation. . . .[65]

Augustine then proceeds to list the pressing jobs that have kept him from getting to what Marcellinus would have him do: the summary of the conference with the Donatists, a letter to the

---

tine's First Contact with Pelagius, and the Dating of the Condemnation of Caelestius at Carthage" (henceforth: "First Contact"), *Vigiliae Christianae*, 8 (1954), 149–53, makes no distinction whatever between Books 1–2 and 3, remarks that Urba and Zycha seem mostly to have "assumed" the date they assign, and argues that *Ep 139* compels our dating the *Mer* as composed sometime in 411: a conclusion valid for the *original* composition of Books 1–2, the *only* books (*pace* Koopmans) which Marcellinus had sent back to Augustine. François Refoulé, in "La Datation du premier concile de Carthage," REA, 9 (1963), 41–49, distinguishes: Books 1 and 2 were already "written," but Book 3 was only "sur le chantier" in February 412 when *Ep 139* was written (pp. 41–42). But Refoulé seems then to assume without question or supporting evidence that Book 3 was both completed and the whole of *Mer* "published" very soon afterward, in 412. Mille La Bonnardière, in "Jérome Informateur," 46n23, accepts this traditional dating (411/412) without demurral. But ferret out the grounds for this "consensus," and the key piece of evidence in each case turns out to be a reading of *Ep 139* which is, in my view, uniformly careless. Inertia works in scholarship as mightily as in physics.
64. There seems little doubt about this dating of *Ep 139* itself. See Goldbacher, CSEL 58, pp. 37–38 (winter 411/412), and Refoulé, "Datation," 41 (before February 28, 412).
65. *Ep 139* 3.

Donatist laity, two long letters, one of them to Marcellinus himself;[66] he has, moreover, still "in hand" the lengthy *Letter 140*, to Honoratus, "On Grace in the New Testament," much more a book than an ordinary letter, and one that must have taken both time and pains to compose.[67]

It is a surprising fact that these remarks to Marcellinus seem the principal basis for a scholarly consensus that dates the *De meritis* as written in the years 411/412.[68] For after reading this letter closely, what exactly can we be sure of? I submit the following. First, Augustine had composed, sometime before *Letter 139* (i.e., before the winter months of 411/412), a "book" on the baptism of infants, and sent it to Marcellinus. Secondly, he had subsequently asked it back from Marcellinus. Thirdly, he had begun, but only begun, a "letter" to be appended to that work, a letter that remained unfinished in the winter of 411/412. Fourthly, he has been very busy, and remains so; he is asking Marcellinus' understanding for past delay, and quite possibly for continued delay in responding to his requests. Fifthly, he claims to have forgotten the reason why he had asked back from Marcellinus the "book" on the baptism of infants; perhaps, he suggests, he might have felt the need to emend it. Sixthly, if emendation was his aim, he has not yet begun on it—indeed, *seems* not even to have checked to see if the work was, in fact, in need of correction.

Other conclusions may be drawn, even on the basis of what we know from *Letter 139*; less certain, they are nonetheless quite reliable, and they are confirmed by what Augustine tells us elsewhere.[69] First, we know that the *De meritis* as it now stands consists

66. Presumably *Epp 137*, to Marcellinus, and *138* to Volusian. See above.

67. *Ep 139* 3. *Ep 140*, in answer to five questions posed him by Honoratus, to which Augustine deliberately adds a vital sixth, was obviously composed carefully and laboriously, with the awareness that it would become a public document. It represents, in fact, a recasting of almost the whole of Augustine's theology, in the light of the challenge Pelagianism represented. It alone would, presumably, have occasioned considerable delay in Augustine's getting to the revisions of his *Mer*, and made Augustine even more keenly aware of the pitfalls involved in making any such revisions. Goldbacher, in CSEL 58, p. 38, argues that *Ep 139* (cf. *Retr* 2.36) speaks of *Ep 140* as *continuo* [*absolvenda*], and it was certainly Augustine's *intention* to finish it as soon as he could. How long, though, did it take him to fulfill that intention?

68. See note 63, above. This is all the more remarkable in the cases of Koopmans and Refoulé, since they both question so many other chronological assumptions, but never this vital one.

69. See below for an examination of the elements drawn from the *Retr* and the *Gest*.

of three books; the first two of them deal with the baptism of infants, and the third is indeed an appended "letter" to Marcellinus. We may safely infer that the "book" referred to in *Letter 139* was really two books, after all, the first draft of the initial two books of the *De meritis*; and that the "letter" appendix spoken of there was the start of a first draft, at least, of what eventually became the third book of that work.[70]

What can be made of Augustine's professed vagueness on his reason for asking this work back from Marcellinus? It is tempting to think, as Koopmans does,[71] of a time delay between Augustine's having asked the work back from Marcellinus, and his writing *Letter 139*; one must leave time for Augustine to have "forgotten" his reasons for asking it back.[72] But once embarked on that course, one must conjure up another, earlier time gap: between Augustine's writing of the "book" and his asking it back from Marcellinus. Of this earlier time gap, we know nothing directly. How long was the work in Marcellinus' possession? But what do we really know of the later one? How much "time" must we give for Augustine to have "forgotten" his reasons for asking the work back from Marcellinus? Or was *time* the crucial factor? Could there have been something "diplomatic" implied in Augustine's claim to have "forgotten"?

Consider that with *Letter 139* we are toward the end of 411 or at the beginning of 412. Grant that Pelagius and his lieutenant Caelestius arrived in Africa sometime in May[73] of 411, and grant further that this question of the baptism of infants was subsequently stirred up by Caelestius' "Pelagian" proclamations on the subject.[74] It follows, then, that even between Augustine's original

70. Bardy, in BA 12, p. 584, observes that in *Retr* Augustine gives the full title as *De peccatorum meritis et remissione et de baptismo parvulorum*, thereby confirming this assumption of identity. But see more on this, below.

71. "First Contact," 151–52.

72. Koopmans, ibid., writes loosely that Augustine's "addressee had returned" these books, so that Augustine has forgotten "why they were sent back." More precisely, Augustine *asked* for them back, and claims to have forgotten his own *reasons* for having done so.

73. As Georges de Plinval suggests on page 13 of his *Pélage: Ses écrits, sa vie, et sa réforme* (Lausanne: Payot, 1943). For confirmation, see Koopmans, "First Contact," 150.

74. Plinval, *Pélage*, p. 239, sees Caelestius as the first to take this precise tack, but (p. 260) views it as a sound "corollary" of Pelagius' own position. Note that baptismal teaching was a particularly sensitive point for Augustine and African Catholics more generally; it was at the center of the fierce Donatist controversy. See Brown, *Augustine*, pp. 344–45.

writing of the "book" to Marcellinus, and his composition of *Letter 139*, no more than six months could have intervened. Between his asking the work back, and this confession of "forgetfulness" in *Letter 139*, the time gap must have been even shorter. And in matters like these, Augustine had quite a remarkable memory. It must be considered a strong possibility, at least, that his "forgetfulness" had a diplomatic quality to it; he may have been a trifle embarrassed to admit outright that the original work to Marcellinus did, in fact, stand in need of correction.[75]

But even if one discounted such a possibility, it is clear from *Letter 139* that Augustine must still verify whether his original work needed emendation, and must still complete the "letter" that now stands as the third book of the *De meritis*. When did he get to these two connected tasks? *Letter 139* does not tell us, but leaves us with the presumption that the press of work Augustine complains of would force him to delay even further. The upshot is that *Letter 139*, far from supporting the conclusion that the *De meritis* was published about the same time, i.e., winter of 411/412, severely weakens it.

Light from Other Sources

So much for *Letter 139*. Turning to the *De meritis* itself, Bardy argues that: "Addressed to Marcellinus, these books must have been published between 410 and 413, *sans doute en* 412." The argument implies[76] that, since Marcellinus met his tragic end in September 413, and the books are addressed to him, we may at least claim confidence for 413 as the *terminus ad quem* of the *finished De meritis*. Augustine would not likely publish a work explicitly addressed to a man who was already dead—this, at least, I take to be Bardy's implied reasoning. But once made explicit, how cogent is it? Would it be all that strange for Augustine to have preserved, in the finished publication, that mark of Marcellinus' original inspiration for the work? Indeed, could he not have thought it a suitable memorial to his slain friend? At all events, the date of Marcellinus'

75. Yet, to do Koopmans justice, there must have been a sufficient time lag to make Augustine's excuse seem plausible to Marcellinus.
76. BA 12, p. 584. I pass on the vagueness of "these books." Is Bardy referring to Books 1 and 2 alone, or to the *three* books of the finished work? And has he taken sufficient account of the distinction between "writing" and "publishing"?

death cannot be invoked as apodictic proof for the latest *possible* date for publication of the finished *De meritis*.

This, then, is all we can learn from the *De meritis* itself, and from *Letter 139*, to Marcellinus. What other evidence do we have to work with? Bardy refers us to *Letter 169*,[77] to Evodius, dating from 415, where Augustine lists his literary accomplishments during the early months of that year. He speaks of having written a "big book against the heresy of Pelagius." This "big book," Bardy assumes,[78] is the *De meritis*. But if that were true, Bardy's original dating (411/412) has unaccountably shifted to 415! That same book, Bardy goes on to tell us, is mentioned in letters of 416, where it is clear that Augustine "addresses a copy" of it to John of Jerusalem and another to Pope Innocent.[79] To our puzzlement, though, only two pages further on, Bardy contradicts what he has just told us: the "big book" referred to in all three of these letters is, in fact, the *De natura et gratia*, and not the *De meritis* after all.[80] A closer look at *Letter 169*, to Evodius, makes it clear that Bardy was wrong the first, but right the second, time. The "big book" against Pelagianism, written earlier in 415, is the very one elicited from him by the queries of the "brothers" Timasius and James. Former disciples of Pelagius, they sent Augustine, in 414, a copy of Pelagius' *De natura*, asking his opinion of it. Augustine replies to them in a work that, as Bardy later comes to see, is clearly *not* the *De meritis* but the *De natura et gratia*.

Letters 169, to Evodius, *177*, to Bishop John of Jerusalem, and *179*, to Pope Innocent, add nothing to our knowledge about the *De meritis*. We are left exactly where we were after *Letter 139*, to Marcellinus, with these three questions: Did Augustine ever "emend" the first two books of *De meritis*? When did he complete the letter constituting the third book of that work? And when was the completed work eventually published?

The *De gestis Pelagii*, written in 417, and the *Retractations*, completed some ten years afterward, in 427, supplement our information about this stage of Augustine's career. Their testimony is fundamentally concordant, but even the slight discrepancies be-

---

77. Bardy, ibid., erroneously prints this as *Ep 269*, but is obviously referring to *Ep 169*.
78. Ibid.
79. See *Epp 177* 6 and *179*.
80. BA 12, p. 586.

tween them may be significant. Combine it with other pieces of evidence, and the sequence of events they describe would appear to be as follows: [81]

Sometime before the arrival of Pelagius and Caelestius in Africa, Augustine hears rumors from Rome about Pelagius' questionable teachings. He feels he must trust his informants, but decides to wait until firsthand word, or some "book" from Pelagius' own hand, provides confirmation of these rumors. Pelagius and Caelestius do finally arrive at the port of Hippo, but at a time when Augustine is away, probably in Carthage. Pelagius, however, is reported to him later as having made no scandalous pronouncements, perhaps in part because he departed Hippo quickly for Carthage. Busy with the Donatist affair, Augustine only glimpses Pelagius at Carthage, once or twice, before Pelagius embarks for Palestine, leaving Caelestius behind in Carthage. Pelagius' followers propagate his teaching in their master's absence, to the growing alarm of Carthaginian Catholics—an alarm that climaxes with a church tribunal condemning Caelestius, in the fall of 411. [82]

He was not, Augustine tells us, at this tribunal of condemnation,[83] but checked the *Acta* of the council sometime later. Condemned but "uncorrected," Caelestius continues with his Pelagian agitation.[84]

Meanwhile, Augustine still abstains from attacking this nascent heresy in "writings," expressing his opposition in sermons and conferences, *sermones* and *conlocutiones*, only.[85] He is still awaiting

---

81. Plinval's chronology of these events, *Pélage*, pp. 261–64, is initially useful, but closer discriminations are necessary for our purpose here.

82. See *Gest* 46, as well as Refoulé's "Datation." Some of Refoulé's argument may need reviewing, however, where it depends on his assumption that *Mer* was completed and published in 412.

83. *Gest* 62; cf. *Retr* 2.33. Since all relevant citations from *Retr* are from this section, I shall write merely *Retr* in subsequent notes.

84. *Gest* 62; cf. Plinval, *Pélage*, pp. 258–68.

85. *Retr* affirms that these sermons and conferences occurred *prius* to any "writings." *Gest* telescopes somewhat, by mentioning "popular *tractatus*" and *libri* as though from the same epoch. It seems sage to honor the more discriminated witness of *Retr* in this connection. Benjamin Warfield, in his Introduction (pp. xxii–xxiv) to *The Nicene and Post-Nicene Fathers* V (New York: The Christian Literature Society, 1888; repr. Grand Rapids, Mich.: Eerdmans, 1956), proposes as the *Serr* in question *175* (412), *174* (413), *176* (414), and *170* (417). J. de la Tullaye and Georges de Plinval, in BA 21, p. 588, mention only *Serr 115*, *292*, and *294*, from the year 413, thus indicating how much more we have to learn about this entire sequence of events.

the reception of firsthand evidence of Pelagius' teaching, and expressly omits mention of any names in refuting the teachings that have been spread abroad in Carthage.[86]

Once back in Hippo Regius, he is besieged by a number of queries sent him from Carthage,[87] and notably from Count Marcellinus.[88] In answer to these queries he finally puts pen to work. *De gestis Pelagii* tells us that the first thing he wrote had to do with the baptism of infants,[89] the topic of the first two books of the eventual *De meritis*. The *Retractations* telescopes things somewhat: "I first wrote . . . three books" on the topics of infant baptism *and grace*— the latter being the focus of the *third* book of *De meritis*, as we have it now. The *De gestis Pelagii*, ten years closer to the events, reflects more accurately the two-stage composition of that work of which *Letter 139* clearly informs us, without, however, clearing up any of the questions that letter leaves us with.

But even in this work Augustine still omits mention of the names of those responsible for the doctrines he is attacking,[90] except for a brief laudatory mention of Pelagius' reputation for virtue, in the letter constituting the third book. The opening paragraph of that third book informs us, also, that Augustine has finally laid hands on the firsthand evidence he has been looking for: Pelagius' *Commentary on St. Paul*.[91] But exactly when did this occur? Alas, we are not told.

We are told, though, that Augustine found Pelagius' method of exposing his own teachings in this work so allusive and indirect that it was difficult to pin him down to a clear position. In adducing the opinion of this or that exegete, was Pelagius espousing it as his own? Only later, *postea*, was Pelagius drawn out to the point of defending as his own a number of the opinions purveyed in his *Commentary* as having been proposed by others.[92] Only then, Au-

---

86. Notice that Augustine's motive for delaying any written refutation was twofold: he was anxious to be sure, from Pelagius' own writings, what he taught, and, in a related concern, was hopeful of correcting rather than alienating him (and, presumably, Caelestius as well).
87. *Retr.*
88. *Gest* 25.
89. Ibid.
90. *Gest* 46–47.
91. *Mer* 3.1.
92. *Gest* 47; cf. *Retr.*

gustine seems to imply, could he feel confident in attacking Pelagius' doctrines with the assurance that he could link them firmly with his name.

Sometime later, Augustine then informs us,[93] he was called upon to preach in the Church of the Majores: the writings of St. Cyprian in hand, he defended the practice of infant baptism for the remission of sins against the Pelagian challenges to that practice: the date of this *Sermon 294*, as well as of the associated *Sermons 293* and *115*, can confidently be fixed as in July 413.[94] We are well after the Carthage condemnation of Caelestius, but Pelagius and he have found another tack. They are now making appeal to the teaching of the learned Eastern Church against the backwater pieties of Africa! That strategy works for a short while; their teachings will seem to be vindicated at Diospolis in 415. Augustine is so shocked by that verdict that he enters into an impassioned correspondence with ecclesiastical authorities in Palestine. Carthage had seen Pelagius in truer colors than the Easterners had!

Meanwhile,[95] as we have seen, Timasius and James inquire for Augustine's opinion of Pelagius' *De natura*. Augustine's answer, the *De natura et gratia*, written in 415, frees Timasius and James of any residual Pelagian sympathies they may have had—a result that may have encouraged Augustine to send off copies of the work, in 416, to Pope Innocent and to Bishop John of Jerusalem, both of them by now equally embroiled in the Pelagius affair.[96]

What does this sequence of events tell us of the publication date of the *De meritis*? Directly, very little, it would seem. Negatively, the evidence lends no support for the common assumption that the work was completed in late 411 or early 412. Indirectly, though, the *De gestis Pelagii* confirms the view that the work was composed in two distinct stages: the first two books in reply to Marcellinus' queries on the baptism of infants, the third book treating of the distinct though related topic of Christ's redemptive grace. One can understand how the *Retractations*, composed some ten years afterward, tended to telescope this two-stage process, without, however,

---

93. *Gest* 25.
94. See Pierre Patrick Verbraken, *Etudes critiques sur les sermons authentiques de saint Augustin* (The Hague: Nijhoff, 1976), pp. 80 and 130–31. (Henceforth: *Sermons authentiques.*)
95. *Gest* 47.
96. See *Epp 177* 6 and *179*, already referred to in note 79, above.

standing in any direct contradiction to the account in the *De gestis Pelagii*. Further, both the *Retractations* and the *De gestis Pelagii* insist repeatedly on two points: that Augustine *first* dealt with the Pelagian heresy in sermons, conferences, and popular expositions generally, only afterward setting himself to "written" forms of refutation; and, secondly, partially explaining the above, that he bided his time before writing, in the hope of obtaining firsthand evidence from Pelagius' own writings.

Now, the first of these writings to come into his possession seems clearly to have been Pelagius' *Commentary on St. Paul*, mentioned at the very outset of Book 3 of the *De meritis*. Was this "find" what prompted Augustine to ask Marcellinus to send back Books 1 and 2? If so, then he may have made this request as far back as winter 411/412, a date which, given Augustine's repeatedly expressed anxiety about working from firsthand evidence, seems the earliest plausible date to work with. But Augustine is dreadfully busy at that time. How long was it before he was able to undertake a serious study of Pelagius' *Commentary*, and to compose his refutation of it?

It might be thought that dating the *sermones* and *conlocutiones* to which Augustine refers might help with this question. He does, after all, assure us that they preceded his first efforts at written refutation, which he identifies as the *De meritis*. But we are left helplessly vague on what *sermones* are being referred to. He expressly mentiones, it is true, *Sermons 294, 293*, and *115* in this connection; if they are the ones he means as having preceded the publication of the *De meritis*, then that publication must have occurred sometime after June 413. But other, earlier sermons, and even "conferences" that never saw publication, could be in his mind, so we are left once again with our doubts and questions.

One final avenue remains: Refoulé has argued that the first book of the *De meritis*—in the version as we now have it—consists of a refutation, point by point, of the six theses defended in Rufinus "the Syrian's" *Libellus de fide*, whom some have been tempted to point to as the real "father" of Pelagianism. Refoulé goes on to conclude that this work must have been in Augustine's hands sometime around the year 411. But his argument rests on exactly the unquestioned assumption that I have tried to show is far from unquestionable: namely, that *Letter 139* entitles us to date the *De meritis* as of 411/412. Again, we are at a dead end.

An Argument from Augustine's Development

It was necessary to survey the extrinsic evidence for dating the *De meritis* before advancing the argument, from intrinsic evidence and intellectual development, that I am about to present for consideration. Since the extrinsic evidence does not foreclose the question one way or another, let me suggest this: Augustine's treatment of the "fall" hypothesis respecting the origin of the soul, in two distinct sections of the first book of the *De meritis*, argues strongly for that book's being a later, "emended" version, a version that Augustine completed and published well after Marcellinus' death.[97]

The fourth of the four hypotheses outlined in *De libero arbitrio* 3 bears strong resemblances to Origen's proposal: that all human souls pre-existed, sinned with sins of various gravity, and were imprisoned in bodies and accorded life-situations proportioned to the gravity of their pre-incarnate sin or sins. Twice during the course of the first book of the *De meritis*, Augustine alludes to this theory, and twice firmly rejects it.[98] His proof-text is the very one that had already rendered similar service in earlier controversies outside of Africa, Paul's reference to Esau and Jacob in Romans 9:11: neither of them had done either good or evil before God's election of Jacob from Rebecca's womb. The application of this text to the Origenist "fall" hypothesis Augustine now clearly sees; without a tremor of hesitation he uses the text to reject the "fall" hypothesis out of hand.[99]

But why the claim that this could have happened only afterward? The reason is this: on at least four "subsequent" occasions Augustine is compelled to grapple with the question of the soul's origin, and to weigh the merits of the "Origenist" hypothesis among others. On none of these occasions does he invoke Romans 9:11, when appeal to that text would have spared him agonies of indecision, and permitted him briskly to eliminate this one, at least,

97. We shall see further on that this final publication seems to date from circa 417/418.
98. *Mer* 1.31 and 69; the result is that from this point forward only three of the original four hypotheses on the soul's origin are left in contention, whereas, after the application of Romans 9:11 in 3.17 only two of the original hypotheses are left.
99. I prescind for the moment from the curious qualification Augustine here enters into this debate: that Paul's words exclude any merits or demerits from our "own lives" (*propria vita*). The force and importance of that qualification we shall have to explore further on.

of the four hypotheses he is obliged to leave "open" for further consideration. Compare that indecision with the unhesitating confidence he afterward shows once this text becomes part of his Biblical armory, and it becomes psychologically implausible, even grotesque, to suppose that he perceived the bearing of Romans 9:11 on the question of the soul's origin as early as the year 412.

But this anticipated conclusion must remain a working hypothesis for the moment; only an examination of the works dealing with the soul's origin can convert it from hypothesis to fully earned conclusion.

Pelagianism and Romans 9:11

How did Pelagius' views bring this text from Romans into such high relief? One by one Pelagius' *Commentary on St. Paul, On Nature*, and, sometime later, his *For the Freedom of the Will*[100] came into Augustine's hands. Additionally, Augustine must have learned a considerable amount about the shape of Pelagianism from reports and queries emanating from Carthage, and also, perhaps, from Rufinus' *Libellus de fide*. What were the issues,[101] and how did they affect the question of the soul's origin?

Pelagius was a moral reformer, certainly; but his legal background had only accentuated both a strong sense of God as "just" and equitable and a coordinate conviction concerning the freedom and responsibility of human moral agents.[102] Any form of determinism which would hem in that responsibility was anathema to him: against the Manichees, he preached the goodness of human nature as God had established it;[103] Origen's claim that our human lives were already partially determined by some pre-incarnate sin, he dismissed as a nightmarish dream;[104] but the transmission of Original Sin and its effects he inveighed against as just another kind of determinism, furnishing human lukewarmness with an excuse to evade the quest for moral perfection he saw as the core of Chris-

---

100. See TeSelle, *Theologian*, pp. 288–89.
101. I present the doctrinal picture substantially as Plinval outlines it in *Pélage*, but with occasional touches gleaned from Gerald Bonner, *St. Augustine of Hippo: Life and Controversies* (London: SCM Press, 1963), Brown, *Augustine*, and TeSelle, *Theologian*.
102. Plinval, *Pélage*, p. 150.
103. Ibid., 149–50 and 234–36.
104. Ibid., p. 152.

tianity.[105] "Give what thou commandest, and command what thou wilt": that phrase from Augustine's own *Confessions*—"a bad book"—Pelagius could speak of only in tones of withering mockery.[106] Does God accord men "grace," then? If "grace" has any meaning beyond God's establishment of human nature as fully furnished for the struggle toward moral perfection, then this at least must be true: God must accord His graces equitably, and therefore in consideration of man's merits.[107]

The transmission of Original Sin and its effects Pelagius directly connected with the "African" theory of traducianism, stemming from Tertullian.[108] Against that view, he set the view of the "more advanced" Eastern Churches: namely, creationism. But, he reasoned, if God created each individual soul afresh for infusion into its body, that soul must come clean and innocent from the creative hand.[109] To speak, then, of the sinful guilt of infants is to insult the goodness of the Creator; to hold infants guilty of the sin of some "other," like Adam, is to insult God's justice.[110] So, whatever infant baptism may be thought to effect, it cannot be "remission of sins" in any genuine sense of those terms![111] And here Pelagius, mostly through the expostulations of his lieutenant, Caelestius,[112] found himself on a collision course with one of the deepest streams of African religious feeling.

His *Commentary on St. Paul* is a curious document: he must explain and explain in the effort to explain away a number of Paul's dark sayings on the sinful condition of the human race. Romans 9:11 was particularly nettling: where were those "merits" of Jacob, in view of which God graced him with "election" over his brother? It is piquant to note that his answer is closely akin to the one Augustine had given, years before, and since abandoned: God *foresaw* Jacob's *future* merits, and graced him accordingly![113]

But aside from that point, Pelagius and his associates gave Au-

105. Ibid., pp. 150 and 234–36.
106. Ibid., p. 227.
107. Ibid., p. 150.
108. Ibid.
109. Ibid., pp. 150–51.
110. Ibid.
111. Ibid., pp. 236–37.
112. Ibid., pp. 239, 256–57, 260.
113. Ibid., p. 153 and notes 1 and 2, quoting from Pelagius' *Commentary* on Rom. 9:11, 11:5, and 8:29–30. Compare Augustine's *ExpRom* as treated above.

gustine much to think about. He might, at the end of the *De libero arbitrio*, have felt entitled to shelve the question of the soul's origin as matter for ivory-tower specialists, secondary in importance to the question of the soul's destiny; but that attitude (if ever he really adopted it) will be permitted him no longer. Pelagianism has placed the question of the soul's origin at center stage, firmly linking it with the question of the soul's innocence or guilt, and need for baptism. Augustine may well discard Pelagius' interpretation of Romans 9:11 as implying God's election through "foreknowledge" of Jacob's merits; but Pelagius compels him to stare hard at that text again. He will come, in time, to see it as implying more than he had previously realized.

3

THE PELAGIANS
RAISE THE QUESTION
OF THE SOUL

MARCELLINUS SEEMS TO ALLOW Augustine no respite. *Letter 143* shows the bishop acknowledging not one, but two, of his letters, both containing theological queries, and both written on the heels of *Letter 139*, in 412.[1] The second of his questions shows that the pace of controversy has quickened. Augustine's Carthaginian critics have moved from the question of infant guilt to the related question of the origin of souls. Their pursuit of that issue has brought them to re-examine the third book of Augustine's *De libero arbitrio*, where he treated this thorny question.

They are aware of his disclaimers insisting that he did not make his defense of God's justice dependent on one rather than another of the four hypotheses current at the time; he had, he claimed, left all four options "open." But this very claim some "critics" of his have called into question; so Marcellinus has informed him. As Augustine's reply also makes clear, his adversaries' objection arises, not from the precise section of the work in which he dealt with these four hypotheses, but from an earlier section, where he may have been writing in less guarded fashion.

All this becomes plain further on in Augustine's reply. It is significant, though, that before dealing directly with the point at issue, Augustine spends considerable time persuading Marcellinus that

1. See Goldbacher, in CSEL 58, pp. 37–38, where he argues (convincingly, I think) that *Ep 143* was written shortly after *139*. Since there were other letters to Marcellinus before September 413, when he was slain, it would appear that the Pelagian controversy had heated up during this period. All references to *Ep 143* will be given in the text.

he should not think him infallible, or set him beyond others' correction; this, Marcellinus' unbounded admiration seems in danger of doing. Instead of applying Cicero's celebrated compliment "He never uttered a word which he wished to take back," Marcellinus— and his co-admirers of Augustine[2]—might more wisely share the "real pain" that saying of Horace causes him, "The word once released cannot return."

> That is why I am holding on to my books, full of the most dangerous questions on Genesis and the Trinity, longer than you desire or [even] incline to tolerate, so that, if it be unavoidable that they have some features deserving censure, they may at least have fewer than if published in headlong haste and without due consideration [3–4].

A letter from Bishop Florentius has informed Augustine that Marcellinus and others have been "pressing for their publication," so that Augustine, while still living, might defend his views against his critics. But they are assuming, of course, that there is nothing in these books "which could be blamed for any valid reason; otherwise you would be urging me, not to publish them, but to carry out a more careful revision." Augustine's aim is to eliminate any "censurable passages" save those which "might escape my notice despite careful scrutiny" (3).[3]

THE OBJECTION OF HIS CRITICS

Only after this lengthy defense of his delaying the publication of both the *De Trinitate* and the *De Genesi* does Augustine take up the objection that had been leveled at the *De libero arbitrio*. That objection, Marcellinus seems to have reported, focused on a sentence in Book 3, paragraph 34 of that work, where Augustine was explaining the "place" of the human soul in the ordered hierarchy

2. Note Augustine's plural *vos*, *Ep 143* 3. This could refer to Florentius, who is mentioned further on, but it seems likely that it refers as well to the "brethren" at Carthage for whom Marcellinus was regularly the spokesman. In any event, Augustine did not have to wait until his sojourn in Carthage during the year 418 to experience the urgings that he publish his *Trin*, as Hendrikx conjectures in BA 17, pp. 560 and 566. See his own implicit acknowledgment of this in connection with *Ep 143*, ibid., p. 564.
3. Hendrikx, ibid., finds this passage supporting his theory that Augustine already had the whole of *Trin* written in "rough"; that support I find fragile, at best.

of spiritual and corporeal creatures. "But the soul," he wrote then, "which, after sin [*post peccatum*], is set in order among inferior and mortal bodies, governs its body, not entirely by choice, but as the laws of the universe permit." Now, it may be true, his critics charge, that in the later sections of that same work Augustine was careful enough not to choose one over the other three competing hypotheses on the soul's origin. But here his pen had surely slipped. The sentence they cite clearly implies some "sin" on the part of the soul which accounts for this limitation on its power of free activity. Such a "sin," however, is featured only in two of those four hypotheses, traducianism and a quasi-Origenist "fall" of the soul into the universe of "inferior and mortal bodies." This sentence then, despite his disclaimers, supposes a preference for one or other of those two "sinful" hypotheses (5).

His critics seem peaceful with his four hypotheses as expressing the accepted terms of discussion at the time; Augustine himself, to clarify his answer to them, sums up (6) those four hypotheses once again. All souls of human beings sprung from Adam

(*a*) are propagated from that first one, Adam's soul (*ex illa una propagentur*)—the traducianist hypothesis; or

(*b*) come into existence (or are made) individually in individuals (*singillatim in singulis fiant*)—creationism; or

(*c*) are created outside, and "sent" (*extra creatae mittantur*); or

(*d*) (created outside, as above) plunge (or "sink") voluntarily into bodies (*in corpora sponte mergantur*)—the "fallen soul" hypothesis.

Now, Augustine's Carthaginian critics are supposing that "sin" on the part of the soul is implied in two, and only two, of these: the first and the fourth, the traducianist and the "fallen soul" hypotheses. It is worth noting that Augustine takes no exception to that supposition, already an indication that he means the terms *in corpora sponte mergantur* as involving a sinful choice on the part of these pre-existent souls; and since he himself is merely re-expressing the original fourth hypothesis of the *De libero arbitrio*, he has implicitly told us what was intended by the terms *veniunt* and *labantur* in that work. But were there any residual doubt on that question, he removes it as completely as one could desire.

THE CRUCIAL PHRASE: *Post peccatum*

For now he moves on his critics' objection: their point is that the *post peccatum* of *De libero arbitrio* 3.34 shows that he had, in fact, "established, and firmly, some certainty about the human soul" after all: namely, "either that it comes by propagation from the parents" (*vel ex parentibus per propaginem veniat*) or that "it sinned by its acts in a higher and heavenly life, and [so] deserved to be shut up in corruptible flesh" (*in actibus vitae superioris atque coelestis peccaverit, ut corruptibili carne mereretur includi*).[4] These two hypotheses, his critics realize, imply some "sin" on the soul's part, and Augustine's phrase implicitly commits him to one or the other of them: either to the traducianist or to the "fallen soul" hypothesis; so, *eo ipso*, he has excluded the other two "sinless" hypotheses, "creationism" and "divine sending." Augustine offers this expression of his original fourth hypothesis with no trace of an objection: it does, and always did, imply for him a pre-embodied "sin" on the part of the soul.[5]

The critics' case seems a strong one. The context shows Augustine explaining the reduced kind of freedom we humans now experience, and the offending sentence works on the assumption that the human will was originally much "freer." Its present subjugation to the rule of "universal laws" and the resultant limitation on its rule over the body are a consequence of its having sinned—*post peccatum*—and having been divinely "ordered" to, i.e., assigned, a penal place among "lower" bodily realities. But among the four hypotheses on the soul's origin, Augustine's critics are arguing, such a "sin" (and punitive consequence) is a feature of

4. Note here the explicit reference to a pre-existent sin. Were we left only with the evidence of *Ep 143*, it might be impossible to decide whether his "critics" were simply impatient with Augustine's delaying tactics or held a counter-theory of their own. But the historical situation argues for the likelihood that these critics were Pelagians, holding a creationist view of the soul's origin, deducing from it the corollary of the soul's innocence, and arguing that Augustine's choice must lie with one or other of the "sinful" theories they repudiated: traducianism or (a variant of) Origen's "fall" theory. Read in the light of this probable polemical situation, Augustine's way of dealing with his critics becomes all the more fascinating—and gentlemanly.

5. This, it appears to me, answers convincingly Father Madec's objection that the fourth hypothesis of the *De libero arbitrio* is not clearly identical with this pre-existent–sin hypothesis; see REA, 21 (1975), 394, and chap. 1, note 40, above. But additional evidence of this identity will be found further on. O'Daly, "Origin," p. 185*n*10, fails to take this correspondence into consideration.

only two of them. This is obvious in the case of a "sinful fall" from a pre-existent state; but the traducianist hypothesis could also be made to imply that our souls were "included" in Adam's soul, so that each of us "sinned" in his sinning. But no such "sin" (on the part of the soul, at least) is involved in the other two hypotheses; whether the soul is "sent" by God from a pre-existent state or newly "created" for infusion into a newly conceived body, its innocence is assured. It is illuminating of Augustine's own understanding of his *De libero arbitrio* that he accepts without demur each of these suppositions his critics have brought to the interpretation of that work, and notably the implicit that his fourth hypothesis did indeed involve a "sin" on the part of the disembodied soul whereby it "merited" its embodied state. What line of defense does all this leave him?

He goes straight to their interpretation of the phrase *post peccatum*. Let them, he counsels, take another, closer look (*diligenter advertant*), for they were not alert enough to appreciate how "carefully phrased" (*perpensa*) the sentence on which they have built their argument was—so carefully, in fact, that it did not "give assent to any of those four opinions" on the soul's origin. They have interpreted that *post peccatum* as though he had written *post peccatum suum* or *posteaquam peccavit*. Either of these phrases, he is implicitly admitting, would have implied a sin committed *by the soul* itself. But the vaguer phrase *post peccatum* can just as validly refer to a sin of Adam and Eve, the soul's "parents in the flesh," and so accommodate itself to the two hypotheses they claim he had excluded (6).[6] For even if the soul itself was sinless, and either "created" or "sent" into a body, that body itself would be drawn from the new individual's "parents in the flesh" and ultimately from those first sinners, Adam and Eve. Hence, the body would be the kind of sinful flesh, mortal body, whose restriction on our free activity all of us experience.

BUT IF ADAM HAD AN "ANIMAL" BODY . . . ?

Augustine is therefore convinced he has demonstrated that in any of the four original hypotheses on the soul's origin, it would be

6. Note that Augustine himself proposes these forms of expression as incriminatory. But other expressions could be thought of, as long as they imply that souls are being punished for a sin they themselves have committed.

true that the will's power to rule the body actually suffered the diminution "after sin" he had argued for in *De libero arbitrio* 3.34. This would follow, he is arguing, whether or not the "sin" in question were the soul's *own* sin.

But now Augustine catches sight of a possible objection to his argument, for the offending paragraph had claimed that the pre-sinful body in question was a superior, heavenly body (*corpus coeleste*). Up to this point in *Letter 143*, he has used the term *spirituale* for that body, but nothing goes to indicate that he meant that term as anything but a synonym for the earlier *coeleste*. He now prefers the terms *spirituale* since (his closer acquaintance with Scripture tells him) it reflects Paul's distinction from 1 Corinthians 15:42–49. Augustine reads that passage as meaning that in *body* the first Adam was "animal," in contrast with Christ, the second Adam, who was "spiritual."

That Pauline affirmation, he recognizes, may run counter to his long-held supposition, the supposition encased in the offending paragraph, that man's original pre-sinful body must have been "spiritual" and therefore "celestial" in nature. It may have been created "animal," but his first interpretation of Genesis (2:10) insisted that it was then transferred to the "life of happiness" sym-bolized by the term "paradise," and transmuted into an immortal, "celestial" body. Now he must confront the possibility that this transmutation had "not yet" (*nondum*) been effected. Yet even on that reformed supposition, Augustine now affirms, his main con-tention in this letter remains untouched. For "Even if [*etiamsi*] the soul of that first man, before sin, did not yet [rule] a spiritual body, but an animal [body], it nevertheless ruled [*regebat*] as it willed"— that is, without the restrictions on liberty we now experience in ruling our sin-infected corruptible bodies (6).

The hypothetical flavor of this sentence evidently betrays a meas-ure of uncertainty on Augustine's part. He does not squarely *affirm* that Paul obliges us to believe that the first man's body was, in fact, "animal" *and therefore not* what he formerly meant by "celestial," but he must allow for that possibility. So, he argues, even if one interpret Paul's words as imposing the belief that the first man bore an animal body, his rule over that animal body must originally have been unhindered; indeed (Augustine's *regebat* in the indicative mood is bold), he *did* so enjoy unhindered rule. And so, the thesis of *De libero arbitrio* 3.34, that the first man experienced "after sin" a diminution of this unrestricted power to rule his body, remains true even on this new supposition.

But Augustine's bold indicative does not bear on the affirmation that the first man did, in fact, possess an "animal" body; he has left himself an escape route on that question. He is speaking in a manifestly hesitant, even hedging, tone of voice at this juncture; one wonders whether he has already begun to face the sobering problems which the *De Genesi ad litteram* will pose concerning the creation of Adam. In any event, his broader acquaintance with Scripture has begun to throw a series of roadblocks in the way of salvaging his earlier, more Plotinian view of man's first sin.

Moreover, when Augustine strives to assure us that Paul's teaching on "animal" and "spiritual" bodies is reconcilable with his own insistence that the soul's freedom was reduced "after sin"— whether the soul itself or an Adam who was "other" committed that sin—the modern reader is tempted to have second thoughts on whether Paul's teaching in 1 Corinthians is equally reconcilable with each of the original hypotheses Augustine has summarized at the head of this paragraph, and particularly with the fourth hypothesis. Augustine sees that, in the Pauline supposition he has entertained, "after sin" would have to mean "after sin would have been committed [*commissum esset*] in the animal flesh." That subjunctive, *commissum esset*, indicates that he is envisaging this possibility in a hypothethical vein; but the precise conclusion he draws is that the reduction of liberty he had affirmed years before would still obtain. But if the sin in question were in fact committed "in the flesh," the pre-incarnate sin of the fourth hypothesis would seem to be excluded, thus incriminating Augustine's claim that his expression *post peccatum* was reconcilable with *all four* hypotheses. There is no indication, though, that he caught scent of this precise difficulty when composing *Letter 143*. The question will return to bother him, however, while writing his *De Genesi ad litteram*.

WHY AUGUSTINE IS DELAYING PUBLICATION

We shall have to return to this exercise in self-defense further on; for the moment, Augustine seems confident that he has satisfied both his critics and Count Marcellinus. Marcellinus may rejoice;

Augustine has triumphed again! But let him be warned: this modest victory must not lull him into thinking that Augustine stands beyond all criticism, either in what he wrote in the *De libero arbitrio* or, *a fortiori*, in other works less carefully written which he may have "published too hastily." One expects him to pursue the question of the soul's origin further. Pursue it he will, but he interrupts the argument to reinforce the original point he was making on the dangers of too hasty publication. He begins with an ironic barb: the only ones with a genuine right to complain of the "carefully phrased" sentence he has just defended are the sort of people who set little value on such a concern with exactitude[7]—the sort who *now* "think that this same delay of mine in a matter so obscure should also be criticized." That obscurity, he assures both Marcellinus and others of his mind, bears not on the soul's immortality, or on its creaturely status; Augustine has "no doubt" of the former, and "hold[s] most firmly" to the latter, as well as to "other truths touching the *nature* of the soul." What, then, accounts for his delay in publishing both the *De Trinitate* and the *De Genesi*? It is, Augustine avows, precisely "the obscurity of this most darksome question about the origin [*exortu*] of the soul which forces me to act thus" (7).

But is this question still so "obscure" to him that he must even now leave all four hypotheses "open"? His critics, obviously, seem confident of some certainties on the soul which they claim have eluded the great Augustine. Does he still have the right to drag his feet on this issue, and deprive his clamorous public of the two great works he has been laboring on for all these years?

A "LESSON" IN EXEGETICAL METHOD

Augustine cannot evade the challenge. He takes it up by proposing an "example" (*exemplum*) to instruct his critics—and Marcellinus also—on the difficulties bedeviling this question. He selects a Scripture text that they will surely admit figures prominently in the debate between them. Ecclesiastes 12:7 speaks of death, when "dust returns to earth" and the "spirit returns to God Who gave it." What

---

7. Marcellinus surely did not miss the irony: he considers Augustine nearly infallible as compared with his hasty Carthaginian critics, and yet would not give him the time required to avoid the sort of hasty composition that would leave him exposed to such criticism. This letter was artfully composed.

does this text tell us about the soul's origin? Take the four hypotheses in turn; which of them does this text support?

The traducianist would presumably argue that "dust" refers to the body, while "spirit" refers to the soul. Let us grant him that for now. Grant, further, that there appears to be a parallelism working in the text: that at death both body and spirit return to where they came from. But we know that Adam's "body" was drawn from the "dust" of earth, and we agree that our bodies have all sprung by propagation from his. So, the traducianist reasons, the parallelism in the text implies that our souls must also have come from his, and by an analogous propagation. Hence, Ecclesiastes could be claimed to be supporting the first, or traducianist, hypothesis on the soul's origin (8).[8]

This same text, however, can be squared with the third hypothesis, i.e., that souls are "created *elsewhere* and given by God individually to individuals" (*alibi creatas singulis singulas Deus dat*). For this hypothesis seems to do justice to the soul's "return" to wherever it was before God "gave" it to its individual body (9).[9]

Prima facie, then, "the two remaining options" would seem to be excluded by this text (*videntur excludi*). Consider the creationist hypothesis first. If Scripture says God "gave" the soul, it is more natural to understand that term as implying that what was given was something first "outside" the body to which it was given. Had Scripture meant us to adopt the creationist theory—i.e., to understand that the individual soul was created "in" its individual body —it would better have said God "made" [*fecit*] the soul than "gave" it. Nor does this hypothesis seem to do full justice to the soul's "return" to God, since in this way of thinking it "never was there before" (*nunquam illic antea spiritus iste fuisse credendus est*). Tenants of the creationist hypothesis are obliged to interpret Scripture's *revertatur* as a simple *pergat* or *vadat*; but their opponents

---

8. Augustine here observes parenthetically that the *body*'s propagation from Adam's body is as clear as the *soul*'s origin remains obscure. Even when fairly exposing the traducianist mode of arguing, he cannot resist firing off this barb against them.

9. Note that while the *singillatim–singulis* language is more normally associated with creationist theory, the *alibi creatas* phrase seems clearly to imply the third hypothesis: that innocent souls are "created elsewhere" and "sent" into bodies. But as time goes on, we shall see, Augustine tends to interpret creationism in his own peculiar way, as a kind of amalgam of these two theories.

The expression of all this in *Ep 143* 9 is more condensed than I report here; I am anticipating the fuller detail Augustine supplies slightly further on.

press their case, insisting on the proper meaning of the term (*urgent verbo et premunt*) (9).[10]

Nor would it seem that the fourth hypothesis (of voluntary sinful "fall") is in a much better state; "it is not easy to explain how souls voluntarily fall [*sponte labantur*] into the body" when Scripture says God "gave" the soul.

Augustine's critics might, at this point, be tempted to conclude that the Ecclesiastes text definitively excluded the second (creationist) and fourth (voluntary–sinful fall) hypotheses. After all, one has a right to some certainties on this question (and Marcellinus, good reasons for nagging Augustine on his hesitations). But Augustine stands to his guns. The foregoing analysis is not so conclusive as it first appears; a more searching examination is still called for. The two hypotheses his readers might think "excluded" are, he admits, in difficulty, even distress (*laborant*). It would take some "work" to bring them into consonance with the expressions found in Ecclesiastes; whereas the first and third (traducianist and "sent–given by God") hypotheses "fit in with those words [of Ecclesiastes] without any labor" being required (*sine labore verba ista coaptantur*).[11] But even so, it would be premature to draw any firm conclusion from those indications. We must go over the ground more carefully, and relate the expressions used here to wider Scriptural usage. Consider the term "gave." Initially, it seems to import that what was given was originally "outside" that to which it was given. But the creationist, Augustine reminds his readers, might legitimately object to that inference. Scripture tells us God "gave" us eyes and ears and hands, but does not thereby compel us to suppose God made a supply of eyes and ears somewhere "outside" our bodies, and only then "added them on, or joined them to," bodies we must imagine as previously without them. No, we understand this gift to mean that God made our eyes and ears "in" the body, to which, nonetheless, He is rightly said to have "given" them (*illic fecit in corpore, cui dedisse illa dicitur*) (10).[12] Surely nothing pre-

10. Notice that Augustine's expression of creationist theory is exact here: the soul did not exist *before* its (simultaneous) creation–infusion into the body. The same is true of his expression of this hypothesis in *Lib*. See note 9, above.

11. Augustine's reliance on the exact force of the Latinisms employed by Bible translators is typical of his exegetical "method."

12. Notice once again the exactitude of his appreciation of creationist theory: the soul is not created and *then* infused into the body.

vents the creationist from understanding God's "giving" of the soul on parallel terms: that God creates each individual soul "in" its appropriate body. Augustine, for his part at least, can think of no solid objection to that proposal. And, he is gently insinuating, his self-assured critics may, on a little reflection, find themselves in a like state of dubiety.

A similar defense can be proposed for the fourth hypothesis as well. Those who "think that souls voluntarily flow down into bodies" (in corpora sponte defluere) may validly claim the right to interpret God's "giving" the soul in the sense implied by Paul's "God gave them up [tradidit] to the concupiscence of their heart" (Rom. 1:24). Souls may sinfully choose to leave their place of pre-embodied existence, while God merely consents as it were to the desire—the "concupiscence"—which draws them down into the bodily world. He "gives them up" or "over" to those desires, yields them to, by yielding to their desire for, embodied existence. Augustine poses no objection to that rejoinder; it bears striking resemblance to his own dimissio motif. Have his critics, though, even considered it as a possibility?

Augustine can now feel that this lesson in exegetical method has shown that, contrary to their overly hasty interpretations, Ecclesiastes does, after all, leave all four hypotheses still "open." But he has not quite finished. One troubling term still creates difficulty (unum verbum relinquitur); that term is revertatur. For, in the creationist view,[13] it is not clear "how that word is to be understood." How can it be said that the soul "returns" to God, to "where it never was before"? Such a "return" in the literal sense would seem to be excluded by the creationist theory that "souls are made, each in its [individual] body." So, "This single word puts one of these four [hypotheses] into difficulties." And yet, one should be cautious still: "I do not think that, on account of that one word, this [creationist] opinion ought rashly to be rejected"—for (again)

---

13. If, as seems more than likely, his critics were Pelagians and therefore creationists, Augustine's maneuvering at this point is a work of art. He first shows them that Scripture, closely read, puts their favored theory into difficulty, then helps them out of the trap Scripture seems to have laid for them, all the while succeeding subtly in making the point he is beginning to see as crucial: it is much more from an attentive interpretation of Scripture and less from their resort to human reasoning that this difficult question must be settled.

a consideration of wider Scriptural usage ought first to be undertaken. "It might be possible to show that this ['return'] could rightly be spoken of" if we uncovered some turn of speech which "Scripture is accustomed to use, such that the created spirit's return be understood as to God as the Author Who created it rather than as Someone with Whom [*apud quem*] it existed originally" (10).[14]

Augustine cannot resist one final volley on the theme of his own indecision about "this most obscure question concerning the soul." Let those who would blame that indecision (*cunctatio*) present him with such evidences from Scripture as "cannot be understood otherwise" than as supporting their position, or such clear proofs from reason "as only a madman would reject." But if they cannot bring such remedies to his ignorance (*imperitia*), let them at least not complain against his hesitation in settling on his own position in the matter.

THE MESSAGE OF Letter 143

Letter 143, therefore, sheds light on a number of questions which, until now, begged for clarification. The question of the soul's origin, Augustine admits, may conceivably be settled by reason, but he demands (hyperbolically?) that the proofs advanced be such that only a "madman" could resist them. The main thrust of his argument, though, is directed toward examining what Scripture has to say on the question, and defending his resolve to persist in his attitude of hesitation (*cunctatio*). The tenor of his argument suggests strongly, moreover, that this open-minded attitude extends to all four regnant hypotheses; the text from Ecclesiastes, he artfully reminds his critics, would even seem to favor, albeit ever so slightly, the hypothesis that our souls are fallen on account of some sin committed in a pre-existent state! But his main challenge to his critics is this: let them produce some text from Scripture which

14. Augustine here makes a more generous concession to his critics than they have made in their interpretation of him. But that concession raises a question: Did he himself, in his earlier understanding of Ecclesiastes' reference to the soul's "return," favor the literal interpretation that would imply the soul's having been created "elsewhere" and therefore having either "fallen" or "been sent" into the body? See, for example, his allusion to this text in his *Retr* comment (1.1.3) on a phrase in *Acad*. It would be perilous to assume that the convert of 386 was as abreast of these issues as the bishop of 427 had become in the meantime.

will unambiguously settle the matter. Is it too adventurous to infer
that he himself, at this writing, knows of no such text?

He will later come to "see" (for a time at least) the text from
Romans 9:11 as peremptorily excluding the "fallen-soul" hypothesis. Once he does so, he begins to apply that text unhesitatingly
and repeatedly to reject that view. Are we to suppose that he was
even now aware of that text as bearing on the issue his critics have
raised, but for some reason forbore to call it to their attention? If
his point was to instruct his critics, not merely to neutralize their
criticism of him, that alternative goes down hard, and it becomes
even more difficult to understand why he would conduct so careful
an exegetical exercise on a text that leaves that offending hypothesis
in slightly better posture than its competitors. In *Letter 140 32*,
written in the same year, he confesses that the question of the soul's
origin remains "obscure" to him; no mention of Romans 9:11 intervenes to qualify that judgment. There is every likelihood, accordingly, that *Letter 143* betrays the same open-mindedness on the
entire question.[15]

But *Letter 143* also conveys more precise knowledge of Augustine's reasons for delaying publication of his *De Trinitate*, and
of his *De Genesi ad litteram* as well. In *Letter 120*, to Consentius,
it seemed to be a matter of wondering how one might rise from
knowledge of the human soul—or, more exactly, its highest spiritual part, the intellectual mind—to an understanding of the Trinity
in whose "image" it was created. Now, in the letter to Marcellinus,
Augustine acknowledges the focus of his difficulty even more precisely: he has seen, or perhaps more recently come to see, that in
both works he is forced to deal with a set of "most dangerous questions"; but then, becoming much more specific, he attributes his
delay directly to the "obscure" matter that has engaged his attention throughout this letter, the origin of the soul (7).[16]

15. "Likelihood" may seem a cautious judgment to draw from all this; my reason
is that Augustine's reply to his critics does seem, after all, on the disingenuous side.
See below.

16. Compare *Ep 143* 3 and 11. This question of the soul's origin, Augustine is
astute enough to see, could not but affect the related question: What is meant by
saying the soul was created in the "image" of God? That related question, we shall
see, lies at the heart of *Trin*; hence, the laborious attempt in the *GenLitt* to resolve
both questions.

A CLOSER LOOK AT *De libero arbitrio* 3.34

But *Letter 143* prods us to learn more, I submit, than Augustine may have intended to tell us. Ecclesiastes 12:7, the very text he later cites in his *Retractations* to fend off a "fall and return" interpretation of his *Contra Academicos*,[17] quite obviously held a different message for him now from what it did later; his last word insinuates that, while that text initially appears reconcilable with any of the four, it speaks, on closer scrutiny, more strongly for the "fall" hypothesis than for the other three. Does this suggest that Augustine, even now, had a preferential lean toward that fourth hypothesis? The point should not be pressed too far. But what of his preference when writing his *De libero arbitrio*? That question calls for a closer look at the argument he presents to defend himself against his Carthaginian critics.

Surely he would have been well-advised to adopt the argumentative strategy he lays claim to here: it would have weakened his case to argue *from* a controversial view on the souls' origin in order to put God's justice beyond the reach of controversy. But our examination of the *De libero arbitrio* brought us seriously to question whether he truly managed to apply that strategy consistently.

Augustine refrains here from mentioning what he admits in *De dono perseverantiae* 29: that his own preferred theory to account for this reduction in the human soul's "freedom" had been, and remained, a "penal" theory—one that would imply a choice between exactly the two "sinful" hypotheses his Carthaginian critics attribute to him. Further, he admits in that work, he let his preference clearly show in writing the *De libero arbitrio*; the most cursory reading of *De libero arbitrio* 3, as we have seen, supports that contention. Everything, up until the introduction of the Adam–Eve objection in 3.53, supposes a direct link between the soul's own "sin" and the just punishment represented by its present unhappy condition. Such a direct link was, in fact, Augustine's most cogent way of demonstrating against the Manichees that God was not unjust; that concern, we have seen, he shared with Origen as well as with others in the *Catholica*, and it *could* have led him, like them, to account for the evils of our embodied existence as punish-

17. *Retr* 1.1.3; see note 14, above.

ments for a sin our souls must have committed in their pre-embodied state. A similar concern for God's justice commanded his first interpretation of Romans 9:11, which was roughly contemporaneous with *De libero arbitrio* 3. Finally, everything in *Letter 143* suggests that Augustine still considers the "fall" hypothesis just as acceptable for a Catholic thinker as its three competitors.

But the *De dono perseverantiae* also claims that he had earlier treated the penal theory in a hypothetical vein. This amounts to asking us to come upon the *si* in his *si naturalis est* of *De libero arbitrio* 3.64[18] and take it as a signal instructing us to supply an absent corresponding *si* much earlier, at 3.51, then to revise our understanding of paragraphs 3.51–52, shifting all their categorical language about our penal condition into a hypothetical key. A structural anomaly, as we have seen; but doesn't it demand of the reader a feat of mental gymnastics that is psychologically almost impossible? Now, however, he is asking even more: he is asking us to perform the same trick as early as paragraph 3.34, and to read a compromising phrase there as though its understanding were commanded by the same attitude of hypothetical abstention for which he will give the reader the appropriate signal only some twenty-two paragraphs further on, in 3.56!

Not only is there no signal whatever as early as 3.34 to prompt the "hypothetical" reading of that paragraph Augustine now requires of us; there are plenty of signals—but they would all encourage exactly the understanding his Carthaginian critics brought to that paragraph, and to its context, both immediate and remote. Augustine is asking us to read his *post peccatum* of 3.34 as though its interpretation were already commanded by the hypothetical suspension governing his treatment of the soul's origin, from 3.56 to 3.63; his critics have no right to infer that the "sin" being spoken of was the soul's "own" sin. But did Marcellinus' report of this criticism focus so narrowly, and with such isolated attention, on that single phrase in 3.34?[19] We cannot know that for certain, but it serves Augustine well to keep the focus exactly that narrow. For

---

18. Note that the "if" (*si*) of *Lib* 3.56 (introducing the "first" hypothesis) could conceivably be interpreted as commanding the entirety of the *preceding* paragraphs 51–52; but the price of that conception would be a structural tangle even more inextricable than the one I am supposing here.

19. It seems likely that Marcellinus sent a condensed report of this whole matter, so that Augustine felt entitled to limit the focus of his reply to the terms of that report.

there are clear signals in the immediate context which point to the view his critics have adopted; indeed, it would be asking the psychologically impossible of the reader to interpret them in any other sense. A review of that context may show what I mean.

Augustine is replying[20] to a third question Evodius had raised sometime earlier (3.9): How can we hold God guiltless of those things in His creation which happen by "necessity"? He has begun his reply to this third question at 3:12. It takes the form of sketching the marvelous "order" prevailing among the hierarchical strata of that creation, from highest angel down through sinful man to brute and material creatures. Some, Augustine takes note, would hold God blameworthy for creating souls He foreknew would sin and would suffer misery as punishment for their sin. That punishment consists in their being consigned to a lower place in the ordered creation than they previously occupied, to govern the inferior bodily realities there. Couldn't one argue that "sin" was "necessary" to ensure the governance of those bodily realities, hence, for the ordered perfection of the universe (3.24–25)? No, Augustine replies, it was souls *qua* souls that were necessary for that hierarchic order, and the punishment of sinful souls takes the form of assigning them the "place" in that order appropriate to them, so that the beauty of the universe remains intact (3.26–27). Augustine presents a few examples of this beauteous order (3.27–31), including that of Christ's redemptive activity, then continues in the same vein. God is Creator of the natures of all beings that exist, and He assigns them functions appropriate to each of them in order to ensure the order of the universe (3.32–35).

It is in this precise section that the litigious phrase *post peccatum* occurs. But notice that from 3.12 forward Augustine has been answering the question why God should be held blameless for creating future sinners whose punishment necessarily makes them correspondingly miserable. The supposition throughout is that their sin was freely committed, and everything conspires to encourage the connected supposition that their freely committed sin was "their own" and not "another's"—Adam's, for example. The possi-

20. My summary here quite deliberately represents a virtual paraphrase of the outline furnished by Father Madec in his edition of *Lib*, in BA 6, pp. 168–69. It so happens that I find his outline a good one, even if a trifle elliptical at crucial points. Those ellipses I have taken the liberty of filling in by consultation with Augustine's text.

bility that Adam and Eve were "others"—not at all necessary to, or necessarily envisaged by, the "fallen soul" theory—enters the discussion only much later, at paragraph 3.53. No indication is given to the reader at any point in the entire preceding development that he should be reading all this with that later consideration kept firmly in mind; every expression authorizes, even imposes, the interpretation that Augustine's defense of the Creator makes sense on the supposition that the sinners being punished sinned freely, and of *their own* volition.[21]

Now, Augustine in *Letter 143* admits that his critics would have a case had he used expressions like *peccatum suum* and *posteaquam peccavit*. But in the very section under consideration, which runs from 3.32 to 3.35, Augustine divides created spiritual creatures into two classes: the "first" never sinned, the "second" did. Both classes have the cosmic function of "governing" the inferior, sensible world, so that *all* created natures should contribute to the universal beauty "whether they willed to sin or not to sin" (*sive peccare sive non peccare voluissent*) (3.32). God foreknew that the "second" class would sin (*peccatura praecognita est*), but made them, not that they might sin (*non ut peccarent*), but that, even as sinners, they should still make their contribution from the place and in the manner appropriate to their changed condition (3.33).

At this juncture Augustine comes to the vital phrase. He speaks of these spiritual creatures of the "second" class as once joined to the "first" class in the government of the lower bodily world, but "ordered" *post peccatum*, "after sin," among "lower, mortal bodies." They still retain a governance function over that inferior world of bodies, but their freedom and power have been diminished. This sinful "soul" (*anima*) has been condemned to wear the vesture of a "slave," is now "weighed down with mortal members, is scarcely able to govern the body that oppresses it" (3.34).[22] That language,

21. See chap. 1, note 20, above; none of these incriminatory phrasings corresponds *exactly* with the two Augustine offers his critics in this letter, but their force is surely as incriminatory as his two examples.

22. Augustine is combining here the well-known Neoplatonic theme of the body as "vesture" of the (fallen) soul, his own interpretation of the clothing of "animal skins" (the vesture of "mortality") the God of Genesis wove for Adam and Eve after their sin, and the image from Wis. 9:15 depicting the "corruptible body" as "weighing down" the soul (note the terms *premit, onerata*). Compare *Conf* 7.23, where in a like context the terms from Wisdom are exactly quoted as *deprimit* and *adgravat*, respectively. Compare Madec, BA 6, p. 449n51.

so similar to that in which the *De Genesi contra Manichaeos*[23] describes man's condition after the fall, leaves little doubt that this second class of spiritual creatures refers to human "souls." That soul now finds its power of operating on other, surrounding bodily entities "far weaker" that it was before sin reduced it to this punitive condition (3.34).

But (the objection returns) this is nonetheless both a "place" and a function that contribute to the beauteous order of the universe: were not man's sin and punishment, therefore, necessary to ensure that this place and function be filled? No, Augustine answers. Even if these human souls "had refused to sin" (*peccare noluisset*), they would still have fulfilled their governing function, but in the higher and more powerful manner they exercised before. But even regarding the class of spiritual creatures whom God foresaw would never sin and by sinning abandon their loftier governance of the lower world, our reason tells us that their abstention from sin is the work of free will, a matter of choice and not of being forced (*a peccato illam libera voluntate abstinere neque coactam non peccare sed sponte*). And, *a fortiori*, the reader is tempted to add, the sin of human souls must equally have been the work of their own "free will," and no one else's. His Carthaginian critics were perfectly entitled to supply the implied "their own" to fill out Augustine's more lapidary, but still incriminating, "after sin," *post peccatum*. For while never actually using the precise terms *post peccatum suum* or *posteaquam peccavit*—terms he has implicitly admitted would have given his case away—Augustine has applied a host of terms which are surely their equivalents.

Letter 143 AND THE FOURTH HYPOTHESIS

A redoubtable Augustinian scholar has recently warned his readers that Augustine's reply in *Letter 143* should make them very wary of the "adventurous" inference that Augustine ever preferred his own fourth hypothesis: that we were "fallen souls."[24] Quite the contrary. Augustine's reply here invites us to look more closely at

23. See *GenMan*, esp. 2.30, and *Early Theory*, pp. 161–66 for documentation and supporting analysis.
24. See Madec, in BA 6, pp. 578–83, esp. p. 582; also, my reply to this precise argumentation, "The Origin of the Soul in Saint Augustine's *Letter 143*," RÉA 28 (1982), 239–52.

the *De libero arbitrio* than he might have liked us to do, and to find
clear confirmation of what he might not have wanted us to find

We have seen that the structural anomalies of *De libero arbitrio*
3, when taken as a real problem, suggest the possibility that the
portions preceding paragraph 3.53 (where those anomalies first
assert themselves) might betray the simpler, more straightforward
intention that presided over the original composition of the work.
Now we have come to see that the very sentence to which Augustine
later appeals to dissuade us from adopting such a view actually
encourages our doing so; it is encased in a context, both immediate
and remote, which unquestionably supposes a penal explanation
of our human experience. That penal explanation, moreover, is
expressed in precisely the terms we would expect, not from a traducianist, but from a "fallen soul" advocate: human souls once
existed as a class of spiritual creatures, governing with the angels
the entirety of the lower, bodily world. They sinned, and God's
ordering power replied to that sin by assigning them a "lower"
place with the more restricted and laborious type of freedom appropriate to that lower world. Now weighed down by the mortal body,
and acting amid and upon other mortal bodies, the soul finds both
its power and "liberty" enfeebled to the point where it can scarcely
govern that very body, the "slave's vesture" it has been "condemned" to wear.[25]

The "ignorance and difficulty" of Augustine's later considerations have already entered the discussion under different names,
but here their genuinely, "properly" penal character is unambiguously affirmed. Complications will later enter to confuse the picture, but at this point Augustine's explanation of our condition is
beset with no such complications or confusions. The hypothesis on
the soul's "incarnation" which he clearly prefers is the fourth
hypothesis: we once dwelt aloft with angels, we sinned, and we fell
into this lower world of mortal and oppressive bodies. The hypoth-

---

25. There is an echo here (*veste* . . . *in honore magno apud dominum*) of Augustine's interpretation of the *stola prima*, the first garment the Prodigal received (*back*)
on his return to his Father. We shall have occasion to see that his interpretation of
that "first garment" (i.e., the spiritual, incorruptible body which the soul wore in
its pre-existent bliss) reflects the very circularity implied by the theory of the soul's
fall and return, with the result that his doubts about that theory are reflected in a
different interpretation of the *stola prima*.

esis earlier proposed for interpreting *De libero arbitrio* 3 has gained the right to be considered a thesis.

But what explains this flare-up of interest in the question of the soul's "origin"? And who were these Carthaginian critics? The background of the times suggests a quite plausible answer to both those questions. It is 412, or 411 at the earliest; by this time Pelagius has come and gone from Carthage, but he has left his fiery lieutenant, Caelestius, behind him. Caelestius pursues his attacks on the African theology of infant baptism "for the remission of sin." Very likely he buttressed those attacks by appeal to his master's view that infant souls were newly created and therefore sinless; likely, too, he proclaimed Pelagius' conviction that the Origenist "fall" of souls was little but a theological nightmare, and traducianism a sad product of Africa's backwater theology. What a delight it would have been to convict Augustine, the current champion of African theology, of one or other of these obsolescent theories! No longer is the soul's origin a harmless issue for leisurely speculation; Pelagianism has turned this "darksome question" into a very "dangerous" one. Augustine's admirers must give him time to make sure his treatment of it, in his *De Genesi* and *De Trinitate*, is unobjectionable.

This seriously altered thought-situation may account for Augustine's less than ingenuous reply to Marcellinus. He once preferred a theory, one that served him well in his polemic against the heretics who thoroughly absorbed his attention, the Manichees. For all he knew then, he had every right to hold it confidently and serenely. Later, he learned of other possibilities, and did his best to deal with them, however maladroitly, as counter-hypotheses tacked on to his *De libero arbitrio*. But now a new heresy has arisen, shocking him into the realization that the question of the soul's origin was far more "dangerous" than he had once thought. Openly admitting[26] that his Pelagian critics were on the right track might

26. We moderns have constantly to keep in mind that a letter, and particularly a letter of this sort, could not in the ancient world be considered a private document. Augustine is keenly aware he is writing for a "public," as much as or even more than when writing to Volusian: see above.

have given them the sort of encouragement that did his African flock more harm than good. Marcellinus, it appears, asked him a very precise question about a very precise sentence in his earlier work. To that precise question, Augustine may have thought it wise to give an equally precise answer, one that did not lie; it simply did not tell the whole truth. But Augustine's reply did more than that; it shifted the discussion from the terrain of "reason," to which the Pelagians so confidently appealed, to that of Scriptural faith. That shift, we shall see, was a decisive one for the future of this entire controversy.

A letter written some years afterward informs us of Marcellinus' reaction to all this.[27] If Augustine cannot settle the issue, perhaps the learned Jerome, in Bethlehem, may shed some light on it. Marcellinus writes to Jerome, accordingly, inquiring about his views on the soul's origin; Jerome replies; that reply is duly communicated to Augustine. But Augustine cannot rest satisfied with Jerome's solution, and so, in 415—some time after Marcellinus' death[28]—he writes bravely to Jerome, "consulting" him on the question.

But in the meantime, events in Africa refuse to stand still, and events from the wider world make their influence felt even more strongly. A messenger from that wider world is about to present himself at Augustine's doorstep; the information he brings will bear on several of the issues Augustine has become concerned with. He will give the bishop much to think about.

27. See *Ep 190* 20–21, to Optatus.
28. It would seem doubtful that Marcellinus himself ever had the opportunity to read Jerome's reply; *Ep 165* was more than likely "forwarded" to Augustine by Marcellinus' family.

4

AUGUSTINE CONTINUES TO HESITATE

PAUL OROSIUS SEEMS, clearly, to have arrived in Africa sometime in the year 414;[1] he was anxious to "consult" Augustine about some teachings both of the Priscillianists and of certain "Origenists," then causing something of a furor in his native Spain. He has summarized these questionable teachings in a *Commonitorium*,[2] and Augustine replies to a selected number of the points presented there.

One of the doctrines attributed to Origen argues that the punishment of the "devil and his angels" will not, after all, be everlasting—and this, despite the Matthaean expression *in ignem aeternum, qui paratus est diabolo et angelis ejus.* The *aeternum* in that expression could, the Origenists argued, be interpreted as meaning "long-lasting" (*diuturnum*), not strictly "everlasting." Augustine replies with a series of considerations on the language of Scripture, both in Latin and in Greek, to refute this contention. He clinches his case, however, by retorting the Origenist contention: for if our merciful instincts persuade us to make "eternal" punishment merely "long-lasting," the same logic could be used to buttress the frightening claim that the eternal reward of the just is equally non-everlasting! "Are we to say that the just, as well, will fall back once more from their sanctification and life eternal into the uncleanness

1. See Augustine's opening to *Ep 166* (reliably dated from 415) introducing Orosius to Jerome.
2. His *Commonitorium* should clearly be viewed as a summary; it would be a mistake to think it contains all that Augustine learned from Orosius. Augustine's reply is contained in *Oros.* I give the paragraph numbers of the latter in the text, reserving text references to Orosius' work to the notes.

of sin and into death?" Away with such unhealthy thinking. *Absit hoc a chrisianae fidei sanitate* (7).

ORIGEN ON CREATION

Among the other Origenisms that engage his attention is the theory propounded to explain the origin of the visible creation. Orosius' sentence here is terse in the extreme: after treating of God's creation of spiritual beings, he adds that the Origenists hold that "The world"—evidently the visible cosmos—"was made last, and in such wise that souls, which had previously sinned, might be purified in it."[3] Augustine, in his reply, links this theory of creation with the related Origenist contention—also presented in Orosius' *Commonitorium*[4]—that all "rational creatures," whether holy angels or unclean demons, or human souls themselves, merited a higher place in this creation in proportion to the lightness (or absence) of their sinful fault. He does not see, Augustine avows, "with what impudence they will try to persuade Christ's Church" of that view.

> It is better, therefore, for us to believe that God was not brought to fashioning the world by sins of rational creatures, lest these absurdities follow, [namely,] that it would have been necessary to have two suns, or three, or four, or whatever number [you choose], if a greater number of spirits had preceded [the creation of those suns] with a freely chosen [sin] of [just] so great a culpability as required their insertion into heavenly orbs [that] similar—

that is, of equal rank and dignity.

It is, then, better for us to believe that

> the world was made by God's goodness, made great, and good, by the highest and unmade Goodness, and that in it all things were made very good, [each] according to [its] nature, some better than others, [but all] ordered in distinct grades from the highest to the

3. *Mundum novissime ideo esse factum, ut in eo animae purgarentur quae ante peccaverunt (Commonitorium* 3). The *ante* seems clearly to imply that souls sinned before the creation of the visible world which was, therefore, created precisely to function as their purgatorial prison. The pre-existent sin of souls is here linked tightly with a view of God's motive in creating the visible world; that linkage must be borne in mind in what follows.

4. Ibid. (the sentence immediately preceding that in note 3, above): [*Dixerunt*] *vel archangelo vel animae vel daemoni locum pro meritorum qualitate datum esse, utentes hoc verbo: "maiorem locum minor culpa promeruit."*

lowest of creatures, so that, in this way, *all* things should exist, since higher realities would not alone exist; and they should [thus] have a limit to their number, which God, the establisher of all created natures, saw in Himself as [the number] to be determined upon, He Who did not [subsequently] learn [from them] that they had been made, but knew them [antecedent to their creation] as what ought to be made [8.9].

It is significant for understanding the exact point of Augustine's reply that he looks on Origen as proposing not so much a theory of the soul's origin as a theory explaining the resulting order of created realities, once one accepts his thesis concerning God's "motive" for creating the visible portions of creation. This is why he marshals here, not a counter-theory about the soul, but his own favorite defense of the *omnia*, the hierarchically ordered "all" that God created.

AUGUSTINE'S PREVIOUS IGNORANCE OF ORIGEN

Mlle La Bonnardière has remarked that "the tone of Augustine's replies" in the *Ad Orosium* "most often manifests the surprise of a man informed for the first time" of Origen's errors.[5] Augustine was, in 398–399, still ignorant of the anti-Origenist crisis in the East; since then, he has repeatedly asked Jerome for light on Origen's dangerous teachings, but our examination of the correspondence with Jerome makes it doubtful how illuminating he was. How unilluminating, Augustine's startled expressions here reveal. The refutations in his *Ad Orosium* do not, as Courcelle has ob-

5. See "Jérome Informateur," 49–50. This would be somewhat difficult to understand had Augustine to hand since 411/412 (as Mlle La Bonnardière believes, pp. 46 and 50) the *De fide* of Rufinus "the Syrian." There, in paragraphs 21 and 27, he would already have encountered Rufinus' censures on several of these doctrinal points. Here, however, Mlle La Bonnardière seems to have reposed too much trust in Refoulé's unquestioning acceptance of 411/412 as the reliable date for Augustine's own *Mer*. Postpone that date, and more coherent sense can be made of Mlle La Bonnardière's presentation of the evidence (pp. 44–45) that Augustine remained ignorant of the anti-Origenist crisis at least until the year 399, and that *Ep 166* (in 415) shows the first peremptory evidence we have that Augustine may finally have taken stock of what Jerome had written against Origen's "fall" theory in the third book of his *Apologia* against Rufinus. The evidence for Jerome's having sent this third book to Augustine as early as the year 402, however, seems to me more porous than this outstandingly careful scholar estimates. See above, chap. 2, note 17.

served, suppose any direct "personal knowledge" of Origen on Augustine's part prior to Orosius' account of his teachings in his *Commonitorium* [6] If he himself had shared, up to this time, any of Origen's own views, he would have done so unwittingly and innocently.

There is another feature of his replies here which is significant for our purposes: whether dealing with the non-eternity of punishment or the Origenist theory of visible creation, Augustine is compelled to fall back on a theological argument. *Absit*, he expostulates in the first instance, and in the second, marvels at the *impudentia* of the Origenist contention; yet, despite this shocked surprise, his only resource is to develop his own theological understanding of eternal beatitude and of God's creation of the visible world against the understanding embodied in the Origenist position. His shock is genuine, but his conclusion must remain disproportionately mild: "it is better [*melius*] for us to believe" otherwise. One senses that, had he a more peremptory way of refuting these views—one unambiguous text from Scripture, say—he would have made much shorter work of them! Origen's adversaries, we have seen, claimed the right to make exactly that short work of this theory; Romans 9:11, about Jacob's "election," testified against him, and that was that. But there is no indication that Augustine has yet seen that text as bearing on this issue.

Suggestive, too, is Augustine's sensitivity to any view that would cast doubt on the unending security of our ultimate beatitude; this he quickly sees as endangered by the Origenist interpretation of the term "eternal." It is unclear whether Augustine has detected that this danger also arises in connection with the Origenist theory of the visible creation; he does not yet seem aware that the "fall" of sinful spirits into the visible world, prepared for them as a kind of "purgatory," is tied up (in Origenism)[7] with a more general cyclic view of the career of souls that would fall, return, and quite conceivably fall again. But when, some time later, he comes to see that implication, his reaction to it will be an even more passionate *absit*. For the moment, though, he does not deal with the theory of the

6. See his *Les Lettres greques en Occident, de Macrobe à Cassiodore* (Paris: de Boccard, 1943), pp. 185–87, but esp. 186n3.
7. As Augustine came later to understand Origen; see below.

soul's pre-existence and fall directly and as such; nor does he show any discomfort directed precisely toward the possibility that our souls *may* have pre-existed their entrance into bodies. Rather, he aims his attack on the more general Origenist theory of God's creation of the visible world. Against Origen's theory he can pit only his personal counter-*theory*: that the visible world was created both great and good, the divine motivation for its creation being God's own goodness, a goodness that willed the ordered "all" to exist, and not simply higher, spiritual realities.

THE *Omnia* ARGUMENT

We have already noted that this argument from the "all" has a history that goes back to the *Confessions* and beyond, to the *De libero arbitrio*.[8] Its compelling force was one reason why the *libri Platonicorum* helped him quash his Manichaean complaints about the very existence of the visible cosmos of "lower" realities. This lower, visible world the Manichees looked upon as an arena of evils and suffering for souls, very like the purgatorial "prison" Origenist teaching made it out to be. The Manichees accounted for our presence in this lower world without assigning any culpability on the part of our souls; but Origenism traced our presence and relative "position" in visible reality to the kind and seriousness of the sin our souls committed in their pre-embodied existence. Augustine, we have seen, had considerable sympathy with this "penal" explanation of our presence in "this" bodily world. But common to both Origenism and Manichaeism was the fundamental conviction that in one way or another the visible world should never have existed, that an all-good God would never have created such a world, unless somehow driven to it.

This was the estimate of the visible world from which Augustine's pondering of Plotinus' *Enneads* had liberated him. He has found Scriptural support for Plotinus' more optimistic view implied in Genesis' phrase that, having finished creating "all" things, God found them, precisely as an "all," very good. But here he seems to betray an awareness that his interpretation of that Biblical expression is partially dependent on taking that view of it which

8. See 3.12–46, but more especially 12–13 and 24–25; see also chap. 1, note 9, above.

Plotinus' argument encouraged. This may be the underlying reason for the rather mild commendation of his conclusion: all he feels entitled to say is that it is "bettei" for us to "believe" this way.[9]

Is it so clear, however, that Augustine's argument from the *omnia* notion so closely parallels Plotinus' own that one must interpret the former in the light of the latter? Opinions will differ on this; but as long as even a reasonable plausibility exists that Augustine's theory is in fact patterned on Plotinus', an air of caution must affect all our inferences about the *Ad Orosium*. It would be tempting to infer that Augustine's rejection of the Origenist account of visible creation logically implies a parallel rejection of the view that our souls were "fallen" into that visible world, owing to some fault committed in their pre-existent state.[10] We must go slowly here. The one position does not logically imply the other, or, at least, did not so imply it in the atmosphere of the time. For Plotinus, who knew something of logical implication, rejected something very like Origen's estimate of the visible world, and still held that our souls' presence in it must be explained—in part at least—as the result of a "fall." This may seem difficult for us to understand; the ambiguities of Plotinus' theory are at times baffling, but it is a hazardous business to impose our inferences on third- and fourth-century minds, like Plotinus'—or like Augustine's. Sagacity recommends that we be more cautious for the moment; the future devel-

9. The expression used of this *omnia* argument in *Conf* 7:19, in a section that bristles with such strong cognitive language as *vidi, cognovi, manifestatum est mihi,* etc., is curiously muted: *iudicio saniore pendebam.*

10. This is the conclusion that Mlle La Bonnardière seems (unwarily, I submit) to have drawn in her "Jérome Informateur," 46n3. She cites a number of texts from works that will concern us further on, but she finds this "rejection" expressed or implied in *Oros* 7 (where Augustine is inveighing *directly* against the non-eternity of our eventual beatitude) and 10 (where his *direct* target is Origen's connected theory of cyclic creation–fall–and–reintegration). One could hold, and it is my contention that Augustine did hold, a theory of fallen soul cleanly divorced from these two objectionable features: so, the only text Mlle La Bonnardière adduces from *Oros* which initially appears directly relevant to that precise issue is from paragraph 9; but I have tried to show that Augustine's direct point there has to do with God's motive for creating the visible world as part of the *omnia*. There is no contradiction between his affirming that creative intention and believing at the same time that our presence in this visible "lower" world is the result of our having sinned and fallen. See my "St. Augustine's Criticism of Origen in the *Ad Orosium*," REA, 30 (1984), 84–99 for ampler treatment of these issues.

opment of this question will show that sagacity to have been wisdom. For the story of the next few years in Augustine's development amply illustrates how uncertain he remained on the precise issue of the soul's origin.

THE SUSPENSE CONTINUES

Augustine's correspondence during the next two years allows us glimpses of his groping progress on this troubling question. *Letter 157*, to Hilarius of Sicily, written in 414, deals with a cluster of Pelagian issues, among them the question that will come more and more to torment Augustine: What of the fate of infants who die without baptism? Hilarius has reported the view of "certain Christians at Syracuse"—obviously Pelagian sympathizers—"that an unbaptized infant cut off by death cannot justly be deprived of heaven, because it is born without sin."[11] No, Augustine replies, it is "better to believe the Apostle than to believe those objectors"—that all, infants among them, are included in the damnation of Adam, just as all are included in the redemption won us by Christ.[12] The Pelagian concern for God's justice is indeed a valid one, but instead of functioning as a premiss to prove the salvation of unbaptized infants, it must take second place *after* the certainty of infant damnation. Paul is too clear on this latter point for our human speculations on divine justice to call it into question.

In *Letter 159*, to Evodius, dated somewhere around the years 414 or 415,[13] Augustine sets about answering a question about the possibility of "seeing" the souls of those departed, and whether this would imply a certain corporeality of the soul after death. He does not have time to go into the issues as thoroughly as Evodius might

11. *Ep 156* 1.
12. *Ep 157* 11. Augustine's *arbitror* and *melius credamus* seem rather moderate, when compared with the firmer tone he will adopt later on.
13. The Maurist editors say only that this letter was written "after" Evodius' *Ep 158*; Goldbacher in CSEL 58, p. 42, conjectures that the entire Evodius–Augustine exchange running from *Epp 158* through *164* would seem to have occurred in the years 414–415, but that the "brief interval" of time so implied may create a difficulty: *haud scio*, he avows, *an recte adfirmaverim*. But the dating of this entire series depends on Goldbacher's undocumented assumption (ibid.) that *GenLitt* was begun in 401 (!) and finished (published?) in 415. He is also working from the assumption that *Trin* was published in 416, a date we now know was far too early. These two assumptions tend to make him "squeeze" this series of letters into what may, on future examination, turn out to be too short a time-span.

like him to; but he promises Evodius that in the twelfth of the books which he has written (*scripsi*) *On Genesis* (which Goldbacher calculates to have been "completed" [*confectus*] sometime around the year 415 [14]) Evodius will eventually find a more exhaustive discussion of such "visions."

> When you read this discussion, you will be able to judge how far our abilities extended, or what we accomplished on this question; [15] on condition, however, that the Lord deign to grant it be permitted me soon [16] to publish [*edere*] those books. . . .

And here he adds a significant qualification: they must first be

> suitably emended inasmuch as I am able, and thus meet the expectation of many of the brethren. [Such a rapid completion of them would avoid] deferring their hopes by protracting a discussion which has already engaged me for a long time.[17]

Augustine still shifts his glance uneasily toward those who are clamoring for publication of his *De Genesi*; he has tried their patience much too long, he feels; and yet, he still feels the need to "emend" that work before being confident that God would "permit" him to publish it. What precise questions are holding him up, he does not say. We know that a similar clamor rang round his ears for the *De Trinitate*, but the topic raised by Evodius does not compel him to mention that work.

Letters 160 and *161* are both from Evodius to Augustine; they are dated by the Maurists as from *circiter* 414 and *videtur an.* 414, respectively, which would make that year one of incredibly busy letter-writing for Augustine's old companion, indeed. Hence, Goldbacher's preliminary uncertainty on the likelihood of that dating.[18]

---

14. This assumption seems to allay the misgivings expressed in note 13, above. His dating of *Ep 159* depends, therefore, on his assumed date for *GenLitt*, and not the reverse. Notice also that Goldbacher pays little attention to Augustine's reference to the work of "emendation" that might be needed before his hope of publishing *GenLitt* could be realized.

15. Curiously, Augustine here shifts into the plural ("we" and "our") for one sentence and only one; the significance of this escapes me.

16. I translate Augustine's *jam* as "soon"; it might have the force of "now," with the suggestion of "at long last." But in either case, Augustine is expressing a hope, so that any conclusions about dating *GenLitt*'s final publication would be premature.

17. *Ep 159* 2.

18. See note 13, above.

Evodius raises several abstruse issues,[19] which others have harried him with, begging for Augustine's light on them. *Letter 162,* "perhaps written in 415," say the Maurists, shows Augustine half-answering, half-excusing himself for not giving as satisfactory an answer as Evodius might surely like. One of his excuses is that he has solved many aspects of the difficulties Evodius has written about "in those books, whether on the Trinity, or on Genesis, which I have not yet published."[20] This would seem to provide Goldbacher additional encouragement for laying aside his misgivings on the surprisingly short interval allowed for the entire series of *Letters 158–164;* he has assumed that we may be confident that the *De Genesi ad litteram* was published in 415 or thereabouts, so that *Letter 162,* written when that work was "not yet edited," *must* date from 415, more or less.[21] But things no longer seem so clear as when Goldbacher penned those lines.

In *Letter 163,* usually dated sometime around 415,[22] Evodius poses a question about the "rational soul" which Christ "assumed" along with the body: Do any one of those opinions apply to Christ's soul, "which are put forth when the question is raised about the soul's origin—if [indeed] any one of them be true"?[23] Or was Christ's soul of so unique a species that none of these usual opinions would apply to it?

Evodius obviously supposes that there is a standard set of "opin-

19. Notably on "Reason," God, and their relationship (*Ep 160*), and on the possibility (even for the risen Christ) of beholding God with bodily eyes (*Ep 161*). Questions of this latter sort begin to preoccupy Augustine quite seriously during this period, for reasons that may well have arisen from challenges critics were directing against the radical spirituality of his views on the "vision" of God. We may have some valuable things to learn about this.

20. This is from *Ep 162* 2, not (as Bardy writes in BA 12, p. 580) *Ep 164* 2. Note that two pages further on (p. 582) he gives the reference correctly. On Bardy's entire argument on pages 584–85, see above, chap. 2, notes 76–80.

21. Note that Bardy (BA 12, p. 582) reverses Goldbacher's direction of argument and unwittingly involves himself in a vicious circle. He first accepts Goldbacher's dating of *Ep 162* (for which Goldbacher had used his assumed date for *GenLitt* as his premiss), and then "infers" that Augustine "must at last have brought out [*GenLitt*] about that time," i.e., 415. But, like Goldbacher, Bardy never seems to have asked how much time the emendations to *GenLitt,* mentioned in *Letter 159,* might have required.

22. But there is some vagueness here: the Maurists reason that this letter was written *paulo post,* "a little bit after," *Letter 162,* "perhaps" *(forte)* in 415. Goldbacher opts for the same year, but see notes 13 and 14, above.

23. Evodius' expression runs: *utrum in una de opinionibus est illis quae proponuntur cum de anima quaeritur, si qua ibi potest veritate fulciri.*

ions" touching on the soul's origin, so familiar to both Augustine and himself that he need not even enumerate them. And yet, he seems also to imply, it is conceivable that no one of these opinions may be true after all!

Augustine's answer, from the same year (415?), comes in *Letter 164*. He is comfortable with Evodius' shorthand manner of asking his question, and runs through three of the standard opinions familiar from *De libero arbitrio 3*. If all human souls, he replies, are "from that one" sinful soul which was Adam's—the traducianist supposition—then either Christ's soul was specially created exempt from the sin Adamic generation passes on to successive generations or else His soul was miraculously cleansed on His assumption of it. Or, in the creationist supposition, it must be human flesh, not the soul, which inherits sinfulness from Adam; in which case, God could simply have created Christ's soul in the same way He creates souls for other humans, but then made it "mingle" (*miscuit*), not with this "flesh of sin," as with other humans, but only with the "likeness of the flesh of sin," as the Apostle makes clear to us (Rom. 8:3), so that Christ's soul was not infected by the sin of Adam, transmitted by the flesh (19).

But Christ's soul was sinless, "whatever opinion about the soul be true," Augustine goes on to say.

> And I am not so rash as to venture to assert any of these opinions at present, except to repudiate that [opinion] which believes that souls, because of the merits of I know not what actions they committed in higher regions,[24] were each thrust into bodies as though into so many prisons [*tanquam in carceres detrudi*] [20].

Now, whatever date we assign to this letter, it comes from a time when Augustine had made some progress on the question of the soul's origin, compared to the position he assumed in *Letter 143*. There, all four received hypotheses were still permissible; now, it would appear, one of them seems to have been discarded, and firmly. But Augustine furnishes Evodius with no grounds for that repudiation; it would have been a simple matter to have cited Romans 9:11, but he does not. The expression *tanquam in carceres detrudi* is hard language for the Origenist theory with which Paul Orosius

---

24. Augustine's phrase is elliptical: *nescio quorum superiorum actuum suorum.* But translators seem justified in supplying the omitted term, "regions."

had acquainted him; it may betray that seizure of revulsion toward that theory which was so manifest in the *Ad Orosium*. It may also be that he hopes Evodius will share his own revulsion.

But even if we assume that this letter dates from as early as 415,[25] the most likely explanation of this abrupt rejection of the "fallen soul" hypothesis would seem to be this: we may have here a letter coming swiftly on the heels of Augustine's exposure to Origen's theory of the soul, thanks to Paul Orosius' visit to Hippo. If that be the case, it remains a distinct possibility that *what* he objects to in that theory, and his *reasons* for rejecting it, had to do more with Origen's theory of creation than with the soul's pre-existence and "fall." Notice, again, that (just as with the *Ad Orosium*) Romans 9:11 never makes an appearance.

Assuming that same date, 415, we have here a letter roughly contemporaneous with Augustine's *Letter 166*, to Jerome, "consulting" him on this very same issue. There, too, he shows a firm inclination to reject the same hypothesis he rejected here. But there, he will spell out his reasons for that rejection, and, in doing so, will clarify how he understands the import of the hypothesis. We shall have to examine that letter very closely, but it will confirm the conjectures we have been compelled to make here.

One final remark on *Letter 164*: it is somewhat curious that Augustine never mentions the "third" hypothesis, whereby souls are created elsewhere and divinely "sent," one by one, into their several bodies. Has he, for all practical purposes, lost interest in this possibility? The answer is unclear for now, but some light will be shed on it soon enough.

---

25. The year 415 represents the "most difficult" date for my hypothesis, obviously; were *Letter 164* to date from a later year, its peremptory rejection of the "fall" hypothesis could more easily be explained in terms of Augustine's having become aware of the relevance of Rom. 9:11 to this issue.

5

AUGUSTINE
"CONSULTS" JEROME:
Letter 166

AUGUSTINE's *Letter 166*, to Jerome in Bethlehem, is surely a *locus classicus* for the investigation of his developing views on the origin of the soul. The story of that letter goes back to Marcellinus once again. Having received Augustine's *Letter 143*, which settled nothing on this ticklish issue, Marcellinus resolves to write to Jerome about it, and other matters theological as well. Augustine seems to have found out about Marcellinus' initiative only later;[1] his first inkling of it may have come when Jerome's reply to Marcellinus arrives at Carthage.[2] It is the year 415 by the time Augustine can answer in turn.[3]

Jerome speaks of Marcellinus' "little" question about the origin of the soul, but then confesses that it is, rather, "a question of great importance to the Church." The theories competing for attention, he makes clear, are five in number; they come down to the four Augustine listed in *De libero arbitrio 3*, plus the Stoic, Manichaean, and Priscillianist opinion that the soul is of the very substance of

---

1. Compare *Epp 166* 8 and *190* 20–21; see also chap. 3, notes 27–28, above.

2. Jerome's reply is *Ep 165* in the Augustine corpus; the Maurist date, "shortly after 410," is plainly conjectural, and probably inaccurate. *Ep 165* was written, obviously, after Augustine's *Ep 143*, to Marcellinus, hence, in 412 or later; and after Marcellinus' subsequent letter reached Jerome—which could have taken some time. It probably arrived after Marcellinus' death in September 413, since in *Ep 166* itself Augustine does not appear to know the story he tells of its history as he has learned of it by the time he writes *Ep 190*.

3. This date is relatively firm, since Augustine speaks of Orosius as its bearer to Jerome, and Orosius' trip to Bethlehem can be confidently dated from the events he describes as happening there during his stay; see Brown, *Augustine*, pp. 356–57.

God. Ignoring this last for the moment, Jerome expresses the other four hypotheses as: the soul

> fell down from heaven [*lapsa de coelo*], as the philosopher Pythagoras, all the Platonists, and Origen think; . . .

> or is long preserved in the treasury of God, as some churchmen are foolishly induced to imagine;

> or is daily created by God and sent into bodies; . . .

> or, at least, is derived from a root stock, as Tertullian, Apollinaris, and most Western scholars claim, holding that, as each body is born of another body, so the soul is born of a soul, and has an origin like that of the lower animals.[4]

Instead of offering his own solution to the question now, Jerome refers Marcellinus, somewhat airily, to his *Apologia* against Rufinus, a copy of which Marcellinus can surely obtain from the priest Oceanus. There his opinion of the matter is made clear; but then, of course, Marcellinus has right at hand that "holy and learned man, Bishop Augustine, who will be able to teach you by the living word, as they say, and will set forth his opinion, or, rather, mine in his own words."[5]

A STORMY CORRESPONDENCE

It is typical of Jerome that, alongside this praise of Augustine's life and learning, there glides the complacent supposition that the bishop would surely be intelligent enough to agree, on this matter, with him—or, perhaps, not bold enough to disagree! For Augustine had already learned what a fearsome man Jerome was to disagree with. True, Jerome's brief, cryptic *Letter 123*, probably written in 410 (five years before), hints that some measure of amity has been restored between these two. His praise of Augustine to Marcellinus would confirm that impression. But Jerome's favor was always a chancey thing; it was never wise to presume too much about it. Augustine, furthermore, seems clear on what Jerome's preferred opinion was: creationism. But this was a position Jerome had adopted, in his own words, "years ago" in his battle against Rufinus'

4. *Ep 165* 1.
5. Ibid.

defense of Origen, and well before the challenge that Pelagianism now represented. Was Jerome aware that Pelagius relied on this very creationist opinion in his argument that infant souls must therefore be sinless? Perhaps; perhaps not. In any event, agreeing with his creationist opinion is not going to be as easy as Jerome seems to fancy. This, one can almost hear Augustine sigh, is going to take some careful doing!

He is older now, he reminds the Jerome who had formerly sneered at his relative youth; older, but still learning, still able to admit (as he hopes, no doubt, Jerome will be) that he has things to learn.[6] As a reminder, too, of the tragic mishap of his first letter to Bethlehem, he introduces Paul Orosius as a man who will surely bring this letter safely to its destination. The wounds may have healed, but scars remain (2).

OPENING THE QUESTION

Now he touches on the question of the soul's origin. This is a question that "troubles many," he observes, including himself. Not that he has no certainties about the soul: let him first make clear what they are, not with the intent of teaching Jerome anything, surely, but merely to clear the ground for what he hopes to learn from him. He is convinced of the soul's immortality, of its immateriality; that it is not part of the divine essence. It is worth observing, in passing, the relatively philosophical nature of these "certainties," as well as the philosophic cast of Augustine's justification of them (3–5).[7]

For his next affirmation takes a decisively Scriptural turn: "I am certain," he says, "that the soul fell into sin, through no fault, no compulsion, on God's part, but by its own personal will, and that it cannot be delivered from 'the body of this death' . . . but 'by the grace of God by Jesus Christ our Lord.'" Hence, "Every soul that departs from the body, no matter at what age, without the grace of the Mediator and His sacrament [of baptism], is destined for punishment . . . " (5). The gauntlet has been thrown down to Pelagian-

6. *Ep 166* 1. All subsequent references to this letter will be identified, by paragraph number, in the text.

7. Augustine may have meant eventually to show his African critics, too, that the hesitations they had complained about did not imply he knew nothing about the matter.

ism, and for fair. Here we have Augustine's "firmest of beliefs" in the universality of Original Sin, the need for grace and baptism—and the damnation of infants who die without baptism.

Augustine is sure that Jerome shares his anti-Pelagianism, that he rejects those "new and absurd opinions, alleging that there is no guilt from Adam that is removed by baptism in the case of infants." But to share that faith is to fall heir to the tormenting question raised by the damnation of infants; and now, Augustine faces Jerome with the central difficulty against his creationist view: "Where [or when: *ubi*] can the [unbaptized] infant soul, snatched away by death, have contracted the guilt [*reatus*] that involves it in condemnation?"

RECALLING HIS EARLIER STAND

He reminds Jerome that some years before, in his *De libero arbitrio*, he himself had outlined four "opinions as to the manner of the soul's incarnation." He sketches them in the familiar and relatively neutral terms of that work. The fourth hypothesis states simply that "souls already in existence . . . fall [*labantur*] into [their bodies] of their own accord." But, he admits, there is a fifth possibility, that "the soul is a part of God," which, "in order to omit none, you have mentioned with the rest in your letter to Marcellinus." Augustine explains that he deliberately omitted this possibility when writing the anti-Manichaean *De libero arbitrio* (6). But two items are now clarified: first, that Augustine is familiar with the contents and terminology of Jerome's answer to Marcellinus; and, second, that he sees no difficulty in equating four of the possibilities Jerome had outlined there with the four hypotheses as he had sketched them in the *De libero arbitrio*.[8]

More particularly, he must now realize beyond any doubt that his fourth hypothesis is substantially identical with the "fall" theory which Jerome has attached to the names of Pythagoras, the Platonists, and Origen. The charged language he uses elsewhere—the soul has been "thrust" into the body as into a prison—betrays the same revulsion toward Origen's theory as when Paul Orosius had exposed it to him; but it does not disguise the fact that he is

8. This is further indication that these hypotheses represented standard thinking at the time. Notice again, however, that for Augustine the problem of the soul's "origin" is identical with the problem of how it became "incarnate."

still speaking in terms of the same four hypotheses he outlined in the *De libero arbitrio*, and that this language of pre-incarnate sin and consequent penal inclusion in the body fits only his fourth hypothesis, which Jerome has now confirmed as Origen's view (11).[9]

He reminds Jerome of the argumentative strategy he had adopted in the *De libero arbitrio*. It was "necessary" to treat all four hypotheses "in such a way that, whichever of them might be true, the decision should not hinder the object I had in view": namely, to free God of the guilty responsibility for our sins, which Manichees contended the Catholic God must bear. This had obliged him then to leave all four of them as open possibilities. But the Pelagian heresy has changed the situation; now he is compelled to inquire which of these "four opinions we ought to choose." He will keep, as the immovable pole of the discussion, the certainty from faith that "every soul, even the soul of an infant, requires to be delivered from the binding guilt of sin" through Christ's grace (7). Does this replace the immovable certainty of God's justice that had functioned in the *De libero arbitrio*? No, as we shall see, it works along with that certainty; indeed, the need for admitting the damnation of unbaptized infants while at the same time not convicting God of manifest injustice is what gives the question its keenest edge.[10]

ON JEROME'S DEFENSE OF CREATIONISM

He now takes up the opinion which, he knows, Jerome favors, creationism, i.e., "that God even now makes each soul for each individual at the time of birth." To foil the objection from Genesis 2:2 that this is unthinkable, God being said to "rest" after completing the work of creation, Jerome was astute enough to oppose Christ's words, "My Father works until now, and I work" (Jn 4:7).[11] How well advised was Marcellinus to write to Jerome on this difficult

---

9. The same inference, we saw, can be drawn from Augustine's answer to his critics in *Ep 143*. The point may seem too obvious to stress, but it has been questioned by Father Madec, as we saw above, chap. 1, note 40.

10. One might wonder, though, whether the defense of God's justice has not taken second place in Augustine's thinking; compare *Ep 157* 11, his answer to Hilarius, treated above, chap. 4. In any event, we shall see Augustine becoming more and more doubtful about the proposition, so dear to the Pelagians, that one could confidently apply human reason's standards of justice to God.

11. Augustine is more eager to praise Jerome than to mention that he himself had used this same tactic in his *Adim*, as well as in *GenLitt*.

question, how gladly would Augustine himself have urged him to do so! Besides, Marcellinus knew well Augustine's own "hesitation to embrace any definite view on this subject"—and that, despite the insistence of many that he solve this question for them. Now, however, "Behold, I am willing that the opinion which you hold should be mine also; but I assure you that as yet I have not embraced it" (8).

A long parenthesis follows on his ignorance and on his humble, ardent desire to know; Augustine is understandably anxious that Jerome not take offense (9). "Teach me, therefore, I beseech you; . . . teach me what I ought to hold as my opinion." And, hoping Jerome's ire will not be aroused, he gingerly inserts his head into the lion's mouth. "Tell me this"—if the creationist opinion be the true one,

> where [or when: *ubi*], in the case of infant children, is sin committed by these souls, so that they require the remission of sin . . . ? Or if they do not sin, how is it compatible with the justice of the Creator . . . that they are so brought under the bond of sin of that other [i.e., of Adam, "from whom the sinful flesh has been derived"], that unless they be rescued by the Church, perdition overtakes them [10]?

Augustine expands upon this difficulty, making it clear how he and, he assumes, Jerome both understand the implications of creationism: a central supposition of the theory is that "new souls, created individually by the will of the Creator, are joined to individual bodies at birth, *with no previous sin of their own*."[12] Now, a number of such souls depart their bodies in infancy, without baptism, when it was "not in their power to be helped by the grace of baptism," and faith tells us they depart for damnation. "What kind of justice is this?" Augustine exclaims, on the part of a God Who, when He created these souls and "gave" them to their bodies, "certainly knew that each one of them, by no fault of its own, would leave the body without the baptism of Christ?" Can we get around this difficulty by suggesting that God either "forces souls to become sinful or punishes the innocent"? Certainly not. Nor are we free to deny that unbaptized infants are in fact "subject to damnation."

---

12. *Nullo suo praecedente peccato*—the emphasis is mine. Note, however, the looser form in which Augustine now begins to express the creationist position; the simultaneity of creation and infusion is becoming blurred.

How, then, can creationism be defended against what appears, at the moment, to be its most serious rival, traducianism (10)?[10]

Before pressing his difficulty further, Augustine diplomatically stresses his areas of agreement with Jerome. In partial anticipation[14] of his De Genesi ad litteram, he resolves the apparent opposition between Genesis 2:2 and John 4:7, arguing that God "rested" from any new creative works, but "works until now" in ruling and governing what has been created (11). Nor does God's "rest" oblige us to side with those who claim that God must create "new" souls only "from that first [Adamic] soul, which then existed, as from some fount or treasury which He then made, and lets them out" one by one into individual bodies. Here Augustine is referring to the third of his own hypotheses, and the third one mentioned by Jerome: that the soul "is long preserved in the treasury of God," as Jerome put it, or, as Augustine puts it now, that God "sends down souls already existing in some fount or other" (12). His only conclusion on this hypothesis, for the moment, is that it is not imposed by Scripture's mention of God's "rest" on the seventh day of creation. But he will return to it shortly. For now, he re-expresses all four hypotheses Jerome had set into competition with creationism, assumes that both he and Jerome would reject them all, and concludes once again that creationism is not excluded by that same mention of the Sabbath "rest" (12).[15]

A second objection to creationism is more delicate. Why does God create souls He foreknows are destined for an early death? Since the objection does not touch specifically on unbaptized infants, but bears on the more general issue of premature infant deaths, Augustine is able to fend it off by invoking his faith in God's artistry as "musical" Creator, weaving our life spans, long or short, into the "wonderful song" of human history (13).

13. Observe that Augustine's language betrays his tendency to think of soul as a substance capable of existence apart from the body; this tendency may account for the gradual slippage we are about to witness in his expression of the creationist position.

14. Or it is more likely that this portion of GenLitt had already been completed to Augustine's satisfaction; see the treatment of that work below.

15. We may be close to the motive which inspired whatever tenets this hypothesis may have had: it safeguarded the "rest" from creative activity Genesis attributes to God, but at the same time avoided an Origenistic "sin" in this pre-existence. Compare Jerome's mocking reference to slumbering "dormice" in his Apologia against Rufinus 3:30, cited in chap. 2, above.

Another objection can easily be dispensed with; it arises from the argument that the soul's immortality *a parte post* proves it must have been created "before time" (14). To yet another objection, proposed by Rufinus, Jerome himself has replied "with a most felicitous illustration," and Augustine hastens to add corroboration of his view from another angle (15). "See how much we agree upon," he seems to be impressing on Jerome; "observe how much I respect this opinion of yours, when I have personally gone to such lengths in digging up replies to objections against it! No one could be more reluctant to disagree with you. . . ." "But"—after five full paragraphs of defending Jerome's opinion, Augustine boldly returns to his objection to it—"But when we come to the penal sufferings of infants, I am embarrassed, believe me, by great difficulties, and am wholly at a loss to find an answer to solve them."

Now, however, he gives the objection greater force than formerly: "I speak here not only of those punishments in the life to come . . . but also of the sufferings which are to our sorrow endured by them before our very eyes in this present life." Surely the creationist must show "how it is compatible with justice that infants suffer all these things without any evil of their own as the procuring cause." The answers that satisfy in the case of irrational animals, or of adults, will not satisfy here, and Augustine shows why (16).

The objection can be brought to even completer form. Not only the sufferings, but the manifest diversity of talents infants possess, diversity taking in some of them the guise of reason's total eclipse— all these inequalities of human existence (which the Origenist position tried to make sense of) the creationist also must try to render intelligible. Perhaps, it might be answered, "the bodies are the cause of these imperfections." But that answer will not work. Yet it *might*, conceivably, if creationist theory allowed for the provision that the individual soul chose its defective body by reason of some "blunder" or was forced to enter a defective body because other souls had already occupied all the available sound ones, as latecomers in the crowd must settle for the poorest seats at the theater. But "We, of course, cannot say and ought not to believe such things." What, therefore, "tell us, what ought we to believe and say" in order to answer this difficulty within the compass of creationist theory (17)?

He had, in his *De libero arbitrio*, treated this difficulty, but in another context, with the view toward defending the justice of God, and was therefore obliged to leave all four hypotheses open. Now that the question has changed to a defense of the creationist hypothesis, he finds those earlier arguments of his no longer serve him. For in the *De libero arbitrio*, he had fended off the objection deriving from infant sufferings, partly by appealing to the "good reward," unknown to us humans, that God might "have in store for these little ones, in the secret of His judgments. . . . [For] who knows what these little ones will receive?"[16] But now he clearly sees that no such reward can await those "children who die, after bitter torments, without the sacrament" of baptism, and are therefore "foredoomed to damnation." The question about these *unbaptized* infants "was not at issue" in the *De libero arbitrio*, but now, if one is to defend creationism while not lapsing into Pelagianism, it is the very nub of the issue (18–20). For again, both the words of St. Paul and the Church's practice of infant baptism clearly proclaim that "all" the newborn are "under the guilt of Adam's offense"; Jerome himself has expressed this same faith in his writings. The question he must try to answer now, therefore, is: "What is the ground of this condemnation of unbaptized infants?" For on the creationist supposition, "I do not see, on the one hand, that they could have any sin while yet in infancy, nor do I believe . . . that God condemns any soul which He sees to have no sin" (21).

Three more paragraphs are spent in discarding an additional possibility of evading the difficulty. The authority of Cyprian is invoked to shelve this possibility; it brings Augustine to admit that Cyprian may not have seen all the necessary aspects of the question. We may be at liberty to differ with him—but not with Paul, not with the universal practice of the Church. And Augustine doggedly comes around to his question again. As to Jerome's opinion concerning the creation of new souls—he is considerably bolder now—"if it does not contradict this firmly grounded article of faith, let it be mine also; but if it does, let it be no longer yours" (22–25).

Now Augustine's boldness reaches its peak; inexorably, he pro-

---

16. Cf. *Lib* 3.66–68. Besides the rewards infants themselves could receive on account of their sufferings (Augustine supposes they have been baptized), those sufferings could provide corrective "admonitions" to their elders. There is also, in 3.66, a suggestion of some *medius locus*, neither heaven nor hell, but the sentence is so involved I can make little of what Augustine is actually holding on the matter.

ceeds to block off all Jerome's remaining escape routes. Creationism, he shows, cannot draw Scriptural support from Zechariah, from the Psalms, or from Ecclesiastes, all of which provide inviting texts, at first blush, for the "opinion I shall gladly see vindicated," but texts which, when pressed, prove far less convincing than they seemed.[17] He would "prevent" Jerome from "endeavoring to deliver [him] from [his] perplexities by quoting passages such as these."

And yet, he assures him once again, "I would wish that this opinion should be true, as I do wish that, if it be true, it should be most clearly and unanswerably vindicated by you." Perhaps it is phrases like this, and *Letter 166* abounds with them, that have encouraged a number of scholars to speak of Augustine's "preference" for the creationist opinion. But the entire burden of the letter speaks otherwise. Augustine's whole point is to bring Jerome around, as diplomatically as he can, to acknowledge the rock-hard difficulty in this theory, a difficulty that Pelagius' reasoning has made him see. It may be Jerome's opinion, and Jerome is certainly to be respected; but Augustine's deepest attitude comes out in the bold observation that, alas, "no man's wishes," not even Jerome's, "can make true what is not true" (26).

THE OTHER THREE HYPOTHESES

Now Augustine turns to an examination of the other three hypotheses on the soul's origin. How do they fare in dealing with this difficulty? To begin with, he treats of the two hypotheses involving pre-existence. If we envisage souls as "sent by Him into bodies"—i.e., if we accept the *third* hypothesis of the *De libero arbitrio*—the supposition is that "being without fault," these souls "go obediently to the bodies to which they are sent" (*inculpatae oboedienter veniunt quo mittantur*). Why, then, "in the case of infants, are they subjected to punishment if without being baptized they come to the end of this life"? The "same" difficulty as attached to creationism attaches to this theory also; in both cases the souls in question are "without fault" of their own.

17. The Eccles text is the same one employed in *Ep 143*. It would be interesting, but not directly relevant to our inquiry here, to write a history of Augustine's interpretation of that crucial text.

His treatment of the fourth hypothesis we shall come to in a moment. What does he have to say of the traducianist possibility? "I will not begin to discuss it unless I am under the necessity of doing so; my desire is that if the [creationist] opinion which we are now discussing is true, it may be so vindicated by you that there shall no longer be any necessity for examining the other," i.e., the traducianist opinion. A curious expression of reluctance, one might think, especially since we know that Augustine recognized this much about traducianism: it claimed to posit such an identity between subsequent souls and the Adamic soul "in which" all of them "sinned" that it removed the very "innocence" of soul that stands as the central objection to both creationist and "sent" hypotheses.[18] Was Augustine so seriously put off by the materialist cast assumed by regnant versions of the theory? The *De Genesi ad litteram* will throw more light on that; suffice it to say that here he chooses to drop the subject abruptly.

CONTENT OF THE FOURTH HYPOTHESIS

What, then, of the fourth hypothesis? The question here is twofold: first, what did this hypothesis imply, in Augustine's eyes; and, secondly, how much acceptability was he willing to accord it?

As to what the fourth hypothesis implied, we are now in a position to pull together a number of strands of evidence. First, both Augustine and Jerome are in agreement that, excluding the Manichaean–Priscillianist claim that the soul is part of God, there are four and only four remaining possibilities to be weighed. Augustine, furthermore, has made it clear from the outset that they are in general agreement on the content of those four theories; his specific handling of creationism, traducianism, and the "divinely sent" hypotheses confirms that agreement about those three. But two of the four hypotheses, they are further agreed, suppose the existence of the soul previous to its incarnate state. What distinguishes these two hypotheses is their mode of explaining the soul's "incarnation." The "third" hypothesis affirms that the soul was "sent" by God into bodily existence, but without any guilt on the part of the soul that is sent, while the "fourth" explains the soul's

18. This explains Augustine's brisk treatment of traducianism in *Lib* as well as his critics' assumptions as dealt with in *Ep 143*.

incarnate existence as the result of some sin or sins the soul committed in its life apart from the body.

This, accordingly, is the essential characteristic of the fourth hypothesis: our incarnate existence is in the strict sense of that term a penal existence, the result of our pre-incarnate sin and God's punitive response to that sin. That characteristic both identifies it and sets it off from the other three hypotheses in contention. That characteristic is common both to the fourth hypothesis of Augustine's *De libero arbitrio* and to the same hypothesis as described by Jerome; it is common, as well, to the Origenist theory as Paul Orosius had explained it to Augustine, a theory which Augustine here finds no difficulty in equating with the theory Jerome, too, has ascribed to Origen.

Now, Augustine can express the central core of this fourth hypothesis in various ways, but without ever obscuring the fact that it is always the same central core he is expressing; indeed, he obviously assumes that Jerome will clearly understand him as in each case referring to the same hypothesis he, Jerome, has described as Origen's. So, where Jerome can say the soul "fell down from heaven," the Augustine of the *De libero arbitrio* can be comparably concise: souls "existing in some place . . . come of their own accord to inhabit bodies"; [19] or, in another expression of it, the soul "comes into the body, . . . falling of its own accord"; [20] or, as here, souls "are joined to bodies of their own accord" (7).[21] But there is no confusion, either in his own mind or in Jerome's, when he chooses to express things somewhat differently: God's punitive response is foremost in his mind when God is said to "bind them [i.e., souls] in the fetters of fleshly members because of sins committed before the flesh" (*pro delictis ante carnem commissis, carneis vinculis compedire*) (12). This paraphrase of the fourth hypothesis is presented in so casual a manner as to leave no grounds for reasonable doubt. Augustine is tacitly assuming that Jerome would understand his earlier formulations this way: souls "came" or "fell" into or "were joined to" bodies "of their own accord," with all the "ignorance and difficulty" that inferior being-condition entailed. But,

19. *Lib* 3.58.
20. Ibid. 59.
21. The soul's "punishment" is clearly being viewed as appropriate in this hypothesis; hence, some sin of its own is implied. Compare the discussion of *Lib* in chap. 1.

Augustine has been arguing from the *De libero arbitrio* onward, souls had no ground for complaining against God since "their own accord" was a sinful choice committed before their entry into the flesh. This, his paraphrase now makes irresistibly clear, is the way he himself had *always* understood such phrases as "come," "fall into," and "be joined to" when qualified by that *sua sponte*.

In short, Augustine always envisaged his fourth hypothesis as implying a sin or sins the soul committed in some pre-existent state.

EVALUATION OF THE FOURTH HYPOTHESIS

So much, then, for the content of the fourth hypothesis. Now our question is: How acceptable does Augustine find this hypothesis now? His evaluation begins in a way that confirms our conclusion on the content of this hypothesis:

> Those who affirm that each soul is, according to the deserts of its actions in an earlier life [*pro meritis vitae prioris*], enveloped in its body [in this life] imagine that they can escape more easily from this difficulty [i.e., arising from infant damnation]. For they think that "to die in Adam" means to suffer punishment in that flesh which was derived from Adam [27].

Just a few lines further on, but in the same paragraph, his expression hardens somewhat, resembling more closely the language of his reply *Ad Orosium* and of his *Letter 164*, to Evodius: "souls sin in another previous life and are therefore thrust down into fleshly prisons." But it is obvious that Augustine is referring to the same fourth hypothesis, and that he fully expects Jerome to understand him that way.

What, then, is his evaluation of it? This much, he admits, is to be said for it: it seems to escape the "difficulty" of infant damnation by eliminating the very innocence of the infant soul which argues against the acceptability of the creationist and "divinely sent" alternatives. For it supposes a pre-incarnate sin for which eventual damnation of certain infants rather than others could conceivably, at least, be an appropriate punishment. And it admits the necessity of baptism for those who will be saved.

Finally, this theory makes at least a plausible effort to explain what St. Paul means by "to die in Adam" (*in Adam mori*),[22] i.e., to "suffer punishments in the flesh which has been derived by propagation from Adam."

But this does not satisfy Augustine. Why? Now he reverts to the very same argumentation he used in his reply to Orosius; now, as there, he focuses, not on the core implications of the fourth hypothesis, but on secondary features that, Orosius had informed him, attended on this hypothesis in Origen's version of it. "I do not believe, do not agree to, do not accept," this view, he exclaims,

> because, first of all, I do not know a more revolting opinion than that these souls should make some indefinite number of trips through an indefinite number of cycles of ages, only to return again to that burden of corrupt flesh to pay the penalty of torment; and, secondly, how could there be anyone who died in the state of grace about whom we should not be anxious lest—if what they say is true—even in the bosom of Abraham he might commit sin after leaving the body if he could do so before entering it [27].

Origen, and perhaps as Jerome had put it, "all the Platonists," had encased the soul's sinful "fall" into the body inside a larger cyclic theory of multiple falls and returns. It is important to note that Augustine's objection, and his revulsion, are aimed primarily at this larger theory. He offers no Scriptural proof to exclude the possibility of a pre-incarnate sin, a proof that would strike at the very core of the fourth hypothesis, making much shorter work of it. This is precisely the attack he mounts repeatedly, as we shall see, once he has grasped the bearing of Romans 9:11 on this question. And given his anxiety to impress upon Jerome that he has scouted this question thoroughly in both Old and New Testaments, it is highly implausible that he would refrain from bringing Romans 9:11 into play at this point had it been an active part of his Scriptural weaponry. The only conclusion to be drawn, then, is this: Augustine must have come to "see" Romans 9:11 in its bearing on

22. The reference is to the Latin translation of 1 Cor. 15:22, and not, as a careless reading might suggest, to the notorious Rom. 5:12, *in quo omnes peccaverunt*. For the history of Augustine's use of this latter text, see below, chap. 8, note 62.

the question of the soul's "origin" only *after* having written *Letter 166.*

As to the explanation of dying "in Adam," Augustine finds it forced. For it is one thing to "have sinned in Adam, for which reason the Apostle says 'in whom all have sinned,' but quite another to have sinned somewhere or other outside Adam, and thence to be thrust into Adam, i.e., into flesh derived by propagation from Adam, as into a prison."

There is, though, one small difference between the argumentation of the *Ad Orosium* and that of *Letter 166* which suggests that Augustine may have been pondering this question, and have made some advance upon it. One could object that his earlier argument was so directed at the cyclic implications of Origen's *de facto* theory that, once those secondary implications were removed, Augustine would be left with no valid objection against the very core contention of the fourth hypothesis: pre-incarnate sin. Here, however, though in the briefest of phrases, he employs an expression that seems to strike at the core contention as well. Anyone, he argues, "might commit sin after leaving the body if he could do so before entering it." Once you weaken the conviction that our soul's beatitude apart from the body is genuinely secure, as Origen has weakened it, then sin, and sinful fall, in principle become possible, and repeatedly possible; before or after life in the body, it makes no difference! This, Augustine seems to have glimpsed, is no mere *de facto* feature of Origen's theory, but an inescapable corollary of his cyclic *kind* of thinking and, indeed, of the kind of thinking common, in Jerome's phrase, to "all Platonists." We shall have to watch for any future appeals to this style of argumentation.

Augustine ends with a passing mention of traducianism—a theory he is "loath to discuss, unless it should be necessary"—and a hope that Jerome will provide such a defense of creationism that it "may not require discussion" (27). But, once more, he implores Jerome to help him with this question, and tells him why. "Some of those opinions might be contrary to what we hold with strongest faith, and might creep into unwary minds." He might once have thought this problem could be shelved, but the challenge of Pelagianism has changed all that. *Letter 167,* written at the same time to Jerome on another matter, admits that the man who fell into the well should be more concerned about how to get out than about how he fell into it in the first place—an illustration that we should want more keenly to know the soul's eventual destiny than its origin. Yet he "thought it wise to raise the question, lest we unwittingly hold one of those opinions about the soul's joining the body" which would argue against the need for infant baptism. So, "if we can discover the cause and origin of that evil [i.e., the soul's incarnation in sinful flesh], we shall be better equipped and prepared to refute the idle prating of pettifoggers"—by whom he obviously means the Pelagians.

It may be the case, however, that God will not grant us any certainty on this question. What then? Patience, Augustine counsels, and submission to His will. There are many things of which he is ignorant and will likely remain so: his only worry about his ignorance on this point comes from the fear that others, deceived into thinking they have arrived at certainty about the origin of the soul, may thereby tumble into the conclusion that infants have no need of baptism for the remission of sin. But that need for baptism, and its corollary, damnation of unbaptized infants, Augustine holds *firmissima fide*, with unshakable faith. And so, he believes, no genuine certainty on the origin of the soul could ever militate against that faith.

We shall see him launched more and more intensely on a campaign to justify his own entitlement to continued doubts on this difficult question. *Defendi cunctationem meam*. "I defended my right to hesitate, still," he will write in summary of several of his works on the topic. Jerome never comes to his aid on the question, his silence perhaps acknowledging that Augustine had a stronger grasp on the issues than he did.[23] But more than one bright young man, finding his hesitation unconscionable, will rush into print to settle what the learned Augustine continued to insist on leaving an open question, only to have their proofs dismantled, their cheaply won certitudes demolished by Augustine's searching replies.

CONCLUSIONS FROM *Letter 166*

In spite of all Augustine's residual doubts on the issue, we can be confident of several things. The first is that Augustine had con-

23. Kelly, *Jerome*, pp. 320–21 cites Jerome's *Dialogue against the Pelagians* on this score, and convincingly.

sistently intended his famous fourth hypothesis to imply that souls pre-existed, sinned in that pre-existent condition, and were punished by being enveloped in mortal bodies. Secondly, he does not yet see the text from Romans 9:11 as peremptorily dismissing this theory. His personal "rejection" of it stems from his "horror" at the cyclical style of thinking which would utterly undermine our security in the bliss that awaits us after having left "this" body.

But, thirdly, Augustine has apparently decided upon what point of Catholic belief must be taken as the starting point for any discussion of the soul and of its origin. That point is Paul's ringing affirmation of universal human sinfulness and the need for Christ's redemptive grace through baptism. This, along with its fearful corollary, the sure damnation of infants who die without baptism, has replaced his earlier conviction of God's "justice" as the immovable pillar that must structure all discourse on this question. Divine justice is far from forgotten, of course; indeed, infant damnation makes defending God's justice an even sorer point than it formerly was for Augustine. But the premiss that God is just never once threatens to overturn the thesis of infant damnation, as it did for a number of Pelagians; they, of course, buttressed their argument with that other premiss, creationism, arguing that such newly created souls could not be sinful.

In sum, one gets the clear impression that, starting from the quite different premiss that, he is now convinced, must dominate the debate, Augustine's preference would still go to some penal theory of the soul's origin if only he could clear away the difficulties he saw attendant on the precise historical forms those theories took. The notion that the soul might have pre-existed its entry into the mortal body does not in the least upset him. But were such a soul "sent" into this bodily world, its very innocence confronts him with an insoluble difficulty. Were such a soul guilty, however, so that its presence in the mortal body were the result of its sinful choice, that would answer to his major premiss far more satisfactorily—if only the theory in question did not go on to threaten that the same horrid scenario would, indeed must, be played over and over, again and again. Few things are clearer than Augustine's distaste for "this life" in "these bodies." Yet no theory coheres more with such a distaste than the one propounded by his fourth hypothesis.

ADAM'S "ANIMAL" BODY

One parenthetical remark: we saw him, in *Letter 143*, momentarily allude to an aspect of Pauline teaching which could have been pressed against the fourth hypothesis, and the third as well. If Paul is taken as teaching that Adam both was created and sinned in an "animal" body, it would make it difficult to embrace either of these theories. For the third hypothesis implies the soul's pre-existence without any such body, and the fourth goes further in proclaiming that the soul's pre-existent sin must have been committed in a "spiritual" body. But Augustine makes no allusion to this Pauline teaching in his letter to Jerome. Why not? Here we are reduced to guessing. Perhaps he never really saw the anti–pre-existence implication that seems clearer to a modern's eye. Or perhaps he felt his argument concerning the soul's secure beatitude was sufficiently persuasive to eliminate the fourth hypothesis, at least in its Origenist form, from further consideration. In that case, one might suggest, he should have used the Pauline reference to Adam's "animal" body against the third hypothesis. But was that phrase of Paul's so sharply etched on his consciousness as all of this supposes? And so on. Such speculations have no end to them. For the moment, no certain conclusion seems to follow; but we must keep alert for possible recurrence of this insight.

That Pauline teaching would also have favored the two hypotheses which eschew all mention of pre-existence, creationism and traducianism. But Augustine does not want even to discuss traducianism; and if he has a single main point undergirding his entire letter to Jerome, he is saying that the creationist view is beset with difficulties, and that Jerome might well have second thoughts on that score.

In any event, Augustine has come to see that the question of the soul's origin has dreadful importance, after all. He may have seemed to dismiss it as a secondary issue when finishing off his *De libero arbitrio* but, he confesses wearily to Jerome, "it keeps coming back." And come back it will, time after time, until the aging bishop is no longer able to lift his pen.

6

Letters 169 TO 174:
PROGRESS ON THE
De Trinitate

Letter 169, to Evodius, furnishes some valuable insights into Augustine's writing activity, and into his preoccupations, during the year 415. In a letter that has been lost to us, Evodius has inquired about the writings his friend is working on, and set him several abstruse questions to answer. Augustine replies that since the days before Lent 415, he has managed to finish Books 4 and 5 of his *De civitate Dei*; he has also completed three rather sizable "volumes" in exposition of Psalms 67, 71, and 77, and his public is breathing down his neck for what *Enarrationes* remain to be done. As a result, he finds himself "unwilling to be called away from these, and slowed down by questions rushing in upon me from another quarter; so much so, that I do not wish at present to turn even to the books on the Trinity, which I have long had on hand and have not yet completed." That reluctance is further explained by the fact that those books on the Trinity "are too laborious [*nimis operosi*], and I believe they can be understood only by a few; hence, they claim my attention less urgently than writings which may, I hope, be useful to a greater number."[1]

In the final paragraph of that same letter, however, Augustine fills out this picture of the press of work besetting him: he has written a "book" (*librum*) to Jerome "consulting" him as to how his opinion on the soul's origin might be "defended," and precisely in view of the universal need for baptism; he has written him a

---

1. *Ep 169* 1. Subsequent references to this work will be given in parentheses in the text.

separate letter (*Letter 167*) inquiring whether the Epistle of St. James lends support to the moral perfectionism preached by the Pelagians; he has also written the *Ad Orosium*, and "a considerable book against the heresy of Pelagius," which *Letter 168* permits us to identify as the *De natura et gratia*, addressed to Timasius and James. All this gives firm support to Goldbacher's dating of this letter in the latter part of 415 (13).[2]

WHY HE DELAYS THE *De Trinitate*

Once again we are faced with an expression of Augustine's reluctance to finish the *De Trinitate*, but his list of works in progress sheds additional light on the reasons for that reluctance. Chevalier and his supporters, we noticed earlier, would trace that delaying tactic to the difficulties Augustine was experiencing in thinking through the relations theory that presides over Books 5 to 7 of that work.[3] That presumption might seem to be confirmed by Augustine's admission that he finds the books he has been composing "too laborious." But *Letters 120*, to Consentius, and *143*, to Marcellinus, concord substantially in suggesting that the "labor" was being expended on another issue entirely: the question Augustine finds difficulty in settling has to do with the soul and, more precisely, with the origin of the soul.

But *Letter 170*, Chevalier points out, which the Maurists date as "perhaps 415" and Goldbacher as "*circa* 415," is concerned with relations theory, and the first Sermon of *Enarratio 68*, which seems to date from 414/415, exhibits a similar concern.[4] We have seen, however, that *Letter 170*, written to a certain Maximus recently converted from Arianism, more probably dates from some time closer to 418, when Arianism flared up as a live issue in Africa,[5] whereas the sections in *Enarratio 68* devoted to relations theory reveal an Augustine brisk and competent, with the main lines of that theory firmly under control. The tone of those sections would prompt one to conclude that the process of working through those problems was well behind him.

Augustine's list of works in progress, moreover, clearly points to

2. See CSEL 58, p. 44: "exeunte 415."
3. See the Introduction above, at note 20.
4. *Relations*, p. 20.
5. La Bonnardière, *Chronologie*, p. 98.

another focus of growing preoccupation. Both *Letter 167*, to Jerome, and the *De natura et gratia* are directly concerned with Pelagianism, and Augustine's own description of the point he had in mind in *Letter 166* confirms the impression gleaned from *Letter 143*, to Marcellinus: that the question of the soul's origin was of immediate relevance to that same controversy.

One might be led to suspect that his resolution to complete his psalm interpretations also had some connection with that controversy. But whatever connection there may have been, it did not lead him to select such psalms as would give occasion to a series of anti-Pelagian thrusts: an examination of *Enarrationes 67, 71*, and *77* will show that Augustine did not work that way. Contrary to Chevalier's tacit assumption that he allowed his intellectual preoccupations to dictate his preaching, Augustine remains substantially obedient to the content of the psalms he is dealing with, limiting his anti-Pelagian remarks to those verses which would naturally inspire reflections of that sort. The same observation, *pace* Chevalier, holds for his allusions to relations theory in the first sermon of *Enarratio 68*; it seems manifestly the content of the psalm itself, rather than some personal preoccupation with the subject, which inspires those reflections.

In a word, Augustine's writing and preaching alike are dictated by the needs of his flock at any given time, much more than by any private speculative puzzle that may be gnawing away at him. Clearly, he thought the cluster of anti-Pelagian works dating from this period were more "useful" and needed by the "many" entrusted to his pastoral care than would be a *De Trinitate* understandable only by Evodius and a "few" like him (1; 13). And the same pastoral sense of responsibility would fuel his burning interest in the question of the soul's origin. Indeed, there are several indications that this temporary halt on the *De Trinitate* may even be symptomatic of a disaffection toward the work of "understanding" he urged so enthusiastically on Consentius in his *Letter 120* five years earlier. That disaffection may prove only temporary, but it could be connected with his dawning awareness that the Pelagian argumentation rested more on a trust in reasoned inference than on the word of Scripture.[6]

6. Compare other signals (like those in paragraphs 1 and 13) to similar effect. Paragraph 2 contrasts the faith of the many with the intelligence of the few; 4 stresses

Chevalier's picture of an Augustine struggling during these years with the problem of Trinitarian relations is, accordingly, more myth than fact. But we have not reached the last of the imprecisions that dog his view of this period. Another of them stems from his interpretation of *Letter 173A*. This letter, absent from the Maurist collection and from Migne, was uncovered by Goldbacher: it treats briefly of the divinity of the Holy Spirit, a question which Augustine has learned is troubling Deogratias and his confreres. It is "dictated in great haste," and Augustine admits his treatment of the subject may be found "inconclusive." If so, he enjoins them, "keep yourselves ready to read the books on the Trinity, which I am now preparing to publish in the name of the Lord; perhaps they may convince you where this brief letter cannot."

That *edere iamque dispono* encourages Goldbacher to date this letter as written shortly before the publication of the *De Trinitate*, which (as we have seen) he assumes occurred sometime around 416.[7] But the evidence we now have makes it virtually certain that Augustine did not publish the *De Trinitate* until sometime after the year 420.[8] *Letter 173A* could conceivably date from an earlier time than Goldbacher infers, a time when Augustine's *hopes* for expeditious publication had not yet been dampened by the difficulties he later saw as besetting his enterprise. This hopeful expression, moreover, could also have been followed by Augustine's discovery that his manuscript had been stolen from him, a discovery which, as we shall see, issued in the temporary resolve to stop work on the *De Trinitate* entirely. For these reasons, it would be hazardous in the extreme to draw any conclusions from *Letter 173A*.

Letters 173A AND 174

But Chevalier does draw conclusions, and he has been followed by others.[9] The result is a nest of obscurities that need clearing up

---

a similar contrast. In both cases Augustine is defending his lean to the "many" who need his pastoral care more sorely. In 12, he makes (somewhat ironic?) reference to Evodius' "avidity" for the understanding he feels obliged to deny him.

7. CSEL 58, p. 45: "Paulo post editi."

8. As Mlle La Bonnardière has convincingly argued in *Chronologie*, pp. 69–72 and 165–77; see her conclusion on p. 166.

9. See, for example, TeSelle, *Theologian*, p. 294, and Introduction, note 31, above.

before we can arrive at any firm notions about how the question of the soul's origin figures into that work on the Trinity. Having accepted 416 as the date for *Letter 173A*, and assumed that the *De Trinitate* was finally published in 419, Chevalier is faced with the anomaly *Letter 174* represents for his entire view of the matter. That letter he dates as from the same year as *Letter 173A*, assuring us that it must have been written "shortly after" its predecessor; here he has faithfully followed Goldbacher's chronology for the *Letters*, but without realizing that Goldbacher is assuming a *different* publication date for the *De Trinitate* itself. Assume, as Goldbacher did, that the *De Trinitate* was published in the year 416— three years earlier than Chevalier assumes—and it is understandable that, working back from that assumed date of the work's final publication, Goldbacher infers, mistakenly, that *Letter 174*, to the "pope" Aurelius, bishop of Carthage, must have been sent no later than the year 416.[10] For *Letter 174* is unquestionably the "covering" letter which, Augustine makes unmistakably clear, accompanied his complete and finally edited version of the *De Trinitate*.[11] But working with 419 as his assumed date of final publication, Chevalier is obliged to interpret *Letter 174* as transmitting, not that final version, but only Books 1 to 12; the other three must have followed some three years later!

Now, *Letter 174* tells us for the first time the depressing story of how his work, in an incomplete state, was stolen from Augustine and published prematurely. He had begun the *De Trinitate*, we are told, while he was still a "young man," and only now, as an

---

10. CSEL 58, p. 45. The Maurists, too, date this letter as "*circa* 415," perhaps following the same line of reasoning as Goldbacher did. Bardy in his turn, BA 12, p. 580, notes that *Trin* 15.48 cites *InJo 99* 8–9, which could date from as late as 418. So, he reasons, there must have been two distinct publications of *Trin*, one from 416 and preceded by *Ep 174*, to Aurelius, and the second from some time later, with new additions and corrections. This strained solution rests, however, on Bardy's having accepted Goldbacher's date for *Ep 174* without noticing that Goldbacher's assumed date for *Trin* was his premiss for assigning that date to *Ep 174*. Bardy fails to see that if you defer the publication date of *Trin*, you must *eo ipso* defer the date of *Ep 174*, so that no two editions are required. Again, Mlle La Bonnardière has considerably advanced this question (see note 8, above), confirming the "unique" date of publication for which Hendrikx argues in BA 15, p. 566, but incorrectly placed in 419.

11. Augustine refers to having (finally) "edited," by which he means "published," his work. There is no mention (*pace* Chevalier) of the work's still being in an incomplete state, and every indication to the contrary. See note 9 above, and what follows here on *Ep 174* and *Retr*.

"old man," has he brought it to completion. *Juvenis inchoavi, senex edidi.*

Indeed, I had laid the work aside after discovering that it had been carried off prematurely or purloined from me, before I had finished it or revised and corrected it as I had planned. I had intended to publish it as a whole, not in separate books, for the reasons that the subsequent books are linked to the preceding ones by a continuous development of the argument. Since my intention could not be carried out because of the persons who had secured access to the books before I wished it, I left off my interrupted dictation, thinking to make a complaint of this in some of my other writings, so that those who could might know that the said books had not been published by me but filched from me before I deemed them worthy of publication under my name.

Now, however, under the insistent demands of many brethren and the compulsion of your bidding, I have devoted myself, with the Lord's help, to the laborious task of finishing them. They are not corrected, as I wished, but as best I could, so that the whole work might not differ too much from the parts which have for some time been circulating surreptitiously. I send it now to your Reverence, by my son and very dear fellow-deacon, and I give my permission for it to be read, heard, and copied by any who wish.

If I had been able to carry out my original plan, it would have been much smoother and clearer, though the statements would have been the same—always, of course, as far as my ability and the difficulty of explaining such matters would allow.

Augustine has made a number of points here which are worth noting. First, he makes it clear that the version which had been stolen from him still, in his eyes, needed revising and correcting. Secondly, he assures Aurelius that later books were linked to earlier by a "continuous development of the argument," a conception that ill accords with Chevalier's hypothesis that Books 5 to 7 were composed out of sequence. Add to this that Augustine claims it was his intention to publish the work as a whole, not in the piecemeal fashion that Chevalier finds more coherent with the case he is making.[12] That intention, however, he must have settled on only after the first five books had seen distribution, for a few lines further in the same letter he informs us that certain people already have in their possession (legitimately, one assumes) copies of the

12. *Relations,* p. 23n2.

"first four or, rather," he corrects himself, "the first five" books; he hopes they will emend them in the light of this final version.

At this point another chock slips out from under Chevalier's case. For the fifth book lays out all the fundamental principles of relations theory, whereas Books 6 and 7 do little more than apply those principles, in relatively unproblematic ways, to the Scriptural data. The portrait of an Augustine still toiling through the thickets of relations theory from the years 413 to 416 has now lost its last measure of plausibility.

Thirdly, Augustine speaks of having left off a labor of dictation that had *already* been interrupted (*interruptam dictationem reliqueram*). This affirmation is consonant with the interpretation given of *Letters 143* to *164*, above, where it was argued that the problem of the soul's origin had begun to throw difficulties into Augustine's path from the year 411 on.

Fourthly, *pace* Chevalier again, he is sending Aurelius the finished work along with *Letter 174* (*opus . . . terminare curavi*).

And, fifthly, the final books he has composed are "corrected," not as he would have wished, but only as best he could, in order that they would not "differ too much" from the earlier parts which had been circulated against his will. And yet—he qualifies this reservation—had he been able to follow out his original plan, the whole work would have been "smoother and clearer," but "the statements would have been the same."

That last set of observations is of capital importance. Not only is there no three-year time gap, as Chevalier found himself obliged to invent, between "earlier" and "later" books of the *De Trinitate*, but there is no warrant for supposing—as I myself once thought there must be—any substantial inconsistency between the theory Augustine espoused in his earlier books and the theory he "would have" espoused in those he later composed.[13] True, he felt obliged to make the closing books "not differ too much" from those which had been stolen from him; but had he been able to follow out his "original plan," the "statements" in those closing books "would have been the same." When we come to interpret his *De Trinitate*, therefore, we must bear this avowal of consistency in mind.

13. See my article "Fallen Soul," which draws this mistaken premiss from the earlier article "Rejection." My mistake was to assume that the scholarly consensus on this whole question was sounder than it turned out to be and that Augustine's temporary rejection of the "fall of the soul" view must have amounted to a final rejection.

Augustine ends *Letter 174* with some indication of where his final additions and corrections introduced some differences between his edited version and the versions that might already be in the possession of others; those with the "good will and ability" will, he trusts, enter those final corrections for themselves. "I ask earnestly," he concludes, "that you order this letter to be used as a preface, separated from but at the head of those same books"—a plea, alas, too seldom honored in contemporary editions and translations.

THE *Retractations* ACCOUNT

Because of the kinships between them, I propose now to skip from *Letter 174* to Augustine's account of this same publication history in the *Retractations*. He begins by saying that he wrote these fifteen books over the span of a number of years (*per aliquot annos*); then he launches once more into the story of the famous theft:

> But when I had not yet completed the twelfth [book], and was holding on to them longer than those could bear who vehemently desired to have them, they were purloined from me, less emended than they should and could have been, when I wanted to publish them.[14] After having discovered this [theft], because still other exemplars of those books remained in our possession, I had decided that I [myself] would not publish them, but so hold on to them that I might recount in some other writing of mine what had happened to me in their regard. The brothers kept pressing me, however, and I was unable to resist; [so] I emended them to the extent I deemed them in need of emendation, I completed and published them, prefacing them with a letter which I wrote to the venerable Aurelius, bishop of the Church at Carthage. In this prologue, however, I explained what had occurred, and what in my own thinking I had wanted to do, and what, compelled by fraternal charity, I did [in fact] do.

14. Mlle La Bonnardière's translation of this sentence (she may simply be following Bardy's), in *Chronologie*, pp. 69–70, runs differently from mine: "Ils me les enlevèrent donc, moins parfaits qu'ils n'auraient dû et pu l'être au moment où je voulais des éditer." But since Augustine has spoken of an already "interrupted dictation," I take this closing phrase as telling us *when the theft* occurred or, perhaps, when Augustine discoveerd it, i.e., at the moment when he had decided to resume his efforts toward publication. Curiously enough, Bardy, in BA 12, pp. 474–75, has a comma in the Latin but not in the French.

Now, the last lines of this paragraph obviously refer to *Letter 174*, and to the fact that Augustine had sent it as his covering letter and intended prologue to the *De Trinitate*. Equally obvious is the fact that the work sent with that letter had at that time been "completed" and was ready to be "published." So much, then, for Chevalier's fancies to the contrary.

SOME REMAINING QUESTIONS

What, though, of the "emendations" he writes of? Mlle La Bonnardière has done as remarkable a job of locating these as anyone could; they consist mainly in new proëmia written for some of the earlier books.[15] We shall have to weigh their import while studying the *De Trinitate* itself.

Once again, Augustine has gone over the story of how the work, in an incomplete state, had been stolen from him. It is regrettable that neither here nor in *Letter 174* does he give any firm indication of when this theft occurred. Mlle La Bonnardière mounts a careful argument for the year 417/418, but as she herself soberly remarks, we could still have more to learn in that regard.[16] As a caution to future scholars of the question, it seems worth observing that her argumentation may have established more solidly when Augustine resumed, rather than when he decided to suspend, his work on the *De Trinitate*. But were we to accept her suggestion that the theft occurred in 417 or 418, then those were interesting years indeed; we shall see why that is so as we go further with this study.

But Mlle La Bonnardière appears to have been much more successful in locating the exact point at which Augustine had interrupted his work. He himself tells us that he had "not yet completed the twelfth [book]," and this meticulous scholar presents a well-argued case concluding that the portion composed before the theft ran up to and included chapter 14 of Book 12.[17] We shall have to investigate the possible significance of that finding further on.

But how long did Augustine suspend his activity on the *De Trinitate*? Here again, our information is fragmentary and all too

15. On these proëmia, see *Chronologie*, pp. 165–77.
16. See *Chronologie*, pp. 168–69.
17. *Chronologie*, pp. 168–69. In terms of paragraph numbers, Augustine's earlier draft would have run up to paragraph 23, inclusively.

scanty. But it seems clear that we must take, not one, but two distinct "interruptions" into account. The second of these, of undetermined duration, occurred as a result of the theft itself; Augustine's anger even brought him to entertain the thought of never finishing the work at all. How long he remained in this frame of mind we are not told. But there was just as clearly an earlier interruption as well; *Letter 174* speaks of his determination to leave off a process of dictation which had *already* been interrupted (*interruptam dictationem reliqueram*). The *Retractations* add confirmation to that reading: Augustine admits having allowed his production of other works to interfere with his progress on the *De Trinitate*.[18] That earlier interruption probably dates from as far back as 414 or 415; we saw that he writes to Evodius in 415 professing his reluctance to resume this laborious work. Indeed, Augustine may have suspended work on his *De Trinitate*, albeit temporarily, even sooner than that. His *Letter 143*, to Marcellinus, in 412, records the impatience his admirers were experiencing over his long delay in publishing a work on which, they knew, he had been laboring for some years, while in 411 he admits to Consentius he is having difficulties.

THE REAL REASON FOR HIS DELAY

But the decisive question to be answered is this: What was it that accounted for Augustine's long delay in finishing the *De Trinitate*? Was he toiling from the years 413 to 416, and presumably until the theft of 417/418, on Trinitarian relations theory, as Chevalier and others have claimed? That hypothesis, we have seen, has been reduced to a shambles. Some of the difficulties besetting it were surely of an accidental nature: Chevalier need not have dated *Letters 173A* and *174* in the year 416, a blunder which then compelled him to half-ignore and half-distort the evidence of both *Letter 174* and the *Retractations*. Nor was it truly necessary to argue that Augustine had adopted a piecemeal method of publication. But there are also substantial difficulties with his view, and they wreck it beyond salvaging. The convergence of evidence he thought he was arguing from has simply dissolved; the "continuous development" Augustine claims from book to book, and the admission

18. *Retr* 2.15.1.

that Book 5 had, apparently long since, been copied and distributed, strike at the very heart of Chevalier's assumption that the sections on relations theory must have been thought through so late as to be composed well out of their natural order. His proposal, in short, turns out to be less a product of scholarship than a creation of the scholar's imagination.

But consider the counter-hypothesis, that it was the problem of the soul's origin which braked Augustine's progress on the *De Trinitate* during those years, and the evidence we have examined for the last five chapters falls into an entirely plausible pattern. *Letters 120, 143,* and *166* all suggest strongly that this was the sticking point; a goodly number of the works to which he accorded such priority that they interfered with his continuing work on his *De Trinitate* were directed against the Pelagian heresy, and his editors have rightly included among them his repeated efforts to gain some clarity about the origin of the soul. Pelagianism had transformed that question, in Augustine's view, from a matter for leisurely speculation to an important and potentially dangerous issue—dangerous, but also very obscure.

Augustine will devote almost three entire books of his *De Genesi ad litteram* to that troubling question; it will be the central concern of *Letters 180, 190, 202A* and of the *De anima et ejus origine*; it will feature prominently in the *De peccato originali* and in those sections of the *De peccatorum meritis et remissione* which, I submit once again, Augustine must have written well after the year 411. All these works and letters, in fact, date from the period between 416 and 419.

Most crucially for our purposes, we shall come to see that the issue of the soul's origin was the very point over which Augustine was laboring when, having reached Book 12 of his *De Trinitate*, he thought it wiser to suspend his efforts and await further light.[19]

---

19. Bardy, BA 12, p. 580, understands *Praed* 13 to mean that Augustine is presently *sending* a copy of this work to Prosper and Hilary; I do not find the Latin patient of that interpretation. But were Bardy's speculation correct, it would insinuate a more approving attitude toward the finished work than *Ep 174* seems to convey. Compare Hendrikx, in BA 15, p. 559, for an interpretation of this episode similar to my own.

7

THE MESSAGE OF
ROMANS 9:11
TAKES EFFECT

WE HAVE SEEN that as early as his reply to Simplician's "various questions," in 396, Augustine had come to the conviction that Paul's words about Esau and Jacob in Romans 9:11 precluded any theory that would make God's "election" dependent on the merits of the one elected. The Pelagian controversy only served to confirm this conviction. Again and again, when faced with this question, he appeals to Romans 9:11 to combat any suggestion that human merits, whether previous or "foreseen" by God, have anything to do with God's election of those whom He will "grace."[1]

Allied to this conviction was Augustine's stand on infant baptism and on the damnation of infants who die without baptism. One can appreciate the scandal this intransigent stand occasioned, especially in the hearts of Pelagian sympathizers, persuaded as they were of the innocence of infant souls, freshly come from the creative hand of the all-good God. But Augustine's writings show that there soon surfaced in the discussion a kind of mid-position, one that suggested that infants, even newborns, were capable of personal sin; the shock of their damnation might, after all, be attenuated. Instead of welcoming this suggestion, though, Augustine goes to war against it, time after time. The infant, he argues, in the normal course of events, does not possess the developed power of reason

1. Augustine uses Rom. 9:11 with this *limited* bearing in *En 134* 5 (from the year 411/412) *Spir* 40 (412/413), *LitPel* 2.15 and 20 (420/421), *Enchir* 98 (421), *CorGrat* 14 (426/427); and in *Epp 186*, passim (417), *194* 34 and 37 (418), *196* 13 (418) and *217* 16 (432?). On *Ep 217*, see Goldbacher's labored argument, CSEL 58, pp. 57–58.

necessary for recognizing sin as sin.[2] He himself makes one concession: that damned though they be, infants dying without baptism will suffer the "mildest of punishments" (mitissima poena).
But to the Pelagian suggestion that God may consign them to some
"mid-place," to an "eternal life" which is neither hell nor the
"Kingdom of God," he stands unalterably opposed.[3]

AN INFERENCE IGNORED

It may seem strange at first that Augustine did not immediately
draw the inference that Romans 9:11 excluded all prenatal sins,
the sin of pre-existent souls among them. Here, however, our
modern tendency to think of the "fallen soul" hypothesis in Origenistic terms may represent a snare. There was, in Origen's effort to
defend God's justice and to keep election from being a totally
arbitrary choice on God's part, a seamless quality that we may not
be entitled to read into Augustine's present thinking. Origen saw
our original life-situations, with all their differences and apparent
inequities, as pointing both backward and forward: backward to
the gravity of our Original Sin, and forward to the spiritual progress
or lack of it that would eventually ground God's election or non-
election of us. His theory worked both retrospectively and prospectively.[4]

It may well be that Augustine's own early thinking, too, worked
in both those directions. But his treatment of Origen's view (or
something very like it) in the reply to Simplician shows the possibility of drawing a distinction. The sin in pre-existence could well
account for our initial life-situation, and even (to all human appearances, at least) for our enjoying uneven capacities for spiritual
progress. But once Simplician's question had compelled him to
make God's election so sovereignly free as in no way to depend on
our faith, works, or efforts and achievements toward spiritual progress, Augustine was still at liberty to think that our life-situations

2. See Epp 279 6, 186 12 and 13, 187 22–26. Note the terms propria peccata and
propria voluntas in 186 13.
3. See Epp 184A 2–3 and 190 6–8. The latter text shows Augustine grappling with
a problem growing out of his increasing anti-Pelagian insistence that all need the
grace of Christ, the "just ones" of the Old Testament and good-living pagans as well.
This universal need of salvation through Christ underlies Augustine's stress on the
universality of Original Sin. See Ep 186 12–13.
4. See above, chap. 2, note 34.

could be explained retrospectively by a "fall" of our souls, *without* that explanation's working prospectively to determine God's election of us.

There may, indeed, have been a second distinction operative in Augustine's mind: between that universal misery which is the common lot of sinful mankind, and the individual, personal quality of God's election of some, not all, of us from out of that universal, common lot. Indeed, the change he admits Simplician provoked in his thinking may, at its deepest level, have amounted to viewing individual election as totally independent of any gradations in the penal misery we all share.

But whether or not this was the way Augustine's mind was working, the facts of the matter are plain: long after the revolutionary insight registered in the *To Simplician* on the question of election, he still lists the "fallen soul" hypothesis as one among four, as though it still enjoyed the same *droit de cité* as the other three.

. . . AND FINALLY DRAWN

But he does eventually draw the inference. Romans 9:11, he comes to think (even if only for a time), appears to exclude all prenatal sin, hence, pre-existent as well. Here too, however, we are left largely to conjecture the routes his mind followed on the way to drawing that inference. It would seem more than plausible that Pelagius, notably with his *Commentary on St. Paul*, helped bring Augustine to the verge of this additional insight. It was one thing to dismiss Origen's theory as the work of a dreamer; Augustine did not have to take Pelagius' judgment of that with profound seriousness. More disturbing was Pelagius' semi-rational argument that from the creationist hypothesis it must follow that infants are born innocent, without taint of Adam's sin; we have seen how seriously Augustine took that contention.[5] It was partly this semi-rational cast of Pelagius' argumentation that persuaded Augustine more and more to make faith in Scripture, and notably in Paul's Letter to the Romans, the foundation of his position on infant sinfulness. Considerations from human reason and all its fragile assumptions

5. This consideration is already implicit throughout *Ep 166*, to Jerome; Augustine refers explicitly to this Pelagian argumentation in *Ep 190* 22. For his contention about infant innocence, without this argument's being adduced, see *Epp 175* (to Pope Innocent), *178* 1, and (to John of Jerusalem) *179* 6.

about how God's justice must work never quite disappear, but they gradually subside into second place in Augustine's thinking. He will argue that infant guilt justifies God in damning them.[6] Mercy is mercy, and grace gratuitous; there is no injustice in God's showing His mercy by gracing whom He will.[7] But in the end, his ultimate appeal is to those "unsearchable ways" that put God's justice beyond the reach of human examination.[8]

That surrender to the "mystery," however, must not be abused. Augustine's fears about the creationist theory never quite desert him; for it is one thing to claim that God's justice is unsearchable, quite another to put forth a theory that makes even that unsearchable justice seem manifestly unjust. The question of the soul's origin, therefore, remains an important one for Augustine.[9] Its very importance, though, is a strong reason for his repeated warnings that care and sound exegetic method must go into any attempt to settle it from Scripture.[10]

Together with his fears about creationism, he maintains a curiously non-committal attitude on his third hypothesis: that souls existing elsewhere are "sent" into their bodies. We have seen in his letter to Jerome that he finds this view embodying the same assumption as creationism: if "sent" by God, the soul is *eo ipso* supposed "innocent," so that all the difficulties involved in creationism afflict this theory as well. It is no surprise that, for a number of years, Augustine makes no express mention of this hypothesis: it almost seems to drift completely out of his attention, as though so unimportant as not to merit mention.[11] He seems content to limit consideration to the two theories that remain, once the "pre-existence" theories have been discarded: creationism and traducianism.[12]

Between those remaining theories, however, Augustine hesitates to the very end, and repeatedly "defends" his right to hesitate be-

6. See, for an example, *Ep 193* 4.
7. See *Epp 194* 4 and *199* 9–12.
8. See *Ep 194* 10 and passim.
9. See *Ep 180* 5.
10. See *Epp 190* and *202A*, to Optatus, *180*, to Oceanus, and *AnOrig*. Also evident in these texts are Augustine's growing reliance on Scripture, and distrust of the human reason on which he thought Pelagius was relying.
11. One wonders how seriously Augustine ever took this hypothesis; and yet, he will reconsider it in *GenLitt*. See below.
12. See *Epp 180* and *190* 1.

tween them.[13] Again and again, he warns of the "logic" to which Pelagius had alerted him, in the creationist position: it could be so understood as to preclude the guilt of infants,[14] and the universality of Christ's redemption, so vital a part of the *fundatissima fides*, the Church's bedrock belief. His distaste for traducianism persists, and its reason becomes more and more plain: he despises its materialistic notion of the soul.[15]

REJECTION OF THE FOURTH HYPOTHESIS

The decisive step in narrowing down the original four hypotheses on the soul's origin to these two remaining—creationism and traducianism—was the rejection of the fourth, "Origenist," hypothesis. Augustine takes that step in two stages: we have seen him move through the first stage in his reply *Ad Orosium*, his brief exclamation in *Letter 164*, to Evodius, and in *Letter 166*, to Jerome. Here he must content himself with what a later age would call a theological "argument," albeit an argument overlaid with revulsion at the cyclic setting of Origen's theory, and its elimination of all security in our final beatitude.

But Augustine's increasing reliance on Scripture rather than reason leaves him less than content with this roundabout and, in the last analysis, human method of excluding this hypothesis. Hence, the alacrity and confidence with which he pounces on Romans 9:11 the moment it appears clear to him that Paul's words categorically exclude any previous merits, and therefore the pre-incarnate sin, so pivotal to the Origenist theory.

WHEN DID AUGUSTINE TAKE THE STEP?

Were accepted notions of chronology to be honored, and the *De peccatorum meritis et remissione* to be dated as published in 411/ 412, one would have to say that the first recorded instance of Augustine's use of Romans 9:11 in this way is found in that work. But, as

13. See *Epp 190* 2 and passim. Could it be that Augustine eventually came to see that, since neither of these remaining theories would do, he must devise a new one on his own?

14. See *Epp 180* 2 and *190* 13, 22–26.

15. See *Epp 190* 14–15, and the treatment of *GenLitt* in the next chapter.

we have tried to argue, that chronology for the *De meritis* is open
to serious question. A similar chronological haziness affects the
applications of this text in both the *De civitate Dei* and the *De
Genesi ad litteram*. Augustine was laboring on both those works
for long periods, and there is always the strong possibility that the
applications of the Romans text which occur in both of them could
be the result of later insertions.[16] It will be sounder method, then,
first to trace the applications of Romans 9:11 to the Origenist
hypothesis in those works that represent little or no dating problem; then we may be in a position to deal more effectively with the
applications that occur in the *De meritis*, *De Genesi ad litteram*,
and *De civitate Dei*.

If we exclude those applications of Romans 9:11 which bear
uniquely on the question of previous merits, without the further
step of excluding the Origenist hypothesis, there are some fifteen
instances where Augustine appeals to this text to discard the theory
of prenatal sin. *Letter 180*, to Oceanus, who had written to inquire
whether Jerome had replied to Augustine's *Letter 166*, would have
been an appropriate opportunity for an application of Romans
9:11, but no such thing occurs; the date is 416, late in the year.

The first occurrence of such an application which we can date
with reasonable confidence is found in *Sermo 165* 6, which Augustine delivered "perhaps" in September of the year 417.[17] In any
event, its anti-Pelagian cast is evident; Augustine is discussing

16. TeSelle, *Theologian*, pp. 70 and 257, dates *GenLitt* 6.14–16 as a rejection
occurring in the year 406; that date he substantiates by adducing a single parallel
from 6.16 with two sections of *InJo* (dated in or around that same year). Such arguments from parallels are always risky, but in this case I cannot accept TeSelle's as
stronger than the evidence from chronological development which I have presented
here. Is it truly credible, to cite but one example, that Augustine would have used
Rom. 9:11 to reject this hypothesis in 406, and then, in 415, written *Ep 166* in the
terms he used there? Note that the newly discovered letter to Jerome (*Ep* 19, in CSEL
88, pp. 91–93), which Johannes Divjak reliably dates from the year 416 (ibid., pp.
lxi–lxii), has Augustine acknowledging receipt of two anti-Pelagian books which
Jerome had recently composed, but making no reference to the question of the soul.
    W. Eborowicz, in "*Ad Romanos 9, 11* et la critique de la théorie du péché de l'âme
préexistante," in *Texte und Untersuchungen*, 103 (1968), 272–76, confines himself to
presenting those texts in which Augustine uses Romans 9:11 to refute the "fallen soul"
theory. Hence, he misses the transition *Ser 165* makes between Augustine's application
of this text to "election" and, now, to the fallen soul (see p. 275). The chronological
gap between *Mer* (which Eborowicz dates from 412) and *Ser 165* creates no problems
for him; nor does Augustine's later usage of qualifying this text with terms like
propria vita. O'Daly, who cites this study ("Origin," p. 187n17) also seems uncon-
scious of any such problems.
    17. Verbraken, *Sermons authentiques*, p. 94.

God's freedom in election, and the mysteries it holds for our human grasp. In an effort to plumb those mysteries, he tells his flock, certain thinkers have invented "fables" that would have us believe that souls "sin on high, in heaven, and according to [the seriousness of] their sins are directed to the bodies they merit, and enveloped in them as in prisons worthy of them." But the Apostle, "meaning to commend grace," contradicts them by saying of Rebecca's twin sons that God's election came to them while "not yet born, nor had they done anything good or evil" (Rom. 9:11). So much, then, for this theory about souls and their alleged conduct (*conversatio*) "in heaven, before they [came into the] body," something which would necessarily entail their doing either good or evil, and being "thrust down into earthly bodies in accord with their merits." The Apostle's opinion is plain, and because of that *evidentem sententiam* the Catholic faith rejects this view.

Here we witness Augustine making the transition from his earlier to his later application of this text; from defending God's freedom in election, it will now be pressed into service to quash his former fourth hypothesis, but quash it at its very root. The same confidence shows in the second such application, which occurs in the *De peccato originali* (2.36). Here, however, the "perhaps" that afflicts our dating of *Sermo 165* can be erased; the *Retractations* (2.50) firmly dates this work as written after the condemnations of Pelagius leveled by Popes Innocent and Zosimus—hence, after May 1, 418. Augustine is inquiring why infants should be subject to damnation; he affirms: "It is not as some Platonists have thought [that this is] because every such infant is thus requited . . . for what it did of its own will [*sua voluntate*] previous to the present life," for Romans 9:11 "says most plainly" that before their birth "they did neither good nor evil."[18] The punishment of these infants, therefore, must be accounted for by their belonging to the "mass of perdition" born of Adam.

The next such use of the Romans text occurs in the year 418/419, in *Letter 190*, to Optatus, a fellow–North African bishop.[19] Optatus

18. These Platonists, Augustine adds, suppose that the infant enjoyed the freedom to live well or ill *ante hoc corpus*, "before [possessing] this body"—i.e., the mortal body of post-Adamic existence.
19. Optatus is inquiring whether Jerome had ever answered Augustine's queries on the soul. Augustine stresses (*Ep 190* 5) that infant damnation, much more than the famous adulterine union objection, is the principal obstacle to holding the

has written to Renatus, a priest and obvious admirer of Augustine's, inquiring about the origin of the soul. Renatus has prevailed on Augustine to answer. It is interesting that Optatus offers only the creationist and traducianist alternatives, and that Augustine quite willingly accepts these terms of discussion.[20] Optatus must understand that Augustine has never dared claim any certainty in choosing between these two theories.[21] But he sets the limits of their discussion by laying down his "certainties" about the soul. The first of these, remarkably enough,[22] is from Scripture: that Christ's redemptive grace is necessary for all without exception (3).[23] Only then does he put forth his more philosophical certainties: that the soul is not part of God; is spirit, not body. At this point he touches directly on the origin question, and in doing so reverts to the Scriptural key:

> The reason why [the soul] comes into this corruptible body which weighs it down is not because it is being driven there in punishment for a previous life badly spent among celestial beings or in some other parts of the universe; for when the Apostle speaks of the twin sons of Rebecca, he says that they had not yet done any good or evil . . . [4].

Augustine's way of expressing himself, that the soul "comes into this corruptible body," leaves something to be desired in the way of precision. It does not strictly fit with either the creationist or the traducianist way of conceiving things.[24] But leaving that aside for the moment, it is evident that Augustine's rejection of this fourth hypothesis has swiftly developed into a firm and confident

---

creationist hypothesis. Note that Divjak, in CSEL 88, pp. lxiv–lxvi, confirms the accepted dating of the works that concern us here.

20. *Ep 190* 1–2 and passim. Further references to this letter are included in the text.

21. In 16, Augustine protests that he feels no shame about his continuing hesitations on this question of the soul's origin. Some sensitivity may be showing.

22. This is the earliest departure I have been able to find from Augustine's former habit of first presenting his more philosophical certainties on the soul; see, for instance, *Ep 166* 3–5. Once again, he is increasingly insistent that these matters be settled from Scripture, with reasoned "understanding" definitely in second place.

23. The damnation of unbaptized infants follows from this as its corollary. Notice the phrase *Unde si origo animae lateat*. Augustine is directing a slant against the Pelagian manner of reasoning from creationism to a repudiation of this Scriptural certainty.

24. As Augustine's earlier, more precise expressions of the creationist hypothesis indicate he must have realized. He may be re-expressing matters quite intentionally. See note 13, above.

intellectual reflex. Whatever reverence he may formerly have had toward these "Platonists" and their theory of the soul's origin, it has yielded to an unquestioning trust in Paul's words to the Romans.

ENTER THE *Propria Vita* DISTINCTION

Or so, at least, it would seem. *His igitur firmissime constitutis*—Augustine begins paragraph 5 of this letter as though the decks had been entirely cleared of the "fall" hypothesis. Whether we opt in this darksome question for a creationist or a traducianist view of the soul's origin, he then goes on to say, our faith is "safe" in holding that no one, infant or adult, can come to salvation unless liberated from the "contagion of that ancient death and the bond of sin which he contracted by birth" into this life.

But in sketching what appears to be his present version of traducianism, Augustine introduces a notion that will have a certain history in his works to come. It may be that our souls were "originally in our parents"—by which he seems to mean Adam and Eve—but "up to that time there were none of them who exercised their own and proper lives" (*cum essent originaliter in parentibus, adhuc ipsi nulli erant qui suas et proprias vitas agerent*). That situation, he is saying, might explain how we contracted the guilt of our first parents' sin, and still not contravene Paul's warning that before being born, we did neither good nor evil. For, his implication seems to be, "we" would then have sinned in our first parents' sin, but since we were not yet living our "own," our "proper," lives, we would have sinned in their act of sinning *before we were an actual "we."* A baffling solution, surely, but to a baffling problem, one must admit! The remark, however, is made only in passing, and in a style so compressed as to be almost cryptic. We shall be wiser to await further clarification of this "proper life" idea.

Having rejected that "fall" hypothesis at the very outset, however, Augustine is still not quite ready to discuss the relative merits of creationism and traducianism; he must deal with the various questions touching on God's "justice" in damning those infants who, it is now clear, "did neither good nor evil" before their birth (5–12).[25] But similar problems about divine justice beset the crea-

25. These questions include the salvation of the "just" in Old Testament times (6–8). Here Augustine emits that hard saying (9–12) that many must be damned in order that the few may properly appreciate the riches of God's grace that saved them.

tionist hypothesis, which Optatus clearly favors.[26] This is the bias with which Augustine opens the discussion of that hypothesis, and it brings him to challenge Optatus to find an answer to this central difficulty, an answer which until now has eluded Augustine (13).

But if Optatus fails to find the answer to this central difficulty, should he then adopt the traducianist hypothesis instead? No. Persist, rather, in the search for that answer; for what could be more "perverse" than the materialist claim of Tertullian and his traducianist followers that the soul is really a body, and propagated by corporeal seed? *Dementia*—madness—is the only word for such a view (14–15)![27] But perhaps one might elaborate an acceptable "spiritual" version of traducianism? Perhaps; but Augustine sees nothing but difficulties in the way of it (15)!

He feels no shame, then, in confessing his ignorance on this issue. But his ignorance has limits. It does not extend to agreeing with the various Scriptural groundings which adherents of both traducianism and creationism have been known to invoke in favor of their views. And here Augustine treats Optatus to a lesson in Scriptural exegesis. He takes up a number of texts adduced by one side and the other, and shows that a closer examination with more rigorous attention to both Scriptural expression and the issues involved deprives both sides of the premature certainties to which they lay claim (16–19).

After a brief account of the exchange involving Marcellinus, Jerome, and himself—he still hopefully awaits a reply from Jerome! —Augustine ends his letter with a warning about the conclusions Pelagius drew from his creationist premiss (20–22) and some final reminders on what the issues in the creationist–traducianist debate really were. The central point is what he had explained earlier. How are we to understand that mysterious truth of which faith makes us inconcussibly certain: that even if freshly created for their individual bodies, and without any pre-incarnate sin, the souls of unbaptized infants are justly subject to damnation (23–26)?

---

26. That this is Optatus' conviction is clear from the language Augustine uses in 13 and 14.

27. It is hard to understand how, in the face of language like this (and that used in *GenLitt* on the same issue), anyone could ever propose that Augustine's favored hypothesis was traducianism.

VINCENTIUS VICTOR'S CHALLENGE

Optatus seems to be only one of many with premature certainties on the soul's origin; the young Vincentius Victor was another. A recent convert from Rogatianism, somewhat carried away by his own rhetorical skills, Vincentius was shocked to hear that the great Augustine professed his ignorance on this important question. This, he suggested, not without a trace of arrogance, was tantamount to admitting he was one of those "cattle" bereft of any knowledge of his own nature and quality.[28]

Again, the priest Renatus seems to have been the clearinghouse for this exchange. Vincentius has transmitted to the priest Peter a book airing his own views on the topic; Peter has communicated this to Renatus, and Renatus in turn sent it off to Augustine. Augustine's reply, the *De anima et ejus origine*, written in the year 419, comprises three distinct parts: Book 1 to Renatus, Book 2 to Peter, and Books 3 and 4 to Vincentius himself.

Pity the poor reader of this work. Besides the tiresome repetitions, Augustine handling many of the same points for all three addressees, there is the additional fact that Vincentius, with a headlong confidence in inverse proportion to his control of either method or relevant information, presented an incredibly messy, inconsistent, and self-contradictory position. The one thing clear about it is his intended opposition to traducianism: beyond that, his position seems to have combined in slapdash fashion elements of all the other three competing hypotheses, along with Augustine's personal *bête noire*, the claim that the soul was corporeal.

The order Augustine observes in his reply is significant. He first points out, to this recent convert, that class of errors which conflict with his faith as a "Catholic"; only then does he go on to a second group—including the corporeality issue—more "philosophical" in nature. As to the hypotheses on the soul's origin, he first discards—what some of Vincentius' unguarded expressions suggested—the idea that the soul is part of God. He then eliminates the Origenist theory of the soul's fall—which Vincentius had somehow succeeded in coloring with a Pelagian tint—applying the Romans 9:11 text,

---

28. Augustine seems to have been stung by this remark. He alludes to it in *AnOrig* 1.26 and 4.2, 8, and 12.

as we shall shortly see. Finally, again without even a mention of the third, "divinely sent" hypothesis, he settles down to a discussion of traducianism and creationism.

The first application of the Romans text occurs in Augustine's communication to Renatus. He has shown that Vincentius' tortured theory puts him in a dilemma: either all infants are saved, or God is convicted of condemning innocent souls.[29] "I affirm that neither of these alternative cases should be admitted," he says,

> or that third opinion, which would have it that souls sinned in some other state previous to the flesh, and so deserved to be condemned to the flesh; for the Apostle has most distinctly stated that "the children [Esau and Jacob], being not yet born, had done neither good nor evil."

Augustine employs the same text when writing to Vincentius himself, who had proposed that "the soul deservedly lost something by the flesh, although it was of good merit previous to the flesh." "Do not, I pray you, believe, say, or teach that," Augustine implores him, "if you wish to be Catholic. For the Apostle declares that 'children who are not yet born have done neither good nor evil' "— and cannot, therefore be of "good merit," or bad for that matter, "previous to the flesh."[30]

THE EFFECT OF ROMANS 9:11

Compare the peremptory quality of these rejections of pre-incarnate sin with the roundabout arguments of the *Ad Orosium* and *Letter 166*, to Jerome, and it is clear what effect Augustine's late-won view of Romans 9:11 has had on his way of dealing with that hypothesis. "The Apostle declares," "the Apostle has most distinctly stated"— these are the expressions of a confident man, who fully expects us to see in Paul's words an unmistakable guideline for us if we "wish to be Catholic."

Augustine's second answer to Optatus, the next year, is, if anything, even more emphatic. Optatus has written to ask him whether he has received any illumination from Jerome on this bothersome

29. Ibid. 1.14.
30. Ibid. 3.9. Note that in 2.11 (written to Peter), Augustine demolishes much this same position by showing up one of the several contradictions in Vincentius' views; in that case, he makes no use of Rom. 9:11.

issue. Augustine quotes part of the cordial but non-committal reply Jerome had sent him. Optatus will understand that, in the circumstances, Augustine prefers not to publish his own *Letter 166* for fear Jerome might still have something to contribute to the discussion. If publish it he eventually does, he hopes that others "will find how these matters are to be examined, and how things not known are not rashly to be affirmed." For until now, Augustine admits, "I have not discovered how the soul derives its sin from Adam, which it is not allowed us to doubt, without being itself derived from Adam, which is something to be carefully inquired into rather than rashly affirmed."[31]

Augustine obviously hopes that his correspondent will take both these remarks to heart, for Optatus appears to have made it clear that he remains a stout opponent of the traducianist position. "But by what reasoning or what evidences from divine Scriptures you prove that view is false, I do not know," Augustine observes. Optatus believes that God "creates" souls, and surely Scripture is on his side in that. But traducianism does not conflict with that faith; it simply affirms that God creates souls in a certain way—i.e., by propagation from the original Adamic soul. It is, then, unclear to Augustine what positive position Optatus is putting forward. But

> God forbid that you should hold that opinion of Origen and Priscillian, or any others who have the same idea, that souls are sent into earthly and mortal bodies in accord with their merits in a previous life. Apostolic authority is quite contrary to this opinion, where it speaks of Esau and Jacob and says that before they were born they had done nothing either good or evil.[32]

"God forbid [*absit*] that you should hold that opinion" for "[a]postolic authority is quite contrary to" it (*prorsus contradicit*). Augustine's confidence in the demonstrative power of Romans 9:11 is reaching its high-water mark. It remains there for the last two applications of this text that I know of. In 423 or thereabouts, he writes to Vitalis of Carthage, admonishing him for some questionable opinions he held about the need for grace. "We Catholic Christians," Augustine tells him, "know [*scimus*] that the yet unborn have, in their own lives [*in vita propria*], done nothing, either good

---

31. *Ep* 202A 6, formerly dated as of 420, but now (see Divjak in CSEL 88, p. lxv) as from December 419.
32. *Ep* 202A 8.

or evil; nor have they come into the miseries of this life on account of their deserts in some prior life, a prior life which none of them individually could have [enjoyed] as their very own" (*quam nullam propriam singuli habere potuerunt*).[33] Augustine has come to connect our "proper" life with a life we each live as "individuals" (*singuli*). Time will tell whether that connection is a significant one.

Augustine's final application of Romans 9:11, as far as I have been able to ascertain, occurs in the *Retractations*, when he is commenting on his early *Contra Academicos*. For reasons that will become clear further on, I postpone consideration of it until later. These, then, are the applications of the text that can be dated with reasonable confidence; what of their occurrence in the *De peccatorum meritis et remissione*?

ROMANS 9:11 IN THE De Meritis

In the first book of the *De peccatorum meritis et remissione*, of uncertain date,[34] Augustine is brought to discuss the fate of unbaptized infants. Why, he is asking (30), do some infants die unbaptized, others baptized, the former to be damned, the latter saved through Christ's redemptive grace? This, he affirms, is nothing less than inscrutable to us, as it was even to St. Paul. Some, he observes, have tried to remove this inscrutability by teaching that "souls which once sinned in their heavenly abode descend by stages and degrees to bodies suited to their deserts, and, as a penalty for their previous life, are tormented either more or less severely by corporeal chastisements." Augustine goes on to show a genuine conversance with the detailed concerns of this view: it tries to explain bodily limitations and intellectual endowments as well as natural moral qualities in terms of the variety of pre-incarnate sins.[35] But, he

---

33. *Ep 217* 16.

34. See the obscurities in dating his work treated in chap. 2, above. I include references to Book and paragraph numbers in the text.

35. Augustine could have been told many of these features of the Origenist position by Orosius, whose *Commonitorium* would then only be a summary of "high points." But enough time may have passed for him to have gained light on the issues from elsewhere.

Note that Augustine's parenthetical admission that believing is an "act of one's own will" (*propriae voluntatis*) seems on the face of it to contradict the position enunciated in his *Simp*. But it appears to me more likely that he has entered into the Origenist position (again, *dato, non concesso*) in order to argue that even on their supposition these defenders of God's "justice" must in the end abandon their

argues, it cannot explain why some morally endowed persons can live in such circumstances as never to have the Gospel preached to and baptism conferred upon them, whereas someone like the "good thief" can live the life he did and still hear, at the end, "this day shalt thou be with Me in paradise." Even the proponents of this theory must ultimately admit the inscrutability of God's "unsearchable ways." But Augustine's argument comes after the single thrust with which he discards this "now rejected and exploded opinion."[36] Holy Scripture, more precisely Romans 9:11, he declares, "presents a most manifest contradiction to it; for when recommending divine grace, it says: 'For the children being not yet born, neither having done any good or evil ...,' " were one of them divinely elected, the other rejected (1.28–31).

Again, in 3.17, when discussing why Christian parents do not automatically beget Christian children, he offers his readers three possibilities: the soul may originate in creationist or traducianist fashion, or it may be "sent" into the body. They will "think one of these things of the soul" as they please, "because, of course, you hold with the Apostle, that before birth it had done nothing good or evil."

This brings Augustine to discuss the acceptability of traducianism (3.18). He quotes Pelagius to show how "circumspect" he was about this "very difficult" question, "rightly determining on so obscure a subject (on which we can find in Scripture no certain and obvious testimonies, or with very great difficulty discover any) to speak with hesitation rather than with confidence."[37] Augustine's opinion here echoes his remarks on the same thorny subject at the end of Book 2, where he raises the question whether traducianism or creationism can better explain the guilt of infants and their need for baptism. "A broad and important subject," Augus-

"reasoned" view and make the appeal to the "O altitudo!" which he himself is obliged to invoke. For it manifestly lies outside our power, he argues, to guarantee our living in circumstances where the Gospel will be preached to us.

36. Compare this language with that in AnOrig 3.9; it seems to hint that there may have been an official condemnation of this doctrine, but I can find no trace of any such in the histories of the epoch.

37. Compare 3.5–6, where Augustine notes the same avoidance of the issue by Pelagius, but interprets his non-committal stance as "perhaps" only welcoming any arguments that might be offered against traducianism. (Given Pelagius' known fondness for creationism, there may be some irony here.) Bear in mind that the traducianists argued that they could explain the transmission of a sin that the *soul itself* committed. That point will become crucial in what follows.

tine concludes, which would "require another treatise." But any such discussion, he warns, "ought to be conducted with temper and moderation, so as to deserve the praise of cautious inquiry, rather than the censure of headstrong assertion" (2.59).

But his way of putting the counter-theory[38] is nothing less than baffling, and the puzzle may be significant. If the soul be not "propagated" as the traducianists hold, we may ask whether the soul (the Latin now becomes extremely condensed and almost untranslatable):

> eo ipso quo carni peccati aggravanda miscetur, jam ipsius peccati remissione et sua redemptione opus habeat, Deo per summam prescientiam judicante, qui parvuli ab isto reatu non mereantur absolvi, etiam qui nondum nati nihil alicubi propria sua vita egerunt vel boni vel mali: et quomodo Deus [in this non-traducianist hypothesis] non sit tamen auctor reatus ejusdem, propter quem redemptio Sacramenti necessaria est et animae parvuli [2.59].

Now, Augustine is asking a question, not making a statement; but the suppositions involved in the question are somewhat surprising. He is entertaining the notion of a "something whereby" [eo quo] the soul, which "had to be weighed down" (aggravanda), was "mixed with the flesh of sin" (which Augustine regularly sees as in fact "weighing down" the soul). Was that "something" an act? an occurrence? even some sin on the part of the soul? We are not told yet; but he clearly hypothesizes it as the "something" that might account for the fact that the soul is "mixed" with sinful flesh, but de jure so mixed since the soul had somehow become (or been divinely judged?) aggravanda, in the gerundive mood. In this hypothesis, he goes on to say, the soul "would still [or: already] have need [jam . . . opus habeat] of remission" ipsius peccati, "of [the] sin itself."

At this point, that vague eo quo ("something whereby"—or "something on account of which"?) seems clearly to have taken on a sinful character. This Augustine connects with the soul's need of a "redemption of its own" (sua redemptione). In this case, the hypothesis continues, "God [would be] the judge, through His lofty foreknowledge, of which infants do not deserve [non mereantur]

---

38. Augustine's expression of the creationist theory has, we have seen, become more and more imprecise; but I cannot be certain he is really referring to creationism here.

to be absolved from that guilt [*ab isto reatu*], even those who, not yet born, did nothing, anywhere, in their own proper life [*propria vita*], either good or evil." Still pursuing his hypothetical question, Augustine specifies that whatever implications we read into it, we must ask how "God would not be the author of that same guilt [*reatus*] on account of which the redemption [by] the sacrament [of baptism] is necessary for the infant soul as well [as for souls more advanced in age]."

Now, Augustine's resort to the language of Romans 9:11 clearly indicates that this sentence was written after the force of that text had dawned on him. But he expresses that force in the same striking phrase he uses in his letters to Optatus and to Vitalis: Paul means us to understand that we did not "do either good or evil *in some proper life*" lived somewhere, or elsewhere (*alicubi*), "before we were born." The phrase *propria vita* has an apparently restrictive force. Is there, the reader asks, some other kind of life we could have led, besides a life that was "proper, our own"?

That question is compounded by another. Romans 9:11 seems first to have forbidden us to think of any kind of merit, or guilt, incurred "before we were born"; but here Augustine is clearly, and seriously, entertaining a hypothesis in which the newborn soul would be the bearer of exactly such guilt (*reatus* appears not once but twice), a guilt that puts it in need of baptismal remission "of its own," "of the sin itself" (*ipsius peccati*). How can Augustine contemplate this possibility as reconcilable with Romans 9:11— unless, as we have begun to suspect, that phrase *propria vita* is in fact being used in a restrictive sense, and he is toying with the unexpressed possibility of our soul's having become *aggravanda* through some guilty act committed in a prenatal, but "non-proper," life?

This text holds a third surprise as well. Augustine proposes an appeal to God's foreknowledge to decide which infants "would merit" release (by being accorded baptism, while others were not) from that guilt; but this, one had thought, was the very position he had rejected in the *To Simplician!* There, however, he had not yet been brought to wrestle with this agonizing question—which his rejection of Origen's "explanation" has made all the more agonizing—why some children are fortunate enough to receive baptism, while others, not so fortunate, are for no apparent fault of their own consigned to eternal damnation. The appeal to God's foreknowledge, then, may hint that Augustine momentarily feels the need of reviewing his earlier rejection of it in the light of what he has subsequently learned; but it also serves to warn us away from suspecting that he means to explain that certain infants "merit" baptism for the reason that their (antecedent) "guilt"—hypothetically envisaged here—was *either greater or less* than that of others. For that would clearly contravene Paul's teaching that our "election" is based on no such *antecedent* merits.

A POSSIBLE MEANING OF *Propria Vita*

But, Augustine's entertainment of this hypothesis suggests, Paul does not directly forbid us to think that our *universal need for baptism* may be traceable to some antecedent "guilt"—so long as we do not think of that *reatus* as incurred in a "proper life" we lived before we were born. That hypothesis, however wild it may initially appear, recalls an earlier mention of the *propria vita* concept that seems to bear on the question. It occurs in Augustine's *Letter 98* 1, to his fellow-bishop Boniface. Can the sin of parents make their child sinful, Boniface has inquired. And Augustine answers with Ezechiel's "The soul that sins, that soul itself will die" (18:4); the child's soul does not sin when his parents sin, without the child's even being aware of their sin (*ei omnino nescienti*). How, then, can the child be said to "contract from Adam" the sin which baptism washes away? The reason, Augustine replies, is that, when Adam sinned, "the [child's soul] was not yet a soul living separately, that is, a soul other [than its father's, as the prophet implies by saying] 'the soul of the father is mine, and the soul of the son is mine.' "

Augustine is saying that our now-individual souls were once not *separatim vivens* and, hence, not truly other (*altera*) than the soul of our father Adam. This is why we could "contract" (*trahere*) Adam's sinful guilt. But, he goes on to say, once a "man is in himself, and has been made other [*alter*] from the one who begot him," that man constituted as *in seipso* cannot be held guilty of another's sin unless he consent to it himself (*sine sua consensione, non tenetur obnoxius*). He goes on to make matters even plainer: "He contracted the guilt [*reatum* of Adam's sin] because he was one with him and in him from whom he contracted it, when [the sin whose guilt] he contracted was committed." We were, Augustine is saying, once "one" both *with* and *in Adam* (*unus . . . cum illo et in illo*), and were that "one" when Adam sinned. That unity, or perhaps "identity" would not be too strong a term, is the metaphysical ground for our being "held guilty" (*obnoxius*) of Adam's sin, the ground for our "contracting" not only the punishment for Adam's sin, but its very guilt (*reatus*). But that same unity-in-identity does not hold for today's child and his earthly parents, for each of them is "other" (*alter*) to the other, each of them constitutes an individual *in seipso*, in him- or herself. That individuated constitution as an "other" self Augustine now sums up in the key phrase that interests us: each of us becomes such an "other" "when each one is living his [or her] *propria vita*." Only then what Ezechiel says becomes true, that the individual soul who sins is the soul that will be punished by death.

Is this the meaning, and the set of implications, Augustine is tacitly conveying by his use of *propria vita* in the works we have been inspecting? It should be noticed that the letter to Boniface, while its date remains somewhat cloudy, could have been written as early as 408.[39] So we shall be wiser to seek confirmatory indications that Augustine is still thinking in these same terms when using the expression *propria vita*. But the letter to Boniface gives us this much assurance: Augustine was quite capable of thinking this way!

THE THIRD HYPOTHESIS RESURRECTED

But the *De meritis* presents us with a final puzzle on the question of the soul's origin. In the sections just examined, Augustine is content to deal with two and only two alternative possibilities: creationism and traducianism. One can understand that, Romans 9:11 having entitled him to eliminate the Origenist hypothesis, his original four hypotheses have been reduced to three; and we have already seen that as time went on he seems to have considered the third hypothesis as hardly worth mentioning, much less discussing seriously. And yet, we have already seen one place (3.17) in the *De meritis* where he still seems to have thought it worth consideration. And, at the end of Book 1, he is discussing the ignorance and weak-

39. See Goldbacher's hesitations in CSEL 58, p. 30.

ness of infants, properties he considers "penal" results of Original Sin. This may be explained by the fact that sinful flesh "oppresses the rational soul"; but that rational soul itself may be thought in its turn to have been "derived from parents, or created in each case for the individual separately, or inspired from above" (*desuper inspirata*). The possibility that souls are "divinely sent" into their bodies seems to be alive and well (1.69)!

THE *De Meritis*: CONCLUSIONS AND PROBLEMS

It may well be that this last anomaly points to a phenomenon we encountered in the *De libero arbitrio*, and particularly in its third book. If the hypothesis proposed here is correct, the *De meritis*, too, would have been composed, and then, several years afterward, emended in the light of much that Augustine originally did not know, but learned in the meantime. The diligent researcher might well uncover other indications, also, where strata of thought early and later succeed one another. Augustine's conclusions from Romans 9:11, then, would represent a later stratum, whereas other passages come from an earlier, and more primitive, stage in his anti-Pelagian polemic. However that may eventually turn out, it seems most plausible, at this stage of our inquiry, to consider the allusions to Romans 9:11 as emendations, much later than the portions of the work which may survive from its original edition, in 411/412.

For the moment, though, several more substantial conclusions suggest themselves. It should be clear that once Augustine comes to see the text from Romans about Esau and Jacob in this new light, one that gives Scriptural ground for excluding the fourth hypothesis on the soul's origin, he applies it with an alacrity directly proportioned to his growing confidence in the text's demonstrative value. His first datable application to this issue, in the *De peccato originali*, betrays the tone of a man who cannot quite believe his good fortune: the Platonists do not have the answer to this conundrum, after all. Once he has made this break with Platonism,[40] his tone swiftly becomes peremptory, apodictic. This is exactly what

---

40. His break, that is, on this precise issue—even it turns out to be a temporary one. And yet, we have seen that Augustine more generally reposes increasing confidence in Scripture rather than in reason.

one would expect of a man whose sympathies with those "Platonists" once led him to adopt the very theory they espoused, and whom the Pelagian controversy has convinced that the Catholic must rely far more on the word of Scripture than on fragile human reasonings. His earlier rejections of Origen's views had much of human reason about them; his pleas to Jerome are those of a man who yearns for the uncompromising clarity only God's word can ground. It would be strange, even fantastic, to suppose that Augustine saw this text in its bearing on an issue that so troubled him when writing to Jerome in 415 or to his fellow-bishop Optatus in 416. What could conceivably have kept him from sharing his "find" with these two men? It would be even stranger to suppose that he made that find in 412, when writing the original two books of the *De meritis*, and that it somehow dropped out of memory, so completely that he does not even think to question Jerome for his learned opinion of that find. In brief, all the evidence seems to support the view that Augustine saw the bearing of Romans 9:11 not much earlier than the spring of 418, when he wrote the *De peccato originali*, or "perhaps" in late 417, when he may have preached *Sermo 165*.

But in line with the adage that every solution creates its own problems, Augustine's fresh understanding of Romans 9:11 left him with the task of understanding how even newborn infants needed baptism for the remission of their sins. The "fall" hypothesis, as he confessed to Jerome, seemed at least designed to answer that question, and answer it more satisfactorily than regnant versions of creationism could. The only other hypothesis that performed this service was traducianism, for which Augustine seems to have a strong aversion. Both "fall" and traducianism, moreover, seemed to answer Caelestius' ringing objection that infants could not be held responsible for the sin of an Adam who was "someone *else*" than they: no one could sensibly be blamed for a *peccatum alienum* of that sort, but only for a sin that was their very own, *proprium*.

This was a serious difficulty, and Augustine's letter to Optatus shows how seriously he viewed it. Could his appeal to the *propria vita* concept represent his mode of probing for some middle way between Paul's apparent rejection of all prenatal sin whatever, and the need Augustine saw for explaining how the sins of infants could somehow be "their own"? Perhaps developments to come will bring more light to that question. But this much should be said for now: Augustine's introduction of this notion comes on the scene later than his originally confident and unvarnished appeals to Romans 9:11; those earlier appeals betray no signs that he felt the Pauline text needed any such restrictive qualification. The need for such a qualification, then, seems to have dawned on him at a more advanced stage in his debate with the Pelagians. Its appearance in the *De meritis*, therefore, furnishes confirmatory evidence that the sections of that work in which it appears were very probably of later vintage than, for instance, *Sermo 165* and the *De peccato originali*.

One final observation: we saw that there was some possibility that Augustine's allusion to 1 Corinthians 15 on Adam's "animal" body, in *Letter 143*, might indicate a dawning awareness on his part that this teaching would preclude any prior sin in a heavenly, "spiritual" body. It is significant in this connection that Augustine quotes from an earlier section of 1 Corinthians 15 in *Letter 190 3*, to Optatus, whereas, in paragraphs 16 to 19, when administering his little lesson in exegesis, the section from that same chapter on the "animal" body goes entirely without mention. The argument is one *ex silentio*, admittedly: but it makes it difficult to entertain the notion that this Pauline idea was tugging at Augustine's mind.

But we have not finished with Augustine's applications of Romans 9:11. He calls it to our attention in both the *De Genesi ad litteram* and the *De civitate Dei*. An odd fact, worth investigating, he entirely omits mention of it in the *De Trinitate*! He was working on these three works concurrently for a number of years; some of his appeals to Romans 9:11 may possibly be later emendations, hence not easy to date. We must attend to his use of this text, but now in the wider context of exploring what these three major works contribute to our understanding of Augustine's final theory of the human condition.

8

THE SOUL IN THE
De Genesi ad Litteram

As in all his commentaries on this work, so in the *De Genesi ad litteram* Augustine confines his interest to the first three chapters: from the Hexaemeron,[1] the account of God's work in the "six days" of creation, to the sin of Adam and Eve and their expulsion from Eden.[2] And, as always, he looks to this section of Genesis as to a rich mine of suggestions on the human being's place in God's creative design. These anthropological discussions occur mostly in Books 6, 7, and 10 of the *De Genesi ad litteram*. Book 10, in fact, represents something suspiciously like a later insertion, an excursus on the origin of the soul, more interrupting than advancing the commentary on the Biblical text.[3] However that may be, Book 10 simply as it stands tells us one thing clear: Augustine views this question as a serious and important one.

---

1. This limited focus was already traditional by Augustine's time. See p. 577 of the first volume of *GenLitt*, edited, translated, and commented on by Paul Agaësse and Aimé Solignac, and published as BA 48 and 49. The English translation by John H. Taylor, s.j. (*The Literal Meaning of Genesis*, 2 vols., Ancient Christian Writers Series 41–42 [New York: Newman, 1982]) (henceforth: *Genesis*) appeared after this chapter had been completed; hence, all translations are my own.
  Citations will be given, in the text for the most part, first according to Book and paragraph numbers as employed by the BA edition and Taylor, then, after a slash, to the numbers in Joseph Zycha's edition, CSEL 28. References to Zycha's numeration are preceded by the letter Z.
2. Note that *Retr* 1.18 informs us that had he completed it, *GenImp* would have been literally an Hexaemeron, i.e., running up to and including the "sixth day" of creation; but his *GenMan* covers temptation and Fall material as well. In any event, it should be clear that Augustine viewed a commentary "On Genesis" in these limited terms, and, more frequently, as including the story of creation, temptation, and fall; compare *Conf* 11–13.
3. See BA 48, pp. 19–20.

CONFUSIONS SURROUNDING THE *De Genesi*

It would be comforting to have more certainty than we do on the publication history of the *De Genesi*. Augustine tells us he began this work after having begun, but completed it before completing, his *De Trinitate*; the beginning of the *De Genesi* can be set with some confidence as later than 404. But the *De Trinitate* publication date remains cloudier than it once seemed, our best information now placing it sometime after the year 420.[4] When Augustine finished the *De Genesi* is a matter for conjecture. It may well be that Books 1 to 9 had virtually been finished for a considerable time; it is quite certain that Books 10 and 12 especially reply to questions that had begun to preoccupy Augustine only after the year 412, the origin of the soul and the vision of God. A close study of Augustine's progress on the latter question might shed considerable light on the dating of Book 12, but we shall confine ourselves here to what his position on the origin of the soul may tell us in that regard.

It is not easy, however, to ferret out Augustine's settled opinions in the *De Genesi*; nothing is more certain than his uncertainties at a number of points. He is continually writing like a man working his way through the successive questions posed him by his effort to furnish a "literal" interpretation of this obscure text, and more than once he appears to adopt a preferred opinion in one book, only to replace it with another later on.[5] There is every indication that the finished work represents a number of strata, both of thought and of composition.[6] Augustine's "musical" mode of composition has been involved in this respect,[7] but that elegant phrase should not be overworked, or applied too indiscriminately. The

4. Note that the speculations in BA 48, pp. 25–31, suppose *Trin* was published in either 416 or 419; they have, therefore, to be revised in the light of Mlle La Bonnardière's more recent conclusions in *Chronologie*.

5. See BA 48, pp. 23–25 and 575–80, for examples and supporting evidence. Compare also the same phenomenon occurring ibid., pp. 647 (on morning–evening knowledge), 657–58 and 688 (on *rationes causales/seminales*), 662–63 (on the *ante–ab–in saeculo* distinction), and 699 (on the "matter" of the soul).

6. See BA 48, pp. 19–20; and BA 49, pp. 45n22, and 530–41, two lengthy "complementary notes."

7. In BA 48, p. 25. Compare Bardy in BA 34, p. 21n3, accusing Henri-Irénée Marrou, who coined this celebrated phrase, of being a trifle "bienveillant" in his application of it. There are some works of Augustine's where from our modern point of view Marrou's original judgment ("Augustin compose mal") seems more to the point.

"music" here resembles more closely the jangle of *De libero arbitrio* 3 than the artful interweave of thematic materials to be found in the *Confessions.* Augustine's candid summary in the *Retractations* says it well: his *De Genesi ad litteram* contains more *quaesita* than *inventa,* and of the *inventa,* only a few are *firmata.* We should look to this book to find more about how the "search" should be carried on, than in hopes of being presented with a series of "firm findings."[8]

We are warned, then, to tread warily. But any hopes of uncovering a finished theory of the soul and of its origin must take account of an additional reason for wariness: the problem of the soul is encased, here, in the wider problematic imposed by the variety of views Scripture presents on the original "creation." A modern, for one thing, recognizes two distinct creation accounts in these pages:[9] the Priestly account of the "seven days" and the subsequent Yahwist account of the creation, sin, and expulsion from Eden of the "man and woman." Augustine's conviction that these two accounts represent a seamless web, with single authorship and presiding intention, will force him at times to try to reconcile the irreconcilable.

THE "DAYS" OF CREATION

But the problem of the "seven days" of creation was to prove even more exacting still. We have seen that, in writing to Jerome, Augustine cites the objection to creationist theory which arose from the statement in Genesis 2:2 that God "rested" on the seventh day from all the works He had "finished."[10] He congratulates Jerome for seeing that John 5:7 suggests the counter-view: the Father "works until now."[11] He was, to an extent, congratulating himself. For in

8. See Augustine's own admission in *GenLitt* 2.1. But the aporetic nature of the work should not disguise the fact that Augustine does make some substantial advances on the interpretation formerly given in his younger *GenMan;* see BA 48, pp. 626, 691, 693–94; see also on *Conf,* BA 48, pp. 586–88 (on the "Heaven of Heaven"), and on *Trin,* BA 48, p. 632 (the "amissibility" of God's image in the soul). Madec, in "The Notion of Philosophical Augustinianism: An Attempt at Clarification," in *Mediaevalia,* 4 (1978), 125–46 (henceforth: "Clarification"), draws an argument from the "undogmatic" character of this work; but the careful reader cannot miss the fact that Augustine would dearly have loved to draw firmer conclusions than he was able to do.
9. See BA 48, pp. 21–23 and 45–46.
10. See BA 48, pp. 639–44.
11. BA 48, pp. 676–80.

his own reply *Against Adimantus*, in 394 or 395, who had claimed these texts showed Scripture in contradiction with itself, he had long since explained the former as referring to the original "creation" of all that God had brought into existence, and the latter, to His providential governance and administration of the created universe.[12] He will adhere, in the main, to that distinction in the *De Genesi*,[13] but he has come to see that his earlier resolution may not get to the root of the matter, after all; for creationist theory seems to imply not only a continued governance on God's part, but a continuous "creation" of new souls. The dialectic of these two key texts must, accordingly, be pushed farther and deeper than he, and presumably Jerome, had once imagined.

But that dialectic will be immensely complicated by the introduction of another text into the debate. For Ecclesiasticus 18:1 affirms, in the translation Augustine depended on, that God "created everything at the same time," *simul*. How could the continued "creation" of new souls, indeed, how could even the "seven days" of the original creation itself, be reconciled with that peremptory *simul*?

Detailed explanation of Augustine's "solution" to these difficulties lies outside the ambit of this study; besides, it is not in the least obvious how satisfied Augustine was with that "solution"—or, better, that series of attempts at solution. Suffice it to say here that the compelling force of that *simul* in Ecclesiasticus *may* not have commanded his first interpretation of the "days" of creation; he *may* have been content, at first, to take each day in a straightforward sense. God's own activity and being are not affected by time, of course, but the succession of creatures spoken of as formed on each "day" is so affected. The eternal act of creation results in the temporal emergence first of Light, then of the firmament, waters and dry land, then of the grasses and trees, and so forth until the "sixth day," when man appears.[14]

12. *Adim* 2.1. The remarks in BA 48, p. 661, could be more precise if this were taken into account.
13. See BA 48, pp. 653–68 and (with respect to "man") 680–90.
14. So Agaësse and Solignac interpret Augustine's procedure; but it would be instructive to make a careful study of how these three texts come progressively into play in *GenLitt* as well as the works leading up to it. Note that *GenImp* 28 already alludes to this *simul*-text, and proposes the provisional explanation (*fortasse*) that

If Augustine truly held to this conception of the six days as implying temporal succession, it soon yields to another. The *simul* of that text of Ecclesiasticus seems to have forced him to the conclusion that everything was actually created on the "first day," "at the same time," so that days two to six must now be viewed as replications of that first day. The succession of days he now accounts for as resulting from the unity-in-multiplicity of the angels' knowledge of the variety of created realities: they oscillate from a "morning" knowledge of all creatures as seen in God's creative Word, to an "evening" knowledge drawn from contemplation of created realities themselves, and it is this oscillation in the angelic knowledge that Genesis would have us understand by the "mornings" and "evenings" of each "day."[15]

AND *Rationales Causales* THEORY

In connection with this "two-phase" or "two-moment" theory of creation, Augustine also finds himself obliged to elaborate his famous proposal referred to as the doctrine of the *rationes seminales.* *Rationes causales*—"causal" rather than "seminal reasons"—does seem to be a happier expression.[16] God, Who exists eternally "before" all times (*ante saecula*), creates, and the original result of God's creative act existed from the beginning of time (*a saeculo*). Into that creature of the "first day" God implants, as it were, the ensemble of causal potencies which would then flower forth into the temporal succession of actual creatures that populate (*in saeculo*) the subsequent history of the created universe. In order to "appear" at their appointed times *in saeculo*, all these subsequent creatures must have been "there" *a saeculo*, from the beginning, if not actu-

---

the time indications may be Scripture's way of expressing ("for slower minds") distinctions among the strata of the "order" manifest in the finished creation. Hence, *pace* Solignac and Agaësse, I suspect that Augustine has this view already in mind in *GenLitt* 1.28 (Z 14) (BA 48, p. 121), where his *ordo formatarum* (the order of "things formed") is mistranslated as "ordre de formation." Compare in this connection the language of 1.29 (Z 15), which supports my view. For this reason, the note in BA 48, pp. 645–53, may require revision. But the point is secondary for our purposes.

15. See the notes in BA 48, pp. 639–44 and 645–53.

16. As ably argued in BA 48, pp. 653–68. This distinction, I suspect, may be even more vital than Solignac proposes, for it leaves Augustine free to abandon his *rationes causales* device while retaining *rationes seminales.* We shall see the bearing of this in *Civ.*

ally existent, then at least implanted in the existing "causal reasons" appropriate to them.[17]

How all this affects Augustine's thinking on the origin of human souls we shall see in a moment. But it is important to recognize that besides the problems that found their "solution" in this "two-phase creation" theory, Augustine is confronting a parallel set of problems as well: precisely those having to do with the Pelagian controversy.[18] He cannot be content to account for the appearance in history of individual post-Adamic souls in such terms as satisfy the data of the creation problem unless those same terms of solution are also in accord with the Church's *fundatissima fides*, its unshakable belief in Original Sin and its transmission from Adam and Eve to all their descendants. A "dangerous question"[19] indeed, and one that he must keep in view, not only in Book 10, but in the earlier books of his *De Genesi* as well.

How, then, does Augustine deal with the "origin of souls" in the *De Genesi ad litteram*? First of all, his general theory of creation brings him to interpret the "Light" that God created on the "first day" as the unity-in-multiplicity of "spiritual" creatures, the community of angels.[20] Their oscillation from morning to evening knowledge and back again will account, as we have seen, for the "succession" by replication of the subsequent five "days." But this "Light" represents two other possibilities as well, and Augustine must deal with them further on. Could this spiritual creature in some way constitute the "matter" required for the formation of those changeable beings that are human souls; or could it furnish the existent ground in which the "causal reasons" of human souls were originally implanted?

17. See BA 48, pp. 662–63, on the *ante–ab–in saeculo* distinction. Note that the *seminaliter* mode of creation for "man" represents, in *GenLitt* 6.17 (Z 10), a *fourth* possible explanation.

18. I may be pardoned for finding Solignac and Agaësse sometimes understressing the importance this question held for Augustine, and particularly for his notion of creationism; see BA 48, pp. 716–17 (on *GenLitt* 7.40–41/Z 28). They do, however, recognize it more clearly in BA 49, pp. 538–39. Compare their remarks in BA 49, pp. 45 and 505–507, and Augustine's own reflections in *GenLitt* 3.24 (Z 15), 4.29–30 (Z 15), 7.36 (Z 25), 8.23–27 (Z 10–11), and, quite especially, on the origin-of-the-soul question, 10.12–39 (Z 7–23) and 11.6 (Z 4).

19. See *Ep 143* 3–4.

20. For Augustine, the community of angels is more "one" than "many." See the explanation in BA 48, pp. 41–44. For the bearing this interpretation has on the origin-of-the-soul question, see ibid., pp. 588–90.

THE ORIGIN OF THE SOUL IN BOOKS 3 AND 6

So much for the matrix of Augustine's thought in this perplexing work. We shall see that one of the difficulties in understanding his explorations on the origin of the soul consists precisely in knowing the extent to which he is thinking out that special problem in the terms dictated by that matrix, for that is not always clear to the reader. Indeed, he may even jettison much of it—the "causal reasons" theory particularly—without giving any clear signals as to when and why he chose to do so. At all events, his two-phase theory of creation and its corollary, his theory of causal reasons, are both in place by the time he has reached Book 6, where the text of Genesis 2:7 obliges him to discuss the formation of "man" from the "earth." [21]

Earlier on, in Book 3, the text of Genesis 1:26 had obliged him to comment on the creation of "man" in the "image" of God; but there Augustine was determined to be brief (29–34/Z 19–22). He argues that the "image" of the Trinity is to be found in that part of man whereby he manifests the superiority that entitles him to "rule over" the lower, brute creation: in his reason, mind, or intelligence (30/Z 20). This prompts him to underline the kinship of "man's" creation with that of that community of spiritual intelligences spoken of as the "Light" created on the "first day" (31–32/Z 20).

Is "man," then, the same sort of "spiritual" creature as the angels? Yes, and no; but first off, yes. Augustine's manner of arguing shows he is initially supposing God fitted man with the kind of "immortal body," different in quality from the bodies of our experience, that would be appropriate to angelic status.[22] Man's sin resulted in his body's becoming "mortal." This raises the questions why even before man's sin God ordained the herbs and other vegetation of

21. Here begins what moderns would regard as the second, or Yahwist, account of creation; on the series of questions forced on him by his conviction that both Priestly and Yahwist accounts came from the same author, see *GenLitt* 6.1 and BA 48, pp. 21–22 and 680–88.

22. Note that the "immortal body" is, for Augustine and for Greek thought, of a different and higher "quality" than our mortal bodies; see BA 48, pp. 266*n*28 and 690. Hence, he can interpret Matt. 22:30, that we shall be "like the angels" in the resurrection, as implying that the angels themselves have immortal, spiritual bodies.

the earth to be man's "food," and how one might conceive of the man and woman, endowed with immortal bodies, engaging in the act of procreation. Both are difficult questions, but the difficulties, he submits, may not be insuperable (33/Z 21).[23] They have given rise to the suggestion, offered by some interpreters of Scripture, that this earlier text refers to the creation of the soul, the "interior" man only, the creation of the "exterior" bodily man being reserved to Genesis 2:7. No, Augustine answers, for even here "male and female" God created—not "him" but—them; that difference between sexes pertains, he is convinced, not to the soul, but to the body. Genesis 1:26 describes, accordingly, the creation of humans both in body and in soul (34/Z 22).[24]

A modern Scripture scholar would object that these two distinct accounts of creation betray different preoccupations and points of view. But since, for Augustine, they are one seamless, "Mosaic" account, he feels obliged to reconcile their conflicting features and to interpret the one in the light of the other.

In Book 6, therefore, when he comes to explain Genesis 2:7, he interprets the text as calling special attention to how man's *body* was formed from the earth, and on the same "sixth" day mentioned in the earlier account. His general theory on the "six days," furthermore, compels him to take this to mean that man's body, created before all time, *a saeculo*, by means of "causal reasons" implanted on the "first" (and only) day, is now being described as "appearing" *in saeculo*, in the course of time. That theory of the six days, coupled with his conviction about the unity of these two creation accounts, forces him to pose questions, and entertain a series of hypothetical answers (1–13/Z 1–8), which are of little interest for our purposes here.[25]

23. Augustine warns that we ought not to conclude that this talk of "food" implies that "man" had only a "mortal" body; also, procreation *might* be conceived of in some way other than we know it now, more appropriate to the immortal body. He will, as Genesis proceeds, have to retract both these suggestions, but his earlier hopes should be clear: he had expected Genesis to lend support to a semi-angelic view of the human soul.

24. Note that the one mind here has two parts or functions, one contemplative, the other administrative of the sensible world. This is good Plotinianism. See Augustine's explanation in *Trin* 12, below, and compare the compromising sections in *Lib* 3.32–35, above.

25. See BA 48, pp. 21–22 and 680–88, for explanatory material.

The Question of Jeremiah's Propria Vita

Suddenly, however, Augustine sets a question that seems to come out of the blue: What can it mean that God "knew" the prophet Jeremiah "before he formed him in the womb" (14/Z 9)? There follows a discussion of this question which has all the appearances of a later insertion, one Augustine felt obliged to make in order to answer a question current at the time. It may well have been prompted by his pondering the objection we saw Rufinus had posed to Jerome: God's "predestination" of Jeremiah seemed to argue for a divine "election" before he was born, an election that supported Origen's theory of the soul's pre-existence and fall.[26]

Augustine offers several possibilities on "where" God would have known Jeremiah before his conception, but in the end confesses that this question is either too difficult or even impossible for us humans to plumb. But whatever the answer to the precise question, he wants to make sure that one point is beyond discussion: that it was only from the day he was "brought forth" (editus) by his parents into *this* world (in hac luce), and not before, that Jeremiah began to "live a life of his own" (egisse vitam propriam). Once again we meet with that curious thought-device, the notion of a person's *propria vita*; we have already seen that it appears to have entered Augustine's thinking processes around the time he composed his *Letter 190*, to Optatus, in the year 418. Here we have another indication that this portion of the De Genesi is probably a later insertion.

But Augustine now goes on to give us more specifics on what this "proper life" implies. Only from his birth in this world could Jeremiah, or anyone for that matter, grow with the onset of years to the point of being able to live either badly or well (qua grandescens aetatis accessu posset vivere seu male seu bene). "For the Apostle has no hesitation in uttering that sententia about the twins in Rebecca's womb, that they were not yet doing anything good or evil." Here, too, we meet with the application of Romans 9:11 which makes its appearance in Augustine's thinking only in 416 or 417. But it comes already qualified by that "proper life" restriction, and now Augustine makes it clear that infants assume their proper

---

26. This is the section TeSelle would date as of 406: see chap. 7, note 16, above.

life only on leaving the womb, and that a certain growth is required before they can reach the stage of moral responsibility. He is, then, still maintaining that infants are as yet incapable of sinning on their own account. So he must face the difficulty arising from his Romans 9:11 insight; how can we sensibly speak of these infants as sinful, and in need of baptism for the remission of their sinfulness?

Augustine answers that question with three quotations from Scripture. Let there be no mistake about it, he affirms, infants *are indeed* tainted with Original Sin; and all God's dealings *are* just; but this must not encourage one to adopt that theory "some have [held], thinking that souls have sinned elsewhere in greater or lesser fashion, and for the variety of their sinful deserts have been thrust into a variety of bodies" (*in diversa corpora esse detrusas*). That opinion does not "accord with the Apostle's words, since he says most openly that those as yet unborn have done nothing either good or evil" (15/Z 9).[27]

This, of course, Augustine remarks, suggests another question: namely, "What did the entire subsequent human race contract of the sin of those first parents, who were only two [in number]?" (16/Z 9).[28] That is another question, and one to be dealt with elsewhere. For now, Augustine hopes to make this much clear: what Paul said of Esau and Jacob is true of all men, including Adam himself; there can be neither merit nor demerit before the individual begins to live "his own" temporal life. Hence, it would be futile to entertain the thought that Adam might have committed that sin of his in that merely potential existence he may be thought to have had in the "causal reasons" explained earlier (16/Z 9).[29]

27. But in 6.15 (Z 9) Augustine adds a peculiar qualification: *quod ad propriam personam pertineat.* Is he envisaging a kind of good or evil that could be committed before birth, but somehow *not* "pertain to our proper person"? Compare the similar possibility suggested by *Ep 98*, to Boniface, and by the *Mer* texts examined in the preceding chapter.

28. *Quid de peccato primorum parentum, quo duo soli fuerunt, generis humani contraxerit universa consparsio.* There is no warrant for the translation (BA 48, p. 467) of *qui duo soli fuerunt* as "qui fûrent les deux seuls à le commettre." The point has its importance for understanding Augustine's thought, as we shall have occasion to see. Taylor, in *Genesis*, I 188, is similarly imprecise.

29. Augustine twice specifies that the individual must live *suo tempore,* "the time span that is his." Compare the qualification: "whatever merits may pass from parents to offspring [*traiiciantur*], . . . no one before birth does any good or evil

Augustine's Governing Assumptions

It is not an irrelevancy to notice here, first, that these were questions and difficulties current in discussions of the time, and that Augustine has placed himself quite specially under the obligation of dealing with them. He has placed man's crucial reality in the mind-soul that makes him the "image" of God; he has twice brought the creation of that image into close association with the creation of the angels on the "first" day; he has reduced sexual differentiation to a secondary human characteristic, traceable to the body rather than to the soul; he has further dissociated body from soul by proposing that the body was created only through the implantation of its "causal reasons," so that it "appears" on the temporal scene only on the "sixth" day; and, even then, man's original "immortal" body has been conceived of in quasi-angelic terms. All this comes dangerously close to attributing to man a pre-embodied reality. Augustine must fend off the implication some might draw that man could merit or sin (and be predestined on that basis) before he was "born" into the embodied, temporal life that is his own "proper" life. But how is he to explain the transmission of Adam's sin to his descendants? Certainly not by appeal to traducianism. The ultra-spiritual cast of his view of man could scarcely consort with that theory. But here he has rejected the only other theory in which the soul itself can be considered "sinful" and its present condition genuinely "penal." It is scarcely surprising that he feels obliged to raise that question; nor is it less surprising that he prefers to postpone dealing with it.

Adam's Animal Body

Instead, he goes on to explain how the formation of Adam's body may be understood in the light of his "causal reasons" theory, but

---

which pertains to his own person" (see note 27, above). Similarly, "Esau and Jacob . . . could not be said to have received some merit from their parents [whether positive or negative] if their parents had done no good or evil." Hence, Adam, who had no parents, could not have contracted guilt except by sinning "personally" (16/Z 9). Augustine's careful phrasing—note the subjunctive *traiiciantur*—scarcely constitutes an affirmation that children actually do inherit guilt or merit from their post-Adamic parents.

that theory now begins to take on both difficulties and complications unsuspected at first (03–29/Z 13–18).[30] His conclusion drawn, he is brought to face a next question: Was Adam's body the kind of "animal" body we have, or a "spiritual" body of the sort we are promised in the resurrection, one that will make us, in St. Matthew's phrase (22:30), the equal of the angels? At long last, he must confront the text he mentioned so allusively in *Letter 143*. Paul's answer to the Corinthians is clear, Augustine now affirms. The first Adam was earthly, and drawn from the earth; his body was an "animal," not a spiritual, body, after all (30/Z 19).

Augustine sees, however, that there may be objections to this flat solution. How, for instance, do we reconcile this view with Paul's other affirmation, that we are "renewed" in Christ? For renewal seems to imply that we are "made new *again*," restored to what we once were. If the term of our salvation involves our donning the "spiritual body" in the resurrection, renewal and restoration would seem to imply that Adam before his sin possessed that same kind of spiritual body. So too, the Prodigal on his return to his father's house was robed in that *stola prima*, the "first garment" that would seem to mean the spiritual body he had formerly possessed and lost.[31]

Those "objections" Augustine is obliged to take very much to heart. For the counter-views he is combating now were his own, and very recently at that: the position he took on Adam's body in Book 3 of this very work clearly implies it must have been an "immortal" body, the very *kind* of body to which he now refers in that coordinate term "spiritual"; and he himself regularly interpreted both the *stola prima* of the parable and Paul's "renewal" expressions in the very way he is flatly rejecting now. But reject them he does, assuring us now that terms like "renewal" and "restoration" have to do with the soul, not the body; Adam's body in paradise was both animal and by nature "mortal," though *promised* immortality out of God's goodness. As far as it affects our body, therefore, our renewal will be a renewal *in melius*; we shall in our

30. See the note in BA 48, pp. 685–90.
31. Compare chap. 3, note 25, above. Augustine here is retracting the suggestions he made in 3.33 (Z 21); see notes 22 and 23 above. Observe, however, that *Trin* 12.16 either retains or reverts to his older, "spiritual body" interpretation of the *stola prima*. Dating that section vis-à-vis this portion of *GenLitt* will be important.

risen lives enjoy a state superior to that which Adam experienced even before his sin (30–35/Z 19–24).[32]

Already, then, Augustine has announced a profound departure from his earlier view of man. But he has not yet faced the full implications of that departure: for if Adam's body be truly "animal," has not man become far less the quasi-angelic being he was up to this point, far more a denizen of this earth? And mustn't Augustine eventually equip him with a "soul" more coherent with that earthly status? But the formation of Adam's body is one thing; now, he proposes to move on to that "very difficult question" about the creation of Adam's soul. Perhaps he means to grapple with some of our questions in this next section of his work. But perhaps not. Augustine frankly avows his doubts whether his exploration of the soul's creation will result in any certainties.[33] But the text of Genesis will not allow him to avoid the issue; so tackle it he must (40/Z 29), in Book 7.

THE SOUL'S ORIGIN IN BOOK 7

The question of the soul, he admits, is an important one, and at the same time very difficult (7.1). He then proceeds to outline his "certainties" about the soul. There are, he says, some (*quidam*) who have interpreted God's "breathing" into Adam the breath of life as implying that He imparted part of Himself; Adam's soul was, therefore, literally a part of God's own substance.[34] But God

32. Clear throughout is Augustine's conviction that the "naturally" immortal body is different in kind and quality from the mortal body; compare note 22, above. Hence, the "promised" immortality he is about to argue for is markedly different from what he has been holding up to this point. It would be helpful to know when and how Augustine came to "see" Paul's text from 1 Cor. 15 as imposing the teaching that the "first" Adam's was in fact an "animal" body. That reading could have been forced on him by those Pelagians who claimed that Adam was made mortal and would have died even had he not sinned. Augustine's position here is a *media via* between his older stand (Adam possessed a spiritual, immortal body) and that Pelagian stand. Adam is now "naturally" mortal but "promised" immortality if he obeys God's command. There is no warrant for reading this new understanding of the matter back into *Ep 143*.

33. This avowal may indicate that he has been over this ground before, without success.

34. These interpreters are Priscillianists and Manichees; see BA 48, pp. 513n4 and 698–99. It might be worth comparing this discussion of God's "breathing" with that proposed by Vincentius Victor in the *AnOrig*. The lack of similarity between them

being immutable, and the soul manifestly mutable, the soul must be a creature made by, rather than a consubstantial reality with, God. If one think of God as corporeal, it might seem to follow that His "breath"—the soul—was corporeal also; but, Augustine affirms, God is superior to creatures both corporeal and spiritual, so that we are not to believe that the soul, which He "breathed" into Adam, was part of His substance, fancied as corporeal or composed of corporeal elements (1–6/Z 1–4).[35]

Was It Made from "Spiritual Matter"?

But one may rightly ask what the soul was made "from"—whether from nothing, or from some "spiritual matter." Augustine leads us through a number of conceivable forms this "spiritual matter" might take; again, he seems to be working through the problem in the very process of composition. One of those possibilities, though, raises a serious question: if one probe the notion of a "spiritual matter," the notion suggests itself that this "matter" could be a kind of spiritual creature enjoying a life of happiness. Again, the soul has been associated with the angelic orders, but this time in a different way, and in a seriously questioning tone. For it would seem difficult to account for the soul's "flowing downward" (*defluxio*) into the life we humans know, a life that is certainly not "happy," and therefore inferior (*deterius*) to the happy life we have supposed that "spiritual matter" once enjoyed. Mysterious, Augustine admits; but one thing is sure: no account of this *defluxio* may invoke the assumption that humans either merit or sin in some pre-incarnate state, i.e., before living their "proper" incarnate lives (7–11/Z 5–8).[36] At this point, Augustine gives us more information on how he understands that crucial term: the soul must have "begun to exercise [*agere*] its proper life"; that is, it must have become (*facta est*) a soul "animating flesh and using its senses as

might indicate that the *GenLitt* discussion was written earlier. A remark in BA 48, p. 698, indirectly raises the question about whence Augustine drew his knowledge of *this* particular feature of Priscillianist teaching (as against their fasting practices in *Ep 36* 28); the answer seems clearly to be, from Paul Orosius.

35. The latter conclusion seems to have been arrived at rather briskly. Note, however, the "philosophical" cast of Augustine's argumentation here.

36. Augustine is in such full possession of his insight, now, that he does not feel the need to invoke the language of Rom. 9:11.

heralds and experiencing itself [*se sentiens*] as living in itself
[*in seipsa vivere*] by its own will, intellect, and memory" (11/Z 8).
He seems to be working toward a description of "individuality"
which is almost convertible with "being incarnate." The implication would be that the soul, previous to its "incarnation," would
not to be an individuated soul! That implication will bear careful
watching.

But perhaps this "spiritual matter" may be conceived of in
another way—as a kind of "irrational soul," or soul not yet arrived
at developed rationality. No, answers Augustine, and the suggestion
sets him off on a rebuttal of those philosophers who see the story
of the soul in terms of cyclic "revolutions," human soul becoming
animal soul and vice versa, in a series of incarnations. Their cyclic
theories they often try to buttress by appeals to our "memory" of
former lives in bodies other than our present one, but such memory
theories are false and deceptive. The Manichaean fantasies on this
theme are, of course, even worse. If there be a spiritual matter
from which the soul is formed, it cannot, therefore, be an irrational
soul. The next possibility to explore is whether the soul might be
made out of corporeal elements (12–18/Z 8–12).

The Soul "Not a Body"

Here Augustine exhibits an acquaintance not only with the history
of thought, but with contemporary "medical" knowledge, which
both impresses and surprises his reader. The *medici* are permitted
to catalogue all those phenomena arguing for a body–soul interac-
tion so intimate and thorough as to argue for the soul's being,
itself, bodily. But Augustine counters their evidence with that
familiar set of Platonist—and Plotinian—observations:[37] that the
bodily senses cannot help but can only hinder the mind in its
properly intellectual activity (xiv.20B/Z 14); that the mind can
lose itself in distraction from sensible objects even when those
objects lie before the gaze of the bodily senses (26/Z 20); that the
whole soul can know itself as a whole in a way which defies the laws
of bodily extensiveness (28/Z 21). All this proves, he concludes,

37. He has used the same insights in his *Immort*, and will use them again in his
argumentation against Tertullian, below. The provenance of this mode of envisaging
the soul–body relation is Plotinus' *Ennead* 4.7, which in turn is indebted to Plato's
Phaedo; see *Early Theory*, pp. 135–45.

that in certain of its activities the soul sets itself apart from, while in others it sets itself in opposition to, the body. Those phenomena cannot be understood except in virtue of a sharp body–soul distinction, a distinction leading to the confident conclusion that the soul itself must be incorporeal; it cannot, therefore, be composed of corporeal elements, however refined and subtle we imagine them to be (29–30/Z 21).

A Limited Conclusion

He ends his meditation on the "matter" out of which the soul might have been made, with a conclusion, but, like so many conclusions in the *De Genesi ad litteram*, it is far from being as conclusive as the argument preceding it might seem to warrant. The soul *may* have been made out of some sort of spiritual matter; or it *may* be the result of a *defluxio*, a "flowing downward," of a spiritual creature (one possible form that "spiritual matter" might take) enjoying a life of happiness; or it *may* have been made, not of any matter at all, but out of nothing! Only corporeal elements and an "irrational soul" have been definitely excluded as conceivable "matter" for the soul's original creation, and no light whatever has been shed on what the soul's creation "out of nothing" might positively entail. But further, the *defluxio* hypothesis has been allowed to stand, despite the difficulty involved in explaining this passage from happiness to misery without invoking any pre-existent sin on the soul's part (31/Z 21).

But now Augustine moves to a distinct, if possibly connected, question: What can have been the "causal reason" of Adam's soul? He recalls the two-phase creation theory that called for such a "causal reason" in the first place, and then proceeds to inquire "where" this "causal reason," if such there be, could possibly be rooted.

One must envisage it, he tells us, as rooted in some actually existing creature; that creature must be either spiritual or corporeal in nature. In the former alternative, Augustine first entertains the possibility of a sort of "spiritual creature" which would have been created on the "first" day. That creature would, however, be devoid of all activity. Notably, it would exercise no governance over the corporeal world, its power of governance remaining unactuated (*vacans*), somewhat the way a man's generative power remains latently present but idle until he actually enters upon the activity of carnal union and conception. Only when man is created in his own "proper nature"—as the soul–body amalgam which "appeared" on the "sixth day"—would that latent governing power come into play.

Reappearance of the Third Hypothesis?

This hypothesis bears evident resemblances to his earlier third hypothesis. It assures that the human soul which eventually "appears" on the sixth day pre-existed, but without performing any act that could be deemed either "good or evil"; one thinks of Jerome's mockery of these souls who "slept like dormice" before being "sent" by God into bodies. Against this possibility, Augustine has two difficulties. The first is drawn from reason. What would such a creature be created *for*, if it exercised no activity of its own (*nihil agebat sui operis*)? Its only τέλος, one might reply, would be that of containing the "causal reason" of future human souls (or soul?), which God would actualize by His creative "breath" on the "sixth day."

Augustine is obviously unsatisfied with this response; but he seems more impressed with a second objection, this time drawn from Scripture. Surely, he argues, the author of Genesis would have made mention of such a spiritual creature in his enumeration of God's works, but he wrote not a word of it (33/Z 22)!

This rejection compels Augustine to ask whether the "causal reason" of Adam's soul might have been implanted in the kind of spiritual creature Genesis does mention: the angelic creation, which God made on the "first day." In this case, the soul would turn out to be "daughter" (*filia*) of the angels. That, Augustine says flatly, is a "hard" word, indeed: *durum*. But he never explains why![38] In any event, he concludes that this hypothesis must be rejected as "absurd."

But the other possibilities in presence are even "harder": *durio-*

---

38. BA 48, p. 715, speculates that Augustine thinks this notion "hard" because it lacks Scriptural foundation; this is the reason he gives for rejecting the same notion in 10.8 (Z 5), but I cannot think this is all Augustine means by *durum*. For some reason or other he finds the notion "goes down hard," but what that reason is I confess I do not know.

res. Are we to think that the "causal reason" of the rational soul could be implanted in some sort of irrational soul? Or that the causal reason of the spiritual soul could root in corporeal elements? Both suggestions he firmly rejects in turn.

The Soul Created on the "First Day"

What, then, are we to "believe"? *Credatur,* Augustine replies— "Let it be believed"—as more "tolerable" for our human understanding that the expression in Genesis about God's "breathing" the soul into Adam's body insinuates the "sixth-day" appearance, *in saeculo,* of the same human soul which was created *a saeculo* on the "first day" when "Light"—the entire spiritual creation—was made (32–35/Z 22–24). That soul, in the meantime, must have remained "hidden" (*latens*) among God's works.

But, in that case, the same question arises as arose for the "latent" spiritual substrate Augustine had considered and finally rejected in paragraph 33 (Z 22). Did this "latent" soul enjoy some interim activity of its own?

Augustine is about to answer that, but before we consider his answer, we, his readers, are tempted to ask whether he has suddenly switched from the position he seems to have embraced earlier: that some kind of "spiritual matter" was required, out of which the soul was created (5–7/Z 3–5).[39] That may or may not be. What is clear is this: that the connection Augustine has just re-established between the "first day" creation both of Adam's soul and of the angels now compels him to face anew the difficulty he had postponed earlier.

The Problem of the Soul's Coming into Body

For if Adam's soul already existed apart from his body, "living" a life of "innocence"—engaging, therefore, in *some* kind of spiritual activity—then how account for its having come from that "better" state to be "inserted" into a body where it would (inevitably?) sin and incur the sufferings of God's condemnation?

39. BA 48, p. 699, suggests this. That suggestion deserves closer study, I think, but the point is secondary for our purposes here.

One way of "understanding" that descent from innocence (and, one presumes, relative bliss) to misery was, of course, Origen's; the soul must have sinned in that pre-incarnate state, and been embodied for punishment and expiation of its sin. But this way of understanding the soul's embodiment, Augustine has seen and said repeatedly, is unacceptable; Romans 9:11 is unambiguous on the point. And yet, there was something sound in Origen's instinct for the question. If God be in His heaven, there *should* be some equation linking happiness and misery with merit and demerit; and, all other things being equal, it is difficult to understand that a spiritual creature, enjoying a life of bliss, would knowingly and willingly exchange it for a life of misery. How can one do justice to Origen's instincts, without falling into Origen's error (36/Z 25)?

The Soul's "Natural" Desire for Body

Augustine's proposal for a way out of this impasse constitutes one of the boldest forays of thought in the *De Genesi ad litteram*. He is almost certainly indebted to Plotinus' inspiration for it,[40] to some extent at least; but daring it remains, nonetheless. He entertains the hypothesis that the soul, even apart from the body, may have a spontaneous, natural desire to rule the body. But that desire would have to be perfectly neutral from the moral standpoint, so that the soul's coming down to unite with the body would be neither a good nor a bad act, neither meritorious nor sinful. In this way Augustine succeeds in eliminating all pre-incarnate "merits" whatever—both the sinful demerit supposed by Origenism and the positive merit implied in the hypothesis that the soul, "divinely sent," comes down "obediently" into the body. The pre-incarnate soul must, in the words of Romans 9:11, have done neither good nor evil (36–38/Z 25–27).

We must pause a moment to take the measure of this suggestion, for it represents a radical change in Augustine's thinking. Even while couching it in the "ifs" and "why nots" of a hypothesis he is entertaining, Augustine is seriously proposing it for consideration,

40. BA 48, pp. 561n37 and 714–17, here corroborates (independently?) an attribution I had made for the same thought tactic in *GenMan*; see *Early Theory*, pp. 169–73. Compare Augustine's search for a neutral *transitus* from wisdom to folly in *Lib* 3.73; see above, chap. 1.

and that is more remarkable a thing for him to do than might initially appear. Notice that in making this desire to govern the body both "natural" to the soul and pre-morally (and presumably pre-consciously) "spontaneous," Augustine has implicitly made it part of the soul's very nature to rule the body, not from aloft, as it were (as in De libero arbitrio 3.32–35),[41] but precisely qua "embodied"; the soul has implicitly been accorded a status in the hierarchy of beings quite different from the quasi-angelic status it has enjoyed until now, a status far more coherent with the "animal" body God made for Adam. He cannot free his mind from thinking of this new genus of soul as nonetheless living in "innocence" and presumably in bliss prior to its coming into the body. It is no accident that the next section will bring him to discuss the creationist theory that undercuts this very way of imagining the soul's "em-bodiment." That discussion will prove inconclusive, but the fact remains that Augustine has entertained here the notion of a soul whose nature and status cohere much better with creationism in its classic form.

But imagining the soul as pre-existing in this "better" state requires Augustine to account for its arrival in the unhappy world of sin and punishment. This passage from bliss to misery Augustine has always felt obliged to account for in moral terms; merit should result in happiness, and misery be the penal consequence of evil-doing. We have seen his sensitivity to this equation showing at several points in the De Genesi itself. But this hypothesis involves the snipping, once for all, of that thread of moral causality. It may be that the soul can pass from bliss to misery without any evil-doing on its part. Augustine is showing his readiness to abandon what has always been one of the most cherished features of his world-view, the central intuition enclosed in that triumph of his early thinking, the dimissio theme. The Pelagian controversy has brought him to feel, for the moment at least, that such human notions of God's just workings may not bear the burden he had always placed upon them.

In every appearance this theme has made throughout the works surveyed here, the "desire" that "weighed the soul down" and accounted for its immersion in the world of mortal, corruptible bodies was clearly of a moral sort; it was sinful desire, naturally

41. This was the section from which his Carthaginian critics drew the objection he discusses in Ep 143; see chaps. 1 and 3, above.

and inexorably achieving what it desired, but finding that achievement itself the punishment of such desire.

Now he is willing to entertain the thought that the desire that draws the soul down into the world of bodies, from bliss to misery, may not be an immoral and sinful desire after all; it may be as spontaneous and natural as the living creature's instinct for self-preservation.

One must not underestimate what this concession must have cost Augustine; but Romans 9:11, coupled with his own determination to think of the soul in the spiritual terms that so appealed to him, exacted no less from him. There are few more eloquent testimonies, I submit, to Augustine's growing willingness to rely, not on human reason, but on what he understood to be the peremptory word of God in Scripture. But it is a nice irony that he should turn back to a master of human reason, Plotinus, to find the suggestion that permits him to do so. For Aimé Solignac is quite correct, I submit, in claiming that Augustine extracted the clue to this reformulation of the *dimissio* motif by re-study of the very section of the very treatise of the *Enneads* which originally "inspired" the earlier version of the theme.

Residual Tensions

There are three additional features of this hypothesis which Augustine feels obliged to specify. The first flows from his present understanding of Romans 9:11: reward and punishment will be divinely meted out to the soul in accordance with its behavior in its embodied life (*vita corporis*). But Romans 9:11 would also lay down that the soul's "coming" at God's command must not be a "good" act of obedience (*Deo volenti obtemperasse*) (36/Z 25). This compels Augustine to add that, before its coming, the soul must not be the sort of being (*genus*) that would foresee its actions, good or bad. It would be "incredible" to postulate a soul "inclined of its own will" (*propria voluntate*) toward a bodily existence, despite its foreknowledge that it "was going to sin, in some respects" (*in quibusdam peccaturam esse*) in that bodily existence. Nor would it be unworthy of God, Augustine is quick to add, to create a soul so bereft of foreknowledge (37/Z 26). But then he is finally brought to ask, what if the soul being "sent" is unwilling to go (*noluerit*)?

Are we to imagine that it would be compelled to go (*compellatur*)? It would be "better to believe," he answers, that the soul wills its own coming into the body, but wills it "naturally," somewhat as the will to live is natural to all of us. That kind of "willing," he hopes we will concede, would be completely neutral of all moral character—hence, neither the "good" nor the "evil" sort of act precluded by Romans 9:11.

These three specifications seem to betray some residual tensions in the hypothesis. The need to eliminate the soul's foreknowledge, coupled with the need to obviate the soul's unwillingness to be sent into the body, confirms the impression that Augustine's earlier language leaves upon the reader. The soul as Augustine now conceives of it, in the "interim" between its first-day creation and its sixth-day insertion into the body, must have been living a life of "innocence" which, though "hidden" among God's creative works, was nonetheless accompanied by some measure of conscious and voluntary activity. Otherwise it could hardly be deemed, as Augustine unmistakably deems it, a "better" life than the one it will eventually lead in the body. But the paradox remains: in this pre-incarnate life, the soul, if conceived of as an "individual" soul, can do neither good nor evil, can do nothing to merit ultimate reward or punishment. Either that paradox has momentarily escaped Augustine's notice, or he is tacitly assuming some species of non-individuated life for souls in their pre-incarnate state. Once again, Augustine compels his reader to attend seriously to that startling possibility. But this time he does so in connection with a thought device almost certainly drawn from Plotinus, for whom there would be nothing startling in that view; his thinking on the "descent" of the soul ran almost exactly along these lines!

The Soul's Creation "From Nothing"

Now Augustine makes one of those returns, so characteristic of this *De Genesi*, to a question previously dealt with. He offers the reflection that, if the solution just proposed has gotten to the truth of the matter, then the earlier question concerning the soul's "spiritual matter" turns out to be an unnecessary one. If (as this hypothesis permits) the soul itself was created on the "first day" along with the rest of the spiritual creation, the soul was made in the same way those other spiritual beings were, out of nothing.[42] But once again, he betrays his continuing uncertainty: even if, he adds, there were some kind of "spiritual matter" involved after all, that matter itself would be God's creation; further, it would be a "spiritual" matter, preceding the formed soul, not in time, but by an antecedence of "origin," the way the singing voice "precedes" but is temporally simultaneous with the song it sings (39/Z 27).[43]

There is something abrupt and inconclusive, even hurried, in the way Augustine closes off this topic, and moves on to another. But move on he does, to ask whether God's "breathing" of his soul into Adam's body can suitably be understood in terms of the "creationist" theory.[44] In this understanding of the matter, the soul would not be created "before" being breathed into the body, but at the very same time.[45] This would obviate the need of supposing the soul's pre-embodied existence, and of having to explain why and how it "flowed down" into the world of bodies. It would also suppose a genus of "soul" whose union with the body was so "natural" that the disproportion between the Augustinian soul and the "animal" body would disappear once for all.

Difficulties for Creationists

The foregoing discussion may well have brought Augustine to see this as an attractive alternative. This may be why his answer has an oblique quality about it. Let the creationists confront the difficul-

42. I take this to be the force of *quae non erant* as Augustine applies it to those "other" spiritual beings. BA 48, p. 565, translates that those other beings "n'étaient pas" which, though literal enough, does not seem to bring out the distinction Augustine is driving at: that these beings, too, were made without any pre-existing "matter" out of which God made them. This makes sense of the qualification Augustine is then brought to add in the next sentence.

43. This, Augustine now feels, permits us to think of the soul as created on that "first day," with no anteriorly existing matter being required.

44. I use the term in a wide sense; strictly, it refers to the origin of post-Adamic souls only. But Augustine is probing that feature of "creationist" theory which makes creation and "infusion" *simultaneous*. He is, therefore, still alert, at least in this passage, to that requirement of creationism when properly understood.

45. See 7.40 (Z 28): *non [facta] nisi cum formato corpore est inspirata*. One could scarcely ask for a sharper awareness of the "simultaneity" referred to in note 44, above. This makes the looser expressions for creationist theory we shall see in Book 10 all the more significant: it is doubtful that Augustine is being simply careless.

ties Genesis puts in the way of their theory, and see if they can meet them more successfully than he has. First, let them explain whether the soul God creates by "breathing" it into the body is created "from" any antecedent "matter." But, second, let them show that their theory, which seems to imply that God "creates" new souls even now, is coherent with Ecclesiasticus' pronouncement that He made everything *simul* and with Genesis' word that He "rested" after creating all that He had created. Up to this point, therefore, Augustine thinks his two-phase theory of creation is still required by these texts, and that those same texts create difficulties against God's creating new souls, even now. But the last word has not been said on either issue (40–41/Z 28).

Having thrown down these two challenges to a creationist view of Adam's soul, Augustine presents a brief résumé of his own theory. God in the beginning, i.e., on the "first day," made all things at the same time, *simul*, creating some of them as actualities, others inasmuch as He created the pre-existing causes from which they would emerge in time. Creation "finished," God's activity— for He "works" until now—becomes that of governing and ruling creatures.

An Escape Route for Creationism

But now Augustine suddenly springs a different view upon us without either warning or acknowledging it is a different view—it would still remain true that God "finished" creating if one chose to interpret that phrase as meaning that He had originally created (*simul*) all the "kinds" (*genera*) of creatures that would ever populate the created universe; this interpretation would leave us free to say that He continues to create, even now, new individuals belonging to those *genera*, just as it is true that He works until now in governing the temporal "propagation" of successive generations of creatures within those *genera*. With a stroke of the pen, he has dropped his chief objection, and provided an opening for creationist theory after all! Now, perhaps aware of the bewildered look on his readers' faces, he admits that someone else may concoct a better explanation of all these texts—in which case, he would not oppose it, but willingly subscribe to it (42/Z 28).

A Tentative Summary

After this summary of his general theory of creation, Augustine finishes with a list of his findings on the particular creation of Adam's soul. It is a comment on the tentativeness of everything he has proposed so far that this list of findings is remarkably restricted: Adam's soul came from God, but is not part of God; it is spiritual; it is a creature and not consubstantial with God; it does not result from God's having transformed either some corporeal reality or an irrational kind of soul; and it is immortal, though not with that unique kind of immortality proper to God alone.

Of what value, then, the lengthy discussions of Genesis he has carried on in this book? For Augustine seems aware of the fact that none of the findings he has just listed actually emerged from his discussion of the text of Genesis: they represent, rather, a series of convictions he had previously reached by routes more philosophical than Scriptural. And yet, he assures us, these efforts to elicit the literal sense of Genesis may have some value, after all. First, they may show how such a search should be carried on, without affirming anything temerarily—particularly, one may think, when dealing with so dangerous a question as the origin of the soul. Or if his own manner of inquiry does not appeal to one or other reader, let it stand as a plea that the reader communicate his own method and findings to Augustine, who will then gladly carry the inquiry forward with him. On this self-effacing note, and with loose ends of theory hanging about in all directions, Augustine brings his seventh book of the *De Genesi* to its inconclusive end. He knows full well he has not finished with its central question, though; he will return to it, and devote the entire tenth book to seeking a more satisfying conclusion (42–43/Z 28).

THE SOUL'S ORIGIN IN BOOK 10

Augustine's introductory remarks to Book 10 attempt, somewhat awkwardly, to connect the topic of that book with the text of Genesis. He has just dealt with the creation of Eve, and observes that nothing has been said about the creation of her soul. This omission, then, rather than something positively contained in the text, is used as a springboard to explore the question of post-Adamic souls.[46] This slightly forced introduction of the problem, however, is only the first of a series of anomalies in Book 10; even when compared with the most tortuous sections that have preceded it, this book is an incredible tangle.[47]

Does the silence of Genesis on the creation of Eve's soul entitle us to infer that she received her soul from Adam in the way traducianists explain the "propagation" of all post-Adamic souls? Augustine's very way of putting the question has been interpreted as betraying his set intention of refuting traducianism in this book, if he can do so successfully;[48] but that interpretation seems highly questionable. In any event, his first step is to neutralize this "argument from silence" by showing that the silence could argue that Eve's soul was drawn from the same *source* as Adam's. This does not close the question, of course; it simply clears the ground for further inquiry (2/Z 21).

A Fresh Summary

Before going further, Augustine presents a summary of "findings" from Books 6 and 7. He reminds us, first, that the formation of Adam from earth and of Eve from Adam's rib pertains to the "second phase" of his two-phase theory of creation. But Adam's soul must have been created in the first phase, on that "first day," simultaneous with the creation of the "Light" which Augustine interprets as the angelic community. He points to various unacceptable conclusions that follow if this view be rejected, the last of them involving the theory of "causal reasons" as it would apply to the creation of Adam's soul. That theory would imply that the "causal reason" of Adam's soul would have to have been implanted in some actually existent creature—either some creature Genesis fails to

46. See BA 48, pp. 19–20, for the same view. But notice that 10.1 is also testimony to Augustine's determination to treat this question, and to the importance he attributes to it.

47. See BA 49, p. 533 for similar observations.

48. So BA 49, p. 531. These remarks would support, of course, my own opinion that Augustine was always profoundly anti-traducianist, and we shall see him show that animus in his treatment of Tertullian further on. But Augustine's attitude here seems, for the moment at least, far more "objective"; the question of how Original Sin is inherited *may* force him to embrace traducianism, or some variant of it, however reluctantly. But Solignac's note stiffens that reluctance into a set intention, without support from the text.

mention as among God's works, or some creature so mentioned. In the latter case, the alternatives are reduced to two: the angels or some corporeal element. This "causal-reason" theory, he admits, does not actually stand in open contradiction to the words of Scripture, but the alternative forms it takes seem "shocking and unacceptable," the conclusion that the soul is "daughter" of some corporeal element being even more "intolerable" than that it be the daughter of the angels. The terms used are far from categorical, but Augustine clearly prefers to exclude, now, the "causal reason" derivation of Adam's soul in favor of its creation on the "first day" (3/Z 2).[49]

The "Three" Hypotheses

As to the origin of post-Adamic souls, then, three hypotheses are left in presence: Augustine's own,[50] which has just been recalled above, traducianism, and the more conventional form of the creationist theory. Which of these, Augustine asks, is the "most acceptable"? Creationism seems, at first blush, to run counter to the interpretation imposed by the words of Genesis, by implying that God is constantly creating new souls in such wise as to deny that He finished creating all He created, and rested on the seventh day. But perhaps the creationist can turn this difficulty after all. Augustine is about to show that the interpretation he sprang on us so surprisingly toward the end of Book 7 must be taken seriously. The creationist might say, for example, that the souls God creates "now" are of the same *genus* as the Adamic soul created in the beginning, so that in this less restrictive sense it may be said He had "finished" creating, after all (5/Z 3).[51]

Having "saved" creationism by this reinterpretation, Augustine feels we can proceed with all three hypotheses as open possibilities. Which of them would Scripture persuade us to favor over the other two? Again, Augustine admonishes his readers and fellow-inquirers on the modest and careful spirit that should characterize such

---

49. Compare this protestation against so "shocking and unacceptable" a materialization of the soul with the analogous *durum* language referred to in note 38, above.
50. That is, the soul was created on the "first day."
51. See above where this notion was suddenly introduced at 7.42 (Z 28), with little warning to the reader that Augustine would eventually embrace it as firmly as he does here.

research and, then, typically, draws up a list of those "certainties" about the soul which he is confident his readers will share with him. That list bears strong resemblance to the list of certainties drawn up at the conclusion of Book 7, as one would expect. But there are some interesting, and puzzling, differences. The soul cannot be "turned into" a body, an irrational soul, or God; nor can any of these be "turned into" a soul. Secondly, the soul cannot be anything else than a creature of God, Who cannot have made it out of a body, an irrational soul, or His own substance. He must, therefore, have made it either from nothing or from some reasonable, spiritual creature (6–7/Z 3–4).

Now he makes an initial reflection clearly aimed at the more conventional form of creationist theory, which he sees as implying that God makes souls out of nothing even now, "after having finished His works, whereby He created everything at the same time" (simul). This seems to do violence to the text of Genesis, first of all, and Augustine does not know whether other clear texts of Scripture can be found to support such a view. There is a certain waffling tone to all this. Augustine does not seem confident enough that his two-phase theory of creation is the only one that can be squared with Genesis, after all; he seems to have in his mind the admission made twice earlier, that creationism could be saved since God would not now be creating souls of a different genus from Adam's soul. In any event, having begun on a tone that promised to exclude creationism as doing "violence" to Genesis, he ends much more meekly, as though ready to examine other Scriptural texts that might support the creationist view.

There follows an utterly baffling sentence concerning "what man is able to comprehend," and then a conclusion on method: "It is safer, therefore, in matters of this sort, not to deal in human conjectures, but to scrutinize the divine texts." Augustine is clearly saying, even if not in the clearest of ways, that he means to rely much more heavily on what Scripture says than on the conclusions of human reason. And with that, he returns to two of his recent reasoned affirmations about the soul, and asks whether Scripture lends any support to the theories that human souls can be "daughters" of the angels, or created from some bodily substrate: his conclusion is negative, as one would expect. But the point about method has been made, and illustrated (8/Z 5).

The "Three" Hypotheses Reduced to Two

The remainder of Book 10, therefore, will consist in an inventory of Scriptural texts, from both Old Testament and New, as they seem to bear on the origin of post-Adamic souls. But now Augustine reframes the question in a surprising way; instead of the three hypotheses he had outlined some paragraphs earlier, he is now prepared to deal with only two, creationism and traducianism.

There is no explanation given for this sudden elimination of one hypothesis, so we are left to speculate about what Augustine had in mind. It is certain that the traducianist hypothesis has not changed its form; it follows, then, that the other two hypotheses have been telescoped into one: creationism in the more conventional form in which its proponents argued for it seems now, in Augustine's thinking, to have merged with his own more personal hypothesis. That personal hypothesis formerly implied the two-phase creation theory, built on the supposition that God could not still be creating new individual souls, as creationism must suppose. But the considerations he has put forward in the meantime have weakened, perhaps even sapped, the force of his objection against creationism. God may be creating individual souls, if they be of the same *genus* as the souls He created in the beginning. This *might* satisfy as a valid interpretation of both Genesis and Ecclesiasticus, Augustine has twice assured us. Now, without ever explicitly turning that "might" into a "does," he seems to be working on the assumption that we will understand that the transformation has been made.[52]

In any event, the remainder of Book 10 is composed as though there were two, and only two, contending theories to be weighed against each other, traducianism and creationism. The only conclusion one can draw is that Augustine no longer sees the need for his general two-phase theory of creation, and has tacitly withdrawn his former objection to creationism, based on the need to explain the "matter" out of which the soul is created.[53] Both theories now in presence, moreover, Augustine defines at the outset in

---

52. See BA 49, p. 163n16, and pp. 533–34, for expressions of puzzlement similar to my own.

53. Note that Augustine had *tentatively* withdrawn this requirement, too, at *GenLitt* 7.39 (Z 28); but this did not prevent him from pressing it against creationism in 7.40 (Z 28)! There may be uneven strata of composition evident in all this.

perfectly straightforward terms: creationism, for example, teaches that God "creates an individual soul for each individual human being, creating other souls as he created Adam's, and without drawing them out of his" (9/Z 6). All talk of a general two-phase creation, involving the need for "causal reasons," is remarkably absent here, and just as remarkably absent, not only from the remainder of Book 10, but from all the other works we have surveyed on this troublesome issue.[54]

Augustine now surveys Scripture in order to judge which of these two theories on the soul's origin finds stronger support from the Bible. That survey, I suggest, can usefully be studied in three distinct movements.[55]

The first movement sees him weighing the import of a number of texts, all drawn as it happens from the Old Testament. One gleans the impression that this selection of texts was not entirely a matter of his own choice: they were, more likely, Scriptural passages to which one or other side had appealed in the conduct of the creationist–traducianist debate. In any event, he examines Isaiah 57:7, Psalm 32:15, and Zachariah 12:1 to find nothing arguing decisively for either side (9–11/Z 6).[56] He comes, then, to Wisdom 8:9–10, where the Scriptural writer speaks of being "allotted a good soul"; this passage seems to speak, as Augustine reads

54. Augustine seems unwilling now to make his solution on the creation of the *soul* depend on the acceptance of his more *general* "causal-reasons" theory; but now that he can abandon the universal theory of *causal* reasons (which is a metaphysical construct forced on him by what he thinks Scripture is saying: everything was created *simul* and yet in "six days") and still retain the more limited theory of "seminal" reasons for those created beings which, *experience* assures us, propagate by and grow from "seeds." This is precisely what I suggest he does in *Civ* (see below) —and that, despite retaining the conviction (in *Civ* 11.9; cf. 7) that all six days of creation are really one single day.

This shift in view may account for a tactic we are about to see him employ repeatedly in what follows: his expressions for creationist theory become less and less faithful to the lines that theory *historically* followed. More imprecision on Augustine's part? Or has he perceived, as seems to me more likely, the need for recasting creationist theory in such a way that it represents a new theory, coherent with the two-phase creation of *man* suggested by Gen. 1:27 and 2:7, respectively?

55. The first of those movements runs from 10.9 to 10.17 (Z 6–10) and concludes with an *ignoro*; the second, from 18 to 29 (Z 11–16), concludes that traducianism is not "absurd" after all; the third, from 30 to 45 (Z 17–26), concludes (39/Z 23) that traducianism "runs even" with creationism, or perhaps has some slight advantage over it. (From 40 to 45 [Z 24–26], Augustine hedges that conclusion somewhat, by presenting a more *philosophic* critique of Tertullian's "materialism.")

56. Again, it is fascinating to see how much Augustine's exegesis relies on the exact force of the *Latin words* of Scriptural translations.

it, of the soul as somehow "coming" as "from above," being "sent" as it were from some reservoir (*fons*) of souls, some good, some bad. Such language consorts ill with the traducianist, much more easily with the creationist, position. But the disquieting thought occurs to him that it seems almost to imply the Origenist hypothesis, whereby the *sors*, or "allotment," of a good soul rather than a bad would depend on the soul's "works" (*opera*) before the allotment was made. But this possibility, he assures us, Romans 9:11 precludes: "God forbid that we should contradict the Apostle, who says the yet unborn had done nothing either good or evil." *Absit, ut contradicamus.* The Origenist alternative firmly discarded, Augustine postpones closer examination of this text until later (12/Z 7).[57]

Psalm 103:29–30 can be argued either way, Augustine concludes,[58] and now takes up the text from Ecclesiastes 12:7, "Let dust return to the earth, as it was, and the spirit return to the God Who gave it." His treatment of this text is far crisper than it was in *Letter 143*, to Marcellinus, the alternatives envisaged more limited, and his conclusion much cleaner: the text favors neither traducianism nor creationism, and that is that.[59] But the text does "teach us" (*admonemur*) that "God made the soul from nothing" (*ex nihilo*) so that, when it "goes back," it has nowhere to go back to except to God Who "gave" it (15–16/Z 9).[60]

It would be difficult, Augustine avows, to claim a total survey of

---

57. Confer BA 48, p. 678, which explains (in connection with *GenLitt* 5.43 [Z 22]) that Augustine thinks of the sometime disproportion between sin and (penal?) misery as a "mystery," and (p. 687) a mystery of "divine will." I suggest he may have thought the proportion much less mysterious at an earlier time. The vicissitudes of the Pelagian controversy have, however, driven him into this somewhat agnostic position.
Note that in this instance there is no mention of our "proper lives," though Augustine does specify that the good and evil Paul refers to cannot have happened "before they began to live in bodies."

58. Augustine does, however, present (in 14/Z 8) a "spiritual" interpretation as an alternative to the more obvious interpretation of these verses; it expresses better, he thinks, the (anti-Pelagian) doctrine of divine grace, but has nothing to do with the traducianist–creationist issue.

59. BA 49, p. 171n21, seems to me insensitive to the subtle, but real differences between this interpretation and that in *Ep 143*; but again, Augustine's progressive interpretations of this crucial text would be worth a study in itself.

60. For an evaluation of how this conclusion relates to Augustine's previous discussions on the "matter" from which the soul may have been created, see BA 48, pp. 699–700. It appears the proposal that the soul was made of "nothing" (and not of some anterior matter), however tentatively one thought it had been made at 7.39 (Z 28), has now become Augustine's firm conclusion.

Scripture on this question of the soul's origin; but even on this admittedly partial showing, he may be justified in claiming ignorance (*ignoro*) about what the Bible would have us believe on the issue (17/Z 10).

This confession of ignorance brings the first movement[61] of Augustine's Scriptural exploration to a close. He has, thus far, adverted to the question of Original Sin and its transmission, but only obliquely. The second movement of his inquiry sets this mystery squarely at its entryway. Which of these theories, creationism or traducianism, does greater justice to the Pauline teaching that we are all condemned on account of Adam's sin, and all saved uniquely through Christ's redemptive grace? This second movement, then, instead of taking account of it almost parenthetically, will be commanded by the anti-Pelagian problematic. And this, Augustine allows, is precisely where the traducianist claims to be on solid ground. For it is "the soul alone that sins," and Paul speaks of Adam "in whom all have sinned" (*in quo omnes peccaverunt*);[62] what clearer evidence for concluding that each of our souls, not simply our fleshly bodies, must be derived by propagation from Adam's soul (18/Z 11)?[63]

At this juncture, Augustine traces out the boundaries of this new phase in the discussion. One must not make God the author of our sins, by claiming, for example (as creationists might stumble

61. This first movement may have been an original stratum in the composition of *GenLitt*, and the subsequent movements (especially the third) later "emendations" called for by his growing concern with the Pelagian aspects of the question. Again, I question whether the commentators of BA 48 and 49 sufficiently underline the connection between Pelagian issues and the question of the soul's origin.

62. Stanislas Lyonnet, in his contribution to the article "Péché" in the *Dictionnaire de la Bible*, Supplement 7 (1963), shows convincingly in cols. 528 and 540 that the principal development of Augustine's own idea of Original Sin took place quite independently of the implications the Latin translation of this text may have had for others, viz., that it was "in" Adam (*in quo*) that all of us sinned. But to make Augustine a "spiritual traducianist," as Lyonnet does (following Michel, apparently) in his article, "Romains V, 12 chez saint Augustin," NRT, 89 (1967), 842–49, esp. 846–48, is going a bit far. Compare Mlle La Bonnardière's suggestion, in private correspondence with Lyonnet (ibid., 848), that any conviction Augustine *may* have had about our "ingredience in" Adam derived much more from 1 Cor. 15:22, that "in Adam we all died"; cf. *En 84* 7 where Augustine embroiders this insight, and see above, chap. 5, note 23. Traducianism made much of this notion of ingredience, of course; but the fact that Augustine also exploits the notion does not necessarily mean he *understands* ingredience *in the traducianist sense*. We shall, I hope, gain a more precise idea of how he understands that notion further on.

63. Cf. Tertullian's *De anima*, 40. BA 49, p. 531, along with the notes to *GenLitt* 10.40–45 (Z 24–26) provide convincing evidence that Augustine was conversant with this treatise.

into claiming), that God "gives" the newly created (and therefore sinless) soul to the sinful flesh derived from Adam, on such terms as to make it inevitable that the soul should sin. Nor may one turn the creationist position into a kind of premiss, as the Pelagians have done, claiming that the newly created soul could not have been "in" Adam as the traducianists hold, and therefore is sinless and in no need of Christ's redemptive grace. The practice of infant baptism tells us that the infant soul, not merely its flesh, stands in need of cleansing; the infant is "Adam both in body and soul," not merely—as a certain understanding of creationism might have it—in body. And since (Romans 9:11 again) infants can, at their age, have done neither good nor evil, it seems to follow that their souls are as "innocent as they can be" (*innocentissima*) unless those souls derive from Adam's by "propagation." It would, then, seem something marvelous (*mirandus*) if the proponents of creationism can find an answer to this difficulty (19/Z 11).

Once Original Sin and its transmission are placed at center stage, then, creationism is seriously on the defensive. Creationists might object that sinful concupiscence is an affair uniquely of the flesh, not of the soul; but Augustine shows that concupiscence characterizes the *ensouled* flesh, is as much an affair of soul as of body. That escape route leads nowhere. And, since we are discussing tiny infants, before they have any capacity to sin by their own free choice, it seems clear, again, that their sinfulness is better understood, as the traducianists would have us understand it, by deriving their very souls from the sinful soul of Adam (19–23/Z 11–13).

An Attempted Defense of Creationism

How can the creationist reply to this indictment? And here, we must suppose, the creationist replying is an orthodox Catholic, not a Pelagian.[64] Well, he might propose, God "gives" newly created souls

64. It will become clear as we go on that this is the only valid supposition one can make to understand the conduct of Augustine's inquiry; it will become plain further on that, at a certain point, Augustine himself takes over the task of constructing this "defense" of creationism. BA 49, pp. 537–39 fails to take this into account, and principally, I suggest again, because Solignac has not followed carefully enough the *connection* between Augustine's exploration of the soul-origin question and the issues raised by Pelagianism. This results in a certain bluntness in his commentary, and quite specifically in his claim, p. 540, that Augustine had a *penchant* for creationist theory. Everything we have seen so far proves that judgment to be a drastic oversimplification.

to this "flesh of sin" so that they may merit, save the very flesh they were given to rule, and bring it to the glory of eventual resurrection. This, of course, and now Augustine inserts a curious condition, this would require that the soul, given to sinful flesh, be "weighed down" by a deep "oblivion," a slumbrous *torpor*. That condition time, growth, and the grace of Christ could eventually overcome, so that God would not be held responsible for any sins the soul would commit in that diminished condition. In this hypothesis, then, the soul would initially be sinful "Adam" only in the flesh, as it were; only if it "neglected" the requirements of moral progress, with the aid of grace, would that neglect make it "Adam in spirit as well as flesh" (24/Z 14).[65]

But, to be orthodox, creationists must admit, and explain, that the infant would stand in need of baptism before coming "of age." And this, Augustine admits, they might successfully do. One might conceive of the grace of the sacrament removing the penal results of Original Sin, a *poena* directly affecting the flesh and indirectly infecting the soul. This sacramental healing could then be thought to enable the soul to overcome the pull of carnal concupiscence and thus grow in merit; in this way the soul's association with the "flesh of sin" would be no insuperable obstacle to it, either in this life or after death (25/Z 14).

So far so good. But there is a damning weakness even in this somewhat ingenious version of the creationist position, a weakness an astute Pelagian would be likely to uncover. What if the infant's parents neglect to have the child baptized? How will the creationist explain that the infant—for our consideration is restricted to infants —dying without baptism would be damned? The supposition in this version of creationism is that the penal results of Original Sin affect the sinful flesh, and then, by a kind of contagion, infect the

65. Compare the "progressive" style of thought Augustine was forced to entertain in *Lib* 3 and in connection with this same creationist hypothesis. See chap. 1, above.
Note also the parallels with Augustine's morally "neutral" theory of how Adam's soul might come into his (sinless) body (7.35–38/Z 24–26). In both cases, the soul is created in some pre-embodied state, enjoys some measure of conscious life (else why should "oblivion" be required to erase its memory?), inclines "naturally" (one presumes) to the embodiment for which it was created, and merits only in its bodily life. But post-Adamic souls enter sinful flesh, and one wonders why Augustine here fails to specify that in their pre-embodied condition they must be deprived of all foreknowledge of their future actions in the body. Perhaps he sees this *oblivio* as somehow meeting the same requirement?

soul; but this is quite another thing from imputing the guilt of that sinfulness to the soul itself. Only if sin can be imputed to the soul can the creationist, or anyone else for that matter, "justify" the eternal damnation of that soul. Traducianists, for their part, as well as "Origenists," evolve their theory precisely in order to be able to impute sinful guilt to the *soul*, but what distinguishes "creationism" from both those theories is its very inability, if not outright refusal, to make that imputation (26/Z 15).

Augustine is at a loss to find any adequate answer the creationist could give to this difficulty drawn from infant damnation (27/Z 15). And now what he has been doing in these last three paragraphs becomes plain. This ingenious defense of creationism is, to some extent at least, his own brainchild, excogitated in a loyal effort to do as much justice as he can to the cause of thinkers unable, in this debate, to speak for themselves; it is the "business of absent ones," *absentium negotium*, that he has been about. One thinks instantly of Jerome, off in Bethlehem, for whose defense of creationism in the face of this very difficulty Augustine has been waiting all these years. Could anyone evolve a stronger defense of creationist theory than Augustine has put forth here? Perhaps, but in any case Jerome must not have any reason to complain that Augustine tried less than his best!

But the creationist may have one more arrow in his quiver. Perhaps God sees to it that certain infants are baptized, and others not, out of His foreknowledge of the good the former class would have done, and the sins the latter would have committed, had they not died prematurely. The Origenists, it will be remembered, tried by their theory to "explain" even this mystery of premature deaths; but Romans 9:11 has blown that theory sky-high (*explosa*), and, with its passing, the fact that some infants die prematurely cannot be used to argue for either of the two remaining theories, for it helps neither creationist nor traducianist (*neutros adjuvat*).

This is Augustine's first reply to the "foreknowledge" gambit. His second reply touches on that point so close to his heart, our eventual beatitude after death. Were the foreknowledge tactic to be taken seriously, no one would ever be judged on the sins he actually committed and on the good acts he actually performed; everyone would have to be judged on the basis of what he *would* have done *had* he lived longer than he did! What certainty is left us, then, about the eternal happiness of those who have died in the peace of the Church, after having lived a good life (28/Z 16)?[66]

Conclusion: Traducianism Not "Absurd"

But perhaps, Augustine admits, someone else can present a better defense of creationism than he has managed here.[67] He hopes others will try. But in that effort, let them respect all St. Paul has taught us about the universality of Original Sin, and of the consequent need of Christ's redemptive grace through baptism; this universality includes infant souls as well. Until such time as he learns of that stronger defense of creationism, then, he is forced to conclude that the traducianist position has nothing "absurd" about it, after all (29/Z 16).[68]

Augustine's "Defense" of Creationism

So the second movement of Augustine's adjudication between traducianism and creationism ends, much as the first one did, with creationism definitely on the defensive. But before going on to the next phase in the discussion, let me suggest an interpretation of what has been going on from paragraph 10.24 up to this point. It would seem that there was a historical position embodying part, but only part, of the position Augustine has elaborated in this portion of the De Genesi. For he speaks, toward the end of this entire section, of "those on whom this question of infant deaths has been pressed." Their answer (respondent), he goes on to say, took

66. Augustine adds the argument from the interpretation he has of Wis. 4:11, where the person who dies young (consummatus in brevi) is held blessed for having escaped the temptations that might have snared him in adult life. There would be, he argues, no benefit conferred by God's taking such young people to an early reward.

It is puzzling that here, as in Mer 2.59 (as we saw above, chap. 3), Augustine seems to have abandoned the far more straightforward rejection of this "foreknowledge" device he expressed in Simp (see above, chap. 2). There he dismissed this same theory by arguing that it made God's election dependent on man's "works," even if those works were "foreknown"; this, he claimed, was excluded by Rom. 9:11. Now his argument has become much more roundabout, but for what reasons I cannot confidently say.

67. Or, he adds, one might reject this inventum . . . quia meum est, thereby admitting that this defense has been, in part at least, a construction of his own. Where, though, has his work of construction begun? He does not make this clear. See my suggestion in note 64, above, and my proposals about this entire section further on.

68. Augustine's expression non absurde credunt may refer to Tertullian's famous credo quia absurdum.

the turn he has already examined: that all those, after Adam, "who lived ill during that time when they could have lived well" were made sinners "according to the soul." Further, they explained the necessity of baptism by saying that it was

> a bad thing for the soul [non expedit] to pass over from this life, even in that age [of infancy], without the sacrament; for the sinful contagion [coming] from the flesh of sin, to which the soul fell heir when it was inserted into the body, would be an obstacle to the soul after death unless it were expiated by the sacrament of the Mediator while [the infant was] yet in this life.

They went on to claim that this sacramental "help was divinely assured to the soul that God foreknew would live piously if it lived to that age when it became capable of believing," although God, "for some reason known to Himself, willed [that soul] to be born in a body, but quickly withdrew it from that body" (28/Z 16).

So much for the historical position Augustine appears to be dealing with. What has he added to it? The effects of baptismal grace in removing the penal effects of Original Sin and aiding the soul to overcome carnal concupiscence would seem in the nature more of logical extensions than of additions to the position he later outlines as historically held. But the remarks about the soul's being "given" to the sinful flesh in order to bring it to salvation and resurrection, with the curious codicil that this would involve a period of "oblivion" for the soul so given to the flesh, seem clearly an embroidery of Augustine's own design. In fact, comparison with similar terms used in the third book of the *De libero arbitrio* strongly suggests that he has adapted a proposal made in that work; but that proposal, back in 395, had to do with another hypothesis entirely, the hypothesis of the soul's pre-existing and being "divinely sent" into the body! Has Augustine somehow gotten these two hypotheses on the soul's origin confused with one another? We shall have to return to that question shortly.

Scriptural Survey: Third Movement

But for now, Augustine is ready with the third movement of his inquiry. We saw that earlier he promised to re-study Wisdom's text, 8:19–20, about its author's claim that he was "allotted" a good soul. That text had an ominous ring to it, seeming to favor neither

traducianist nor creationist, but the Origenist, theory of pre-incarnate sin: a theory in which Romans 9:11 forbids us to believe.
Augustine repeats that appeal to Romans 9:11 here: if one set the
Origenist theory firmly aside, then which of the two remaining
contenders does Wisdom's expressions favor? Augustine finds
nothing decisive for either side, except that the Church's practice
of infant baptism for the remission of sin—a consideration that
entered only obliquely in his earlier examination of this text—
seems to him now to weigh slightly in favor of traducianism (31/Z
17).[69] An examination of Hebrews 7:4-10 and John 3:6 is equally
inconclusive. *Ambigo*, Augustine confesses wearily again (34-38/Z
19-22); he cannot find grounds for opting one way or the other.
And still he submits, somewhat defensively one may think, that he
is not bereft of all firm opinions on the soul. It is not body, not
bodily property, not "harmony" of the body; and so long as God's
help keeps him thinking straight, no man's eloquence will ever
persuade him of the opposite![70] The Scriptural texts and reasoned
arguments he has examined seem to leave the scales even, or nearly
even, except that the practice of infant baptism—an apostolic tradition, and to be taken seriously—seems to weigh slightly in favor
of the traducianists (39/Z 23).

A Plea to Traducianists

This brings Augustine to address the tenants of the traducianist
position. Let them reflect upon themselves, and come to see at least
this much: that their souls are not bodily realities. For this was
Tertullian's error—an error the logical extension of which leads
to thinking God Himself is a bodily reality, indeed, to thinking that
unbodily reality can be no reality at all! But, says Augustine after
an extended refutation of Tertullian's materialist position, he has
dealt with this question of the spirituality both of soul and of God
in numerous of his other works, and will likely deal with it again

69. A subsequent paragraph (33/Z 18) develops the suggestion that this text may
apply, prophetically, to the soul of Christ; Augustine then goes on to show that
questions proper to the origin of Christ's soul do not affect the present debate, since
His soul represents an exceptional case.

70. True to the alternatives envisaged in *Immort*, these semi-materialistic counter-
positions (37/Z 21) are the only ones he can envisage as competitors to his own substantialist conception of the soul as "spirit." Notice Augustine's embarrassed awareness, however, that he has shifted onto philosophic grounds.

(40–45/Z 24–28). We are reminded, in fact, that this ability to think of "spiritual" realities in appropriate terms lay at the very center of the "intellectual" conversion Augustine recounts in the *Confessions*.[71] This single conviction, that spiritual reality truly exists and must be thought of in its proper, unsensual, and transphantasmal terms, comes very close to Augustine's way of defining himself as a thinker. It is reason enough, and more than enough, for his ineradicable suspicion of a traducianism that defined itself in the very opposite terms, materialist, sensual, phantasmal in its way of thinking everything. Had the Pauline statements on Original Sin ever compelled Augustine to admit that he must become a traducianist of this stamp, it is scary to imagine the intellectual crucifixion that would have represented for him.

But subtending his "intellectual" conversion in the *Confessions* there ran another, deeper conversion. Call it moral or ethical, for it is at least that. But Augustine would determinedly characterize it as religious. His inability to admit of the reality of the spiritual, he came to see, was rooted in an attitude of heart. It was his passionate attachment to sensible realities and to the happiness he sought and fleeting delights he found in them which beclouded his mind's eye, preventing it from "seeing" that his heart's true happiness, enduring delight, could be found only in the embrace of a higher, spiritual reality: the enrapturing beauty of God.[72] This aspect of his conversion lives on in all his preaching and writing. The human being's most tragic loss would be loss of this beatific vision; our most devastating blunder would be to set our hearts on the fleeting beauties of this world, and fail to attain to the Beauty that awaits us "there." The inability, or refusal, to acknowledge the reality of that higher spiritual world can have, accordingly, momentous ethical and religious consequences.

That burning conviction drives Augustine even now. We see him, in his later years, returning in letter after letter to the radically spiritual, trans-phantasmal nature of this vision of God.[73] Though connected only in the remotest way with his exegetical task, the

---

71. I use this term despite my conviction that calling *Conf* 7 and 8 accounts of Augustine's "intellectual" and "moral" conversions, respectively, is deceptively superficial; see below for more on this.

72. This ethical or, better, religious conversion Augustine presents as the condition of possibility for his (so-called) intellectual conversion.

73. The classic example, of course, is *Ep 147*, "On Seeing God."

entire twelfth book of the *De Genesi ad litteram* is devoted to the subject of the vision of God. The *De Trinitate* begins with the vision of God as the goal of all life's journeying, and devotes no fewer than eight of its fifteen books to demonstrating that the soul, as "image" of the Trinity, is contemplative soul, made for union with its divine source in the vision that will be its unabating bliss. And all human history is nothing else but the record of humankind's baffled, faltering, but insatiable quest for this same City of God, where we shall "rest and see, see and love, love and praise . . . in the end without end."[74]

Intimately connected with this lofty view of man's ultimate beatitude, however, was Augustine's obdurate conviction that man was primarily, when all is said, a contemplative soul for whom such a destiny was uniquely appropriate. When asked about man, Augustine's first impulse is to define him as soul, made in the "image" of God; man's incarnate character regularly occurs to him in a kind of afterthought. The Book of Genesis, as we have seen, compels him at a number of points to attribute greater weight to that afterthought than he had done formerly; so did the problem of the soul's "origin." But Augustine's growing acknowledgment of man's incarnate status has all the aspects of a stubborn rearguard action. His last word, in the face of traducianism's insistent appeal, is a defiant "however." Origen's brand of spiritualism has been barred to him. Adam's body was an "animal" body, not an immortal, "spiritual" body, after all. Our "first garment," *stola prima*, was not what he had long thought it was. Our renewal and restoration is not the term of a circular "pilgrimage," nor concupiscence uniquely a property of sinful "flesh." Creationism, the only viable alternative left to explain the soul's embodied status, was fraught with difficulties. But let God keep him thinking straight, at materialism, as he envisaged it, he drew the line.

So Augustine brings to an end his effort to decide between creationism and traducianism—an effort that leaves the scales slightly tilted toward traducianism, but toward a traducianism which, in his day, dressed itself in a materialism that he found intensely repulsive. It would be tempting to speculate on how, and whether, Augustine's theory of "causal reasons," if applied to post-Adamic souls, might have produced a theory of "spiritual" traducianism

74. *Civ* 22.30.

which could have answered all his difficulties on this troubling question; but perhaps his two-phase theory of creation,[75] and certainly his insistence on viewing man's creation "in the image of God" as uniquely affecting the creation of man as "soul," stood in the way of his taking that imaginative leap of thought.

A Reconception of Creationism?

That proclivity for thinking man *qua* "soul" may help us to understand an anomaly to which allusion was made earlier. Augustine almost seems at one juncture to have confused the creationist theory with the theory of soul as pre-existing and "divinely sent" into the body. When excogitating his defense of the "absent" creationists, he speaks of the soul as "given" to the body to govern it, merit, and thereby bring the body to fulfillment in the resurrection; he appends, moreover, that curious proviso (with which he assumes his creationist friends would agree) that the soul so "given" would have to undergo a period of "oblivion" from which it would gradually emerge.

Such talk of "oblivion," forgetfulness, is of course stock in trade of all Platonist theories of the soul: the soul "pre-existed" its embodied state, but somehow has "forgotten"—forgotten, but not completely forgotten—that blissful condition. Augustine's frequent references to "memory" and "forgetfulness" in his early works strongly suggest that he was then thinking of our souls as having existed prior to their embodied state. But we have seen in this study a number of changes in Augustine's later theory of man. It would be highly questionable method, though, to read Augustine's later views back into his earliest works.

At all events, there is nothing strange about Augustine's invoking a period of "oblivion" when speaking of the soul as "divinely sent" into the body; the supposition involved in that hypothesis is that

---

75. As a *general* two-phase theory of how creation *as a whole* occurred, and occurred *simul*, Augustine's appeal to *rationes causales* seems to have been dropped. He very likely thought of that device as unnecessary once he adopted the view that on the "first day" God created all *genera* of creatures *simul*, but continues to create *individual* instances of those *genera* "even now." But with respect to Adam's soul, at least, he still feels obliged to hold a (more *particular*) two-phase theory; a first-day creation "in the image of God" and a sixth-day insufflation of that soul into the body. It may be that he has simply carried over that theory on Adam's soul to the creation of post-Adamic souls as well.

the soul "pre-existed," but Augustine seems now to imply that our experience tells us we have no direct memory of that pre-existent state. Yet there does appear to be something strange about his mentioning that same phenomenon of oblivion in a discussion centered on the creationist alternative. Was it, one wonders, a mere slip of the pen, or, more accurately, a slip of the mind?

Consider, in this connection, the series of expressions the Augustine of Book 10 uses of the creationist hypothesis: that the created soul may come from "some secret [treasury?] of [God's]" (9/Z 6); that God "sends the soul [once it is] made" (11/Z 6); that souls, in creationist theory, "are believed to come to bodies from above," as though the souls "in that reservoir of souls, if any such there be" were some of them good, some bad (12/Z 7); that creationists "assert that souls come, God sending them" (13/Z 8); and that the soul, finally, is "given from above" (17/Z 10). At first it would appear there was simply an unguarded quality in all these expressions, as though the limitations of Augustine's philosophical imagination compelled him to express creationist theory in terms more congenial to his own substantialist view of soul as "other" and radically independent of the body to which it "comes." And yet, Augustine can still show an acute awareness of the exact lines of creationist theory: right in the midst of this very discussion he makes the creationist claim that God forms each soul and "sends it," or (vel) —the rephrasing is significant—"forms it in the very [body? individual person?] to which He sends it" (10/Z 6). Not only is this latter, consciously emended form of expression more accurate; it is the only genuinely fair way of formulating the creationist position as it was historically held by its proponents. For it did not in the least require, and some proponents of the theory seem sedulously to have avoided all suggestion, that God first created, or formed, the soul, and then sent that fully formed soul into the body. The looser, two-phase manner of viewing the soul's origin brings the creationist hypothesis into remarkably close neighborhood with the third hypothesis, which views the soul as a fully constituted being even apart from, and prior to its being divinely "sent" to govern, the body.

It is into just such an imprecise notion of creationism that, on one view of the matter, Augustine would seem repeatedly to have slipped, if slip he did; and the fact that the slip was repeatedly made might seem to suggest only that this was the way in which Augustine most naturally and comfortably thought of the soul: as a fully constituted being, created apart from and prior to its being sent by God into the body. Any other way of envisaging the soul's relationship to the body, his altercation with Tertullianism broadly hints, would seem to reduce it to a "property" or "harmony" of the body, a "materialist" conception that he qualifies as simple "madness" (41–45/Z 25–26). Between these two extremes Augustine seems never—even when speaking of the soul's "natural" desire for body—to have entertained the notion of some mid-position, one that, like Aristotle's entelechy concept, might have done greater justice to the creationist position, for one thing, as well as to the more flexible forms a traducianist theory might assume.[76] For in neither creationism nor traducianism does the question of the soul's "origin" come down to "how the soul became incarnate"— the form in which the question seems always to have presented itself to Augustine's mind.[77]

But there is another possibility to ponder: that Augustine's re-expressions of the creationist theory were a matter far less of inadvertance than of deliberate policy on his part. He has set himself the task of defending creationism as loyally as he can; but he may have come to the conviction that the price of any such defense must be a reformation of the very theory being defended. Arguing for that reformation there would be, of course, the spiritual and substantialist view of soul that was always so dear to Augustine's way of thinking. But Romans 9:11 may have introduced a new, and even stronger, motive for recasting the form creationism historically took.

Again: The Soul's "Proper Life"

For Augustine, we have observed, has shown his awareness again and again, from the *De libero arbitrio*, through *Letters 143* and *166*, and now in the tenth book of his *De Genesi ad litteram*, that historical forms of creationism insisted that the soul's creation, infusion into the body, and therefore the inception of the newly

76. This, I remain convinced, was owing to Augustine's limited acquaintance with the Greek philosophic tradition out of which the Plotinus of *Ennead* 4.7 was working. See *Early Theory*, pp. 135–45.
77. We shall witness the same tendency operative in *Trin*; see below.

conceived's "proper life" were all absolutely simultaneous; there was no possibility that the soul could pre-exist, even for an instant, prior to its actual ensoulment of the body.

Now, Romans 9:11 seemed clearly to preclude any sin on the part of human beings "before they were born." And yet, we have seen Augustine more and more regularly, insistently, introduce a peculiar qualification into his understanding of that text: it precluded any sin before we entered on our "proper" lives. That notion of "proper" life he has progressively unfolded. Whether it be Jeremiah, Adam, or ourselves, we must all live "our time" as souls "animating" the body, using its senses, experiencing ourselves as living "in ourselves," with a will, intellect, and memory that are "our own"; further, we must progress in "age" until such time as we can assume responsibility for our moral actions; only at the state of incarnate human development can we be said to "do either evil or good."[78]

Once again, it should be clear that this qualification must be meant to restrict the bearing of Romans 9:11; now, Augustine seems to be insinuating, not *all* prenatal sin is being excluded by that text, but only such prenatal sin as would suppose we were already living our "proper," individualized, embodied lives. But this leaves open a surprising possibility: that the soul may have lived some kind of pre-existent life which was not "proper" in the sense Augustine attaches to that term. That, in turn, hints at some interval between the soul's creation and its divine sending—or infusion—into the body of its proper life. That interval would then allow for what creationism in its historical forms precluded: some pre-existent sin, though not of a "proper" kind, which would explain the guilt which our *souls*, not merely our post-Adamic bodies, bear on entering "this" life. That guilt traducianism explained, but at the cost of a materialism Augustine could not stomach. Creationism, though, with its insistence on the simultaneity of creation, infusion, and the inception of our "proper" lives, left no opening for understanding how our souls could have contracted any such guilt. And if there is one thing the Pelagian controversy has borne in upon Augustine's mind, it is this: no theory of the soul's origin can satisfy unless it permit us to account

---

78. See again *GenLitt* 6.14–16 (Z 9), 7.11 (Z 8), and 10.12 (Z 7), along with the treatment of *Ep 98* and *Mer* 2.59 in chap. 7, above.

for that guilt and for our need of Christ's baptism for the remission of sin.

If this was Augustine's intention, it would explain a number of anomalies we have seen crop up in his writings once the force of Romans 9:11 dawned on him.[79] Confirmation of this suggestion, however, must await examination of the works we are about to study. Yet the hypothesis itself may sharpen our reading of both of them.

79. See notes 44, 45, and 54, above, where this proposal began to take shape.

9

THE
De Trinitate

Augustine almost certainly began work on his *De Trinitate* as early as 404, after completing the *Contra Felicem Manichaeum*, which dates from that year. If he began it earlier, as a number of scholars have opined, then one thing is even more certain: the problem of the soul's origin was even farther from being the deeply troubling preoccupation it became for him later. I opted for the hypothesis that this, far more than the difficulties of relations theory, was the problem that forced him to delay publication of his *De Trinitate*. We have seen the apparent convergence that supported the relations hypothesis progressively disintegrate, only to receive its *coup de grâce* in *Letter 174*, which strongly suggests that Book 5, the foundational book on relations theory, had long since seen at least limited circulation. At the same time we have seen that in writing to Consentius, and then to Marcellinus, Augustine points to this question of the soul, and then more precisely to the problem of its origin, as his real sticking point. To Evodius, moreover, he writes that he has suspended work on his *De Trinitate*, and sent off his important letter to Jerome, "consulting" him on this very problem. The Pelagian controversy has passed from initial simmer to rolling boil; the question of infant damnation has made the origin of the soul an inflamed and dangerous question.

THE ORIGIN OF THE SOUL AND THE *De Trinitate*

But what could the problem of the origin of the soul have to do with the composition of a work on the Trinity? Our knowledge of the Trinity, Augustine tells Consentius, must pass upward from the knowledge we may glean of that "image" of the Trinity, "man," or human soul, precisely as "intellectual" soul. But there is a gigantic supposition involved here: that this is truly the nature of the soul God made in His "image." For there is at least one theory on the soul's origin which appears to state that the opposite is the case, indeed *must* be the case, if we are to understand correctly how even newborn infants inherit the guilt that calls for baptism. Tertullian and his traducianist followers claimed that this transmission of Adam's guilt required us to think of the soul in bodily, even materialistic terms.

There were, of course, other opinions on the origin of the soul. Origen had the merit of thinking our souls were spiritual beings, and explained our guilt as resulting from their sinful fall into the world of bodies. Or perhaps our souls pre-existed as spiritual beings and were divinely "sent" to govern mortal bodies; their spiritual nature remained intact, but their inheritance of Adam's guilt became a problem. Creationism, finally, though reconcilable with the soul's spirituality ran up against a similar problem; the Pelagians, indeed, argued *from* their creationist thesis to the innocence of infant souls. But in every case, this much was clear: any opinion one held on the origin of the soul went hand in hand with a corresponding opinion on its nature, and the *way* it should be thought of as an "image" of the Trinity. If this was the point of Augustine's hesitation, as one may guess that it was, it was certainly a valid point.

For though initially it sounds paradoxical, the *De Trinitate* is at least as much an exploration into the nature of the soul as it is a probe into the Trinitarian Godhead. Augustine begins by summarizing and putting into order—his order—what the ecclesiastical tradition presents to him as the Scriptural Catholic faith on the Trinity (Books 1–4). He moves from there, typically, toward an effort to "understand" that faith. His first step is a negative one. He exploits the Aristotelian theory of relation in order to show that there are no incompatibilities or contradictions in viewing God as one in nature, three in persons (Books 5–7).

But then Augustine sets out in hopes of offering a more positive understanding of the faith in God as triune. He reasons from the pronouncement in Genesis that God made "man" in His own "image." One should, therefore, be able to obtain some understanding of that Trinitarian God, however dark and enigmatic, through one's knowledge of His created image, man. This task will occupy him for the closing eight books, more than half the *De Trinitate*.

But what is "man"? Whatever confidence Augustine may have felt earlier in replying to that question, it has been steadily eroded in the interim. Pelagius has forced him to examine many of his assumptions, brought him to see that one's stand on the "origin of the soul" implied an answer to the larger question about "man." Augustine had begun his *De Trinitate* years before Pelagius and Pelagianism woke him to the dangerous implications of that question; the years 411 to 413, when we see him protesting most passionately against hurrying the publication of this work, were the very years when he began taking the measure of this new challenge to his "understanding" of the faith. But then, in 417 or 418, the "brothers" lose their patience, and he discovers, to his dismay, that the major part of his *De Trinitate* has been placed in circulation. And this was just about the time when we can be sure that St. Paul's text in Romans 9:11 had brought him to think that any theory of man portraying him as "fallen soul" must be rejected.

Augustine's reaction to that "theft" is one of furious indignation; he resolves, for a time, to give up entirely on the *De Trinitate*, and spray his angry expostulations around in other, later writings. Mere snit? Or was there some deeper reason, after all, for that stubborn refusal to publish that work before he felt it was ready?

The "brothers" finally prevail upon him to complete his work. But even then, he complains unhappily to Aurelius, he felt constrained to finish it off in such a way as to leave it substantially consistent with the version that had been stolen from him. He insists, accordingly, that this letter of consignment be placed at the beginning of the final version, warning his readers of what he had been compelled to do. That final version, our best information tells us, was completed sometime after the beginning of 420—after his *De anima et ejus origine*, and his letters to Optatus on the soul and its origin. We are left to guess, or ferret out, how differently Augustine might have written his *De Trinitate* had he been free to start it afresh in 420.

To educate our guesswork, Augustine has left us a trail of indicators, both in his letter to Aurelius and in the finished *De Trinitate*. We can be fairly confident, for instance, that the portion finally composed afresh began with Book 12, chapter 14. Augustine clearly says, moreover, that new *proëmia*, introductory sections, were composed for each of the first five books. Of the *exact* extent of those new *proëmia* we can be less confident, but we do not need that exact knowledge to catch their drift. A dominant theme recurring in them all echoes the message of *Letter 174*. Augustine is alerting the reader to be cautious; he is more sorely conscious than ever before of his own fallibility in the matters under discussion. *Caveat lector!*[1]

MAN AS "IMAGE" OF GOD

Augustine begins his probe into man as image of God with the same exegetical supposition we saw active in the *De Genesi ad litteram*: that Genesis 1:26—the proposal to create man in the "image" of the Trinity—must be interpreted in the light of the second member of that verse, endowing man with the power to rule over the brute creation. The "image," then, must be situated in the soul whereby man exercises this superiority over the animals, *and not* in any properties or characteristics man possesses in common with brute creatures. This rules out from the very start any notion that man *qua* incarnate—the soul *qua* embodied in the "animal" body of the *De Genesi*—is to be regarded as the seat of God's image.

We are already alerted to Augustine's conviction that his project is not so simple or so obvious as it might sound at first. This first step of discerning how the term "man" must be understood for the purposes of this inquiry will be followed by a series of similar discernments on what "soul" is to mean. The business of exploring

1. See Mlle La Bonnardière's effort to delimit these *proëmia* in *Chronologie*, pp. 169–77, as well as her remarks on their tone and content. But it would be enough to read the opening paragraphs of Books 1 to 5 to catch the note I speak of.

Citations will be given, in the text, by arabic paragraph number when it is clear what Book is being discussed. The BA edition uses the same numbering as William I. Mountain in his edition, CCL 50 and 50A (Turnhout, 1968).

what soul *truly* is will entail sifting out and excluding all irrelevant or alien features one might confusedly entertain as characterizing the soul's authentic essence, until the soul itself, stripped of all adventitious excrescences, stands forth stark and clear in its image character. But at that point, a further discernment will be required: Where is it *in the soul* itself that its image character is situated? In its embodied existence the soul uses sense perceptions, phantasms; it believes and hopes; it not only administers its own body, but acts upon and among other sensible realities as well. Do these strata of activity declare it has been made in the image of the Trinity? No, Augustine is convinced, and all his efforts from Book 8 to the end of Book 14 constitute an "exercise of the mind" aimed to bring us to that same conviction.[2]

AUGUSTINE'S SEMI-ORIGENISM

That conviction, be it noted, was not unlike Origen's: the soul's errant persuasions that it was *de jure* an embodied or even bodily, sense-using, active being were all results of its sinful "fall"; God's original creative intention was that the soul remain disembodied and engaged in direct contemplation of the divine splendor. There is a gap between the soul's present *de facto* situation and the ideal situation it should *de jure* still enjoy, the situation for which God intended it. But the ideal situation, corresponding to God's creative "idea" of the soul, was one the soul originally enjoyed, and to which it is destined, once redeemed, to return. Quite literally, then, the soul can say: "In my end is my beginning." The history of the soul is perfectly circular; the Pauline terms "renewal" and "restoration" are understood in their most literal sense.

We have seen how Augustine has been compelled in his *De Genesi ad litteram* to correct his former understanding of such circular terms and to reinterpret the "first garment," the *stola prima* of the Prodigal parable; Adam's body in paradise was not the "spiritual" body which we are destined to wear in the final resurrection, however much Augustine may formerly have thought,

---

2. Madec, "Clarification," 128, correctly stresses the "spiritual exercise" intention of *Trin*, but one should balance his remarks with the recognition that Augustine was also straining to incorporate as much truth value as he could into the affirmations he was making there.

and said, so. Yet despite whatever efforts he may have made to "emend" his earlier version of the *De Trinitate*, one interpretation he gives of the *stola prima* in the finished work (12.16) remains the "circular" one he rejected in the *De Genesi*. We may be touching, here, on one motive for Augustine's anger at the pious theft and premature publication of his work. Begun as early as 404, or even 399, it could well reveal an Augustine tranquilly assuming that a semi-Origenist explanation of the soul's incarnate condition was an acceptable Catholic view and, indeed, the most plausible of the four hypotheses on the soul's origin.

THE SOUL'S "KNOWLEDGE" OF ITSELF

Take that proposal as a working hypothesis for now: Is there any evidence in the *De Trinitate*, even as it stands, that it was once Augustine's preferred position?

To answer that question, it should be noticed that Augustine's exploration of the soul's authentic reality is situated squarely in that classic line of philosophic inquiry hearkening back to the Delphic oracle's command to "know thyself"—*nosce teipsum*, as the Latins put it. And from the outset of Book 8 until Book 10, chapter 5, he seems content to pursue this *notitia sui*. At that point, however, he finds himself obliged to introduce a distinction that had not seen service in those earlier books; now he finds it necessary to differentiate between that *notitia sui* and a more advanced, refined stage of the soul's self-knowledge, *cogitatio sui*. The distinction arises from his conviction that the soul cannot but have *notitia sui*, an "awareness" of itself concomitant to all its conscious activities. But that ineradicable self-awareness does not guarantee that the soul "truly knows itself" in that stronger sense of know, a sense of the term implying that the soul knows genuinely *what* it is, can really form an exact notion of its own authentic reality, can really *cogitare se*. And, it is clear from Augustine's development, this self-*cogitatio* must be achieved in the light of the divine creative idea of "soul."

Indeed, Augustine argues, the soul may have a self-present *notitia sui*, and be unable correctly to *cogitare se*; it may, in fact, have an idea of its own reality which is false, confused, overlaid with those extraneous features that must be distinguished out as "adventitious" to the soul precisely as soul—features that do not pertain to its authentic reality as soul created in the image of the Trinitarian God.[3]

THE SOUL NOT A BODY

The first type of misconception of itself which Augustine chooses to deal with arises from the soul's proclivity to think of itself as a bodily reality. He comes to this temptation in the course of Book 10, but he has found it necessary to deal with an analogous temptation in Book 8. For the same temptation as affects the soul's self-knowledge also affects the God in Whose "image" the soul is created; as with the image, so with God Himself, we are often tempted to think of Him in terms of bodily images and phantasms.[4] It is, Augustine warns, difficult to transcend this mode of thinking about God. *Ecce*, he urges the soul, "Behold, see if you can, O soul weighed down by the corruptible body [*anima praegravata corpore quod corrumpitur*] and laden [*onusta*] with earthly thoughts many and varied; behold, see if you can, that God is Truth."

That "seeing," Augustine warns, is to be accomplished, not with bodily eyes (*isti oculi*), but interiorly, with the "heart." Unless it be the heart that sees, then all at once the "mist of bodily images and clouds of phantasms stand in the way" (*se opponant caligines imaginum corporalium et nubila phantasmatum*). These trouble only the clarity of insight that dawned, in the *primo ictu*, on the soul's eye contemplating God as "Truth."

> Behold, in that first flash [*in ipso primo ictu*] how you were bedazzled as though by a lightning-streak [*quo velut coruscatione perstringeris*]. Remain [*mane*] that way if you can; but you cannot. You fall back into those accustomed and earthly [ways of thinking] [*relaberis in ista solita atque terrena*]. What weight is it, pray, that makes you fall back, if not the stickiness of the filth contracted through your cupidity and the errors of your wandering [*Quo tandem pondere, quaeso, relaberis, nisi sordium contractarum cupiditatis visco et peregrinationis erroribus*] [8.4]?

3. Compare the analogous observations in TeSelle, *Theologian*, p. 306.
4. Augustine stresses this connection in his remarks on Tertullian in *GenLitt* 10.45 (Z 24–26). But *Ep 120*, to Consentius, emphasizes its relevance to the task of the *De Trinitate*.

God, Augustine counsels, is the Supreme Good. Now he leads our minds upward, in an ascent from lower to higher and higher goods, and is confident that we can follow him in that ascent. But do we truly understand what we have been doing? Do we realize, Augustine asks us to reflect, that we have throughout that ascent been making "judgments" of value, finding this good superior to that, another superior to this, and so on up the scale? But such "judgments" would be impossible for us to make unless "there were impressed on us the notion of goodness itself, in accord with which we approve this or that, and set one thing over another" (*nisi esset nobis impressa notio ipsius boni, secundum quod et probaremus aliquid, et aliud alii praeponeremus*) (8.4). And, he concludes, that *bonum* whose *notio* is impressed on our minds is none other than God—not a good soul, not a good angel, not a good heaven, but the "good good" itself, the *bonum bonum* and nothing less than that.

This, Augustine continues, is the "good" toward which the soul must freely turn in order to become a "good soul"—the "good," other than itself (*quod ipse non est*), which it "loves, and desires, and attains" (*amat, et appetit, et adipiscitur*). But let us suppose that the soul has turned away from this good (*se avertit*);[5] it thereby becomes a "not-good" soul, since it had turned from the good it was meant to love, desire, attain. Suppose now we try to conceive of the soul's "amending" itself, of its correcting that first "aversion" by a "conversion." How can we even conceive of such an emendation and conversion unless we also conceive of that divine "good of all goods" as still enduring, still being "there," as it were, the unchanged and unchanging "whereunto" for the return pilgrimage of the converted soul? God must, in a word, "remain in Himself" if we are to have a *terminus ad quem* for our conversion (*nisi maneat in se illud bonum [scil., Deus], unde se [scil., anima] avertit, non est quo iterum, si [scil., anima] voluerit emendare, convertat*) (8.4).

The Latin of that last sentence has defied more than one translator,[6] but the meaning comes straight from Augustine's emphasis,

5. I omit here treatment of the *rursus* contained in the text; it refers, if I am right, to Augustine's theory of the "creation"–"formation" of the soul by a process of "conversion" to God for its constitution as soul, i.e., for its initial being as creature. But the omission does not affect my argument; nor does this interpretation of the *rursus*.

6. Compare the translation by P. Agaësse in BA 16, p. 34 ("à moins que demeure en elle ce bien dont elle se détourne," the "elle" referring to the soul), and that by Stephen

throughout the *Confessions*, on the link between God's genuine immateriality and His integral omnipresence to every item of the lower created world, and the equally firm link between His integral omnipresence and His property of "remaining in Himself." *Manens in se*, He constitutes the *mansio* to which the fallen soul may always "return."[7]

COMPARISON WITH THE *Confessions*

But the other key elements of this entire complex of language, imagery, and thought-drive are equally familiar from the *Confessions*. There, for instance (7.1), Augustine describes his efforts to think of God as a substance familiar to him from corporeal sight (*quale per hos oculos videri solet*). He knew enough even then to value (*praeponebam*) the immutable, incorruptible, and inviolable over their opposites; but though he bent every effort to put to rout the crowd of unclean *phantasmata* that beclouded his spiritual eye (*obnubilabat acies mentis*), thinking that this could be accomplished in one stroke (*in hoc uno ictu*), still, in the twinkling of an eye (*in ictu oculi*) those phantasms came swarming back again to block his spiritual vision.

Shortly afterward (7.13ff.) he comes upon those *libri Platonicorum*, and finally makes the breakthrough to a genuinely spiritual conception of God, that beatifying *bonum* forever remaining in Himself (*in se manens*) (7.16–17) and therefore integrally omnipresent to all His creatures. He marvels that it is God he now loves, not so many *phantasmata* in His stead. But a momentary glimpse is all he is allowed. The "weight" (*pondus*) of carnal custom (*consuetudo carnalis*) drags him down to the familiar bodily world (*ruebam in ista; redditus solitis*) (7.23), for, he explains it there, as here, "the corruptible body weighs down the soul" (*corpus quod corrumpitur adgravat animam*). He pursues the implication of the value judgments he has been making (*unde adprobarem . . . praeferendum . . . praeponeret*) and sees, *in ictu trepidantis as-*

McKenna in *The Trinity*, The Fathers of the Church Series 45 (Washington, D.C., 1963), p. 249 ("unless the good remain in it [the soul] from which it has turned away").

7. See, for instance, *Conf* 4.31, a paragraph situated in a development running from 4.1 to 5.2, all of it under the aegis of Augustine's "integral omnipresence" conception. For my grounding of this view, see *Early Theory*, especially, touching this section, pp. 82–85. Also, *Odyssey*, pp. 55–58.

pectus, the Divine Light, *quo lumine aspargeretur*, that empowers even the sense-bound soul to make those judgments. But the radiance of that Light is too much for his infirm spiritual eye (*aciem figere non evalui et repercussa infirmitate*); he is beaten back down to the shadows of the sense world (7.23).

As in the section of the *De Trinitate* from which all these cognate expressions are drawn, the Augustine of the *Confessions* is diagnosing the epistemological difficulty that had prevented him, until now, from gaining a genuinely spiritual insight into God's immateriality and, consequently, into God's integral omnipresence. But an inability to think out God's immateriality, Augustine is persuaded, is inevitably linked with the inability to think out the soul's immateriality as well; indeed, if the soul be made "in the image" of God, one would expect the one difficulty to be interwoven with the other! But in the *Confessions*, and now in the *De Trinitate*, these interconnected difficulties have the identical root: in the soul's condition as "fallen" from the higher spiritual world into a world of sense and "mortal" body.

FROM *notitia* TO *cogitatio sui*

The evidence for that last contention only becomes stronger when Augustine comes, in Book 10, to diagnose the difficulties the soul encounters in coming to knowledge of itself. First, he must show that the soul already has, and must have, *some* knowledge of itself, some *notitia sui*. His argument for this is interesting, and it parallels the famous Platonic argument stemming from the *Meno*: to look for anything, one must already know what one is looking *for*. So, if the oracle's command *nosce teipsum* is to have any sense, the soul must in some sense already "pre-know" what it is being bidden to "come to know"; the command to know oneself must, therefore, mean that the soul is bidden to pass from its mere self-awareness (*notitia sui*) to a knowledge of what its true reality is (*cogitatio sui*) (10.5–7).

But some would claim—materialists, for instance—that the soul is a bodily entity. This erroneous way of *cogitatio sui* soon equates with a "forgetfulness" of self. Thus Augustine sets up the problem as one not merely of correcting the materialist's error, but of accounting for how such "self-forgetfulness" may have come about.

And, once again, an epistemological error is rooted in the soul's "fallen" condition.

It is a base cupidity (*cupiditas prava*), he explains, which brings the soul to be so forgetful of itself (*tamquam sui sit oblita*). The soul begins by beholding (*videt*)—in its original state—the invisible beauties of the Divinity; but instead of resting in that contemplation, it conceives the desire of attributing those beauties to itself instead of to God (*volens ea sibi tribuere*), of playing God, as it were (*ex seipsa esse quod Ille est*), instead of being content with its status as God-created image of God. The impulse is obviously one of pride, the *superbia* which, in Augustine's early theory, is his counterpart of the Plotinian τόλμα. That pride prompts the soul to "turn away" from God (*avertitur ab Eo*), to pass from the stability of contemplative enjoyment (*stare debeat ut . . . fruatur*) into the "movement" of fall (*moveturque et labitur*). The fall carries it into a realm of diminished reality, ontological poverty (*egestas*), a realm that wears the deceptive appearance of "more and more" while, in reality, it is "less and less" (*in minus et minus, quod [anima] putat amplius et amplius*). For instead of being a realm of assured contemplative possession of God, this is the realm of all-absorbing action and "unquiet delights" (*inquietas delectationes*) and, hence, the realm of *curiositas*, "curiosity," though, in the double Augustinian (and originally, Plotinian) sense, for it is at once the realm of "care" (*cura*) and "curiosity" in the sense of striving to acquire sense knowledge for its own sake (*cupiditate acquirendi notitias ex eis quae foris sunt*). Extended fond familiarity with these "exterior" bodily beings begets, in the most literal sense imaginable, a growing attachment to them. It is as though the soul were "glued" to them by a *glutinum curae* (or a *glutinum amoris*) (see 10.10), to such an extent that it begins to think of itself as sharing the very nature of these appendages to itself; it thinks of itself as "bodily" (10.7; cf. 10.8–9). And yet, despite this blindness to itself, the soul retains (here, as in the *Confessions*) the capacity to "judge" on the relative superiorities amid the sense beauties that surround it (*servat autem aliquid quo . . . judicet*). Its forgetfulness is not entire, therefore; but, as is obvious from the passage, the soul begins by "seeing" (*videt*) but its fall deprives it of the enduring vision it once enjoyed, of those invisible beauties of divinity.

PARALLELS WITH EARLIER WORKS

Again, the images, thought-drive, and the very language, all dupli-
cate Augustine's earlier descriptions of the soul's fall from contemplative eternity into temporal action—descriptions which, I have
tried to show, stem from his having conflated Plotinus' own descriptions of that fall into "time" and "genesis" as they occur in *Enneads*
5.1 and 3.7.[8] In the related section of Book 8, he had stressed the
tumor, the "self-inflation," of our *superbia*, the Original Sin from
which Christ came to rescue us (8.7); a little further on (8.11) he
had expanded on the soul's impious delight in its own power
(*propria potestate*) which goes with that sin of pride and persuades
the soul "proudly to prefer the power to do what an angel can rather
than devotedly to be what an angel is" (*malunt enim superbe hoc
posse quod angelus, quam devote esse quod angelus*). Was the soul,
then, prior to this impiety, the equal of the angel? The conclusion
would, once again, be perfectly consonant with Augustine's earlier
theory.[9]

"ANIMAL" OR "CARNAL"?

But even taking the *De Trinitate* on its own terms, in abstraction
from all continuity with Augustine's early works, it is difficult to
see how these affirmations can bear any but a semi-Origenist sense.
Augustine, obviously, is addressing his readers, asking them to
check whether his analysis rings a response in their own experience.
Do they find themselves tempted to think of spiritual realities, like
soul and God, in phantasmal terms drawn from sense realities? Yes,
the reader could calmly reply, but can that not be explained as an
inevitable consequence of the soul's incarnate condition? Has Augustine himself not come to admit that Adam's own body was
"animal" rather than spiritual, that Adam ate and drank, would
even have procreated, as we do now? Where is the difficulty in admitting, then, that our souls' intimate association with the animal
body involves such a dependence on sense knowledge[10] as to make

8. See *Early Theory*, pp. 173–82.
9. See *Early Theory*, pp. 158–59 and 270.
10. We saw in *GenLitt* 7.11 (Z 8), characterizing the *propria vita*, Augustine came
very close to such an incarnate view of man. But that as yet mysterious expression
still awaits further elucidation; see below.

these epistemological shortcomings understandable? They can, if Augustine's analysis be sound, be corrected by purely epistemological considerations. What warrant do we have for tracing them to the body as "corruptible," to the "stickiness and filth contracted through ... cupidity"—and a "base cupidity" at that? What warrant is there for claiming that the root of such errors must be sin— whether pride, or cupidity, or "curiosity"? Only if the human soul was originally so situated that it directly "saw" and sinfully "turned away" from that vision of God, only if this is the meaning Augustine attributes to our *peregrinatio* (our wandering away in the Prodigal's "land of want" and pilgrimage back to our Father's "mansion") does this entire analysis make sense—the kind of sense Plotinus saw in it and, like him, Origen.

Augustine resorts to similar language at the beginning of Book 11. His task here is to explore the possibility (and his intent is to eliminate it) that man as "image" may mean the "exterior," bodily man—more precisely, the sense-using man one might expect from a soul joined to an "animal" body. St. Paul, he reminds us, discourages such an idea from the outset. It is the "interior" man that will be "renewed" in its image quality—the "spirit of our mind," not our body. But still, some "trace" (*vestigium*) of the Trinity may be found in the body also. "For it is not in vain that this is called [exterior] man, since there is in it some similarity to the interior [man]." But there is further reason for pursuing this inquiry:

In the very order of our condition, whereby we have become mortal and carnal [*quo mortales et carnales effecti sumus*], we deal more easily and familiarly with visible realities than with intelligible realities, since the former are exterior, the latter interior, and we perceive the former through bodily sense, while we understand the latter through mind [*mente*]. We, minds [*animi*] as we are, are not sensible, but intelligible, beings, since we are life [*vita*]. Nevertheless, as I said, our habitual familiarity with bodies [*in corporibus consuetudo*] has become so great, and our attention [*intentio*], constantly falling outward in a way to be marveled at, so projects itself upon these [bodily realities], that, once we turn it away from the uncertainty of bodies to rivet it upon spirit [where it enjoys a kind of] knowledge far more certain and stable, it [nonetheless] flees back to these [bodily realities], and there, whence it contracted its infirmity, seeks its repose [11.1].

"We must accommodate our procedure to this sickness," Augustine goes on to say, and seek amid the world of sense what analogies it may furnish for the spiritual realities we aim to understand. But, once again, the attentive reader is inclined to protest, Augustine has traced our greater familiarity with sensible beings to sin and the punishment of sin. For the "order of our condition" is one whereby we have become "mortal and carnal"—*become*, have been "turned into" (*effecti*, not *creati sumus*[11]) that. The implication is that, before the "ordering" power made us become so, we were other than "carnal and mortal," were, in effect, "spiritual and immortal." Augustine is using here, not the language of "creation," but the *dimissio* language[12]—familiar from the *De ordine*, the *De libero arbitrio*, and other works—of that Divine Providential action that responds to sin by "ordering" the sinner, "placing him at the level of the universe suited to his sinfulness. "Mortal," "carnal"—these are terms of opprobrium for Augustine. He might say, as he does in the *De Genesi ad litteram*, that God makes man "bodily" in the sense that He clothes the soul with an "animal" body, but only sin can make the soul "carnal." Likewise, for the early Augustine, the Augustine before the Pelagian controversy, only sin could strip the human soul of its *stola prima*, the immortal body, and plunge it into the realm of "mortality." The soul's familiarity with the sense world is, not something "natural," not a result of God's having "created" it both bodily and mortal, but quite literally a sickness (*infirmitas, aegritudo*), the inexorable resultant of its sinful attachment to the sense world, "whence it contracted its infirmity," and into which *relabens*—refalling, continuing and confirming the movement of its original "fall"—its "habitual familiarity" (*consuetudo*) impels it to seek the "repose" (*requies*) it can truly find only in the God Whom it has deserted.

Here, I submit, we may be tempted to think we are contemplating a shard excavated from a much earlier stratum of Augustine's thought, from a phase of his intellectual development the Pelagian controversy urged him to outgrow. For the only way of making sense of this fragment is to reset it into the larger picture from which it was drawn: the picture represented by the *De libero*

11. BA 16, p. 161, mistranslates *effecti* as "créés," thus destroying the sense.
12. Which he had seemed to abandon (temporarily) in *GenLitt* 10.36–38 (Z 20–23); see above.

arbitrio's fourth hypothesis. Once spiritual and clothed with immortality, the soul has fallen, and by its fall been ordered into a
penal condition of carnality and mortality; in that condition it
constantly re-enacts and extends the original movement of its fall,
by seeking its rest among the realities whose bewitching fascination
originally infected it—drew it down to become mortal, carnal, and
sickly, and induced that habitual familiarity with the objects of
sense perception that all of us experience.

BOOK 12: "FALL" AGAIN

In the early portions of Book 12, Augustine once again resorts to
the same language of "fall." At this point in his inquiry, he is asking
whether the "image" quality of the soul may be found in the mind
inasmuch as the mind possesses *scientia*, the "knowledge" that is
directed toward the guidance of "action." His conclusion is negative, as things turn out. It is mind precisely as contemplative, as
possessing "wisdom" (*sapientia*), which truly images the Trinity.
He admits that a kind of "trinity" may be detected in mind-active,
but this is only a "derived," not the genuine, "image" trinity we
should be looking for (12.4).

The relationship of mind-contemplative to mind-active brings
Augustine to discuss the symbolism of "man" and "woman," the
Adam and Eve of the original creation. His discussion here shows
striking parallels with, along with subtle differences from, that
symbolism as he had dealt with it years before in the *De Genesi
contra Manichaeos*.[13] In the *De Trinitate*, "woman" is a figure no
longer of the "sensible" element, but rather of the mind—part of
the "interior" man—mind, however, as actively involved with "realities bodily and temporal." This brings Augustine to observe that
"too great a *progressio* into these lower realities is dangerous"
(*periculosa est nimia in inferiora progressio*) (12.10). The dangerous quality of this involvement in "action" he then spells out, and
once again in the language and imagery of the soul's "fall." If
mind-active is not adequately restrained by mind-contemplative,

13. Compare Augustine's own admission in this connection in *Trin* 12.20. A good
critical edition of *GenMan* remains a crying need in Augustinian studies; only then
can we hope for a close comparative study of how Augustine interprets Genesis at
varying stages of his career. The results in terms of our understanding of his theory
of man would be invaluable.

it can happen that it "falls into exterior realities through a *progressus* beyond measure" (*immoderato progressu nimis in exteriora prolabitur*). So doing, it "grows old among its enemies," i.e., the demons, and even contemplative mind is deprived in consequence of that "vision of eternal realities" (*aeternorum illa visio ab ipso etiam capite . . . subtrahitur*). So both mind-contemplative and -active, like Adam and Eve after their sin, are "stripped naked of that truth illumination" they had previously enjoyed (12.13).

Through a love of its own active "power," therefore—the *dimissio* motif is at work again—the soul "falls" (*prolabitur*) from the *universum* it once possessed in "common" with other souls to the "private part" of reality it has chosen for its own. Its pride, the *initium peccati*, has brought it to "apostasy"; it yearned for "more than the *universum*" and now, in accord with the righteous laws of the *universitas*, it is plunged into "caring for only a part" (*curam partilem truditur*). Its "avarice" and "concupiscence" for "more" condemns it, ironically, to possession of "less." That lesser "part" it has chosen in preference to the *universum*, Augustine intimates, may be the body that the soul "possesses as its own"; "through its very own body, . . . which it possesses as its part [of the universe]" (*per corpus proprium, . . . quod partiliter possidet*), the soul now presses its "proper" concerns against the common good of the *universitas*. Having placed its delight in "bodily forms and motions," moreover, the fallen soul can become increasingly enmeshed in the network of its sensible images and phantasms, and thus plunge even more deeply into the kinds of activities inspired by pride, concupiscence, and curiosity, the very same triadic sin (as Augustine orchestrates even more fully in the following paragraph) to which he attributed the soul's "fall" in his early works and in the *Confessions*.

The fallen soul, Augustine goes on to say (12.15), should strive to return to the contemplative "perception" of those "interior" and "superior" riches it may once again enjoy in "chaste embrace" and in "common" with other souls. But its desire for "private" possession, at once proud, concupiscential, and curious, can entrap it in a tangle of errors, luring it to "empty itself" of its interior forces in a succession of activities which Augustine denominates as "fornication."[14] By seeking to become the center (*medium*) of its own universe, it has fallen from its original "mid-rank" station (*medietas*), where God alone was above, and the entire sensible universe was below, it. That fall Augustine now feels entitled to describe in two ways: from one point of view, the soul has been "propelled into the lowest of realities, as a punishment" (*poenaliter ad ima propellitur*); but also, from another, distinct but coordinated, point of view (his *dimissio* motif is at work) the soul has become "inflated" by its concupiscential desire for experimental knowledge of temporal realities, so that, overburdened by this additional weight, it is "expelled from beatitude" (*praegravatus animus quasi pondere suo a beatitudine expellitur*).[15]

LOSS OF THE stola prima

Two connected results follow: fallen souls lose their "first garment," the *stola prima* of the incorruptible body, and are deservingly clothed in the "tunics of skin" appropriate to their mortal,

14. Plotinus, in *Ennead* 3.7.11, depicts the soul's fall from its contemplative possession of the "All" in eternity into the active pursuit of part-for-part in time, as like to a "seed," all its richness within it, uncoiling into a weaker greatness, and losing its inner riches in this process. Augustine, I have tried to suggest, finds this image strikingly paralleled in Ecclus. 10:9–14, where the "proud" man—or soul—is portrayed as "spewing forth its insides" (*projecit intima sua*). (See *Trin* 10:14 for the *superbia* reference [Ecclus. 10:10], but in the predictable context.) As time goes on in Augustine's career, the text from Ecclesiasticus slowly gives way to the text of Ps. 58:10 which urges the soul to "preserve its *fortitudinem* for God"—and not, therefore, to "empty itself" of its inner riches—as the Prodigal Son did—in the "fornication" that consists of taking temporal realities as the objects of its *frui*. (Compare the application of these two texts, but in identical contexts, in *Conf* 7.22 [Ecclus 10:10] and 4.30 as well as 10.53 [Ps. 58:10]). I would wager that the study of how the one text begins slowly to take the baton from the other would be highly illuminating. On the import of Ps. 58:10 for an understanding of Augustine's view of man as active, temporal, and artistic, see my *Art and the Christian Intelligence* (Cambridge: Harvard University Press, 1978), p. 213n171.

15. For Plotinus, the question of whether the soul was "fallen" or "sent" was an important one; he opts for a solution in which both are true, and, looked at in depth, identical. This is a highly idiosyncratic view, hence, a hallmark of his personal position on the matter. Augustine takes the same position (see *Early Theory*, pp. 169–73), thereby pointing to his indebtedness to Plotinus in this regard. It is interesting to see him, at this late stage in his career, going out of his way to stress the profound identity between the soul as *propulsus* (sent: by way of punishment by God) and *expulsus* (fallen: as though by its own "weight," seeking its natural place).

penal condition (*nudati stola prima, pelliceas tunicas mortalitate meruerunt*).[16] But, along with this, there is some positive fruit from the fall, for the soul comes to learn "experimentally," as it were, the gap between the good it has abandoned and the evil it has committed (*per illud suae medietatis experimentum poena sua discit quid intersit inter bonum desertum et malum commissum*).[17]

But, having "poured forth and lost its [original] forces" (*effusis ac perditis viribus*),[18] it is, like the exhausted Prodigal Son, unable to "return" (*redire*)—for "this life," Augustine assures us, should be like a road we walk in order to return home[19]—except through the salvific work of Christ. For only Christ's grace can "liberate the unhappy soul from the body of this death" (*infelicem animam liberabit a corpore mortis hujus*) (12.16).

AUGUSTINE'S FINAL *emendatio*

This text provides a striking revelation about the work of final redaction Augustine brought to his published version of the *De Trinitate*. He complains to Aurelius, in *Letter 174*, of the need to compose the remainder of the book in a way consistent with the earlier portion that had been stolen from him and published against his will. But the question still arises: How much emendation did he bring to that earlier portion, if any? The indications from the section just examined are unsettling: the story of the soul, of its original state, its fall, and its return, is told in those perfectly cir-

16. In this way Augustine accounts for the "opacity" of soul to fellow-soul in this "mortal" body. (See *Early Theory*, pp. 161–66, and my *Art and the Christian Intelligence*, pp. 39, 58, 96–99, 100–106, and 197*n*42). This permits of dissimulation and therefore "lying" (*mendacium*). The complex of ideas and images still holds true in this passage of *Trin*, even if a trifle more subtly. On the (Prodigal's) *stola prima*, see chap. 8, note 31, above.

17. Plotinus, in *Ennead* 4.8.7, seems to have found it necessary to "justify" the fall of the soul in terms of this fruit of its "experience"; Augustine, in his early *GenMan*, responds to that same feeling of urgency—as he seems to do even here. See *Early Theory*, pp. 156–61. But this experience of evils also helps to guarantee the permanency of our ultimate beatitude.

18. Again, Ps. 58:10 is at work, and, as customary, in connection with the image of the Prodigal Son, his "fornication," and subsequent exhaustion. See note 14 above.

19. See *Trin* 12.15 (the paragraph immediately preceding): *Et magnum est hanc vitam degere, quam velut viam redeuntes carpimus.* The Prodigal image still threads its way through.

cular terms embodied in Augustine's earlior exegesis of the Prodigal parable and, notably, of the *stola prima*, the "first garment" featured in that parable. Once vested in that garment of the spiritual, incorruptible body, the soul has fallen into the realm of mortality, and is covered with the "animal skins" proper to that realm; its principal task is now, with God's help, quite literally to "return" to the Father's mansion it once deserted, in the hope of being robed in that *stola prima* once again. But this was the very circularity, and the principal image for it, that Augustine came to reject in the *De Genesi ad litteram.* Yet here it stands, in uncorrected form. Was it an inadvertence on the old Augustine's part? Or did he feel obliged to leave, unemended, even this unmistakable clue that the *De Trinitate* had originally proposed a view on the soul's origin that time had brought him to repudiate? If this was his reason, the decision must have cost him dear. We can understand his anger that it was forced upon him. Or has he further surprises in store for us?

But there is still another revelatory feature here. Augustine's portrayal of the soul's fall has left unaltered the *dimissio* view which the *De Genesi ad litteram* seemed either to reject or at least to take pains to circumvent. That same view, however, clearly lies behind Augustine's observation that the fall may be expressed in either of two ways: the soul becomes "heavy" (*praegravatus . . . pondere suo*) so that by its weight it is "expelled" from the lofty region of its blessedness; or it is "penally propelled" by the eternal law of God's ordering activity into the "lowest" of realities it had longed to possess as its very "own." This interlock of sinful desire and divine ordering was what the Augustine of the *De Genesi* came to think was excluded by Romans 9:11, but here it stands, uncorrected, with all those older implications still intact. Now a surprising new possibility suggests itself: Was Augustine's repudiation of this older view only a temporary one? Has he, in the *De Trinitate*, actually reverted to the view that we are "fallen souls"?

FINAL STRATUM OF THE *De Trinitate*

Mlle La Bonnardière has ably argued that the "substantial portion" of the *De Trinitate*'s Book 12, which Augustine tells us was composed before the theft of his earlier version, runs up to and includes chapter 14;[20] if confirmation were needed for the results of her painstaking labors, the "dated" character of the views we have been examining might be thought to furnish it. From chapter 15 on, accordingly, at the point after Augustine winds up his discussion of "knowledge and wisdom" (*scientia et sapientia*), we must be alert to possible shifts in the doctrinal winds. Indeed, the fact that in the sections presumably dating from before the famous theft he conferred the title "knowledge" on our acquaintanceship with the changing world of temporal realities may argue that he had already given it a higher status than that of mere "opinion"; for that was the term he regularly used for such sense-dependent knowledge in his earlier works.[21] I do not mean to press that point here, beyond remarking on the methodological dangers involved in reading the *scientia–sapientia* distinction, and its implications, rearward into Augustine's earlier thought.[22] The question obviously calls for a full-scale study on its own merits.

REJECTION OF PLATO'S THEORY IN THE Meno

But in rounding off Book 12, Augustine might seem to be warning his readers away from thinking of the soul as pre-existent. Plato, he reminds us, writes of a thought experiment Socrates conducted with a slave boy, in order to show that all learning is remembering. The reference is obviously to Plato's *Meno*, where the suggestion is evolved that the slave boy's geometrical insights might stem from the fact that he, like the rest of us, might be remembering what he once learned in some previous life "here," in the bodily, temporal world. In this way, as Augustine tells it, Plato tried to persuade us that "human souls lived here [*hic*], and before they bore these bodies [*ista corpora*]"—the bodies of our present experience. Augustine has relatively easy game in refuting both this and the similar theory attributed to Pythagoras. His mode of refutation is significant. The genuine experience of "reminiscence," he claims, has to do with remembering intelligible realities only, not with remem-

<hr>

20. See *Chronologie*, pp. 167–69. The newer sections would then begin at paragraph 24.
21. See *Early Theory*, pp. 241–42.
22. As Madec strives to do in his "*Christus, scientia et sapientia nostra*," RA, 10 (1979), 77–85; his position on the same issue in the later "Clarification" appears much less vigorous in its claims. See my *Platonism*, pp. 4–8, for more detailed treatment.

bering the things of sense experience. But if this theory of the "souls' revolutions" were true, it would imply that we were "placed here before, in other bodies" than the ones we now inhabit, and would remember the sense realities we experienced in our former bodily lives; but this, Augustine is convinced, is manifestly not the case. But his animus is plainly directed against this "cyclic" view of *repeated* falls and returns.

He makes no mention of the altered theory of reminiscence put forward in the *Phaedo* and *Phaedrus*, one which limits reminiscence precisely to those "intelligible objects" Plato calls his "Forms"; one wonders whether Augustine was even aware of that theory as Plato's. It is, in any event, an overstatement to say that he is here refuting the theory of "Platonic reminiscence" *tout court*.[23] He never, even in his earliest works, showed any sympathy for this view of the repetitive cycle of souls, even when he must have found it in Plotinus; indeed, he tends to look on it with something verging on horror.[24] But in Books 1 through 12 of the *De Trinitate*, he seems clearly to be defending the same theory as he found it expressed in Plotinus, the theory that runs through his earlier works and the *Confessions*: we did exist once, as souls, in a heaven not unlike that world of Forms, clothed with a *stola prima* of a transparent, incorruptible body; we have sinned and fallen from that sublime state into "this" life and "these" mortal bodies; our life is a project of "return." But once returned, we shall not fall again; the experimental knowledge gained from our fall will, in part at least, see to that.

And one key piece of this theory is the "memory" we retain of the intelligible realities that were once the object of our direct vision, but are no longer; and still, that "memory" is what empowers us, even in the relative "forgetfulness" of our fallen state, to "judge."

FALL, MEMORY, AND FORGETFULNESS

Augustine returns to that theme of memory in Book 14. Book 13 and the opening sections of Book 14 have brought him to locate the

23. On the confusion such scholars as Bardy and O'Daly have introduced with this vague term, see my "Pre-Existence."

24. See his first reactions to this cyclic theory as Orosius presented it to him, above, chap. 3; the horror seems to stem precisely from the non-eternity of our eventual beatitude all such theories imply.

genuine Trinitarian "image" quality in the soul's memory, understanding, and love of itself. At this point, he poses an objection to his own position. It might be urged that "memory" is an inappropriate term for the mind's self-present awareness of itself; in good Latin, one might contend, "memory is concerned with the past and not with the present." Augustine had once before entertained an analogue of this difficulty, but with respect to the soul's memory of higher, intelligible realities. Those, too, the objection ran, are "eternally present," and therefore not correctly termed the object of "memory." His answer then was in terms of our once-enjoyed "vision" of those realities; our fall has put that vision into our past, even though the intelligible world remains eternally "present." It is, then, the past-ness of our lost "vision" which makes "memory" an appropriate term for our "recall" of that intelligible world.[25] Obviously, though, that answer will not serve him here, since the soul's "self-awareness" is as "present" as its object, the soul itself. His choice of a reply to the objection in the *De Trinitate* is not without a certain aura of the ironic; one wonders if it might have been meant to convey an arch hint as to where Augustine originally drew the notion. For he quotes from Vergil (a man who could be counted on to know the correct meaning of Latin words, like "memory"), and his choice falls on a line portraying Ulysses (that classic metaphor for the "wandering soul," as Augustine well knew from Plotinus' *Enneads*[26]) as "not forgetting," hence as "remembering," himself (14.14). The conclusion is that memory can properly be said to pertain to present realities as well as past and, more to the point, that the soul can be said to "remember" itself. All necessary reference to the "past" had been dispensed with, therefore.

But, Augustine continues, what is crucial is that the mind, as *imago Dei*, must be said not only to remember itself, but to remember, understand, and love the God in Whose image it is made. It cannot be that the soul has forgotten God "completely" (14.16). For if that were the case, Augustine argues, no "reminder" (cf. *commoneat*) could ever succeed in awakening that lost memory. But, one might object, Psalm 9:18 seems to suggest such a total forget-

25. See my "Pre-existence in Augustine's Seventh Letter," REA, 15 (1969), 67–73, esp. 70–71.
26. Especially, of course, from *Ennead* 1.6.8, which we know burned its way into Augustine's consciousness. See *Early Theory*, pp. 9, 19, 34, 39, 73, 85, 173, 206, 207, 225.

fulness, for it reads: "Let sinners be converted to the lower world
[*convertantur in infernum*[27], all the nations that forget God
[*obliviscuntur*]." Augustine counters this objection with Psalm
21:28 to the effect that: "All the ends of the earth shall be reminded
[*commemorabuntur*] and shall be converted [*convertentur*] to
God." Even sinners do not, accordingly, *totally* forget God, else
they could never effectively be reminded of Him. By "forgetting,"
Augustine explains, and precisely in the measure of their forgetfulness, "they have been converted to death, that is, to the lower
world" (*infernum*) of the bodily and temporal realities in which
they intended to find their happiness (14.17).

The human mind, therefore, was so created (*sic . . . condita est
mens humana*) as never to be entirely forgetful of itself (14.18). But
the same must be said of the mind's memory of God. True, the soul
has "deserted" (*deserendo*) the God above it, "for Whom alone it
could preserve its force," as Psalm 58:10 expresses it. It has become,
in consequence, sickly weak and darkened over (*infirma et tene-
brosa*); it has "fallen" (*laberetur*) into the realm of realities inferior
to itself (14.18), into a life where it is "vainly disquieted" (*vano
conturbatur*) (14.19). And yet, though weak and wandering (*infirma
et errans*) and "evilly loving and pursuing realities inferior to
itself" (*quae sunt infra ipsam*), it never completely ceases to love
itself. But that implies that it must retain some residue of self-
knowledge and self-memory, even if it has lost that "understanding" of itself, i.e., that *cogitatio sui* whereby it would recognize
itself as "image" of God and capable of cleaving to Him for its
beatitude.[28] For this was its original station in reality, not "spatially," but in the order of natural dignity, to have nothing save God
as its superior and as object of its felicity. *Sic enim ordinata est.*
Augustine is speaking of the soul's authentic reality as "image,"

27. Translators are frequently tempted to render *infernum* by "hell," "enfer," and
the like. But the context shows, here as elsewhere, that souls may "return" from this
infernum, and that Augustine is plainly talking about souls like our own! He merely
means the "lower" of the "two worlds" of Neoplatonism, i.e., the world we "inhabit"
after our "fall."

28. The text is tricky here: I have taken the semi-colon before *nec se intelligeret*
perhaps too seriously, thereby equating the *intellectus* in question as at the level of
cogitatio rather than mere *notitia*, as most translators take it. But the point has no
importance for my argument here. I mean only to urge another look at the text by
a better Latinist than I claim to be.

the station God in His creative intention meant it to occupy—and the station it has, obviously, deserted in its movement of "fall." Hence, he can move into the future tense: when the soul shall cleave to God, it will both share His immutability and be so filled with His riches as never again to find delight in sinning (*numquam peccare delectet*) (14.20). Again, Augustine's antipathy to Origen's "cycle of souls" theory is evident; once "arrived," he insists, the soul will never fall again.

CAN THE "MEMORY" BE RECALLED?

But the question arises: Does the soul hope to regain a felicity which it still somehow "remembers"? We come, at this juncture, to what seems to me a significant adjustment of the theory of memory unfolded in his *Confessions*. To outline that adjustment, though, we must divide the above question into two: and first, is it clear that Augustine is saying that the soul *once enjoyed* the kind of comtemplative felicity it now hopes for? Everything we have seen thus far in Book 14 would argue for an affirmative answer to that question; but if any doubts remained, Augustine is prepared to clear them up. He argues as follows: the soul is *misera*, unhappy, in its present state; he seems confident we will all agree on that. Now, he continues, God being both good and all-powerful, the soul's present misery must be accounted for; and, he concludes, it must be the result (not of the original creative design of God, but) of the soul's own sin and God's just punishment of the soul in view of that sin (*peccatum suum et justitia Domini sui*).[29] The hidden premiss would seem to be the familiar one: a "good" God would not create souls for a state of misery; hence, that state must be a "penal" one. But have we truly come back to that position? Augustine's expression *peccatum suum* seems to imply exactly that, and even in this "second" stratum of his *De Trinitate*!

The soul in its present situation, he continues, "cannot endow itself with the justice it has lost; that justice it received [as God's gift] when it was created as human, and lost by sinning." The soul itself sees clearly that it could not have fallen except through some voluntary deficiency of its own (*nonnisi suo voluntario defectu*

29. Observe the *peccatum suum* which *Ep 143* admitted would be incriminatory.

cadere potuisse), just as now it cannot rise from its sinful condition except through God's grace.

There is a clear anti-Pelagian cast to all this; its likely significance we shall have to discuss shortly. But for our purposes at the moment, Augustine is claiming that the soul, when first created as "human" (*cum homo conderetur*), received "justice"[30] from God; but justice, even when conferred by God as gift, "merits" in its turn the reception of "beatitude" (*Accipit ergo justitiam, propter quam beatitudinem accipere mereatur*) (14.21). The soul "received" beatitude, therefore, when it was created as "human" soul; it sinned, and was justly punished for that sin; its present misery is the merited result of that sin, which can have no other explanation than as the result of God's just punishment for its having sinned.

The first of our two questions, therefore, has its answer: the soul *did*, once, enjoy felicity; *it* sinned, and lost the justice that once entitled *it* to that felicity! We must keep those phrases in mind. But now the second part of the question arises: Does the soul retain any "memory" of the beatitude it once enjoyed? The memory theory of the *Confessions* would seem to imply that it does;[31] the *De Trinitate* now resolutely states the opposite. And the reasoning Augustine presents in this connection is both interesting and suggestive. *Non sane reminiscitur beatitudinis suae: fuit illa quippe et non est.* That beatitude, Augustine is saying, "was," but "is no longer," and he appears to be giving this as the reason why "the soul has thoroughly [*penitus*] forgotten it; [that beatitude] accordingly cannot be recalled to mind" (*ideoque nec commemorari potest*). Only faith can assure us that we once were happy; the soul "believes" (*credit*) that its beatitude once held true, and believes it on the word of Scripture and its historical tradition (*historica traditione*). For Scripture does recount "the felicity of paradise, and that first [i.e., primordial] good and evil," man's original happiness and sin. Genesis' account of Adam and Eve, therefore, is still, in Augustine's eyes, a Scriptural account of "our" souls' primordial felicity and fall into misery.[32]

30. This, as we saw, was the revised interpretation of the Prodigal's *stola prima* which Rom. 9:11 (temporarily?) compelled Augustine to elaborate in *GenLitt* 6.31 (Z 20); see above, chap. 8. But it would seem that his use of the term in its older sense at 12.16 prevented his mention of the *stola prima* here.

31. See *Odyssey*, pp. 120–34.

32. Here it begins to become clear that Augustine's rejection of his earlier circular anthropology was only a temporary affair, after all.

But while he insists that the soul cannot remember its original state of beatitude, he is claiming that the soul nonetheless retains a memory of God: *Domini autem Dei sui reminiscitur.* And the reasoning, again, is significant: *Ille quippe semper est, nec fuit et non est, nec est et non fuit. . . . Et ubique totus est; propter quod ista [anima] in illo vivit, et movetur, et est* [cf. Acts 17:28], *et ideo reminisci ejus potest.* God always "is"; it cannot be said of Him, unlike our beatitude, that He "was once and is no longer"; nor can it be said that He "is now, but [once] was not." To be "remembered" by the soul, Augustine appears to be arguing, God must be not simply existing in the present (as though He were some present temporal reality), but, like the entire intelligible world, eternally present in His existence. But this seems to be an incomplete statement of the conditions for the soul's memory of God. He must, in addition to the above, be integrally omnipresent. "And He is totally everywhere," Augustine adds, "for which reason [*propter quod*] [the soul] lives, moves, and in Him has its being: and this is why [*et ideo*] the soul can remember Him."

What, one is tempted to ask, has God's integral omnipresence got to do with the soul's capacity to "remember" Him? Augustine explains: "The soul remembers, so as to be converted to its Lord, as though to that Light by which it is somehow touched, even when it has turned away from It" (*Sed commemoratur, ut convertatur ad Dominum, tanquam ad eam lucem qua etiam cum ab illo averteretur quodam modo tangebatur*). Were the soul simply to have "fallen" from its contemplative union with God into this lower world, and were that the whole story, it could be thought to follow that it had lost all contact with the higher world and with the God from Whom it fell away. Did the soul remember its own once-enjoyed beatitude, as the *Confessions* seem to suggest, some line of residual contact would be assured by that route, but that line of contact the Augustine of Book 14 has cleanly severed. How, then, account for this residual memory of God, when the soul's memory of its past "vision" of God has been thoroughly (*penitus*) forgotten? These seem to be the lines of the new problem Augustine has set himself by altering the theory he presented in the *Confessions*, and, indeed, throughout the early books of the *De Trinitate* itself.

Now, the notion of God's integral omnipresence is surely central to the *Confessions*, as to his other early works; but, I submit, it is never called upon to render the exact service Augustine requires of it in the *De Trinitate*: to assure this line of contact with God as "remembered." Now he makes that "omnipresence" of God interlock with the soul's residual power to make value "judgments." For, he points out once again, even unjust souls, souls that have chosen to "turn away," to absent themselves from God, as it were, still make correct judgments on the "justice" of others' and of their own lives. Even "the soul that does not do justice and nonetheless sees how [justice] should be done, this is the soul that has turned away from the [Divine] Light, and is, nonetheless, touched by it" (*ab illa luce avertitur, a qua tamen tangitur*) (14.21). That Light of Truth, therefore, must be not only a Light of supernal, otherworldly Truth, but a Light of Truth present everywhere (*ubique praesentis veritatis*), so that the soul is "reached" by it (*attingitur*) even in the lower world to which sin, and the punishment for sin, have thrust it down.[33]

SUMMARY OF BOOK 14

To summarize before going further: Does the Augustine of Book 14 of the *De Trinitate* still consider human beings, i.e., the human beings of our experience, as "fallen souls"? One step toward answering that question would consist in underlining the language and imagery of "fall" which we have seen him using throughout the book, a language and imagery which matches up with the language and imagery of the earlier books, of the *Confessions*, and of the earlier works in which he came to his first formulations of this theory. Thus, for example, he evokes the image of Ulysses, the

33. This development may partially explain the disappearance of a theme which had considerable importance in Augustine's earlier "fall" theory: that not all souls were equally "fallen," some being more "deeply" fallen than others. It follows from this view that "less fallen" souls retain a greater sensitivity to divine "admonitions" to "return." Translated into the terms Rom. 9:11 introduced into this debate, this greater sensitivity could be viewed as an advantage (as it was in Origen's theory), influencing *prospectively*, or even in part determining, God's "election" of less-fallen souls; this may well turn out, on closer examination, to be a feature of his earlier theory (and of Origen's, accordingly) Augustine definitively rejected. See *Early Theory*, pp. 152–55, and *Platonism*, pp. 13–20.

"wanderer," when that evocation seems almost gratuitous; when, in fact, he would have been better advised to avoid it *if* he were rejecting the "fall" theory he had previously held. He connects the dynamic of *oblivio* and *memoria* with the soul's *aversio* and *conversio*, from and to God, and still, in this memory connection, uses terms like *commonere* and *admonere* to mean "reminders"; the *infernum* the soul finds itself "converted" to in consequence of its "aversion" from God is, when read carefully, the realm of realities "inferior" to the soul, realities bodily and temporal; the soul's presence in this lower world is the consequence of a "fall," and for an Augustine, who put such a value on the exact use of words, terms like *cadere, labi,* must have been used only after some reflection; that "fall," in turn, implied a "voluntary defect" on the soul's part *(suum),* an "evil" which is nothing less than a "sin" *(voluntarius defectus; malum; peccatum);* that sin brought in its train the working of God's "justice" *(justitia);* and the consequence is man's loss of the beatitude he once enjoyed and has now utterly "forgotten," hence man's present state of "misery," a misery one of whose hallmarks is the "vain disquiet" the earlier Augustine regularly connected with the soul's fall into the realm of time, action, and "curiosity."

So much, then, for the language and imagery of the "fallen soul" theory. What of the substance of Augustine's view in Book 14? Here I must ask the reader to retrace my "reading" of Augustine's argumentation. He has eliminated all necessary reference to the "past," and thereby introduced a major adjustment to the theory of "memory" proposed in the *Confessions.* That adjustment compels him to put his familiar stress on integral omnipresence to a new task, i.e., that of accounting for the soul's continuing ability to be "reminded" of the God it has "deserted" but Whose Light still reaches down to touch it, and empower it to make "judgments" of value. But the substance of his view of the human condition would seem essentially unaltered for all that. The "image" of God is to be found in the soul as mind, and mind precisely as contemplative mind. This, and precisely this, is what it means to say that "man" is made "in the image" of God—which is to say, this is what "man" is when viewed against the background of the divine creative idea of man, man as he was "created human" *(cum homo conderetur*), man as God intended him to be and to remain, man before he sinned, and "fell," and became the kind of "man" we now, erroneously, are tempted to think we "are."

It is difficult to see in all this anything other than a theory of man as "fallen soul." Granted: Augustine has introduced several modifications to his earlier presentation of it, but the theory remains substantially faithful to that contained in his earlier works. And yet, setting the *De Trinitate* against the background of Augustine's entire later development, one would scarcely have expected him to cling to this view; there is even some surprise in his having abstained from emending those earlier sections of his work where it plainly persists. True, his anger at the theft of his incomplete work *could* indicate his reluctance to compose the remainder of the work in substantial consistency with what went before, but was he compelled, against his better judgment, to stretch consistency quite this far? Perhaps a more careful re-reading of these closing portions of his work will yield a more satisfying clarification of the matter.

A CLOSER LOOK AT TWO CRUCIAL PASSAGES

The sections that clamor loudest for explanation are chapters 15 and 16 of Book 14. They occur after Augustine has expanded on his meditations about *scientia* and *sapientia*, knowledge and wisdom, into Book 13's full-scale review of the economy of fall and redemption. Here, at a number of points, he seems clearly to be treating of Adam the *man*, body and soul, and the man from whom we, body and soul, are historically sprung. There is an incarnate and historical cast to this entire exposition that might be thought to contrast, even conflict, with the notion of man as image-soul which prevails throughout the earlier books.[34] It was this historical Adam, Augustine seems to be reminding us, who sinned, and we have inherited the punishment of his sin. But there must be more to it than that. For how could it be affirmed with any truth that

---

34. There is, as we shall see, a great deal of reality to the incarnate and historical cast of *Trin* 13; see, for example, the treatment of death (16, 20) and of "happiness" (25) as affecting precisely "man" rather than "soul." Compare that sentence of "mortality" whereby (as Augustine reminds us later, in 14.24), we all die "according to Adam."

"we sinned" in the sinning of an Adam who, precisely as historical individual, must be "other" than ourselves?

This is what Augustine expressly says in chapters 15 and 16 of Book 14. He is speaking now of the "mind, weak and wandering" (*mens . . . infirma et errans*) (14.20). The most obvious implication is that he is addressing us, his readers. It is *our* mind-soul that is being talked about. Our soul is "unhappy" (*misera*), which shows it must be changeable, for otherwise it could never change from being miserable to being happy, or from being happy to being miserable. "But what could have made it miserable, under a God both all-powerful and good, save its own sin [*peccatum suum*] and the justice of its Lord?" It can "merit" happiness—again—but only if God graciously confer upon it the lost "justice" it does not now possess (*quam perditam non habet*). That justice it "received" when it was created human, and lost surely by sinning (*Hanc enim, cum homo conderetur, accepit; et peccando utique perdidit*). For the soul can be sure, *pace* Pelagius and his colleagues, that it "cannot rise up except by an affect [*affectu*] freely[35] conferred by Him, as it could not have fallen except by its own voluntary defect [*nonnisi suo voluntario defectu cadere potuisse*]. It does not remember the bliss it once enjoyed, but it did indeed possess it" (*fuit illa quippe, et non est*). It is faith that assures the soul of this—*credit*—faith in the Scriptural story of that "bliss of paradise, and that first good which man [received] and first evil which man [committed]" (*de felicitate paradisi, atque illud primum et bonum hominis et malum . . .*) (14.21).

AUGUSTINE'S CIRCULAR ANTHROPOLOGY

Now Augustine is at pains to remind us that this story is an "historical tradition" (*historica traditio*). He is not interpreting the fall of Adam in an allegorical sense, as typical of the "fall" each one of our individual souls experienced. That was his manner in the *De Genesi contra Manichaeos*, as well as in the thirteenth book of the *Confessions*; but the labor of the *De Genesi ad litteram* has brought

35. That *affectus* is the "love for God poured forth" to us through the Holy Spirit, a love *for* God that remains, on close examination, a "desire" for God as object of our contemplative beatitude.

him to see that the "historical" character of Genesis, and the equally historical reality of Adam, Eve, and the original paradise, command respect first and foremost. And yet, the repeated use of the possessive *suum* clearly indicates his conviction that the bliss of that historical person, Adam, and his sin can truly be said to have been "ours" as well. The term he uses for the soul's "rising up" from its fall—*surgere*—reminds one forcibly of the same term's occurrence in the Prodigal parable. But he carefully abstains from any suggestion that the *stola prima*, the "first garment" of the incorruptible body, was something lost in that "fall"; that "first garment" has become the original "justice" God conferred on Adam—and on our souls as well. And yet the circularity once expressed by the *stola prima* would appear to have yielded, but only to another circularity;[36] the return is now to a "justice" and a "bliss" originally possessed not only by our historical first parents, but by us as well.

A similar circularity runs through the expressions in chapter 16. Having remembered the God they can still remember, souls are "converted to the Lord from that deformity" whereby, through their temporal cupidities, they were "conformed to this world." This "reformation" and "renewal" pertains to the mind-soul, to that part of "man" whereby he was created in God's "image," but its circular character is still in evidence: "By sinning, [that mind-soul] lost justice and sanctity; . . . it receives them [back] when it is reformed and renewed" (*peccando . . . amisit; . . . recipit, cum reformatur et renovatur*) (14.16.22). Augustine's long quotation from Cicero's *Hortensius* at the end of Book 14 may indicate how peaceful he is with this circularity; for Cicero speaks plainly of the soul's "return" (*reditus*) to heaven, and Augustine echoes him by alluding to its *regressus ad Deum*. The Augustine of the *Retractations* will be far warier about both those terms; that only makes the puzzle of the *De Trinitate* more baffling still.

REVISIONS TO HIS EARLIER THEORY

Still circular, the circularity of the mind-soul's story is different from the one which characterized Augustine's earlier theory. Per-

36. But a circularity that excludes, and fiercely, the "cyclic" *repetitions* characteristic of Origen's theory (13.12); Augustine makes explicit reference here to his treatment of that same cyclic theory in *Civ* 12, where the lesson learned from Orosius is plain to read.

haps a study of those differences will bring us closer to an understanding of this later theory. First, in Book 14, Augustine seems intentionally to have replaced the *stola prima* of the spiritual, incorruptible body, just mentioned in 12.16, with a "first garment" that is now "justice" and "sanctity." Secondly, the soul has no "memory" of the bliss it enjoyed before its sinful fall, though Scripture assures us it did enjoy such bliss. Everyone, Augustine insists, knows somehow what we mean by the term "happiness" (*beata vita*). That common knowledge led him, in the *Confessions*, to conclude that we all somehow "remember" the happiness we once enjoyed in common. That argumentation has been studiously ignored or silently discarded here (see 13.6–9). Indeed, the claim Augustine once made, that memory in its proper sense implies a necessary relation to *some* past or other, has been firmly contradicted here. The crucial "memory" he now feels entitled, and perhaps obliged, to stress, is the soul's residual memory of *itself*. But that memory of itself he goes on to link with the soul's memory of God. This he tells us is implied in the very logic of the mind-soul's reality as "image" of the Trinity. But if we are to rise from knowledge of the soul as "image" to some understanding of the Trinity itself, it must be that, however deeply plunged into sinfulness, the soul never totally loses its character as image. The *De Genesi* had, unguardedly perhaps, suggested the opposite,[37] so Augustine twice proclaims the reverse of that suggestion.[38] The *Confessions* had traced our memory of God to the vision we enjoyed of Him, again in the past, when in that other, loftier realm, the Heaven of Heaven;[39] the *De Genesi ad litteram* resulted in a different interpretation of that Heaven of Heaven,[40] and now the *De Trinitate* takes the further step of grounding our memory of God in His omnipresence to us, even in our sinful state, here "below."

What seems to be implied in all these modifications of his earlier theory is this: Augustine has drastically reduced the "distance," as it were, between our prior unfallen state and our present fallen condition. Adam possessed an animal, not a spiritual, body; there

37. In *GenLitt* 6:38 (Z 20), where it may be that Augustine meant to deny *in directo* his older *stola prima* interpretation, a denial that led him (semi-carelessly) into the denial, *in obliquo*, of the persistence of the "image." Compare *GenLitt* 3.32 (Z 20). But the reversal here of *GenLitt*'s denial loses little of its interest, for all that.
38. *Trin* 14.6 and 11; cf. *Retr* 2.24.2.
39. See above, chap. 8, note 8.
40. See again, BA 48, pp. 586–88.

might even have been controllable movements of concupiscence in paradise;[41] he ate and presumably drank, and was even made to procreate physically. The semi-angelic quality of unfallen "man" as Augustine originally envisaged him has been brought much closer to the familiar human scale. And the semi-angelic Plotinian linkage even fallen man enjoyed with the over-world he once inhabited has been seriously attenuated. We do not remember our former happiness in any way whatever, and our memory of God is of a God, not "there," but omnipresentially "here." The "fallen" world is not nearly so dark a place at it once was. The soul remains the "image" God intended it to be, remembers itself as image even now, and, "touched" by that divine Light omnipresent to the lower world, can accept the grace that fires it with charity's "affect" and empowers it to "rise up" again.

THE SOUL AS "SPIRITUAL"

Each of these modifications Augustine was brought to introduce in response to his growing acquaintance with Scripture and under the pressure of a Pelagianism that rinsed out of his thinking an entire array of features his earlier dependence on Plotinus had encouraged. But there is a limit to the concessions he feels obliged to make. That limit, it would seem, he saw in Tertullian's "materialistic" view of the soul. And so, despite his animal body, Adam's creation as the "image" of the Trinity must refer not only primarily, but properly, to his soul: soul as *capax Dei*, ineradicably capable of contemplative union with God.

That view of the human soul prompts Augustine to present, over and over again, not one but two definitions of "man": he is body and soul, embodied soul; but in the deeper reaches of Augustine's thought and affect, man remains much more a soul "using" a body, a contemplative soul with so slack a relationship to the body, its senses, imagination, feelings, and involvement in the temporal world of action, that Augustine can still employ a language of "fall" to warn us against "immoderate" immersion in any of those incarnate activities.[42]

---

41. *Trin* 12.23.
42. *Trin* 14.18; compare Gilson, *Introduction*, pp. 44–45, and *Christian Philosophy*, pp. 35–36.

That continuing stress on man as soul-contemplative, and the associated slackness of the soul–body relationship, are key elements in accounting for the obstinate circularity that marks even his later theory of man. Bodily, temporally, and historically, we are individuals distinct from our historical father, Adam, each of us living our own "proper" life; but as souls, our identity mysteriously transcends those obvious limitations. The obscure mystery surrounding the origin of our souls permits Augustine to read such texts as Romans 5:12 the way he did, at least for a time: that "in" Adam all of us sinned, fell from "justice" and its attendant "bliss"; we must, at least to that extent, literally "return."[43] When speculating on what might account for the soul's "memory" of God, Augustine initially toys with the possibility that such a memory might stem from the soul's having "known [God] in Adam," or "somewhere, elsewhere, before life in this body," or from "when it was first made for insertion into this body" (*quod eum [scil., Deum] noverat in Adam, aut alibi alicubi ante hujus corporis vitam, aut cum primum facta est ut insereretur huic corpori*) (14.21). These ways of accounting for the soul's memory of God Augustine rejects, but precisely for the reason that the soul "remembers nothing whatsoever of any of these; whichever of these may have been the case, it is obliterated by forgetfulness" (*nihil enim eorum reminiscitur; quidquid horum est, oblivione deletum est*).

But observe the phrase "whichever of these" three possibilities "may have been the case." Augustine abstains from *eliminating* any of these three possibilities, just as he abstains from stating any *preference* for one over the others. Again, as he had once hoped to do in treating the four hypotheses on the soul's origin in the *De libero arbitrio*,[44] he seems to be standing back from making a choice, whether negative or positive.

He has, however, given us an idea of what he would now consider as three (not four) ways of envisaging the soul's lost, and forgotten, state of beatitude. The terms are manifestly drawn from the controversy on the soul's origin. The phrase *in Adam*, one conjectures,

43. Lyonnet, "Péché," sees this text as influencing Augustine *only* later in his development on Original Sin. It may have been that Augustine was beginning to see a non-traducianist way of interpreting that "in Adam" which encouraged him to make freer use of this text.

44. But again, this abstention may not be used to argue against Augustine's having had a personal preference in the matter.

Augustine may see as most properly verified in tiaducianist theory, but he may have some surprises for us on that score. A soul *facta ut insereretur,* made in order to be inserted into the body, is being viewed from the creationist standpoint. But again, Augustine has reformulated that theory: the soul may have been made "somewhere, elsewhere, before life in this body," made "in order to be inserted"—in a second moment—into the body. The two hypotheses, that the soul was "created" or was "sent," are in danger of coalescing into one! And yet, that obdurate expression stands out: "we" sinned. Whichever of these hypotheses one chooses, it must be so understood as to allow for that fact. Has Augustine, one asks, reverted to some variant of Origen's, or Plotinus', "fall of the soul"?

No, it might be suggested, the circularity we have observed in Book 14 of the *De Trinitate* would seem to imply that Augustine has chosen some form of traducianism.[45] For in that hypothesis, too, one can speak of "our" sin as identical with Adam's. The traducianism need not be Tertullian's; it could be of a spiritual sort, envisaging our souls as somehow contained—*seminaliter?*—in Adam's soul, and therefore sinning *in* his very act of sinning. The suggestion is a tempting one, but not so irresistible as it seems at first. For Augustine is interpreting Romans 5:12 as implying that we did indeed sin "in" Adam, while at the same time shying away from the inference that the Pauline "in" imposes a traducianist explanation of that inclusion, and no other. We have seen him twice driven, in his *De Genesi,* to the reluctant admission that traducianism seemed to have the advantage over creationism, and nevertheless turn on the traducianists to lecture them at length on the dangers of their materialism. And writing to Optatus, he explicitly outlines the difficulties he sees in the way of any "spiritual" form of traducianism, then goes on to counsel him away from any flirtations with that theory.[46]

A CONSPICUOUS ABSENCE; ROMANS 9:11 AND *propria vita*

The *De Trinitate,* curiously enough, sheds very little direct light on the question of the origin of our souls, beyond this clear affirma-

45. As Lyonnet, "Romains V, 12," mistakenly concludes.
46. In *Ep 190* 14–15, Augustine could scarcely have been plainer about the difficulties he perceived in all forms, including the "spiritual" form of traducianism. This leads me to the hypothesis mentioned in note 43, above; that hypothesis, we shall see further on, seems to be confirmed by the evidence of his later works.

tion that the sin of Adam must be considered our sin as well. Another curious omission: there is not a single allusion that I have been able to find to Romans 9:11. This may partially account for another omission: Augustine is never compelled to bring into play his notion of our "proper life," a notion, we have seen, that seems to function as restrictive qualifier on Paul's exclusion of prenatal merits.

Proprium AND *commune*?

The only application of the *proprium* notion that may turn out to be enlightening occurs in Book 12, where Augustine attributes our fall to the proud desire of abandoning the "universe" we blissfully possessed "in common," in order to possess some part of that universe as our "very own," our *proprium* (12.15–16). Augustine's fondness for the *proprium–commune* antithesis is familiar enough; but does it truly illumine what he may be setting over against our *propria vita*, our "proper life"? The suggestion may sound strained, but let us pursue it nonetheless. Is he suggesting, or toying at least with the possibility, that we may all have enjoyed a "common" life—and committed a "common" sin—before entering upon this life that each of us recognizes as his or her "very own"? Could this be what he has at the back of his mind when he writes of our all having sinned "in Adam"? And if so, how does he reconcile that notion with Romans 9:11?

Perhaps the *De civitate Dei* will cast some light on those puzzling questions and on Augustine's final view of the human condition.

10

THE CONDITION
AND DESTINY OF
HUMANITY IN THE
De civitate Dei

THE *De civitate Dei* stands in an interesting, but complex relationship to the two works we have just examined. It would be gratifying to be able to affirm from the outset that, published well after both of them, it might safely be taken as Augustine's finished statement on the story of humanity. But the facts may call for a more nuanced position. We saw, for example, that the *De Genesi ad litteram* may have to be considered as in some respects earlier, in others later, than the *De Trinitate*; the latter's interpretation of the *stola prima* as an immortal body, along with its attendant portrayals of the soul as "fallen," may antedate the *De Genesi*'s rejection of both; and yet, in composing Book 14 of the *De Trinitate*, Augustine took the opportunity to correct the *De Genesi*'s suggestion that the "image of God" in the soul could be totally lost.

A similar priority–posteriority mix seems to hold for the *De civitate* as it stands to the *De Genesi* and *De Trinitate*.[1] Its earlier books seem to have seen publication in piecemeal fashion, from the year 412 or thereabouts on, so that the Augustine of either 426 or 429 (however one dates the final publication of the work) may not have been able to "emend" his earlier statements to bring them into line with the latest positions toward which his thought was evolving. So, for example, chapter 26 of Book 5 speaks as though the

1. See Bardy in BA 12, pp. 587–88, and, with more detail, BA 33, pp. 23–24. The latter, the first volume of *Civ*, was published in 1959, some nine years after BA 12; hence, the occasional differences between them.

first three books had already been published, and presumably during Marcellinus' lifetime, by 413. *Letter 169*, to Evodius, informs us that by 415, Books 4 and 5 have been completed; Orosius, in 417,[2] speaks of Books 1 to 10 as fully composed. *Letter 184A*,[3] from 417/418, intimates that the first ten books may have already seen publication,[4] states that Books 11 to 13 have been written and that Book 14 is underway—*in manibus*—and promises that his "literary agent," Firmus, will be sending off copies of the completed books of the *De civitate* to his correspondents shortly.[5] Parallels found in other works of the period appear to confirm that sections, at least, of Book 14 had been written by 420, and sections, if not all, of Books 15 and 16 by 419. The *Retractations*[6] speak, in 427, of the whole work as "terminated" by then, but a recently uncovered letter to his agent, Firmus, detailing how the volumes should be bound in order to respect the structure of the argument, could date from as late as 429,[7] and a chronological indication found in Book 18 argues for the same date.[8] These minor discrepancies may well be ex-

2. In the Preface to his *Adversus Paganos*, written in 417. Note Bardy's obvious misprint, 405 for 415, relative to *Ep 169*.

3. See paragraph 5, not 3 as Bardy writes in BA 12, p. 587; I have also kept closer than Bardy does to the exact wording of Augustine's text. Note the mention of Firmus, now his "literary agent," ibid., 7.

4. Again, Bardy does not advert to this distinction between "written" and "published."

5. Bardy argues in BA 12 that the actual citation of *Civ* 12.20 in *Trin* 13.12 argues for a date of 417. But whereas in BA 12 he is supposing *Trin* was published in 417, he admits in BA 33 that this date could be later than 419, thus anticipating the 420/421 (or later) conclusion Mlle La Bonnardière has more recently argued for in *Chronologie*.

6. *Retr* 2.43.1 employs the non-technical, hence somewhat ambiguous term, *termi natum*.

7. Bardy, in BA 12, dates this letter as "sans doute" from 429; but he seems to base this conjecture on the article (to which he refers) of Cyrille Lambot, "Une lettre inédite de saint Augustin, relative au *De Civitate Dei*," in *Revue Bénédictine*, 51 (1939), 109–24, where I can find no foundation for that dating. The letter is to Firmus, specifying details of *Civ*'s final publication. In BA 33, Bardy makes no allusion to this letter or to the dating inferences he had previously been tempted to draw from it.

8. In *Civ* 18.54 Augustine mentions the consulate of Manlius Theodorus as dating from thirty years before, in 399, which would mean that this book was being composed as late as 429. That date, however, Bardy (BA 12, p. 588) finds impossible, since "it is very certain" (presumably from the witness of *Retr*) that *Civ* was completed "well before 429." Augustine's "thirty years" must have been a "round number" only. In BA 33, he argues that closer study of the indications Augustine furnishes for Manlius Theodorus' consulate yield the date 395 rather than 399, thus allowing us to take that number thirty literally, and date Book 18 in 425, a much more acceptable figure. But the situation remains cloudy. Aside from Bardy's more recent failure to deal with the problem raised by the letter to Firmus, which *could* still

plained by assuming that Augustine had revised the entire work before sending this finished copy to Firmus, so that the work was "finished" by 426/427, but "published" in its final form only several years later.

But we may take these questions about final publication as relatively secondary for our purposes. Two dates are of primary importance, and one could wish we had more clarity about them. The first of these is the year 417/418. This is the earliest year for which we have firm evidence that Romans 9:11 had persuaded Augustine that he had Scriptural grounds for rejecting the theory of the soul's "fall" into the body. This insight could, of course, have occurred earlier, or slowly dawned on him over months or years, but it is highly unlikely that Augustine had seen the text as having this force when writing, in the year 415, his *Ad Orosium* and *Letter 166* to Jerome, or in late 416, when replying to Oceanus.

It would be comforting to know the second date more precisely, but since we can be confident that the final publication of the *De Trinitate* must date from sometime *after* 420, we must be content with that for now. Take it as a working hypothesis, then, that Books 1 to 5 of the *De civitate* were both written and published and Books 1 to 10 at least written, and possibly published also, before Romans 9:11 took effect on Augustine's thinking. And assume for the moment that Books 11 to 16 were very probably written, and possibly published too, before Augustine had finally published the *De Trinitate*. This is not much to go on, admittedly, and we may have to correct these two hypotheses further on, but they furnish us with initial touchstones to sharpen our inquiry into the *De civitate*. But they also furnish us with an initial reason for comfort: Books 11 to 22 all seem to have been thought out and composed after Augustine gained his insight into the force of Romans 9:11; and, as we shall see, those are the precise books in which he sets himself to deal with the questions that directly concern us in this study. In that sense, then, the *De civitate* may yield Augustine's "last word" on the subject, after all.

---

date the actual publication of *Civ* as late as 429, there is the possible distinction betweeen the *Retr* allusion to having "finished" the work (hence, by 427), and finally "publishing" it (perhaps in 429). Lambot, "Une lettre inédite," 115–16, argues from differences in the *Civ* manuscript families to something like this two-stage process. Again, we have things to learn in this connection.

THE MISERY OF BEING HUMAN

The *De civitate*, that "great and arduous work" as Augustine described it, touches on virtually every facet of the human condition.
But running through the entire work, from earliest portions to
latest, is Augustine's persisting conviction that the human condition is one of "misery," unhappiness. This is partly owing to the
exalted notion he has of happiness, for nothing less than the unremitting rapture of the beatific vision will do for that. Our mortal
life is a condition of transiency, in which nothing is ever securely,
tranquilly possessed (9.14–15; cf. 4.3); once born into this life, we
begin to die, the whole course of our lives is shot through with
change that makes them tend—literally, race—toward death (13.
9–11). Our days and years, though traversed with fleeting joys and
loves, are darkened over with sadness and fears, disturbances of
soul beyond our power to avoid or control. None of us lives as we
truly desire to live, and the Stoic counsel to limit our desires to
what we actually possess is merely a formula for being "patiently
miserable" (14.8–9, 25).

True it is that Augustine is directing this work against that
querulous rearguard of pagans who complain that the Christians
have abolished the cult of those gods who guaranteed the temporal
prosperity of the Roman empire; these are people superficial
enough to think that human happiness was meant to be found in
this life. But the animus with which he returns again and again to
this topic of human misery cannot be accounted for only by citing
those adversaries; this was Augustine's own ripened judgment on
the human scene, deeply held and intensely felt. Even Cicero in
his *Consolation*, he tells us, was inadequate to this task of portraying
how endangered all health and grace and beauty of body are; how
fragile is our hold on sight and hearing, on intelligence and sanity;
how even our virtues are means for an unremitting war on our
vices and weaknesses. Even the Stoics, at one moment preaching
that the evils of life are not genuinely evil, admit in the next that
the wise man may commit suicide in order to escape them: "Oh
happy life, which seeks the aid of death to end it!" exclaims Augustine (19.4). Everywhere, in social life and friendship, in the pursuit
of truth, in the barriers of language and the tragedies of war, even
the wisest and best of humans encounter the transiency, insecurity,

treachery, that make our lives one long trial (19.5–10). No, not simply trial, it is a temptation and entirely a punishment (tota poena), into which we appropriately enter, as newborn infants, not with laughter but with tears. Why punishment? "A heavy yoke is laid upon the children of Adam," Scripture assures us; "this life has become penal in consequence of the outrageous wickedness which was perpetrated in Paradise," and it is "by the sin of one man we have fallen into so deplorable a misery," into this "war" between flesh and spirit (21.14–15).[9]

A PENAL CONDITION

The root of our present misery is, therefore, that ancient sin of our father, Adam. But if that is so, the original human condition must have been other than the one we know. Yes, answers Augustine, and he describes the creation of Adam. For God created the human race starting from this one man. After the disquisitions on human misery, and on its penal character, one might expect that Augustine would stress the individuality of Adam in order to ground humanity's unity in misery and sin. But no. God chose to draw all subsequent humanity, even Eve, from this one man "in order to commend more effectually the unity of society and the bond of concord, men being bound together not only by similarity of nature, but by family affection" (12.21). God foreknew that Adam would sin, and propagate a race of mortals who would run to "enormities" of sin unknown even among the animals; but He foreknew as well that "by His grace a people would be called to adoption" and, "justified by the remission of their sins, would be united by the Holy Spirit to the holy angels in eternal peace" and "derive profit from the consideration that God had caused all men to be derived from one, for the sake of showing how highly He prizes unity in a multitude" (12.22).

THE SOUL'S ORIGIN

Now, God made man (at Genesis 1:26) "in His own image" in the sense that "He created for him a soul endowed with reason and

9. Cf. 22.22–23 on the miseries, and 24 on the blessings of this life, despite its "penal" character. On balance, it must be said that the penal character of this life wins out. Only by citing the final paragraph without all connection to the two preceding ones could one give the opposite impression.

intelligence," the mark of his "excellence" above all the creatures of the animal world. "And when [at Genesis 2:7] He had formed the man out of the dust of the earth, and had willed that his soul should be such"—formed it, that is—"whether He had *already* made it, and now by breathing imparted it to man, or rather made it *by breathing*, so that the breath which God made by breathing . . . is the soul—He made a wife for him, to aid him in the work of generating his kind . . ." (12.24).

Augustine, then, still thinks of the soul, endowed with reason and intelligence, as the seat of God's "image," for he thinks of this creation "in the image of God" as immediately associated with, and illumined by, the ensuing divine command to "subdue" the earth and all the lower orders of creation. It must be, then, those very potentialities that constitute man's "superiority" to the lower creation that also constitute him the "image of God." All this remains faithful to the *De Genesi ad litteram*, and to the *De Trinitate* as well. But there is no mention of creation *in general* as having implied two phases, and the implantation of *rationes causales* as linking those two phases. The apparatus of the *De Genesi*, once elaborated, seems to have been discarded quietly.[10]

But a possible two-stage creation *of man* enters by another bias. It could be that God (at Genesis 1:26) had "already made [man's soul] and now [at Genesis 2:7] by breathing imparted it to man."[11] Or it could be that God made man's soul "by breathing" so that His "breath . . . *is* the soul."[12] Now, it cannot be that Augustine means this last phrase to insinuate that man's soul is in any way of God's very substance; we have seen too much of his enmity to that position to take such a possibility seriously.[13] How, then, does he see the difference between these two interpretations of God's

10. Augustine recalls his theory of the angels' morning and evening knowledge (11.7), as well as the view that creation occurred entirely on "one day" (11:9), which would seem to call for his *rationes causales* insight; but that thought device is never brought into play. The reason may perhaps be this: the point he is making *in directo* is the identification of the angelic creation with the "Light" of the "first day," without concerning himself directly with the problem provoked by the *simul* of Ecclus. 18:1. That text, it may be significant, is never involved in this version of his creation story.

11. *Iam fecerat*, Augustine writes, and now *insufflando indidisset*; the two stages seem clearly distinct.

12. *Sufflando fecisset eumque flatum, quem sufflando fecit, . . . animam hominis esse voluisset*.

13. Everything we have seen above and, most recently, *Trin* 13.24 makes this abundantly clear. But *Civ* 13.24 is explicit on the matter.

"breathing"? Could the familiar creationist–traducianist debate have taken a new form of expression? Hardly; there is nothing in either phrase to suggest a traducianist interpretation.[14] He could mean us to understand both expressions in the creationist sense: the first of them betrays his now-familiar penchant for thinking of the soul as created prior to, and apart from, the body; the second of them admits that this two-stage process might conceivably give way to the single-stage process whereby God "breathes," and breathes "into" the body, a soul that has no existence prior to its existence "in" the body it ensouls. Augustine is not wedded, then, to the two-stage interpretation of the creationist hypothesis, after all, even if his mind moves more naturally along those lines.

"IMAGE" OR "INCARNATE" SOUL?

Augustine, then, still situates the image of God in the soul rather than in the body–soul composite; and yet, he himself admits, the term "man" more correctly designates that composite rather than one or other "part," even if the "superior" part.[15] How "incarnate," when all is said, is the De civitate's portrayal of the human being? There are still tensions in the picture, but along with them an array of elements that go to stress the incarnate character not only of humans in the fallen state, but of both Adam and Eve in their "ideal" condition in paradise. Paradise itself, Augustine insists, was a real place, its four rivers actual rivers, its trees visible and tangible trees. One may take flight into allegorical interpretations of all these, if one will, but never to the denial or denigration of this "historical" sense of Genesis' affirmations (13.21). But when it comes to such spiritual interpretations of "man" and "woman," his realism is, if anything, even more exigent. He is plainly reluctant to give any encouragement to interpretations—like his own in the De Genesi contra Manichaeos—which would see "man" as the ruling or contemplative mind, "woman" as the subordinate, or active principle

14. Again, traducianism in the strict sense is an irrelevancy, since it has to do with the creation of post-Adamic souls, only; I am alluding here to the quasi-traducianist form God's original creative act might take.

15. See 13.24. Etienne Gilson, in Introduction, pp. 44–45, and Christian Philosophy, pp. 35–36, presses the unitary implications of this affirmation (and of the "definition" of man in Trin 15.11) much harder than I can find justifiable; he seems anxious to bring Augustine much closer to a Thomist view of the human composite than the facts of Augustine's development truly warrant.

in the idealized human.[16] We have here an actual individual man, an actual individual woman, and let us be clear on that!

That man and woman are both moreover unambiguously incarnate. Augustine repeatedly assails the suggestion that their bodies were "spiritual" rather than "animal" (13.19–23), were like the bodies the saints will enjoy in the resurrection rather than the sorts of bodies we experience now. They had to nourish themselves from the various trees in the garden, in order to fend off hunger and thirst; they were both fashioned and intended to have intercourse and to procreate, even in paradise. The allegorical interpretations that would make their "procreation" a purely spiritual affair producing purely spiritual offspring—these Augustine firmly excludes (14.21; cf. 26).[17]

THE BODY

But even if their bodies were more like our own than like the "spiritual" bodies of the final resurrection, there were two notable differences from the bodies we experience. They were, first of all, immortal.[18] If they had remained obedient to God, and nourished themselves on the "tree of life," they would never have known the decaying process of aging, never have experienced death,[19] but at some appropriate moment their "animal" bodies would have been transformed into the spiritual bodies proper to risen existence (13.13). Secondly, they knew nothing of the war of flesh against spirit, the unruly "disobedience" of the sexual members, particularly, which Augustine expresses in the term *concupiscentia*. As long as the soul remained perfectly obedient to God, the body was to remain perfectly obedient to the commands of the soul (14.10).[20]

16. It would be worth some scholar's while to conduct a comparison of this theme as it appears in *Civ* 14.22 and in *Trin* 12, but within an overall study of the theme in Augustine's developing thought.

17. Augustine does say (14.26) that this procreative power was not actualized until after the banishment from Eden; he grounds that affirmation on the text of Genesis.

18. But "immortal" has changed its sense. It no longer requires that difference in kind and quality implied in *GenMan* and in the earlier stratum of *GenLitt* 3. This immortality retains the same "gift" quality as that in *GenLitt*.

19. Augustine's meditation on death (13.1–12) is full of interesting observations, including the admission (7–8) that martyrs to the faith can be saved without sacramental baptism—a development, surely, on his earlier anti-Pelagian views.

20. Compare ibid. 21–26, and 17. Augustine introduces a distinction here (for the first time?) between "flesh" and "corruptible flesh." But it would be hazardous to read that distinction into his earlier works, where "carnal" regularly has the pejorative connotation betokening sinfulness, penality, and "fallen-ness."

THE FALL

God had given Adam and Eve only one commandment, a command-ment "easy" for them to observe, and one given to them as constant reminder of the thankful obedience they owed Him. It was pride, the insubordinate will to live "according to themselves" and not "according to God," which introduced the evil disposition that made them willingly vulnerable to the serpent's temptation. How great a sin when obedience was so easy; no wonder the results of their sin have been so cataclysmic! Cataclysmic for them, first of all. The first punishment the rebels experience is the rebellion of their own bodies in those stirrings of lust which Augustine still thinks makes intercourse a topic of instinctive "shame" for all of us. The second punishment consisted in being banned from paradise and from the tree of life that nourished their animal bodies with im-mortality; they began their own personal "race" toward death (13.13).

KINSHIP WITH ANGELS?

There are passages in the De civitate, though, when this incarna-tionism appears to be skating on thin ice; several of them have to do with the soul's kinship with the angels. When discussing with the "Platonists," for example, he commends them for having so agreed with St. John's Prologue: the soul is not itself the Light, but like the Baptist, witness to the Light from which it receives its contemplative beatitude (10.2). Some pages further on, this precise comparison is given about the angels and their bliss (11.9). So, when Augustine comes to the creation account from Genesis, and explains the "six days" as the "first day" replicated through the (angelic) creature's morning and evening knowledge of creature-in-God, creature-in-itself, and back again (11.7), we are prompted to look carefully at what he says of the creation of "Light." Here his proposal that the "Light" of that first day of creation is the angelic host is far less confident than it seemed in the De Genesi ad litteram; what is more, there is no intimation that human souls were also included in that spiritual community (11.9). The contemplative bliss we shall achieve in heaven will be the same as that which the good angels never lost, but there is no suggestion that it is the kind of bliss we once enjoyed. Like the Prodigal, we are called to "return" to the Father's house, but the "circular" implications so often hinted at in Augustine's earlier interpretation of that parable fail to appear. Romans 9:11, one may think, has accomplished its task.

OBJECTIONS TO ORIGEN

And yet, the only application of that text occurs when Augustine is treating of the Old Testament, and comes to the story of Esau and Jacob. That story, he reminds us, the Apostle Paul saw as an instance of "grace," of God's sovereign freedom in "electing" from condemned humanity those whom He will (16.35). There is no mention in this connection of Origen's theory of pre-incarnate sin and the fall of the soul. The theory of the soul's origin Augustine is supposing here may eventually tell us why.

Indeed, the only treatments of Origen's theory[21] occur in quite other contexts, the first of them when Augustine is treating of creation. Here it becomes even more evident than in the *Ad Orosium* that this is precisely the bias along which Augustine primarily views the theory of which Orosius first informed him: it is at bottom, to Augustine, a theory explaining God's "motive" in creating the visible world with the precise kind of "order" it reveals. The whole of Book 11 is devoted to the "beginnings" of the "two cities," and Augustine feels obliged to go back to creation itself. From 11.4 onward, he takes up a series of questions touching on the notion of creation, on Genesis' account of it, and on the beauteous order—the *omnia*—to which even evils are made to contribute.

This brings him to assail, once more, the Manichaean complaints about such evils, but then to avow his surprise that Origen, who like Augustine and unlike the Manichees, believed that "there is only one source of things," should nonetheless have "refused to accept with a good and simple faith this good and simple reason of the world's creation, that a good God made it good." Origen's theory

21. Origen himself is mentioned by name three times: in 11.23, where Augustine repudiates his theory of "cycles"; in 21.17, where he repudiates his "merciful" theory as imperiling the eternity of the saints' beatitude; and in 15.27, where Augustine cites approvingly his exegesis on the measurements of Noah's ark. There may be a reference to Origen's *De principiis* in 12.13 (on cyclic theory again), and an allusion to Origen himself in 13.20, but this seems to me less certain. Compare the note in BA 35, pp. 483–86.

of the soul's sin and fall runs counter to that simple faith—but *precisely* inasmuch as it claims that "this is the reason for creation, not the production of good things, but the restraining of evil." Astonishing, Augustine exclaims, when "authoritative Scripture, in recounting all the works of God, regularly adds, 'And God saw that it was good.'" So ran his first objection to this theory, when writing his *Letter 166*, to Jerome (11.23).

But even as a reasonable explanation of the shape creation took, Origen's theory leaves much to be desired, and here Augustine enlarges on the second objection he had made in writing to Jerome. Can we, for instance, really accept that our universe boasts just one sun, because only one soul was capable of hitting on that "fine quality of sinning" that entitled it to be embodied in that lustrous orb? No. When asking of any creature, "Who made it? By what means? Why?" Augustine repeats, "it should be replied, God, By the Word, Because it was good."

But *Letter 166* proposed a third objection to Origen's theory; it expressed Augustine's "horror" at what the cyclic trappings of this view implied concerning our happiness after death. Augustine lays the foundations for his refutation of this view in Book 12. He is still concerned with the topic of creation—the creation of the angels, then of man—and finds himself compelled to face the theory which "some" (some "philosophers"?) have proposed, that the entire cosmos is a cyclic affair. After refuting this general cosmic view, he passes on to its "impious" corollary, that "after evils so disastrous, and miseries of all kinds have at length been expiated" in this life, and we have "entered into bliss," it should inexorably happen that "we should lose all this" and "be cast down from that . . . felicity to infernal mortality" once again, and "endlessly again and again." Once more, Augustine's horror shows: "Who can listen to such things? Who can accept or suffer them to be spoken?" But Origen's name goes unmentioned (12.11–20).[22]

Having gotten this indignation out of his system, he can treat Origen's theory of the end-times in its proper place, in Book 21. Here he is concerned with the eternal punishments destined for those who are never incorporated into the "city of God." Those

---

22. The "some" of 11 is left indeterminate, but in 13 Augustine expressly mentions "philosophers." The final exclamation of shock occurs in 20.

punishments are, he insists, eternal, and not as some "tender-hearted Christians" have argued, "longer or shorter according to the amount of each person's sin." "Origen," he notes, "was even more indulgent" in this respect, teaching that even the devil and his angels would eventually be delivered from hell. "But the Church, not without reason, condemned[23] him for this and other errors, especially for his theory of the endless alternation of happiness and misery." For instead of being merciful, as he may have intended, Origen denied to the saints themselves that "true and secure joy" which depends on the "fearless assurance of eternal blessedness" (21.17).

But, for some reason, Augustine never in the *De civitate* brings Romans 9:11 to bear in order to refute that precise contention of Origen's, so often the target of attack in his other works, that our souls' presence in mortal flesh was the outcome of some sin we committed in our pre-incarnate existence. Should we take that omission as a significant one? The least we can do is bear it in mind.

A CURIOUS OMISSION: HYPOTHESES ON THE SOUL

For that omission is part of an even larger one. It is striking that the *De civitate*, a work so tirelessly comprehensive that it sends Augustine down a hundred byways of *excursus* after *excursus*, never once presents the reader with an explicit discussion of the competing hypotheses on the origin of the soul and of their relative merits. Not once does Augustine set creationism against traducianism, as we have seen him do repeatedly, not even to warn his readers that he is unable to resolve the issue. Indeed, to my knowledge he does not even mention them by name. Did this just "happen" that way, or does it reflect a strategic decision on his part?

For everything we have just seen argues that he owes us some such discussion. Our unhappy condition, he has assured us, is a penal one; Adam's penalty and Eve's devolved upon us, their descendants. The death that was punishment for them became, for us, a "natural consequence," and their disobedience inflicted on us the corrupt-

23. Augustine leaves us wondering what Church "condemnation" he is referring to, and, more to the point, when and how he came to learn of it, and what those "other errors" were *in addition to* the one he is attacking here. Too many scholars, as we have noted before, slip into the lazy assumption that whenever Augustine attacks some "error" of Origen's, it is the fall of the soul he is (also?) attacking.

ible flesh that so often refuses its obedience to the will's commands
(13.3; 14.3, 18–20).[24]

But, to put the question in Caelestius' bold terms, why should we
inherit the punishment of a sin committed by those "others" long
ago? How does the Augustine of the *De civitate* help us to understand the mysterious transmission whereby the punishment meted
out to our first parents should afflict us as well? An initial cryptic
answer is given in Book 13, which contains the remarkable statement that: "This first death, which is common to all [*communis
est omnibus*], was the result of that sin which in one man became
common to all" (*Quod in uno commune factum est omnibus*) (13.
23). Not only is the punishment "common," but Adam's sin "became," or "was made," common to all of us. Caelestius is silenced,
but there is scarcely a great deal of illumination on how that
"common" sin is to be understood. Somewhat later, Augustine
speaks of

> that first and great sin—that sin from whose evil connections
> [*nexus*] no one can escape unless God's grace expiate in him indi-
> vidually [*in singulis*] that which was perpetrated to the destruction
> of all in common, when all were in one [man], and which was
> avenged by God's justice [*Quod, cum omnes in uno essent, in com-
> munem perniciem perpetratum est . . .*] [14.20].

Now the rhetorical antithesis involving the "individual" and the
"common" has gotten a step further: the reason why the sin committed "in one man" could bring on a *pernicies* "common to all"
is that we post-Adamic humans were all "commonly" *in* "one man,"
Adam. But what can it mean that we were "all in one man"? A few
paragraphs later, Augustine suggests an answer, but it is couched
in metaphor: God discriminates the saved from the eventually
damned, "not now by merits, since the whole mass [*universa massa*]
was condemned as if in a vitiated root [*radice*], but by grace . . ."
(14.26).

24. I translate *naturaliter sequeretur* (13.3) as "natural consequence" (compare
13.23 also). The entire section 14.3–20, and especially 15–17, should be read in this
connection.

We are all of one "mass" or "lump," all from one "root." The
"mass" metaphor derives from Romans' illustration from the potter's wheel (9:21–23): God, the divine potter, is perfectly free to
fashion, out of the same "lump" of clay, either "vessels of honor" or
"vessels of wrath"; the clay that is formed into a vessel of wrath is
only receiving a just punishment; it can have no complaints if God
freely chooses another portion of the "lump" for the exercise of
His mercy.[25] The "root" metaphor, however, works in a slightly
different way. It stands to reason that a rotten root will bring forth
only a diseased tree; the tree, given its natural dependence on it,
can be no healthier than the root.[26] What Augustine has done here
is cross these two metaphors: the infection of the "root" accounts
for the "damned" character of the "mass" or "lump." A similar
"natural" mode of thought seems to lie behind his explanation that:

> The first humans, though created for immortality, having become
> sinners, were so punished with death, that whatsoever sprang from
> their stock [eorum stirpe] should also be punished with the same
> death. For nothing else could be born of them than that which
> they themselves had been.[27] Their nature was deteriorated in
> proportion to the greatness of the condemnation of their sin, so
> that what existed as punishment in those who first sinned became
> a natural consequence [naturaliter sequeretur] for their children.
> . . . [For] as man the parent is, such is man the offspring. In the
> first man, therefore, there existed the whole human nature [uni-
> versum genus humanum fuit] which was to be transmitted by the
> woman to posterity. . . . [But] what man was made, not when he
> was created, but when he sinned and was punished, this he propa-
> gated, as far as the origin of sin and death is concerned [13.3].[28]

25. This metaphor does not help to answer the question facing us here, for it
supposes that the entire *massa* is infected with sin, rather than making intelligible
how it could have become so infected.
26. The "root and stock" metaphor comes *closer* to answering the question at issue,
except that the transmission of a disease may be explainable on radically different
terms than the transmission of—or, better, common participation in—an act of "sin."
It would, I am suggesting, be naïve to suppose that Augustine's mind was too primitive to grasp the inadequacy of these two metaphors, even when combined as he
combines them here, to satisfy the mind on a question which Caelestius' objection
had so sharply posed.
27. This comes down to a far more confident and categorical affirmation of what
Augustine had so embarrassedly expressed in *Lib 3*, in answer to essentially the same
objection. See above, chap. 1, note 35.
28. Note here a clear instance of the distinction between *facere* and *creare* to which
I called attention above, note 11 of chap. 9.

The "stock" having become diseased (at the root, as it were), It became naturally impossible for the branches to be any healthier than the ruined "stock." If, therefore, we conceive of our relationship with Adam as that of branches to stock, tree to root, then we can understand (and presumably accept) why we could never expect to be immune from the diseased state to which their sin reduced both him and Eve. This may explain the universality of the penal "deterioration," but not yet the "common" nature of the sin itself. There may be a hint enclosed in the phrase, that the "whole of human nature" was in Adam, but it remains only a hint.

Something of that "natural" cast of thought runs through the next, and final, text we must examine; but it ties up all that we have seen, and goes well beyond it.

"Man," Augustine tells us,

> corrupted and justly condemned, begot corrupted and condemned children. For we were all in that one man, when we were all that one man [*Omnes enim fuimus in illo uno, quando omnes fuimus ille unus*] who fell into sin by the woman who was made from him before the sin. . . . For not yet was the form created and distributed to each of us, in which each of us was to live [*Nondum erat nobis singillatim creata et distributa forma in qua singuli viveremus*], but already the seminal nature existed from which we were to be propagated; and this being vitiated by sin, and bound by the chain of death, and justly condemned, man could not be born of man in any other state [13.14].

From Adam's misuse of his free will, then, originated the "whole train" of evil and miseries which "convoys the human race," excepting those freed by God's grace, "from its depraved origin, as from a corrupt root, on to the destruction of the second death."

HOW WE SINNED "IN COMMON"

Here Augustine is once again arguing from the "natural" incapacity of a "condemned and corrupted" "root" to bring forth offspring superior in quality. But he goes further than this: we were, he affirms, not only "in" that one man, Adam, we "were" that man! We did not have the "form" in which we were to live as "individuals"; that was to be "created and distributed" only later; but the "seminal nature" from which all of us unfolded in the course of subsequent history was already there, in Adam. In Adam, that seminal nature was "vitiated," "enchained," and "condemned," which explains why we too come forth from Adam's root stock blemished with those same properties.

Augustine uses the same device later on, when speaking of infants in the final resurrection. The infant, he explains, lacks at birth the perfection of bodily size; but "this perfect stature is, in a sense, so possessed by all that they are conceived and born with it—that is, they have it potentially, though not in actual bulk"—for "in this seminal principle of every substance there seems to be, as it were, the beginning of everything which does not yet exist, or, rather, does not appear, but which in process of time will come into being, or, rather, into sight" (22.14).

The thinking involved here closely resembles that which Augustine applied when explaining the function of "causal reasons" in his two-phase theory of creation in the *De Genesi ad litteram*. But we have seen that, even in the course of that work, and particularly when discussing the "origin" of post-Adamic souls, he seems to have slackened his hold on, perhaps even lost confidence in, his "causal reasons" theory. Are we witnessing a revival of it now, in the hope it may serve to support our "unity" in and with Adam? Here, I submit, we must distinguish between "causal reasons" and "seminal reasons," for while the latter may be thought a sub-class of the former, and operate in almost identical ways, their existence and operation may be affirmed on quite different, and far more solid grounds. The "causal reasons" theory in its widest scope depends far more on Augustine's "metaphysical" approach to the textual difficulties in Genesis, and on the two-phase theory of creation those difficulties initially compelled him to forge. But "seminal" reasons may be affirmed only of those living beings that reproduce by "seed," and the cogency of the theory in this narrower application derives from our observations of the development of such beings, in regular and lawful patterns, from seed to mature specimen. Augustine could, then, still hold on to a conviction about "seminal reasons," even while having his doubts about that far more universal theory of "causal reasons."[29]

29. The explicatory notes in BA 37, pp. 798–801 and 840–42, do not take sufficient account of the distinction between "causal" and "seminal" reasons, as Solignac suggests, and I have contended above (chap. 8, notes 16 and 54). Augustine may *now* feel entitled to retain the more limited (and experientially based) doctrine of seminal

But, one may ask, does even this more limited theory of "seminal reasons" allow us to understand our oneness with Adam in the way required to solve Augustine's problem here? For he claims not only were we "in" that man, we "were" that man. The language recalls Augustine's sporadic appeals to Romans 5:12, whose *in quo* he tended to read as assuring us we were indeed "in" him when he sinned and, therefore, "sinned in" his very sinning. Such talk of being "in" Adam, we saw, seemed to support the traducianist rather than the creationist position; and since traducianists held that our very "souls" were one with the soul of Adam from which they derived, they felt entitled to claim that we and Adam constituted a single moral agent: "we" sinned in his sinning. Traducianism, therefore, could argue that the implications of their theory would permit them to say, with Augustine here, not only that we were "in" Adam, but that we "were" that man. Do Augustine's parallel expressions support the inference that he has finally surrendered to the appeal of traducianism? Augustine never evokes those conventional terms in order to tell us; besides, everything he has said about the *imago* properties of our souls runs counter to the materialism he found so repulsive in Tertullian's proposal. Can it be that Augustine has found a way of breaking clear of the very terms in which the traducianist–creationist debate has become bogged down?[30]

---

reasons without committing himself to the more comprehensive theory of causal reasons which, as we saw, was a metaphysical construct forced on him by a view of creation as occurring *simul*. But the exegetical problem which forced him to adopt (temporarily) his "causal reasons" theory vanished as a problem from the moment that he could admit that God's creation of all things *simul* (and before "resting") *could* be understood as meaning He created individual instances of all the *genera* which would eventually fill the earth (*GenLitt* 10.8/Z 5). The very real possibility that Augustine's thought developed on this score is not even envisaged by either Bardy or Thonnard, in their respective contributions to BA 37. Bardy, for example, cites *Civ* 14.14 without noticing that the *ratio* Augustine speaks of there is quite precisely a "seminal" *ratio*; he cites 22.19 as well, but there is no mention of "causal" reasons in that text. One should notice that *Trin* 3.13 and 16 speak of the "seeds" of all living beings as possibly contained in the corporeal elements—something very close to "causal" reasons thinking—but that text probably antedates the development that may have begun with *GenLitt* 10.8. In *GenLitt* 10.35 and 37 (Z 20 and 21), moreover, Augustine can speak of Levi as contained *seminaliter* in Abraham without implying the wider theory of causal reasons. This, I suggest, is just one more instance of where Augustine needs to be read with an eye to finer discriminations than have customarily been brought to that reading.

30. See once again chap. 8, note 62, referring to Lyonnet's conclusions, and the suggestion of Mlle La Bonnardière. It would be worth exploring whether Augustine's discretion about appealing to Rom. 5:12 until only *later on* in the development of

OUR ONENESS AS ADAM

We must be open to that possibility. And here that remarkably durable article on our "sinful condition" by Aimé Solignac provides a clue.[31] Solignac lists the various "schémata" whereby Augustine argues to our relationship to Adam. One such relationship is expressed in the "biological" terms we have been exploring. Propagated from, generated by, parents, themselves ultimately generated by Adam, we draw upon the same "seminal nature" that was contained in him, and therefore inherit the contagion spread by his original sin. In more "juridical" terms, Adam incurred a debt, and as his inheritors we are liable for that debt. For the purposes of the problem we are discussing, this kind of relationship is essentially the same as another schema Solignac presents: human nature became "vitiated" and "depraved" as a result of Adam's sin; and Augustine would ready our hearts to accept the inevitability of our own depraved condition by pointing to the "psychological–ethical" consideration Solignac also lists as a distinct schema: the sinful concupiscence that is part of that vitiated nature still infects every act of human generation.

But each of these modes of expressing our relationship to Adam shares the same weakness: for in each of them, we are linked to, related to Adam, but Adam remains "other" than we. Our linkage to him may help us understand why we inherit the disease, are liable for the debt our first father contracted, and find our individual natures as vitiated and depraved as he passed them on to us by the now-tainted act of human generation. But Adam's irreducible "otherness" makes it impossible to get our minds around the fact that we are held "guilty" of his actually having contracted the disease or debt in question. But this is the rock-bottom question that bothers Augustine, and he is groping his way toward some answer to it. Two steps toward that answer we have seen in the

---

his thinking on Original Sin may have stemmed from his suspicion of the way traducianists used it to argue for the precise kind of (materialistic) "ingredience" implied by their theory. His resort to this text might then indicate his growing confidence that something like that ingredience could be entertained in a non-materialistic way—in a way, I am suggesting, coherent with his more confident grasp of the distinction implied by his notion of the *propria vita*. We shall meet further on with several suggestive texts arguing in this sense.

31. "La condition de l'homme pécheur d'après saint Augustin," NRT, 78 (1957), 385–416. Henceforth: "Homme Pécheur."

claims he makes that "the entire human genus was in Adam" (*in illo universum genus humanum fuit*) and that the sin itself, *peccatum*, "committed in one [man]" became, or was made, "common to all." For both these lead us closer to the fundamental and quite remarkable claim that we not only were "in" Adam, but "were" Adam.

THE DOUBLE ADAM

That claim did not escape Solignac's alert eye,[32] and he saw some of its implications. He lists five distinct texts in which Augustine tells us outright that we "were" that one man, Adam, and in his concluding explanation[33] asserts that Augustine is asking us to see Adam as a "transindividual personage," at once himself and, in virtue of a link both biological and juridical, "he is humanity entire." But this, I submit, reduces markedly the most fundamental claim Augustine is making, and feels obliged to make, for the juridical and biological "link" we have with Adam may still leave Adam "other" than we. As subtending that link, Augustine is asking us to accept a *metaphysical* identity with Adam as "transindividual" Man. And the device he applies to help us "see" this is put to work in virtually all the texts Solignac cites in this precise connection, but fails to bring into clear focus. That device is implied by that cryptic term *propria vita*.

OUR *propria vita*

That phrase we have seen Augustine invoking more and more frequently since the force of Romans 9:11 dawned on him. What Paul forbids us to accept is that God's election depends on what we have merited either well or badly—or, more precisely, merited before we were "born." Does that mean we could have merited in the womb? Augustine has firmly rejected that possibility, rejected also that infants can merit by consciously and voluntarily doing either good or evil before they have reached a certain stage of maturity. It takes *time* for us to ap-propriate our individual incarnate lives, make them truly "our own" (*propria*). Thus far, the

---

32. For some analogous insights, see Rist in "Free Will," pp. 230–31.
33. "Homme Pécheur," 384.

antonym implicitly supposed by that *proprium* would appear to be the *alienum* of Caelestius' objection to our being held guilty of "another's" sin. That objection seemed to gather strength from Cyprian's assurance that infants were the more easily liberated in baptism since the sacrament remitted *aliena peccata*. In his *De peccatorum meritis et remissione*, Augustine must deal with that seemingly compromising statement: Cyprian was correct, the infants' sins are *aliena*, in the sense that "at their age they committed no [sins] in their own proper life" (*per suam propriam vitam*) (3.10).[34]

The same answer is later given to Julian of Eclanum: the newborn "contract" Adam's guilt, but "without [any act of] their own will" (*sine propria voluntate*).[35] But, the *De meritis* goes on to explain, these are called *aliena* sins, not as though they did not "pertain" to the infants. The reason is that by virtue of that power implanted in him (*insita vi*) whereby Adam gave rise to us all (*gignit omnes*) "we *were* to that extent all of us *that one* [man]" (*adhuc omnes ille unus fuerunt*). These sins, then, are called *aliena* "because [these infants] did not yet live their own lives [*vitas proprias*], but whatever existed in [his] future progeny, the life of [that] one man contained" (3.14).

Solignac is correct in finding Augustine endeavoring to *support* the metaphysical claim of our identity with Adam by appealing to the propagational "schéma"; but the metaphysical claim of identity is the one Augustine feels compelled to make, in order to preserve some right to say that infants *are* somehow guilty with the guilt of Adam's sin. And to make that metaphysical claim, his instinct tells him, the *propria vita* device must be invoked. Julian will later object that the generational linkage is inadequate to support the claim of our identity with Adam; the son is not "rightly said" to have "done" what his father did. This brings Augustine, in another text Solignac cites, to propose something about our generational link with our own parents that sounds very surprising. It can "rightly be said" that "Those also did it in the parent, because when he did it, they existed in him; and so they were, to that extent that

34. Compare *Ser* 294 19, and the comments of Athanase Sage on pp. 78–80 of "Le péché originel dans la pensée de saint Augustin, de 412 à 430," in REA, 15 (1964), 75–112.
35. *JulImp* 5.40.

one [man]" (*in illo fuerunt; ac sic ipsi ille adhuc unus fuerunt*).³⁶ This comes very near to saying that we can understand our ingredience in Adam from the analogy of our more ordinary ingredience in the parents who gave us birth. But in his more alert moments Augustine views our identity with Adam as so unique that it alone can help us understand how we can truly have sinned "in" his sin.

So intense is that identity, in fact, that it must be said that "Through the evil [act of] that one [man's] will, all sinned in him, when all were that one [man]" (*Per unius illius voluntatem malam omnes in eo peccaverunt, quando omnes ille unus fuerunt*); then, in a variant on the *propria vita* motif, Augustine explains: "because of that, each individual contracted [the] original sin from him" (*de quo propterea singuli peccatum originale traxerunt*).³⁷ Here that claim of identity is supported by appeal to the "concupiscence" schema, but in the *De civitate* explanation of it, we each become "individuals" (*singuli*) through the later creation and distribution of that "form" which makes us our individual selves, living (we may now infer)³⁸ our own "proper lives"—the same device Augustine was driven to apply elsewhere in his debate with Julian.

But even in that *De civitate* text, Augustine terminates this line of reasoning by turning our attention once more to the "seminal nature" schema. He never, in fact, makes the claim of metaphysical identity with Adam, or resorts to the *propria vita* concept, without appealing to one or other of Solignac's schemata as a kind of sup-

36. *JulImp* 2.177.
37. *Nupt* 2.15. In the light of my suggestion in note 30, above, it is significant that Augustine confidently invokes Rom. 5:12 as proof text for this ingredience identity with Adam here, in *Nupt* 2.15, as well as in *Mer* 3.14 (quoted in text) and *JulImp* 2.177 (see note 36, above); in the latter two cases, furthermore, the only two in which the argument compels him to do so, he falls back on the distinction implied in his *propria vita* notion.

It should be noted, though, that Augustine's reliance on Rom. 5:12 for this ingredience-identity proof appears to have been short-lived: see *AnOrig* 1.28 where he explains that it might prove only (by metonymy) our being in the "flesh" of Adam, and *LitPel* 4.17, where consultation with the Greek behind the somewhat deceptive Latin translation inserts doubts about the appositeness of his *in quo* inferences. So too, in *Civ* 16.27, 21.25, and 15.11 Augustine appeals to Rom. 5:12 without once drawing the inference we have been examining, i.e., from that text. And yet, his conviction about our ingredience-identity in Adam remains unshaken.

38. Observe that Augustine makes use of this *propria vita* restriction on Rom. 9:11 as late as in *Ep* 217. If Goldbacher's dating of 423 (see above, chap. 6, note 1) is sound, this notion had greater durability in his thinking than his ingredience-interpretation of Rom. 5:12. Hence, perhaps, the endurance of ingredience thinking remarked on above, note 37.

port for them: this is what justifies Solignac in never having isolated either the metaphysical claim or the *propria vita* manner of supporting it from the more juridical or biological linkages that are always in the immediate neighborhood, often as ostensible premiss for the metaphysical claim.

Indeed, it could be argued that in his own mind Augustine may never clearly have disengaged the sort of thinking implied by the *propria vita* device from the other sorts of thinking conveyed in juridical and biological metaphors. But however true that might be of Augustine's psychology, the logic of the matter, I suggest, may have been otherwise. It is plain that none of the other schemata, whether juridical, biological, psychological, or ethical, gives adequate support for the bold statement that "we" sinned in Adam's sinning. They all link us with Adam, help us understand why our sharing in his punishment is an inevitable consequence of his having sinned; but each time Augustine advances along one or other such line of argument, and ends by announcing that we *sinned* because we *were* that man, we experience a mild shock. Somehow a leap has been made for which the preceding thought process did not prepare us; we gape at an Augustine who has suddenly materialized on the far side of a chasm, and stupidly wonder how he got there. Or—to change the metaphor—we begin to suspect he has played this round with an extra card in his hand.

That extra card, I am suggesting, was the line of thinking implied by the *propria vita* notion, a line of thinking that parallels those traced out by his other arguments. But instead of receiving support from them, it may, on the contrary, have lent them in his eyes the extra force we fail to see in them—force enough to conclude, as Augustine was determined to conclude, that we *were* Adam, sinned in his sinning, and truly merited the penal condition in which we find ourselves.

Propria vs. *communis*

Thus far the *propria* seems to call for *aliena* as its antonym. But several of the texts, particularly from the *De civitate*,[39] hint at a moment in Augustine's thinking when the *proprium–alienum* antithesis orbited into the magnetic field of his well-known and cher-

39. See 13.23 (*commune factum est omnibus*) and 14.20 (*in communem perniciem perpetratum est*), cited above.

ished *proprium–commune* antithesis. We live our own "proper" lives in the body into which individually (*singuli*) we are born, and for the time given us to live in that body. But (taking advantage of Solignac's suggestion) the Adam who lived his own "proper" life is at once an historical individual "other" than our proper selves, and, as primal font of our humanity, the "transindividual" bearer of a life we not only inherit from, but possessed "in common" with, him. This would explain why that sin "in one man became common to all," was "perpetrated to destruction of all in common."

But in such a case, Augustine intimates, we must try to think of ourselves as we were when "that form" which constitutes us as "individuals" was "not yet created and distributed" to each of us as individuals. We must try to think of a "we" before it became a "we," of our distinct individualities before they were differentiated into distinct individualities. For, Augustine goes on to say, even if we did not exist as individuals, "the seminal nature already existed out of which we were to be propagated" (13.14).

That this was actually Augustine's thought process is more clearly reflected in another text Solignac brings to bear: from *Enarratio 84* 7. Augustine is indirectly acknowledging the difficulty involved in merely "biological" or "juridical" linkages: normally, he admits, sons once born (*nati*) are not held guilty of their fathers' sins; but (before any of us were born) the case was different: "That Adam we all of us *were*. . . . For we were not yet *ourselves*, but *we existed* in Adam; . . . we *existed* in him" (*Adam ille omnes nos eramus. . . . Non enim eramus jam nos, sed eramus in Adam; . . . in illo fuimus*).

ONLY A "POTENTIAL" EXISTENCE?

But this claim that we enjoyed some kind of "existence" in Adam might seem at first to run counter to what Augustine tells us elsewhere. In the *De civitate*, for example, he appears to imply that the later actualities present in the infant's "seminal nature" are present only "potentially";[40] and the *De Genesi ad litteram* has rejected the idea that Adam may be thought to merit, do either good or evil, when present only "potentially" in his "causal reasons."[41] The later "form," moreover, which when "created and distributed" makes us

---

40. 22.14, cited above.
41. *GenLitt* 6.14–15, treated above, chap. 8. Note that the case I have been making for Augustine's having possibly abandoned his wider theory of causal reasons does not

"individuals" (*singuli*) endows us, in that other terminological register, with the *propria vita* that constitutes us our "own" incarnate and temporal "selves." Has Augustine moved back into implying that "we" could truly sin while enjoying a merely potential existence in the seminal nature embodied in Adam, and in that way (*pace* Romans 9:11) "do either good or evil" before we were "born" and came to live our "own, proper lives"?

That question may be answered stepwise. First, is Augustine here telling us that our penal condition is due to the fact that "we" did indeed "sin"? This, however difficult to believe, is nonetheless the clearest element in the case I am making here. This was the surprising affirmation we saw him make in the *De Trinitate*, and the affirmation he makes in the *De civitate* as well; remarkably, too, Book 14 of the *De Trinitate*, and Books 11–22 of the *De civitate* (from which all the relevant texts have been drawn) were all written well after Augustine had come to see the dangers involved in this question of the soul's origin, and even after he had come to "see" the bearing of Romans 9:11 on the issue.

That same dating applies to all the other texts, including those taken from the *De peccatorum meritis et remissione*, which we have dealt with here.[42] The affirmation that "we" sinned in Adam's sin cannot have been made carelessly, or without full awareness of the implications. Caelestius' objection could not have been that easily forgotten: portray our present human condition as "penal," and you must be implying that "we," somehow, not someone "other," were the guilty parties; and there can be no question that Augustine, in the *De civitate* and in the finally written sections of the *De Trinitate*, portrays our condition as penal, with none of the hedging qualifications he felt obliged to enter in the *De libero arbitrio* III. The affirmation that we *did* sin followed from the implicit premiss that it *must* have been "we" who sinned.

But that sin must have been committed before we were "born" and lived our "own, proper life." Nothing could be clearer. But

make a text like this any less a difficulty against establishing the point I am trying to argue for now. He could still have retained both his theory of seminal reasons and the conviction that the cast of thought reflected here applied to seminal as well as to causal reasons; neither is the full flowering, so to speak, of the eventual being that emerges from them. Again, we may have to allow for development on his part.

42. Indeed, by the sort of non-vicious circularity that applies in the verification of hypotheses, the evidence that this insight dawned on Augustine relatively late may be thought to confirm the later date I postulate for the *Mer.*

then, one might object, it must have been committed when we existed only "potentially" in the "seminal nature" Adam embodied, and Augustine seems clearly to have denied this possibility in the *De Genesi ad litteram*. Granted. But we have seen how frequently Augustine reversed positions taken in that confused and exploratory work, both in the course of writing it and afterward. The *De Genesi*'s denial of this possibility, moreover, occurs well before the exegetical labors of Book 10 compelled Augustine to acknowledge, reluctantly, the surprising strength of the traducianist claim. Could he have changed his mind?

OR "INCHOATIVE" EXISTENCE?

The phrasing of his description of the seminal nature in the *De civitate* may be significant in this precise connection: when speaking of how actualities, later unfolded from the infant, are present in its seminal nature, he starts by referring to them as "what does not yet exist," and immediately corrects that expression to read "rather, what does not *appear*." Similarly, he starts by saying these later actualities "will come into being," and immediately corrects that expression to read "rather, what will *come into sight*." This is exactly what one would expect from a man trying to warn us against thinking of those later actualities as present *only* potentially. They must be thought of more as "beginnings," inchoations, more "actual" than the phrase "only potential" would imply. So, too, our presence "in Adam." Rather than individuals who did not yet "exist," who had yet to "come into being" as individual selves, we must have existed in some twilight kind of reality, hovering uncertainly between potentiality and full actuality; we must have been present in Adam as what had not yet "appeared," "come into sight." A difficult notion, admittedly, even a hazy one. But the mystery of our relationship to Adam, Augustine might have replied, quite obviously defies formulation in any easier, clearer way; and *some* justice must be done to the traducianist insight, while sedulously avoiding the materialism of its conventional formulation.

UNDERSTANDING ROMANS 9:11

But how can this be reconciled with the import of Romans 9:11? First of all, it must be conceded that Augustine had that text clearly in his sights; he has brooded long and hard upon it; its bearing on the question could not have escaped him. Moreover, we have seen his later meditations on it regularly couched in that curious turn of phrase, *propria vita*. Augustine must, therefore, have come to *some* interpretation of the Romans text that squared, in his mind, with the affirmation that "we" did sin, after all, in Adam; and the most promising lead on what that interpretation might be lies in that term *propria vita*.

From that point on the best evidence we have points to the distinction between our "proper" lives and the "common" life we must have lived in Adam. The hypothetical probe Augustine sent out in *De meritis* 2.59 appears to have found its target: before living our "proper" lives, we not only could, we must, have sinned. But now the proposal made to Boniface in *Letter 98* has found full articulation: it appears we sinned a "common" sin. The penal consequence of that sin was that we all, without exception, were enclosed in the *massa damnata*. Romans 9:11, Augustine may, even must, have come to see, says nothing directly to deny that precise way of understanding things, for it *supposes* our universal presence in the *massa damnata* as an accomplished fact. What it bears on directly is God's merciful "election" of this rather than that individual *from out of* the *massa*, saying that this election has nothing to do with the merits or sins of our "proper" individual lives, or of some life lived individually before we were born. Hence, the only application he makes of this text in the *De civitate*: Jacob precisely *qua* Jacob, Esau *qua* Esau, had done "neither good nor evil" and could not have. But the reason is that the individualizing "forms" that made them Jacob and Esau were "not yet created and distributed."

At all events, some such theory as this would entitle Augustine to say all the things he says in the *De civitate Dei*: that our human condition is penal, that "we" sinned in Adam's sinning, that Origen's explanation for all this must be rejected, and, finally, that Romans 9:11 indicated God's sovereign freedom in electing Jacob rather than Esau. With that same sovereign freedom He elects out of the *massa damnata* those He chooses to grace, without any regard for previous merits, or any semblance of injustice toward those He chooses should remain vessels of wrath. The message of Romans 9:11 has been not only respected, but at last exactly understood.

A DIFFICULT SOLUTION TO A DIFFICULT PROBLEM

Was this what the aged Augustine was actually thinking, or perhaps struggling to formulate? The theory is difficult, but the years had taught him that easier explanations shattered before this mystery; it is ingenious, as well, but we have met with instance after instance of Augustine's ingenuity, even in the limited ambit of this study. But would he have left it so hazy and vague as this, allusive to the point of being elusive? He might have seen advantages in that: he had been wrong before, but had always been granted the opportunity to correct his earlier missteps; he is about to write his *Retractations* to warn believers about where he no longer agrees with his earlier self; he cannot count on many more years to live. This "word released" he might never be able to "call back." Present a clearly articulated theory now that the future proves wrong, and Catholics might be tempted to think God's ways with us sinners were not only unsearchable, but as arbitrary and absurd as both Manichees and Pelagians claimed. Better, therefore, to point out a line of solution, but keep it suitably vague and flexible; the mystery is vast, and our human minds are so small.

THE PLOTINIAN HALLMARK

But if what I have presented here bear some resemblance to Augustine's final word to us, the message is hauntingly familiar. The *De civitate* leaves no room for mistaking it: the Archetypal Man was *also* an historical individual who lived his "proper" life, among real trees in a garden in a real someplace, wearing an "animal" body like our own.[43] But before our individual incarnate lives we pre-existed in that Man; our subsequent individualities were somehow present there. But more important and real was the reality

---

43. Solignac was largely right, therefore, in the proposals he made on pp. 376–81 of his "Homme Pécheur" article, though less right in failing to detect the strong resemblances between Augustine's Adam and Origen's "Homme Idéal." Compare Sage's observations in "Peché Originel," pp. 80–81, that the earlier Augustine frequently refers to Original Sin as *peccatum naturae*, and connect those texts with those adduced in his "Peché originel: La Naissance d'un dogme," REA, 13 (1967), 211–48, at 223–25 on *peccatum hominis* or *peccatum animae*. All these texts, reread in the light of what I am proposing here, are perfectly consonant with the thought ways which both Origen and Plotinus imbibed at the feet of their common master, Ammonius Saccas.

that made us one. That common "One" sinned and fell, and our later individualities, each living its proper life, became uniformly parts of the *massa damnata,* all of us punished for that common sin. The modifications are serious and seriously meant; but the Plotinian aroma is unmistakable.[44]

SOUL'S "NATURAL" DESIRE REVISED

But the last time we uncovered such clear traces of Plotinian influence was in *De Genesi ad litteram* 7.38, where Augustine briefly entertained the hypothesis that souls, existing elsewhere, might come down through a desire for embodiment that was "natural" in the sense of morally neutral. How does Augustine's final view compare with that hypothesis? If the theory I am proposing is correct, it follows that in the *De Genesi* Augustine was momentarily experimenting with that hypothesis, and that the assumption governing his experiment was precisely the one imposed by his earlier and simpler understanding of Romans 9:11—that the soul's descent into body must be neither a "good" nor an "evil" act.

Augustine was perfectly aware, however, that even while conducting that experiment under Plotinian auspices, he was using Plotinus' thinking in a deliberately unilateral way. For the section from the *Enneads* which spoke of the soul's "natural" desire for descending into the body appointed to it did not mean to deny that its descent would *also* be an "evil" brought on by the soul's own τόλμα, or arrogant self-assertion. It was not Plotinus' point to deny this "fault" on the soul's part, but to integrate it, rather, into the all-embracing network of cosmic lawfulness. This was precisely what Augustine was convinced his own earlier theory succeeded in doing by means of his elegant *dimissio* motif. The soul's fall was prompted by the sin of *superbia,* pride, but a pride that "weighted" the soul to go, "naturally" and inexorably, to the "place" amid lower, bodily realities appropriate to that weight. As with Plotinus, so with Augustine's earlier thought: individual "fault" and the working of cosmic—read "Eternal"—law were, not opposed, but perfectly harmonized with each other.

This, we saw, is precisely what lent such poignancy to Augustine's brave experiment with the soul's "natural" desire for embodiment;

44. For fuller development of this suggestion, see the Appendix.

it came with a high price-tag, demanding a readiness to scrap one of his most cherished insights. But it would be wrong to take that as his last word on that matter, for now his *propria vita* distinction has freed him once again to think of the soul's descent as a genuinely *evil* act, albeit an act committed by none of us individually, but by all of us "in common" with, as literally "one" with, that Archetypal individual named Adam.

Despite some changes in secondary features, then, this final theory represents Augustine's return to the "fourth hypothesis" he had step-by-step encased in the works that antedated his "insight" that Romans 9:11 forbade his clinging to it as his "preferred" theory. This was the view, we saw, which undergirded the original stratum of his *De libero arbitrio*, before later emendations entered to muddle its argumentative line. One might object that the distinction between our "proper" lives and the "common" life we enjoyed as one with Adam constitutes an important revision of that earlier view; it should be left as a point of secondary importance, but I suggest that "refinement" would be more accurate than "revision." Augustine has merely come to sharper awareness that the implicits of his earlier view, if once made explicit, were adequate to meet the challenge of Pelagianism within the boundaries of Pauline thought, properly "understood."

CLEARING UP AN ANOMALY

It may in some measure confirm the interpretation given here that it permits of clearing up several anomalies in Augustine's text. The first of them is this: despite the confidence with which Augustine formerly applied Romans 9:11 to reject outright Origen's theory of pre-existence and fall, we saw him abstain from that peremptory tactic in the *De civitate Dei*. Perhaps now we can understand why. There is enough of an Origenist flavor in his own mature solution to the problem of the soul's origin to deter him, now, from applying Romans 9:11 that way. He has come to see that Pelagianism imposed the necessity of elaborating some understanding of how each of our souls can have shared not only in Adam's punishment, but in the guilt of his actual sinning. Wrestling with that text from Romans, furthermore, Augustine began to see that restricting its bearing to our *propria vita* allowed him both to respect the force of that text and still to find room for a sin each one of us committed "before we were born," but also while "one" with Adam, before we were actually our subsequent individuated "selves."

At the culmination of this thought development, therefore, he has come to see not only that he was no longer obliged to apply Romans 9:11 to exclude *all* prenatal sin whatever, but also that his earlier applications in this sense betrayed too simple an interpretation of Paul's teaching. Romans 9:11 still preserved God's sovereign freedom in election—hence, Augustine does apply it with *that* force in the *De civitate*; but he has come to realize it as most urgent that we understand that text in a way which harmonizes with, and leaves room for, that equally Pauline article of the *fides fundatissima*: that all of us without exception stand in need of baptism for remission of the sin itself *(peccati ipsius)*, the *reatus* of which we had contracted through our relationship to Adam.

AND ANOTHER

The second anomaly this theory may explain occurs in that lengthy section of the *De Trinitate* 13.13–23, where Augustine describes the redemptive work of Christ Incarnate. The incarnate cast of that description, we remarked earlier, coheres perfectly with what would seem to be a picture of an equally incarnate Adam, and an equally incarnate portrayal of the human drama of fall and return. No thought of man as fallen soul *here*, one is tempted to judge.

But if the theory we have since uncovered be the correct one, this apparent difficulty is obviated. For the view Augustine was elaborating even then has this remarkable virtue to it: it permitted him to integrate a radically spiritual fall of the "interior" man with an "outward" act of disobedience whose guilt, and penal consequences, both, could be shared in and transmitted to all of incarnate Adam's incarnate and historical descendants.

A THIRD ANOMALY

That reply, however, presupposes the solution to the third anomaly spoken of above. It crops up in Augustine's explanation of the Fall in Book 14, chapters 11 to 13, of the *De civitate Dei*. Permit me, however, to take this as an occasion not only for resolving that anomaly, but also for summarizing the main lines of Augustine's final theory on the origin of the soul. So that our end may also be our beginning, I hope also to point out in passing how that final theory compares with the one explained in our first chapter, as implied in the original stratum of the *De libero arbitrio*.

Augustine repeats some details already given in Book 13 in his analysis of the Fall in Book 14, chapters 11 to 13, but the two accounts are perfectly coherent. To begin with, his description of the original human couple insists on the fact that the "paradise" they inhabited was—allow me the expression—"doubled." It was a paradise whose lower storey, so to speak, was "corporeal," its upper storey being "spiritual." On the corporeal level it contained "bodily goods," and goods for the "exterior" senses, while its spiritual level contained goods for the "mind" and for the "interior" senses. Paradise "was clearly both," Augustine argues crisply, "because of both"—that is, both these levels of the human being; if "man" be "doubled" in his constitution, paradise must have been so as well (11).

How, though, does Augustine now envisage that "doubled" constitution of "man" or "human being"? At this juncture, he departs from his earlier theory in two important respects. First, he repeatedly insists, and expressly cites Paul's teaching in 1 Corinthians 15 in support, that man's body was an "animal" and not the "spiritual" body he had held for in his first *De Genesi* and in the original stratum of *De libero arbitrio* 3 (13.23). We saw that as late as the third book of *De Genesi ad litteram* he still proposed that earlier doctrine; there he had to confess that it was "difficult" to reconcile that view of the first man's naturally "immortal" body with the facts that he ate and drank, and was intended to beget children. Now, on the contrary, he roundly declares that Adam's "animal" body was not the kind of "spiritual" body promised us in the resurrection; we would be wrong to think—as he had formerly thought—that it was originally a spiritual body and became "animal" only as a consequence of sin (13.23). He even appeals to the fact that Adam ate and drank as a premiss from which he can confidently conclude that his body must have been "animal" (13.20).

But, he goes on to say, that animal body must, before the Fall, have been perfectly obedient to governance by the soul; hence, the act of bodily copulation—which he was earlier tempted to suspect was unworthy of paradise—must have been possible to Adam and Eve without any of the unruly upsurge of the concupiscence which we, fallen children of Adam, experience to our shame (14.16–17).

The second difference is this: in his first *De Genesi* he interpreted Adam and Eve as symbolizing a "double" constitution of "human nature," but of a quite different kind; for Adam then referred to the governing mind and reason, while Eve stood for the lower powers of sensibility which God intended to remain "obedient" to reason. His explanation of the Fall then flowed from this allegorical interpretation: the tempter was able to approach "Adam," the higher, contemplative "reason," only through "Eve," the inferior power of sensibility. Augustine now explicitly rejects that view. Adam was truly an historical individual man, and Eve, truly an historical individual woman (13.21). But Genesis does describe the tempter as making his initial approach to Eve and, through her, to Adam. We shall have to see what Augustine makes of that teaching shortly.

Adam and Eve, then, were a genuine couple. But Eve had been drawn from Adam. He, therefore, was the original individual from whom all human beings trace their descent. We can almost see Augustine's mind oscillating back and forth between these two Scriptural affirmations (13.1); that oscillation may entitle us to adopt a more economical form of expression and speak, as he sometimes does, of the fall of Adam as the fall of "Man."

ADAM'S ORIGINAL CONDITION

Both Adam and Eve, therefore, or, to adopt the protocol above, Adam was "doubled" in constitution. His "upper storey" was "mind," and it becomes obvious from Augustine's expressions that he views that mind as primarily "contemplative" in nature and activity. The superior level of paradise held forth "goods" for his "mind"; his "love for God was unclouded" and "from this love flowed a wonderful delight" because he "always enjoyed what was loved." This was not yet that "higher felicity which is enjoyed by the most blessed angels," but precisely because there was not the "sure assurance that no one would sin." And yet, had Adam not

sinned, the "saints" among his descendants "would have lived [as
he presumably lived] . , . as now they live in the resurrection"
(14.10)

Adam, moreover, had been made "upright" and, therefore, with
an (habitual) "good will"; he lived "with God for his rule," his will
"truly free" as God had given it to him (11). The only prohibition
God laid on him was "easy to keep" and "found no resistance to
its observance in lust" (12). He should have continued to "cleave
to God" as his "end," and not have chosen to become a "kind of
end to [himself]," for as "unchangeable good" God would then
have continued to "satisfy" him more than himself. His "will"
should have "remained steadfast in the love of that higher and
changeless good by which it was illumined to intelligence and
enkindled into love" instead of choosing to "please himself as if he
himself were Light," and so "turn away from that Light by which,
had he followed it, he would himself have become Light" (13).

In Book 13, when refuting the contention of some "Platonists"
that true happiness could not be enjoyed while the soul was still
encumbered by a body, Augustine had concluded that this was true
of the corruptible and mortal body, but not of "such bodies as . . .
God contrived for the first man" before he sinned (13.17). Yet while
the body in its final, resurrected condition seems to resemble Adam's
"animal" body in being "subject to the spirit with a perfect and
marvelous readiness of obedience" and responsive "to the will in
all things," Augustine is swift to add that it will "surpass the bodies
of our first parents before they sinned." But why? Because, Augustine specifies, Adam and Eve "used food as men do now, their bodies
not being spiritual, but animal only"; they needed to take that
nourishment so that "their animal bodies might not suffer the discomfort of hunger or thirst." (In our risen bodies, Augustine assures
us in 13.22, we shall be *able* to eat food when we choose, and even
enjoy it, but there will be no such necessity for doing so.) They also
ate of the "tree of life" to forestall both death and the decay that
comes to us with aging; in that respect, then (the "doubled" paradise presides over Book 13 as well), the tree of life "would seem to
have been in the terrestrial paradise what the Wisdom of God is
in the spiritual," since they both are in their respective realms what
Scripture describes as "a tree of life to them that lay hold upon
her" (20).

The portrait of Adam before his sin is rigorously consistent: as "mind" and "will" he dwelt on a level of contemplative happiness to rival that of the angels. God both illumined his mind and enkindled his love, filling him with the unclouded joy of knowing and loving Him. His "animal" body offered no hindrance, the generation of children would have been accomplished without any unruly stirrings of concupiscence, and if he needed to eat and drink, it was not to prevent decay or death ("eating" from the tree of life took care of that) but only to avoid the discomfort of hunger and thirst. On the spiritual level, therefore, his contemplative mind-soul enjoyed unbroken union with God. One thinks of Porphyry's claim that Plotinus, too, even while in the body, could go about his daily business in habitual union with the One.

The only shadow on Adam's beatitude on this spiritual level came from the possibility that he might sin and lose it. It should have remained the faintest of shadows, so simple and easy was the single commandment God had issued, and so admirably equipped was he to keep it (14.12). But the shadow was real. Illumined by the Light, he was still under the necessity to "follow after" that Light in order to become, in perfect security, the Light in God's own Light that the blessed angels were.

In summary, Augustine has limned Adam's contemplative bliss in substantial fidelity to his much earlier conception of the "unfallen soul." He has had to take account of the "animal" body, but he does so without having to alter his earlier picture essentially; he must show more explicit recognition of the soul's insecure beatitude, but that was already implicit in his earlier view.

THE MECHANISM OF THE FALL

The same fidelity shows in his explanation of Adam's "fall." Again, though, that fall boasts a "doubled" character. Inasmuch as Adam was embodied in a paradise whose lower level was equally corporeal, his sin took the "outward" form of an *opus*, the externally observable "work" of disobedience (14.13). Inwardly, however, his sin is described almost exactly as in Augustine's first *De Genesi* and *De libero arbitrio* 3. Its root and "beginning" was pride—the *superbia* that Augustine's old warhorse text, Ecclesiasticus 10:9–13, imaged as the soul's "standing away" (*apostatare*) from God, its true Light, and turning toward itself. Instead of continuing to "cleave" to God, its true *Principium*, the soul "became pleasing" to its own gaze, proudly took its own excellence as the object of its contemplative delight, and freely chose to make itself its own self-governing *principium* (14.11–13). But it was not the Light, so that its turn away from the Light that formerly had both illumined and enkindled it axiomatically implied that it became both cold and darkened over. But the laws of the *omnia* God "disposed" in "number, measure, and weight" require that "cold" realities belong in the lower and darksome "places" of the universe. Inexorably, then (the *dimissio* theme has rewon its *droit de cité*), the soul "falls" (14.12).[45]

That fall implies what it did earlier, the soul *deficit*, becomes lesser and inferior in its very being; from the "immutable good" by which formerly it was both "illumined" and "enkindled" (*illustrabatur, accendebatur*) so that, "cleaving" to God it shared in His immutability and thus remained "stable" (*stabilis*), it sinks downward and away from those bright and blazing heights it once inhabited, into the realm of change. That defective movement, Augustine goes on to say, is possible only because the soul was made from "nothing"; and yet, as in his earlier works, he thinks it necessary to caution that the soul's fall never reduces it to the absolute nothingness toward which it tends, but brings it "closer to nothing" than it formerly was (*nihilo propinquare*) (14.13).

At this point we come to a third anomaly in Augustine's final theory. He goes to some lengths to insist that a certain *mala voluntas* must have "preceded," in "hidden" fashion, Adam's "outward" sin of disobedience. That "evil will," he tells us, must have had its beginning (*initium*) in pride (14.13).

INNER AND OUTWARD SIN

When one stops to think about it, that qualification is peculiar. Either Augustine is saying that an "interior" *act* of the will is necessary to command any "outward" bodily action, in which case the reminder is so banal and obvious as to be unaccountably super-

---

45. For ampler treatment of this cosmic image, see my *Imagination and Metaphysics in St. Augustine* (Milwaukee: Marquette University Press, 1986).

fluous; Augustine writes better than that, surely. Or he could be
saying precisely what he does say: that in the case of Adam and
Eve, a "hidden" evil *set* of the will must have—not commanded,
precisely, but—actually "preceded" the outward act. If that is what
he intends by this *voluntas mala*, then he is saying something far
from banal or obvious. But how are we to understand it?

He makes it plain that he is talking about a set rather than a
mere act of the will by specifying that Adam and Eve had already
"begun to be bad" (*mali*), and that they would never have performed the bad action of eating the forbidden fruit "unless [they]
were bad already" (*iam mali erant*). The tree's fruit, he cites the
Gospel metaphor, would not turn out evil unless the tree itself
was already evil; so this "evil act" of "open disobedience" would
never have been done unless our first parents were "already secretly
corrupted," "were already wicked" (14.13).

What is Augustine getting at? And how does this peculiar qualification fit with the theory as he has now come to formulate it? His
first point, I suggest, is this: he was obliged to depict the sin of the
incarnate Adam and Eve as an "open" sin of disobedience since
Genesis describes them as embodied and, as Paul reminds us, in
"animal" bodies. But the body, for Augustine, is the "outward"
instrument through which the "inner" soul expresses itself. Inasmuch as he was embodied, it was commensurate that Adam's sin
take overt expression in an *opus*, a "work" which was equally embodied. And (Augustine is implying) what more ideally consonant
bodily expression of the soul's interior sin of pride than an outward
sin of disobedience?

One result of his doubled constitution, then, implies that this
incarnate Adam, an historical individual, was caught up in a web
of incarnate historical relationships to all his descendants. This is
the level on which Augustine's mind was working in *De Trinitate*
13.13–23.

But, so embodied, Adam must have been an individuated human
being, living his "proper life." As the sin of someone already living
his *own* proper life, Adam's "outward" act, *as act*, could not be
shared by his descendants once they, too, had entered on their own
"proper lives." His resultant corruption, the punishment and debt
incurred by his sin—these might be shared by them, but not the

very guilt of his sinful act. But would the same be true of the "in-ward" act that might account for his, and Eve's, being "already bad"?

To answer that, consider once again the implications of Augus-tine's having "doubled" both Adam's mind–body constitution and the spiritual–corporeal paradise he inhabited. In line with his mature theory, this doubling would imply that, *qua* embodied, Adam was an historical individual living his own proper life and, therefore, an individual distinct from any and all of his descendants. But *qua* contemplative soul, dwelling on the luminous heights of the "spiritual" paradise, this incarnate Adam could simultaneously be what Plotinus would describe as the transtemporal and trans-individual Man, contemplative Soul (or segment of contemplative Soul). This would permit him to be the totality of "human nature" in which we all once commonly participated; as such, "his" fall from the spiritual paradise of contemplative union with God could indeed be "our" common fall, as well.

That fall, Augustine assures us, was due to a "hidden" sin of pride which occurred in the "spiritual" paradise; that "secret" sin, he is arguing, must in some real (but not necessarily temporal) sense, have preceded its expression in the "outward" act of dis-obedience Adam committed as incarnate individual in the "corpo-real" paradise. But it is necessary for the theory he now advocates that there be such a spiritual, antecedent sin; for God could impute to no one of us subsequent individuals the guilt of Adam's "out-ward" sin, committed in *his* "proper life." But God could, and does, impute to us the preceding sin of pride that had made both him and Eve "already wicked" and makes each one of us similarly "wicked" even "before" our entry upon own "proper lives." And He does so, Augustine is implying, because that preceding sin was committed by Adam *qua* contemplative Soul, the totality of the human race which was contained in him in "common" pre-individuated form. This, I submit, is why Augustine so repeatedly insists on this "spiritual" sin of pride as preceding, and rooting its "outward" expression in, the sin of disobedience.

One might object to this, as Boniface may have implied, that children, in their proper lives, may knowingly consent to sins their parents commit in their proper lives. But now Augustine has fully articulated the theory implied in his *Letter 98*: in such cases the children themselves "commit," not strictly their parents' sin, but a sin of "their own" in imitation of their parents' sin. And history records Augustine's cold rejection of this "imitation" theory of Original Sin.

One final comparison with his earlier theory, and we are done. In his first *De Genesi* Augustine explained the serpent's address to Eve rather than to Adam as directed at the lower and weaker component of the single "human nature" their *coniugium* symbolically represented; the rational soul, he contended there, could not have been solicited to fall except by that route. Now he explains that address to Eve as made to "the weaker part of the human alliance," granted, but Adam's yielding to Eve's invitation to eat is now explained in far more interpersonal terms. It was the "drawings of kindred," of "husband to wife, of one human being to another" that won him over. For, Augustine sums it up movingly, "the man could not bear to be severed from his only companion, even though this involved a partnership in sin" (14.11). The old man is far more human than the young theoretician of the *De Genesi contra Manichaeos*.

Thus far Augustine's view of the soul's origin in the *De civitate Dei*. But anyone acquainted with his *Retractations* knows the nagging question that must still be faced: How does all that I have presented above cohere with what Augustine tells us in his own retrospective examination of his writings?

EPILOGUE

ON READING
THE
Retractations

THIS STUDY is the conclusion of a long meditation on St. Augustine's theory of the human condition. It began with my *St. Augustine's Early Theory of Man, A.D. 386–391*, and was continued in a more hypothetical vein in *St. Augustine's* CONFESSIONS: *The Odyssey of Soul.* The reason for that hypothetical approach was the nagging awareness that the later Augustine seemed clearly to have repudiated the theory—that we humans are "fallen souls"—which I had proposed as applying to his earlier period. When, why, and exactly how that repudiation came about remained unclear. Hence, I determined to test that early theory for what possible explanatory value it might have for illumining the problems besetting any interpretation of the *Confessions*.[1] But Augustine's later repudiation of this view of the human was taken as the premiss for what I considered the weightiest objection to my view of Augustine's early theory. Though it was frequently advanced in various guises by others, I was especially grateful for the formulation that Robert Russell gave it:[2]

> it is from Augustine's own literary history that more serious objections to [the] thesis of the "fallen-soul" may continue to be raised. From his first mention of the four theories on the origin of the soul in the *De libero arbitrio*, completed in 395, where no reference to a "fall" is included under the two pre-existing theories,

1. The present work, if cogent, may now be viewed as having raised the underlying hypothesis of *Odyssey* to the status of a "thesis." This does not mean, of course, that there are no details in that work I should wish to change.
2. In his review in *Thought*, 44 (1969), 303–305, at 304. Father Russell has always been a model of that courteous criticism that furthers the common pursuit of truth.

up to the *Retractations* (426–427), and his last unfinished work against Julian, Augustine uniformly acknowledges his inability to reach a decision. Even if we assume that he had at an earlier period accepted the "fallen-soul" theory, it seems incredible that the scrupulous redactor of the *Retractations* would not have expressly repudiated an error for which he was later to censure Origen, as opposed to "Apostolic authority" (Ep. 202A).

That objection, carefully phrased and temperately expressed, summed up cogently what other scholars had proposed in slightly different terms, and I felt obliged in an article[3] some years ago to suggest what seemed to me then the general direction in which an answer might lie. But too much in that answer—or cluster of answers, really—remained ill-defined and even problematic. For one thing, I was constrained in a subsequent study candidly to admit that the apparent persistence of Augustine's "early" theory in the *De Trinitate* faced me with a problem that I was unable to unravel.[4] Hence, the need for this full-scale study on an issue narrower than, but central to, Augustine's later theory of the human—the issue, moreover, which drew the heaviest fire from the critics of my original study. My answer to Father Russell's objection I think stronger now than it was earlier, but this closer look at Augustine's maturer views has also shown a number of points where my earlier attempt at an answer was inconclusive, imprecise, and sometimes just plain wrong.

But I would hope that this study, imperfect though time will undoubtedly prove it to be, has managed to locate a number of points where the prevailing wisdom in Augustinian matters, too, was itself unexamined, imprecise, and sometimes in need of serious revision. And Father Russell's objection embodied, explicitly or by implication, a heavy cargo of that prevailing wisdom: first of all, that none of the four "hypotheses" in *De libero arbitrio* 3 contains reference to the "fall of the soul." Augustine's own *Letters* *143* and *166*, to Marcellinus and Jerome respectively, give the lie to that. But the Augustine of the *De libero arbitrio* refused to choose one out of these four hypotheses as preferable to the others.[5] Examination of what Augustine himself later tells us of his argu-

3. "Rejection."
4. "Fallen Soul."
5. See Gilson, *Introduction*, pp. 66–68 (and *Christian Philosophy*, pp. 50–51).

mentative strategy in that work, followed by close examination of how much that strategy introduced inconsistencies into the third book, suggests the strong possibility that he started with one as his preferred theory, only later saw the advisability of taking a more hypothetical stance, abruptly shifted register, and finished off by emending the work as best he could. *Letter 143* seems on the face of it to deny this possibility, but following the very leads it gives for a re-examination of the *De libero arbitrio* actually confirms the interpretation of the work that Augustine seems to be denying. Instead of confirming another item of the conventional wisdom, then, that the Augustine of the *De libero arbitrio* could not have been thinking of our souls as "fallen," *Letter 143* when examined closely seriously undercuts, if it does not soundly demolish, it.

Implied, but never made explicit, in this prevailing wisdom is the tacit assumption that Augustine must have been aware of Origen's similar theory of the soul's "fall," of the disfavor it had met with among Catholics, *ergo* . . . Hence, the need for exploring the issues of the Origenist controversy, and the knowledge Augustine, across the sea in Africa, might have gleaned of them. Surely Jerome *must* have apprised him of the dangers others had seen in the "fall of the soul" hypothesis; but no, Augustine's reply to Orosius' revelations on Origenism confirms what a study of the correspondence with Jerome already suggests: Origen was, to him, until 414/415, a relatively unknown quantity. If he himself preferred the theory that we humans were fallen souls, he did so in perfect innocence. In any event, about this time Augustine has entered a long period of hesitation on this question; its "dangers" have persuaded him to suspend work on both the *De Trinitate* and the *De Genesi ad litteram*.

Later, though, he does "censure" Origen's view, "as opposed to 'Apostolic authority' "; again Father Russell, and conventional Augustinian wisdom, are on target but just outside the bull's-eye. There is a story to that rejection, and it is not a simple one. For when Augustine first makes the acquaintance of Origenism, through Paul Orosius in 414, his instincts of repulsion bear rather on its cyclic and "fantastic" account of creation and of God's motive for creating the visible world; Origen's account of our souls as "fallen" does not move directly into his critical sights. For several years afterward, in fact, it is more this wider setting of Origen's theory which repels him, but his only resort is to attack it with theological arguments: far "better" to believe otherwise.

Even as late as the *De civitate Dei*, these are the features of Origenism against which Augustine aims his strongest batteries. But by that time he has come to "see" the "Apostolic authority" of St. Paul as sparing him the need for roundabout theological argument: Romans 9:11 appears to exclude any thought of prenatal sin or merit. How did he come to "see" this text that way? For his earlier meditations on it show that it did not always have that force in his eyes. The answer to that seems manifestly to lie in the progress of the Pelagian controversy, which very early brought him to re-examine his position on the origin, or embodiment, of the soul. The terms of that re-examination were defined for him by the four *sententiae* regnant in the discussions of the time; of those four, Augustine seems clearly to have favored one of the two penal explanations, leaving him a choice between either traducianism or the "fall of the soul." And in all his discussions of the four hypotheses, he takes no pains whatever to disguise his profound revulsion toward traducianism. Yet neither of the other two theories, that the soul was "divinely sent" or immediately "created" for infusion into the body, seems to answer the question Pelagianism has brought him to sharpen considerably: the guilt that afflicts even infants seems to commend more strongly than ever some penal theory or other. But which of them can truly furnish the reply to Caelestius' objection, and show that we are being punished for a sin "we" ourselves committed? Underlining to Jerome the difficulty that weakens his creationist view, Augustine indicates where "fall" theory seems to fit that bill, but not so precisely as he may once have imagined. Traducianism, however, he simply refuses to discuss, and the *De Genesi ad litteram* among other works makes the reason for that refusal clear: Tertullian's materialism is nothing less than madness, *dementia*. And yet, he is eventually compelled reluctantly to avow, that same *dementia* may not be so absurd as it initially seems, for it does furnish a way of thinking out how "we" might all have sinned *in* Adam's sinning.

But this admission is wrung from him in the course of the *De Genesi ad litteram*; something has occurred since he wrote to Jerome in 415, to make him take traducianism far more seriously than he was previously inclined to do. What made the difference?

The evidence indicates that the course of the Pelagian controversy must have come round to fastening on the very text that had already featured so importantly in the anti-Origenist movement outside of Africa: Romans 9:11, on the election of Jacob rather than Esau. For suddenly that text crops up again and again in Augustine's works and letters, cleanly and confidently undercutting any appeal to prenatal sins or merits: "before they were born they had done neither good nor evil." But that left only one "penal" theory still open: traducianism, alas!

The year 417 seems to have been a fateful one for Augustine. At the very time when he came to acknowledge "Apostolic authority" as excluding any "fall of the soul," the early books of the *De Trinitate*, where in serener times he had encased that very theory, are stolen from him and circulated among the brethren. He is furious, and for a time refuses to put a conclusion to the work. Fortunately, his *De Genesi ad litteram* is still in hand, and he goes about emending those sections in Books 6 and 7 in the light of what Romans 9:11 has brought him to see. He may already have written the initial portions of Book 10, as well; his earlier handling took some notice of the Pelagian question, but it seems likely that he decided to add an entire movement to his treatment of the soul's origin, now frankly commanded by the issues Pelagianism had inflamed.

Again, Romans 9:11 threads its way through these emendations, rejecting all appeal to prenatal sin, but at the same time insisting that all, even infants, share the guilt of Adam's sin. But now a subtle change asserts itself. The question has arisen why certain infants are born in circumstances that favor their being baptized, while others are not. God is certainly justified in damning all who share Adam's guilt, but how to explain that some infants, through no fault of their own, are never fortunate enough to be granted the remission of that guilt through baptism? An unsearchable mystery, Augustine cries, one to which even Origen's theory, despite all its initial attractions, was unequal, one that defied even Paul's understanding.

But this seems to have been the question that invited Augustine to inspect Romans 9:11 even more carefully than hitherto. Did it in fact exclude *all* appeal to prenatal sin? "As yet unborn"—he begins to explain that phrase with another: "not yet having lived their own life" (*propria vita*). Was this an opening? He returns to his

De peccatorum meritis et remissione to emend it, raising the hypothetical question that suggests that even infants may be guilty with a guilt that is their own, and yet a guilt contracted in a life that was not their "proper" life. By the time he writes the relevant portions of his *De civitate*, that hypothesis has hardened considerably. Augustine's final view seems to have been that "we" all sinned in Adam's sinning, not as our "proper" selves, but in a "common" life we lived in that Archetypal Man. This, I suggest, was the view that permitted him to write the final books of the *De Trinitate* in substantial consistency with, but injecting subtle modifications into, the theory that presided over the earlier books: we did indeed sin, but our "fall" was not the fall of some quasi-angelic creatures; Adam was "man," with an animal body like our own. Within the limits imposed on him by his enduring conviction that man as "image" was primarily "soul" and spiritual "mind-soul," Augustine could rest content that the finales of his *De Trinitate* and *De civitate* portrayed "man" as fallen from a bliss once enjoyed in Adam, and bent upon a "return" that was truly a "re-newal" in the genuine Pauline sense of the term: a "renewal of our minds," importing a progress toward an even better bodily state than Adam had enjoyed, a renewal in *melius*.

This final theory, I submit, or something very like it, provides the vantage point from which we can better understand not only Augustine's final criticisms of Origen, but the other observations he makes in the *Retractations* on the origin of the soul and associated issues.

The first such observation occurs when Augustine lifts out a sentence from the first paragraph of his *Contra Academicos*. There he wrote to Romanianus that "it has been so established [*comparatum*], whether on account of our merits [*pro meritis nostris*] or on account of natural necessity [*pro necessitate naturae*], that the divine mind-soul [*divinum animum*] [while] attached to mortal realities [*mortalibus inhaerentem*] can in no way whatever be received into the haven of philosophy."[6] The sentence is of interest because it shows Augustine already toying with the two possibilities that might explain our unhappy arrival into the world of mortal bodies: sin, and the working of cosmic—read "divine"—law. He

<hr/>

6. *Retr* 1.1.1. Observe that the term *divinum* when applied to the soul is far less innocent than is usually supposed; see *Early Theory*, pp. 112–31.

takes no exception to those same possibilities as he speculated on them in the *De beata vita*, possibly because they may have been omitted from the "incomplete" copy of that work he has on hand. But these were the two mechanisms used to explain the soul's fall in Plotinianism, and we have already seen that Augustine soon succeeds in forging them into the unitary interlock of human and divine action he came to express in the term *dimissio*. He seems to have lost faith momentarily in this rich notion in Book 10 of the *De Genesi ad litteram*. What is his evaluation of it now?

> I ought to have said nothing of these two [merits and natural necessity], for the sense would even so have been complete without them; or it was enough to say "on account of our merits," in the sense in which that is true of the misery inherited from Adam [*sicut verum est ex Adam tracta miseria*], and not added "on account of natural necessity," even though the hard necessity of our nature sprang from the merit of the iniquity that preceded.

But does this constitute a repudiation of the offending sentence after all? For Augustine here admits the appropriateness of tracing our mortal misery to Adam and, at the same time, to "merits" that he finds no difficulty with terming "ours"; on the other hand, he must admit there is some sense in using the term "necessity," for our misery is "merited" by the "iniquity" that preceded it. In the universe supposed by his *dimissio* motif that moral causality is as much a "natural necessity" as the movement of a "weight" from higher to lower. What seems to bother him here, however, is the impersonal character of that expression *necessitas naturae*. He may have found this term, inherited from the pagan philosophical universe, like the term *fortuna* the use of which he criticizes later on,[7] jarring with the profoundly religious and Christian universe he would prefer his readers' minds to dwell in. But the substance of the problem, and the continuing validity of the *dimissio* notion that responded to that problem, have not really been called into question.

His next criticism of interest to us touches on something the *Contra Academicos* said about the soul. *Securior rediturus in caelum*, he wrote then: the soul 'will return more securely to heaven." "I would have been safer in saying [*securius dixissem*]

7. *Retr* 1.1.2 and 1.3.2.

iturus rather than *rediturus*," Augustine admits; the soul "will go" rather than "will go back"—and that, "on account of those who think that human souls have fallen or been cast down from heaven, and thrust into these bodies by reason of their sinful deserts" (*putant animos humanos pro meritis peccatorum suorum de caelo lapsos sive deiectos in corpora ista detrudi*). He did not, Augustine assures us, hesitate to use the expression he used, for it could mean the soul would return to the God Who made it; Cyprian, after all, used similar expressions, and the author of Ecclesiastes tells us that "The spirit returns [*revertatur*] to the God Who gave it." But his own mode of expression "must of course be understood [*utique intelligendum est*] in such a way as not to contradict the Apostle when he says [of Esau and Jacob]: 'when not yet born, they had done nothing either good or evil.' " But on the question of the soul's origin, "how it came about that it is in a body"—whether creationism or traducianism be true—"I did not know then, nor do I know even now."[8]

Now, everything we have seen in this study makes one admire this masterpiece of careful statement. In reading it, we must not forget what Augustine has told us just above. His expression of Origen's theory still contains that telltale *detrudi*, but here he is using Romans 9:11 to undercut the precise "fall of the soul" feature in that theory, without any need to concentrate on its wider implications. "Apostolic authority" forbids our holding *the sort* of prenatal sin Origen supposed; there is no need to mention that prenatal sin as such is not excluded by that text, so long as the "merits" that brought us into "these" bodies, "attached" us to them, are not thought of as incurred by us living a "proper" kind of life, disembodied in the "heavens." Augustine would have been "safer" to avoid the expression "return," but only "safer"; he need not here enlarge on the fact that his own mature theory involves a different *kind* of soul's "return" in a quite literal sense of that term. The familiar text from Ecclesiastes, with its suggestive *revertatur*, may serve to excuse his own similar expression in the *Contra Academicos*. There is no need to mention that, as late as his *Letter 143*, to Marcellinus, he suggested an interpretation of the *dedit* in that

---

8. *Retr* 1.1.2. Augustine cannot resist using the pejorative *ista* when designating the sort of bodies we bear in this post-Adamic world. Compare the explanation of *ista sensibilia* further on, *Retr* 1.4.3.

text which strongly recalled his cherished *dimissio* motif, and viewed that *revertatur* as tilting the scales ever so slightly in favor of the theory—still an open possibility then—he now rejects. Nor is there any need to admit how much later than the *Contra Academicos* Augustine himself saw Romans 9:11 as possessing the demonstrative force he brings to bear now. He would urge us to "understand" what he had written a full thirty years afterward in such a way as not to "contradict" the interpretation of that text to which he came at the price of such long and hesitant labor. But what was his *original* intention when writing that *rediturus*? Augustine refrains from saying, one way or another. But the changes we have seen his mind go through on this "dangerous" question bid us to be very cautious.We may not simply suppose that the *Contra Academicos* originally meant what the aged Augustine—or we ourselves—would wish it had meant. We must clear our minds of questionable presuppositions, and read the work carefully for ourselves. The marvel is that the *Retractations* finds in it so few expressions to criticize.

But how can Augustine say that between creationism and traducianism he does not know even now which theory to choose? He may have *thought* once that he did know, but he has come to see he did not (*nec tunc sciebam*). But the same thing is literally true even now, for his personal suggestion toward the answer contains elements of both competing theories, yet in a unique combination that makes it both and neither. Our "ingredience" in Adam—as individual as well as Archetypal embodied "man"—has a traducianist ring, but what is needed over and above that ingredience is a later "creation"—not so much of individual "souls," apparently, as of the individualizing "forms" that endow us with our "proper" selfhoods. *Nec adhuc scio*: "I do not know even yet"; the statement is perfectly true. Indeed, it seems doubtful whether Augustine's is any longer a theory of the "origin of the soul" in the conventional sense supposed by both parties in the controversy; he may have come a good way toward explaining the origin of that "whole man" (*totus homo*) who, body and soul, was the incarnate subject of the "original sin."[9]

9. Again, Solignac's instincts on pp. 376–81 of his article "Homme Pécheur" are correct: Augustine's emphasis on the origin-of-soul problem, but also, I would add, his effort to deal with it in terms of the four hypotheses regnant at the time, blocks his way toward solving the connected problem of how we inherit sinfulness from Adam. But we see him here anticipating the *totus homo* considerations to which

Augustine's handling of the difficulties he found when reviewing his *Contra Academicos* already gives us a taste of the "manner" he will adopt at a number of points in his *Retractations*. Something very like that manner is illustrated in his treatment of the *Soliloquies*. He ought to have avoided (*cavendum fuit*) the expression *penitus ista sensibilia fugienda*, "we must flee entirely from these sensible realities," lest he be thought (*ne putaremur*) to be holding the theory of that false philosopher Porphyry, who taught that "we must flee from everything bodily." In his own defense he notes that he did say *ista*, "these," in the pejorative sense of "corruptible sense-realities," so that his expression need not import a flight from the kind of sensible realities that will exist in the "new earth and new heaven of the age to come"; but he ought to have been more explicit at the time (*hoc potius dicendum fuit*). He has "saved" his earlier expression; but he has told us nothing on the exact intent of that expression when he wrote it.[10]

But his next rejection is couched, as Bardy puts it, in far more "formal" terms. The reminiscence theory of the *Soliloquies* had allowed him to claim that learners in the liberal arts "bring forth and dig out again" (*eruunt . . . quodam modo refodiunt*) knowledge that is covered by forgetfulness; all such learning is therefore "remembering" what we once "knew." *Hoc quoque improbo*, Augustine stays firmly and flatly; "I disapprove of this also." Plato and others like him, he explains, were of the opinion that "unlearned" people, when properly questioned—the slave boy in the *Meno* obviously comes to mind—could reply with true answers on such subjects (like geometry); this seemed to indicate that they "had known [those truths] at some time [in the past] and forgotten them." But there is a more credible—*Credibilius*—explanation: that the "light of eternal reason, where they see these things as true," need not be supposed as something they glimpsed in their past, but "is present to them to the extent they are capable of receiving it." This, he advises his readers, is substantially the explanation of the remi-

---

Julian of Eclanum eventually forces him: see *JulImp* 5.4.17 (not, as Solignac writes, 5.5.16). But pursuit of this insight would have put the question to Augustine's stubborn determination to view the soul as "spiritual" in a substantialist sense of that term.

10. *Retr* 1.4.3.

niscence phenomenon he proposed in his *De Trinitate*, Book 12.[11] As indeed, we saw, he did.

But what was Augustine's intention when writing this phrase in the *Soliloquies*? One need only consult his *Letter 7*, to Nebridius, which is roughly contemporary with the Cassiciacum dialogues, to find him stoutly defending the view that "memory" in the proper sense of the term implies just such a "past vision" of "eternally present realities" as his comment here seems, but *only seems*, to be denying. Indeed, Augustine has made his work of criticism easy for himself, by alluding to the earlier sort of reminiscence theory Plato briefly entertains in the *Meno*, a theory which would involve our having lived a former life "in these bodies." But this is neither the *Phaedo* nor the *Phaedrus* theory on which Plotinus drew, and gradually refined in writing his *Enneads*. That theory, in bald terms, implies exactly the "past-ness" of our "vision" and the simultaneous "presence" of the "eternal realities" that still illumine our minds in their "fallen," embodied state. And this, I still submit, is exactly the theory—in which "memory" from the unfallen past is at bottom one and the same as persisting "illumination" in our fallen present—which Augustine embodied in the *Soliloquies*. His substitution of the *Meno* theory has all the airs of a tactical distraction to screen the more precise question that is at issue; the incredible confusion his comment here has begotten in the minds of many an excellent scholar bears witness that he succeeded.[12] How "scrupulous," in Father Russell's phrase, is the author of the *Retractations*? Here, at all events, one may not accuse him of excessive candor.

Soon afterward, he issues another warning bearing on reminiscence theory. He had proposed in his *De quantitate animae* that the soul brought all the *artes* with it into this life, so that "learning" (*discere*) is nothing other than "remembering and recalling" (*reminisci ac recordari*). That phrase, Augustine warns, is "not to be taken as implying approval" (*non accipiendum est quasi ex hoc approbetur*) of the teaching that the soul at some time lived, either "here" in another body or "elsewhere either in a body or without

11. *Retr* 1.4.4. Bardy's characterization of these remarks is from BA 12, p. 144.
12. See my note on "Letter 7" in REA, 15 (1969), 67–73, and the subsequent note on "Pre-Existence."

one," so that responses like that of the slave boy in Plato's *Meno* point to his having "learned them before in some other life" (*in alia vita ante didicisse*). The phenomenon can be explained, he goes on to assure us, as he later explained it in the *De Trinitate*; besides, there are obviously some *artes*, like much of medicine and all of astrology, which involve much more than the grasp of intelligible realities, so that there is no substitute, in them, for experiential learning.[13]

Now Augustine's earlier smoke screen has parted somewhat. We are given a glimpse of a reminiscence theory which would imply a past vision of intelligible realities in "another life," possibly lived "without a body"; here in our embodied lives we would still retain the "memory" that would enable us to "learn" at least those *artes* that deal in purely intelligible connections. Augustine would not have us "accept" his earlier expressions as implying approval even of this more "Plotinian" (and *later* "Platonic") version of reminiscence. But has he merely changed his earlier view, and is that the most natural "acceptance" we would normally bring to those expressions as they occur in the context of the *De quantitate*? Our only resort is to read that earlier work with this more sharpened question in mind.

Augustine's final two comments on the "origin of the soul" refer to his *Letter 166*, to Jerome, and to his later refutation of the hapless Vincentius Victor.[14] He was, he assures us, "consulting" Jerome, and in the second instance "defending" his right to remain as uncertain on the question as Jerome's well-guarded silence left him. But we have seen the fuller story of his growing doubts about this question, as well as the evidence for thinking he was not always so hesitant about his views as later events compelled him to become. These two observations need not detain us further.

It would be tempting to extend this inspection of the *Retractations* into Augustine's expressions implying a certain "divinity" of the soul; his repeated suggestions that the "wise man" can be perfectly happy even during this life if only he live in accordance with what is highest and "best" in him, his mind; his claim that there is more than one "way" to arrive at Wisdom, and so on.[15] His em-

---

13. *Retr* 1.8.2.
14. *Retr* 2.45 and 46, respectively.
15. These are among the connected assemblage of features that betray Augustine's early anthropology as "Plotinian" in inspiration. It is perhaps understandable that

barrassment on rereading such expressions is real; they, and a
number of others to which he does not call our attention, are symptomatic of a theory I submit he once held, but now is anxious to
warn us against adopting.

For this anxious concern appears to have been uppermost in
Augustine's mind when writing about this "dangerous" question
in his *Retractations*. He has "expressly repudiated" the "fallen
soul" theory, as Father Russell's objection would have him do; he
has never lied or distorted the truth in any way; he simply has not
told all the truth he could have. A more modern understanding of
the term "retractation" would demand of him a greater candor,
perhaps verging on something like self-laceration. But for an influ-
ential bishop, still hip-deep in the fires of the Pelagian controversy,
and whose primary concern was sustaining the orthodox belief of his
flock, that more modern approach would have involved a trace of
self-indulgence that Augustine could ill afford. "Scrupulous" this
entire performance may not seem to contemporary eyes, but scruples
can be tyrannical masters. Say, rather, that the entire procedure was
apostolically effective and responsible, prudent and discreet—in
a word, "conscientious." With that wiliest of debaters, Julian of
Eclanum, hotly eager to seize on any stick to thwack him with,
Augustine could easily have thought it foolish to be anything else
than that.

There is little new in this interpretation of Augustine's procedure
in the *Retractations*. Long ago, Gustav Bardy warned us of how
risky a business it would be to assume that Augustine's expressions
of dissatisfaction, or outright disapproval, always enlighten us on
the original intention behind the texts he is correcting. As Bardy
remarks on two of the texts we have considered, "the manner in
which they are explained in the *Retractations* does not instruct us so
much as we would like on their original meaning." [16] *Hoc quoque
improbo*, Augustine can say in one instance, and the very style
of his retractation gives us to suspect that the text in question can
scarcely be interpreted except as implying the very reminiscence

---

critics have chosen to aim their fire at the central claim I have made, that Augustine
thinks of us as "fallen souls," but there is much more involved than that core doctrine. For evidence that other scholars, Oliver DuRoy and André Mandouze among
them, have pointed to such features of Augustine's early views without succeeding in
identifying them as Plotinian, see *Platonism*, pp. 13–15, 18–20, and notes.

16. BA 12, p. 144.

doctrine, with its implications of pre-existence, that he now warns his readers to avoid. But *non accipiendum, cavendum fuit, dixissem securius,* here his language is more guarded; Augustine never comes right out to say he *did not then* intend to convey the meaning he now, years later, finds reprehensible or suspect. What apostolic purpose would it have served?

John Burnaby, in his brief but luminous study of the *Retractationes,* years ago called attention to the very tendency I am alluding to. Augustine starts by announcing his intention to "censor" his earlier works with *iudiciaria severitas,* the severity of a judge; a modern expects the bulk of his remarks to take the style of *reprehensio.* Yet as he went on, Augustine allowed other motives to encroach upon that original one. Burnaby points to several unmistakable instances where Augustine can "slip from *reprehensio* to *defensio,*" a reprehension in one locus, a defense in the next, despite the fact that it is manifestly a question of the same "error" in both. "[I]t was inevitable," Burnaby goes on to point out, that with this process in full swing, "defence should too often take the form of that same kind of forced interpretation" as Augustine, and other Fathers, were in the habit of using with respect to texts of Scripture. The result, in Burnaby's terms, was that Augustine "becomes *acceptor personae suae*; the *iudiciaria severitas* is sadly relaxed." [17]

"Sadly," I am now inclined to think, may be too strong a term; Augustine might legitimately have rewritten it "prudently." He is reviewing his earlier works in the light of much that he has learned since, dexterously suggesting distinctions and applying Scriptural interpretations that were clearly not part of his intellectual armory years before, all in the interests of extracting what poisonous barbs he was now, after years of experience, in a position to see embedded in his more youthful writings. Those years had been punishing years, scored with agonies of doubt and protracted, stubborn hesitation. *Defendi cunctationem meam.* Laying bare what his original intentions had been could have done considerably more harm than good. He has come to see, specifically, this question of the soul's origin as a "most dangerous" one; equally dangerous, I submit, he came to see his earlier "answer" to that question. I question whether Burnaby's adverb accurately measures that sense of danger Augus-

<hr/>

17. See "The *Retractationes* of St. Augustine: Self-Criticism or Apologia?," in AM I, pp. 85–92; the final judgment quoted is from pp. 89–91.

tine felt about it, and about other questions that could still divide
believers of the time. But aside from that, both Bardy and Burnaby
leave us with a sobering conclusion: the *Retractations* hardly represent a reliable school for learning what Augustine said and meant to
say in those early works. Indeed, the reverse may be true: a careful
reading of those works may be one of the best schools for learning
how to read the *Retractations*.

But what holds true for his earlier works holds equally for the
later writings studied here. What Augustine wrote, he wrote, and
no inferences drawn from the *Retractations* can succeed in unwrit-
ing it. Our souls are sin-laden from before conception in our
mothers' wombs, guilty with a guilt we could never have contracted
in our "proper" lives, guilty because we were one in and with
Adam, *were* Adam in his primal act of sinning.

How, then, are we to understand that sweeping *nec tunc sciebam,
nec adhuc scio* of his *Retractations*? Perhaps Augustine is simply
warning us that the final theory he elaborated on the subject was
the best he could do, but not to be taken as Gospel truth. But this
will not entitle us to deny that it was his theory, one on which he
toiled tenaciously from the year 417 on. For Pelagianism had convinced him that the Church required *some* explanation of how
each of us, as infants yet incapable of sinning "on our own," still
stood in need of the baptismal grace of Christ to bring us home
again to God.

APPENDIX

PLOTINUS AND AUGUSTINE'S FINAL THEORY OF SOUL

THE PLOTINIAN HALLMARK on St. Augustine's final theory of our relationship to Adam is, I have suggested above, unmistakable. To help the reader evaluate that suggestion, I must first clarify what I suppose in making it, and what I do and do not mean by it.

First, I suppose what I have tried to prove elsewhere: that Augustine very early both read and reflected on many more than the "very few books" of Plotinus to which some scholars still imagine he was restricted. Secondly, I suppose that his readings and reflections were inspired by the confidence that he would find Plotinian thought-ways for the most part congenial to the task he set himself from Cassiciacum forward, the understanding of the Biblical faith much in the "spiritual" cast it had been preached to him by Ambrose of Milan. Finally, I assume the reader will accept, for the sake of argument at least, that among the *Enneads* familiar to Augustine one may list treatises 4.3–5, on the soul; 6.4–5, on omnipresence; and 5.8, on intellectual beauty.[1]

So much for my assumptions; now to the import of my claim. The relationship between the individual human and the Archetypal Man of Plotinus' overworld is a nettling one, and contemporary scholars, with all their technical mastery at the ready, find it difficult to agree on the matter.[2] But even did they agree entirely,

1. Justification for appeal to these treatises can be found in *Early Theory*, pp. 6–10, 31–86, and 152–83. On the inclusion of *Ennead* 5.8, see my further observations in *Platonism*, passim, but especially notes 47 to 62.

2. For the latest *status quaestionis* on this issue, see the article by A. H. Armstrong, "Form, Individual, and Person in Plotinus," in *Dionysius*, 1 (1977), 49–68. Armstrong takes up a highly technical discussion inaugurated by scholars like Rist, Blumenthal, and Igal, and mounts a strong argument for the consistency of Plotinus' thought on

it would be a serious mistake to judge the "Plotinian" character of Augustine's own view by the yardstick of what contemporary scholars would require. For Augustine neither was, nor was profoundly interested in being, a "Plotinian" in that technical sense; his shaky knowledge of Greek, and his relatively amateur acquaintance with the resources of Greek philosophy Plotinus was bringing into play, would have made that impossible for him even were it what he most desired. But more pertinently, his interest in Plotinus, and in other thinkers as well, was both selective and highly focused: he concentrated purposefully on those elements of their thinking which he found serving his task of understanding the faith—or more precisely, understanding the reality the lines of which, he trusted, both the Biblical faith and all true philosophy presented for acceptance by reflective human beings.

In the case of our relationship with Adam, Augustine, I submit, would interest himself much less in trying to ferret out a theory which would mark him as a competent and faithful disciple of Plotinus than in choosing, from the *Enneads* that promised to serve him, those elements he hoped would aid him to think out that relationship in the terms which he believed his faith imposed upon him—in this instance, his *fundatissima fides* in our universal need for the remission of sins accorded by baptism in Christ. He would feel free to adapt what he found in Plotinus, but his having found those elements in the *Enneads* would at the same time encourage him in thinking that the "understanding" he had come to merited serious consideration by reflective believers.

Where, in the *Enneads*, would he be tempted to look for those elements? At this point in my argument, we would seem to launch out into the depths of conjecture. While everything I have proposed to this point can, I am convinced, be supported by careful study of Augustine's actual practice, the evidential base for what I am now to propose is admittedly more slippery. But there are several considerations which may help to establish boundaries to conjecture, and keep it in fairly reliable touch with the realities.

First, Augustine was likely to have gone back to the Plotinian

---

this relationship. Note that while concentrating on whether forms of "individuals" *exist* in Plotinus' overworld, Armstrong and company nonetheless suggest which *Enneads* would best illuminate the question of our relationship to the "Ideal Man." But they also illustrate how difficult it is, even for contemporary scholarship, to decide what is "Plotinian" in cases like this.

treatises that were already familiar to him, and which influenced—positively, he must have thought—his earlier thinking on the question at hand. We may have confirmatory evidence for this suggestion in the fact that, when writing his *De Genesi ad litteram* compelled him to question his early *dimissio* insight, he appears to have reconsulted the very section of *Ennead* 4.3 which initially furnished him with the vehicle for expressing that insight.[3]

But further confirmation may be found in the peculiar coincidence whereby contemporary scholarship points to three Plotinian treatises that bear most directly on the issue that concerns us here: three treatises for which there is persuasive evidence that they influenced Augustine's early thinking on our relationship, as temporal-historical individuals, with that atemporal figure, the Plotinian Archetypal "Man." I have already mentioned them above: *Enneads* 4.3–5, 5.8, and 6.4–5.

Consider first *Ennead* 4.3. There Augustine would have renewed his longtime familiarity with that pecular relationship Plotinus establishes between our individual souls and Soul Universal: we are like parts without actually being parts of that unique Soul, distinct both from it and from each other, but at the same time not truly divided off from either. In matters like these, Augustine would have been reminded, the understanding must be prepared for paradoxical solutions. But division and multiplicity, he would also have been reminded, are more dominant in this lower world of our fallen experience, whereas the higher world is dominated by their opposites, unity and undividedness. Even "here" it remains *truer* to say that our souls are all one than to say they are many; but "there" that unity is far more real-ized than it ever could be here. Plotinus here is supposing what he had already proved in a previous treatise, *Ennead* 4.9. Augustine, for his part, had early shown his sensitivity to this view about the unity of our souls despite the apparent division attendant on our fallenness, in *De quantitate animae* 69. However much of a shock it is to our accustomed thought-ways when Augustine assures us we are one with Adam, and even implies that our unity with him is more real than our individual diversity from him, there is nothing outrageous in such a statement to one who has gone to Plotinus' school.

That paradoxical unity of beings in the overworld was familiar

3. See above, chap. 8, at note 40.

to Augustine from the treatise we shall next examine: *Ennead* 5.8. But from this point forward the exact wording of Plotinus' text assumes critical importance. For *Ennead* 5.8, I shall take as my base the translation by A. H. Armstrong; but for the treatises from the Sixth *Ennead*, which have not yet been published in Armstrong's translation, I shall go back to the Greek of the Henry–Schwyzer critical edition, and consult the translations made by Stephen MacKenna, Emile Bréhier, and Richard Harder,[4] in hopes of conflating as literal a translation as possible. That method offers the best chance of capturing what Augustine would have read in the Latin translation, presumably by Marius Victorinus, which nourished his reflections.

The texts I present are selected with a purpose. They all have to do, of course, with what Plotinus says about the relationship we bear as temporal individuals to that Ideal or Archetypal Man that is one aspect of Augustine's final view of Adam; but they are also selected with the more precise purpose of illuminating the steps through which Augustine's mind could conceivably, perhaps even plausibly, have gone toward expressing that relationship in terms of the distinction whose import concerns us: between the *propria vita* each of us lives as historical individuals and the "common life" he envisaged our once having lived "in" and, indeed, "as" Adam. Hence, I shall present a number of texts, but all from two treatises familiar to Augustine, whose expression of that relationship of Ideal to historical man may have tempted Marius Victorinus to employ the term *proprium*, or something very akin to it. Augustine's thinking, I am more and more convinced, was far more word-centered than has always been acknowledged.

The procedure may initially seem arbitrary. On what grounds could one argue that here, or there, Victorinus would have felt obliged to use the term *proprium*, or some variant sufficiently akin to it, as to "key" Augustine's word-sensitive style of thinking? Put that abstractly, the obstacle seems insuperable. But we shall see, in

4. See *Plotini opera*, edd. Paul Henry and Hans-Rudolph Schwyzer, 3 vols. (Oxford: Oxford University Press, 1982); *The Enneads*, trans. Stephen MacKenna, 3rd ed. (London: Faber & Faber, 1962); *Les Ennéades*, trans. Emile Bréhier, 6 vols. in 7 (Paris: "Les Belles Lettres," 1924–1938); and *Plotins Schriften*, trans. Richard Harder, 5 vols. (Hamburg: Meiner, 1956). The translation of *Ennead* 5.8 is taken from *Plotinus*, trans. A. H. Armstrong, 3 vols. (Cambridge: Harvard University Press, 1966–1984).

a number of concrete cases, that it can be gotten round, and quite persuasively.

In any case, the second treatise to which contemporary scholars point to illuminate the relationship of our individualities to the Ideal is *Ennead* 5.8. There Plotinus describes our once-blissful state in his overworld. "There," he explains to us (5.8.4), each being sees

> all things, not those to which coming to be, but those to which real being belongs, and they see themselves in other things; for all things there are transparent, and there is nothing dark or opaque; everything and all things are clear to the inmost part to everything, for light is transparent to light.
>
> Each there has everything in itself and sees all things in every other, so that all are everywhere and each and every one is all and the glory is unbounded [4.4–8].

"Here," on the contrary, in our visible world,

> one part would [not]⁵ come from another part, and each would be only a part; but there each comes only [or: eternally?] from the whole and is part and whole at once; it has the appearance of a part, but a penetrating look sees the whole in it, supposing that someone had the sort of sight which it is said that Lynceus had, who saw into the inside of the earth, a story that speaks in riddles of the eyes which they have there [4.21–24].

One consequence of this dominance of unity over diversity, Plotinus goes on to point out, is that the bliss these beings enjoy is not mutually exclusive, for "things are not different from each other so as to make what belongs to one displeasing to another with different characteristics [or: proper-ties]" (4.29–30). It is only once we have "become [a] man" that we have "ceased to be the All"; but once we have "ceased to be a man," we shall once more "belong to the whole [or: All]" and again administer the Cosmos entire (7.32–35).

Now, Augustine early established a connection between our having "fallen" out of the desire to possess something exclusively "our own"—something that would "belong to us" and not to others

---

5. The text of Henry and Schwyzer has a "not" (οὐκ) which Armstrong translates, but which Bréhier omits and Harder brackets, as I have done here; but their note *in loc.* (II 274, line 21) explains the matter in such a way that the same sense results as Armstrong, Bréhier, and Harder elicit from the text. Here, part is only part; "there" each part is the whole.

—and our having been relegated by that fall to possession, and governance, of some "part" or "particular fragment" of the universe we once blissfully governed "in common" with others and as a "whole."[6] That "proper" part of the universe, however, is clearly the mortal body each of us now bears, the body which, as we have seen, makes us incarnate individuals, using senses and living our own temporal "proper" life. If he reconsulted this treatise during the process of hammering out his *propria vita* distinction, one would expect all these connections, already familiar to him, to have come to the fore.

But apart from setting the background for what was eventually implied in his notion of *propria vita*, these two treatises fail to suggest many specifics toward illuminating the precise avenues of its elaboration. Suppose, hypothetically, that Augustine found it useful to reconsult the *Enneads*. Our question must now take a far more specific turn: What help would he have found toward thinking out our relationship, as individuals living our *propria vita*—our "very own" incarnate and temporal lives—with Adam? In answering that question, it must be borne in mind that if Augustine's faith is to be adequately understood, Adam must now function in a double role: he must be not only the Ideal Man, atemporal and pre-temporal Archetype for all our individual humanities, but somehow, also, the historico-temporal individual from whom all our individualities are generated in time.

It may seem surprising, but the richest contribution to the *propria vita* notion could well have, and perhaps did, come from one of Augustine's longtime favorites, the double treatise on omnipresence: *Ennead* 6.4–5. There Plotinus is striving mightily to help us transcend all imaginative ways of thinking, in order to understand in appropriate fashion how every item of the intelligible world can be *integrally* present to every item of the lower sense-world. His thesis obviously applies to the Ideas of his Second Hypostasis, Νοῦς; but again and again, by illustration and by argument, he applies the same rules to the soul's presence to the bodily world, as well. Keeping in mind that this was the nub of Augustine's problem, I shall in the following texts speak of Plotinus' prescriptions as applying to the soul in its relationship to individual bodies.

One of the commanding rules for understanding omnipresence

6. See *Early Theory*, pp. 177–81.

may seem paradoxical: for the soul to be omnipresent *to*—not *in*—
the body, it must "keep its distance," so to speak, "remain in itself,"
and never enter into such an intimate relationship to the body as
to become the form, possession, or "property," of the body. Plotinus
most regularly expresses the excessively intimate communion of
soul with body by using the lapidary genitive: the soul must not be
thought of as becoming "the body's," or something "of" the body's.
But translators, anxious to alert us to what the genitive implies in
context, frequently find themselves compelled to employ less condensed and more explicit forms of expression. Consider Plotinus'
early statement of this law, in *Ennead* 6.4.3: if any item of the Real
world, including soul,

> became the form of some particular thing, it would cease to be the
> all, to be entirely in itself; it would be, as accident [the property?
> possession?], of another. Since it is not [the property or possession]
> of any of them, and since [those other] beings aspire [rather] to be
> its, it approaches as nearly as can be to those it wishes;[7] but it does
> not become [the property or possession] of this one any more than
> of that one, but remains the aspired-after [6.4.3.12–17].

In this translation, Plotinus' genitives are reproduced with brutal
literality. It is easy to understand why translators would find the
result intolerably awkward. And so, where I submit only tentative
suggestions within brackets, we find Mackenna employing such
terms as "belong to," become the "property of," the "chattel of,"
the body possessing the soul by "appropriation." Bréhier is forced
to similar shifts, the soul becoming "l'être d'une autre chose," so
that it "appartient" to one being rather than to another, and, indeed, "à elle seule," with that exclusivity that makes it, in Augustine's sense, the *proprium* of that being. Harder does the same job
with terms like "gehören," "angehören," and "Eigentum." Is it too
wild to conjecture that Marius Victorinus, too, would have appealed to similar "property" terms? That same ideal relationship
between lower and higher Plotinus sketches in the image of "Erôs
waiting at the door" (6.5.10)—in a section that burned its way into
Augustine's imagination, and became the climax of that first

7. Again, the text established by Henry and Schwyzer differs from Bréhier's, but
their note *in loc.* (III 139, lines 15–16) admits they are proposing a doubtful version:
locus nondum sanatus. Harder relies on a Greek version different from both the
above, but the resulting translation agrees with Bréhier's and with the one I give here.

344 THE ORIGIN OF THE SOUL

lengthy *exercitatio animi* on the *proprium/commune* antithesis he executed in the second book of the *De libero arbitrio*. That image he connected, in that early work, with an embroidered version of one found further on in the very same paragraph of this treatise: for there Plotinus excludes the illusion that our pursuit of the beatifying good is like that of a crowd of people pushing each other out of the way to get at that good (6.5.10.47–48).[8] It is scarcely a great imaginative leap to conjecture that Augustine connected this mode of thinking with what he had found in *Ennead* 5.8: that the community-in-identity of souls in the overworld precluded their possessing the object of their beatifying contemplation as their exclusive "property."[9]

Plotinus returns tirelessly to stress the non-possessive character of the omnipresence relationship implied in a genuine notion of "participation." Here, however, is an instance where his lapidary genitive yields to more explicit expression: when any lower reality participates in higher, it does not mean "receiving some portion of that reality, since it belongs to none of them as ἰδίου αὐτὸς ὄντος" (6.4.8.41–42). No conscientious translator can avoid that term ἰδίου. So Mackenna translates with the term "appropriated"; Bréhier, with "appartenir en propre"; and Harder, with "Sondereigentum." Could Marius Victorinus have used anything but some such "proper-ty" term?

But the alert reader must have noticed that all these variants on "property" terms seem to be working, thus far at least, in exactly the *opposite* sense from the one required for my argument. For Plotinus, in the grip of his omnipresence insight, is regularly excluding the soul's becoming a "property" of the individual body, whereas Augustine's earlier depictions of the soul's fall have the soul taking on the individual body as *its* "property." So, in his later thinking, he is consistent in stressing that our "proper life" begins when the soul is individualized through receiving "its very own" body. Would Augustine have found any encouragement here for *reversing* that property relationship?

---

8. See *Lib* 2.20–25, 33–38, and *Early Theory*, pp. 51–58.
9. Augustine uses the paradigm of our higher senses and their ability to *know*, i.e., see and hear the entirety of any common object of attention, despite our individuality. The paradigm was suggested, however, by Plotinus himself, who observes: "So our many eyes can all take in the same undivided spectacle; our many ears all hear the totality of the same spoken word" (6.4.12.1–8).

That encouragement comes when Plotinus himself is compelled to reconcile the soul's "remaining in itself" with the possibility (which he seems so far virtually to have *excluded*) that our souls have "come down," "fallen," into this realm of particularity. Toward that reconciliation we are about to watch him labor now.

For excluding any such "property" relationship provokes an objection. How would the soul of *this* body be distinguished from the soul of *that*? "By what is added on [to the essence of soul in each of them]" (6.4.6.4–5), Plotinus replies.

Paradoxical notion, that; a diminishing addition. Plotinus must further clarify it. He does so in the closing paragraph of *Ennead* 6.5, while stressing one final time the theme of our true and primal one-ness. How then, his "objector" asks, are we to experience the Omnipresent? Plotinus answers:

> in that you have entered the All, and do not remain in some part of It. Nor do you say [of yourself] "This much [of the universe] is me"; but leaving aside [or behind] all "this-muchness," you become the All. And yet, you were that [All] from the first. But because some other thing was added to you, that addition diminished you; for that addition came, not from Being—one cannot add anything to Being—but from non-being. Having [thus] become some-one and [become that] out of non-being, you are not the All until you put aside that non-being. You become greater, therefore, by putting aside the others . . . [6.5.12.16–24].

For, he reminds his reader again, the All does not have to "come" to us, since it was we who "departed"—departed, not in the sense of going someplace else, but, all the while "present to It, you have turned yourself around to [Its] opposites" (6.5.12.28).

But still another objection has to be faced: for if soul is one, and everywhere the same soul, how does each body have its own "proper" soul (ἴδια) (6.4.14.1)? "Proper" is more exact than Mac-Kenna's "particular"; Bréhier translates "en propre"; and Harder, "seine eigene." In reply, Plotinus first emphasizes that he will not compromise on the unity of soul. There is not, he insists, a real "division" or "sharing-out" of that unique soul; rather "it *appears* to the recipient that there is such a division" or sharing-out (6.4. 14.13–14).

But this seems to contradict much of what he had written elsewhere about the "descent" or "fall" of the soul into a relationship very like this "proprietary" association with some "part" of the universe. How can his omnipresence insight be reconciled with that classic teaching? Now, it may be that contemporary scholars could successfully argue that Plotinus is entirely consistent on this point; but his re-expression of the "fall" from this omnipresence stand-point seems to have a certain embarrassed tone to it. So, at least, consciously or otherwise, Augustine may have read it.

For Plotinus now explains (6.4.16) that the soul does not "come down" into the body; it is, rather, the corporeal nature that rises like an intruder, as it were, to a more intimate form of communion with the soul. "So, the 'coming down' of the soul [means] that the soul comes to be in the body, as [older philosophers] speak of it as coming to be in the body." And yet, this "coming to be in the body" must, he insists, be understood in the sense of the soul's

> giving to the body something of itself, without, however, becoming [the property?] of the body's. . . . But that [closer] communion with the body is [an] evil, and release from it [a] good. Why? Because although the soul [in this communion relationship] is not [a property] of the body's, it is said nonetheless to be the soul of *this* [body]; thus it becomes in some fashion particularized soul, having come out of the All [6.4.14–24].

In this fallen condition, Plotinus goes on to admit, the soul's activity is not directed toward the All, as it formerly was and should have remained. And now, in language very like his earlier language for the "fall," he describes the soul as having "broken away," "leapt down," from the All, so that it becomes taken up with the governance of that fragment of the universe, its own part-icular body. This interpretation of the "fall," however, must be read in the light of what he had written two sections earlier:

> Before we had our becoming here we existed There, men of another sort [ἄλλοι], . . . pure souls and intelligences united to the entirety of Being, parts of the Intelligible [World]; but parts not separated or cut off from each other, but all [of them] of that Whole. Even now, we are not separated [off from each other], but another man, desirous of existing, approached that [Ideal] Man that we were, and he has wrapped himself about us and added himself on to that Man that each of us was, then. . . . [A]nd we have become this coupling [of two men], we are no longer Him we were before; and sometimes, when the First Man is no longer

active and is, in a sense, no longer present, we are only the second man we added on to the first [6.4.14.17–31].

Here again we see Plotinus faithful to his stress on the primal unity of our souls in the overworld, and to that corollary of the omnipresence insight: that the soul does not so much "come down" as the "inferior" ascend intrusively to take possession of it, insofar as that is possible. But this "diminishing addition" has now been portrayed in ultra-vivid terms: it is an "other" man that adds himself on to the Ideal Man that is our primal reality, "wrapping himself about" that Ideal Man to produce a monstrous kind of συνάμφω. This "double man," this Jekyll–Hyde, is what we have now become—and sometimes only Hyde! The omnipresence insight, which seemed originally to preclude the soul's ever entering such a relationship, has given way to a very much "closer communion" indeed, and one which Plotinus was justified in deeming an "evil." Yes, he will remind us nervously, even in this new situation the soul is not truly "[property] of the body," but some of the sting seems to have gone out of his earlier assurances. In any event, the gap between "fall" and "omnipresence" styles of thought seems to have closed considerably. The soul is "said" to be the soul of "this" body—and rightly. For it has become "in some fashion particularized"; it has in some fashion "come out of the All" and become preoccupied with governing a fragment of the lower world, the body which, Augustine would have felt entitled to translate, has become its "very own," its "property" (proprium). The relationship of soul as body's property is beginning to call forth its reciprocal. Once readmit the possibility of some "closer" and "evil" communion of soul with body—a possibility required if one is to think of the soul as "fallen"—and the particularized soul does become something much closer to the "property" of its individual, particularized body, after all. And once that has occurred, it becomes newly possible, even unavoidable, to think of that particular body as the soul's "very own," its exclusive "property."

But there were also rich suggestions in that notion of the "double man." We were all originally that single Ideal Man; but now we have become this strange amalgam of Ideal wrapped around by an "other" man. Plotinus obviously does not mean to suggest that our identity with that Ideal Man is thoroughly severed or abolished, but the experience of fallen particularity compels him to admit that there are times when that Ideal Man seems to be so inactive as to be almost "absent." One in and with Adam as Ideal Man, Augustine could translate for the purposes of his problem, we have become "particularized" to the extent that our one-ness with Adam fades entirely from consciousness. But our being this "other" man, distinct from Adam, does not militate against our also being in our deepest reality identical with Adam; *fuimus ille unus*, and, indeed, we still "are" that First Man.

This, however, was not Plotinus' final bout with that problem of particularity. In *Ennead* 6.5.6 he is brought to wrestle with it once again:

> It is as though the [Ideal] Man, having come [down] into some particular man, became that man, but still remained the [Ideal] Man. The material man, derived from the unity of the [Ideal] Man, produces [by generation] many men identical with himself, all in accord with the Idea [of Man], and the same single reality is [ingredient] in many, somewhat like the one stamp of a [same] seal upon many [6.5.6.6–11].

That way of envisaging our particularity, though, may well have become associated in Augustine's mind with one Plotinus presents shortly afterward, in 6.5.7.

"We," and all that is "ours," go back, reductively it would seem, to "the [one] Being." We go back to It as from It we came. We are, all of us, Beings, all of the same Beings; indeed, "we are all one." Why, then, do we remain ignorant of that unity? Because, Plotinus replies, we "look outward," to the "outside" of the single Being in which we, all of us, root. Then, in a striking image that left its mark on Augustine's imagination earlier, Plotinus likens our individual selves to "many faces turned outward, all having, were we to look inward, [the same] one head" (6.5.7.10–11). But did one receive a lucky "tug at the hair" from Athena, say, one would, turned inward, see that unity of all with all.

That remarkable image of many faces but one head, I have argued elsewhere, along with the "tug of the hair" that would twist our heads about again, made a deep impression on the Augustine who wrote the *Confessions*.[10] But there may also be a suggestive analogue of it in his *Letter 190* 15: writing to Optatus in 418 on the origin

10. See *Early Theory*, pp. 62–63 and 68–70.

of our souls, he speculates about whether God made all our souls
from the one soul of that First Man, "as He fashioned men's individual faces but from the body of that First Man" (*sicut fingit singillatim facies hominum, ex uno tamen corpore hominis primi*).

But however sound that suggestion may be, it does point to a
kinship between these two depictions of our relationship to that
First Man, one that may well have permitted Augustine to round
out his own thought on the matter. For we are, to begin with, all
that Ideal Man, but at the same time different outward-looking
"faces" on that single "head," each of our individualities like so
many "imprints" from that single "seal."

But that Ideal Man too, Plotinus suggests (less guardedly than
he might have wished?), may be thought of as having "come down
into some particular man," indeed, as having "become that man,"
and then as having generated the whole procession of other historical individual humans we know as the race sprung from his loins.
So, Augustine would have been encouraged to conclude, Adam the
Ideal can indeed become Adam the historical individual as well;
he, too, can take on a "proper life," and in that proper life generate
the entire cortège of proper lives, each individual and so distinct
from him as historical individual, yet each, in their deepest reality,
identical with him as the Ideal Man he "still remained." But if that
Ideal Man "came down," he must have existed as Ideal Man "before" his coming down inexorably resulted in his entering upon
his "proper" temporal life.[11] And if we ourselves came down with
him, and in his very coming, we too did that in virtue of our identity with him as Ideal Man, but equally "before" we received the
proper lives transmitted to us by generation[12] from that "double
man" which Adam and, later in His own way, Christ, quite
uniquely were. "We" sinned, but "before" we had become a genuine "we." For as Augustine puts it, *fuimus ille unus*; we were "that
one man." Hence, our sin must have been one with the sin of that
Ideal Man—a sin as "common," therefore, as the bliss we once shared
when we were, not yet our proper selves, but only him.

11. Both Plotinus and Augustine, when arguing in strictest terms, would question
whether the soul's supra-temporal existence should be thought of as "before" its
temporal state; I am here alluding to Augustine's use of the term *nondum* in *Civ.*
13.14, where some kind of anteriority is implied.
12. *Civ* 13.14 refers to the "creation" of our "individual forms"; but that divine
creative act, one assumes, must somehow be associated with the generative act of
Adam and subsequent human parents.

Plotinus, it may be, had suggested here the finishing touches to the saga of human history Augustine had so long and hesitantly labored to decipher. It may be, but did it actually happen as I have conjectured? To make a claim that bold would be close to madness. But that point, I submit, may remain secondary for our purposes.

For the essential point I mean to make by this conjectural reconstruction is this: that the interpretation I have presented, out of Augustine's own text, of what he implied by our "proper lives" was one which the intellectual atmosphere of his time would have found entirely plausible, even respectable. And, secondly, but definitely in second place, there is the fact that all the materials for this reconstruction come from a limited number of *Enneads*, all of which we can confidently claim Augustine had read and pondered. And, thirdly, the *De Genesi* hints clearly that he reconsulted *Ennead* 4.3, while in the *De civitate* he not only refers to, but actually quotes from, the *Enneads*.

All this suggests strongly that Augustine's elaboration of his *propria vita* notion and of its implicits could have taken *some such* route *like* the one I have proposed. In that event, the hallmark of his final theory seems unmistakably Plotinian, after all.

BIBLIOGRAPHY

Armstrong, A. H. "Form, Individual, and Person in Plotinus." *Diony-sius*, 1 (1977), 49–68.

Bonner, Gerald. *St. Augustine of Hippo: Life and Controversies*. London: SCM, 1963.

Boyer, Charles, s.j. "Dieu pouvait-il créer l'homme dans l'état d'ignorance et de difficulté?" *Essais sur la doctrine de saint Augustin*. Paris: Beauchesne, 1932.

Brown, Peter. *Augustine of Hippo*. Berkeley: University of California Press, 1967.

Burnaby, John. "The *Retractationes* of St. Augustine: Self-Criticism or Apologia?" AM I. Pp. 85–92.

Chevalier, Irénée. *Augustin et la pensée grecque: Les relations Trinitaires*. Fribourg: Librairie de l'Université, 1940.

Courcelle, Pierre. *Les Lettres grecques en Occident, de Macrobe à Cassiodore*. Paris: de Boccard, 1943.

Dinkler, Erich. *Die Anthropologie Augustins*. Stuttgart: Kohlhammer, 1934.

Duchesne, Louis. *Early History of the Christian Church* III. Trans. Claude Jenkins. New York: Longmans Green, 1924.

DuRoy, Olivier. *L'Intelligence de la foi en la Trinité selon saint Augustin*. Paris: Etudes Augustiniennes, 1966.

Eborowicz, W. "*Ad Romanos* 9, 11 et la critique de la théorie du péché de l'âme préexistante." *Texte und Untersuchungen*, 103 (1968), 272–76.

Fortin, Ernest, a.a. *Christianisme et culture philosophique au cinquième siècle: La quérelle de l'âme humaine en Occident*. Paris: Etudes Augustiniennes, 1959.

Gilson, Etienne. *Introduction à l'étude de saint Augustin*. 3rd ed. Paris: Vrin, 1949.

——. *The Christian Philosophy of Saint Augustine*. Trans. L. E. M. Lynch. New York: Random House, 1960.

Hendrikx, Ephrem. "La date de composition du *De Trinitate* de saint Augustin." *L'Année Théologique Augustinienne*, 12 (1952), 305–16.

Kelly, J. N. D. *Jerome: His Life, Writings, and Controversies*. New York: Harper & Row, 1975.

Koopmans, Jacob H. "Augustine's First Contact with Pelagius, and the Dating of the Condemnation of Caelestius at Carthage." *Vigiliae Christianae*, 8 (1954), 149–53.

La Bonnardière, Anne-Marie. *Recherches de chronologie augustinienne.* Paris: Etudes Augustiniennes, 1965.

———. "Jérome Informateur d'Augustin au sujet d'Origène." REA, 20 (1974), 42–54.

Lambot, Cyrille. "Une lettre inédite de saint Augustin, relative au *De Civitate Dei.*" *Revue Bénédictine*, 51 (1939), 109–24.

Lubac, Henri de, S.J. "Note sur saint Augustin, *De Libero Arbitrio.*" AM III. Pp. 279–86.

Lyonnet, Stanislas. "Péché." *Dictionnaire de la Bible.* Supplement 7 (1963). Cols. 486–567.

———. "Romains V, 12 chez saint Augustin." NRT, 89 (1967), 842–49.

Madec, Goulven, A.A. Review of Robert J. O'Connell, S.J., "Augustine's Rejection of the Fall of the Soul." REA, 21 (1975), 394.

———. "The Notion of Philosophical Augustinianism: An Attempt at Clarification." *Mediaevalia*, 4 (1978), 125–46.

———. "*Christus, scientia et sapientia nostra.*" RA, 10 (1979), 77–85.

Meer, Frits G. L. van der. *Augustine the Bishop.* Trans. Brian Battershaw and G. R. Lamb. New York: Sheed and Ward, 1961.

Moreau, Madeleine. "Le Dossier Marcellinus." RA, 9 (1973), 1–181.

Montcheuil, Yves de, S.J. "L'hypothèse de l'état originel d'ignorance et de difficulté d'après *De Libero Arbitrio* de saint Augustin." *Mélanges théologiques.* Paris: Aubier, 1946. Pp. 237–71.

O'Connell, Robert J., S.J. *St. Augustine's Early Theory of Man, A.D. 386–391.* Cambridge: The Belknap Press of Harvard University Press, 1968.

———. *St. Augustine's* CONFESSIONS: *The Odyssey of Soul.* Cambridge: The Belknap Press of Harvard University Press, 1969.

———. *Art and the Christian Intelligence in St. Augustine.* Cambridge: Harvard University Press, 1978.

———. *St. Augustine's Platonism.* Villanova: Villanova University Press, 1984.

———. *Imagination and Metaphysics in St. Augustine.* Milwaukee: Marquette University Press, 1986.

———. "Pre-Existence in Augustine's Seventh Letter." REA, 15 (1969), 67–73.

———. "*De Libero Arbitrio* I: Stoicism Revisited." AS, 1 (1970), 49–68.

———. "Augustine's Rejection of the Fall of the Soul." AS, 4 (1973), 1–32.

———. "The Human Being as 'Fallen Soul' in St. Augustine's *De Trinitate.*" *Mediaevalia*, 4 (1978), 33–58.

———. "When Saintly Fathers Feuded: The Correspondence between Augustine and Jerome." *Thought*, 54 (1979), 344–64.

———. "Pre-Existence in the Early Augustine." REA, 26 (1980), 176–88.

———. "The God of St. Augustine's Imagination." *Thought*, 57 (1982), 30–40.

———. "The Origin of the Soul in Saint Augustine's *Letter 143*." REA, 28 (1982), 239–52.

———. "St. Augustine's Criticism of Origen in the *Ad Orosium*." REA, 30 (1984), 84–99.

O'Daly, Gerald J. P. "Augustine on the Origin of Souls." *Platonismus und Christentum*. Jahrbuch für Antike und Christentum Supplement 10. Pp. 184–91.

Pépin, Jean. *Ex Platonicorum persona: Etudes sur les lectures philosophiques de saint Augustin*. Amsterdam: Hakkert, 1977.

Plinval, Georges de. *Pélage: Ses écrits, sa vie, et sa réforme*. Lausanne: Payot, 1943.

Plotinus. *Plotini opera*. Edd. Paul Henry and Hans-Rudolph Schwyzer. 3 vols. Oxford: Oxford University Press, 1962–1982.

———. *The Enneads*. Trans. Stephen Mackenna. 3rd ed. London: Faber & Faber, 1962.

———. *Les Ennéades*. Trans. Emile Bréhier. 6 vols. in 7. Paris: "Les Belles Lettres," 1924–1938.

———. *Plotins Schriften*. Trans. Richard Harder. 5 vols in 11. Hamburg: Meiner, 1956.

———. *Plotinus*. Trans. A. H. Armstrong. 3 vols. Loeb Classical Library 444. Cambridge: Harvard University Press, 1966–1984.

Pope, Hugh. *Saint Augustine of Hippo*. London: Sand, 1937.

Quasten, Johannes. *Patrologia*. 3 vols. Westminster, Md.: Newman, 1960.

Refoulé, François. "La datation du premier concile de Carthage." REA, 9 (1963), 41–49.

Rist, John. "Augustine on Free Will and Predestination." *Journal of Theological Studies*, 20 (1969), 420–47.

Russell, Robert P., o.s.a. Review of Robert J. O'Connell, s.j., *St. Augustine's Early Theory of Man, A.D. 386–391*. *Thought*, 44 (1960), 303–305.

Sage, Athanase. "Le péché originel dans la pensée de saint Augustin, de 412 à 430." REA, 15 (1964) 75–112.

———. "Péché originel: La naissance d'un dogme." REA, 13 (1967), 211–48.

Schmaus, Michael. *Die psychologische Trinitätslehre des hl. Augustinus*. Münster: Aschendorff, 1927.

Solignac, Aimé. "La condition de l'homme pécheur d'après saint Augustin." NRT, 78 (1957), 385–416.

Taylor, John H., s.j. *The Literal Meaning of Genesis.* 2 vols. Ancient Christian Writers 41–42. New York: Newman, 1982.

TeSelle, Eugene. *Augustine the Theologian.* New York: Herder & Herder, 1970.

Verbraken, Pierre Patrick. *Etudes critiques sur les sermons authentiques de saint Augustin.* The Hague: Nijhoff, 1976.

Warfield, Benjamin. "Introduction." *The Nicene and Post-Nicene Fathers* V. New York: Christian Literature Society, 1888. Repr. Grand Rapids, Mich.: Eerdmans, 1956.

INDICES

1. SUBJECTS AND NAMES

2. SACRED SCRIPTURE

3. WORKS OF ST. AUGUSTINE

(In Chronological, i.e., *Retractationes* sequence)